S0-AGV-022

THE USSR AND LATIN AMERICA

Written under the auspices of
the Center of International Studies
Princeton University

THE USSR AND LATIN AMERICA

A Developing Relationship

Edited by
EUSEBIO MUJAL-LEÓN

Boston
UNWIN HYMAN
London Sydney Wellington

Unwin Hyman, Inc.
8 Winchester Place, Winchester, MA 01890, USA

Published by the Academic Division of
Unwin Hyman, Ltd,
15/17 Broadwick Street, London W1V 1FP, UK

Allen & Unwin Australia Pty Ltd,
8 Napier Street, North Sydney, NSW 2060, Australia

Allen & Unwin (New Zealand) Ltd, in association with the Port Nicholson Press Ltd, 60 Cambridge Terrace, Wellington, New Zealand

First published in 1989

Library of Congress Cataloguing-in-Publication Data

The USSR and Latin America: a developing relationship / edited by Eusebio Mujal-León.
p. cm.
Includes bibliographies and index.
ISBN 0-04-445165-2
1. Latin America—Relations—Soviet Union. 2. Soviet Union—Relations—Latin America. 3. Soviet Union—Foreign relations—1945- 4. Communist strategy. 5. Geopolitics--Latin America. I. Mujal-León. Eusebio. 1950-
F1416.S65U84 1988
303.4'8247"08—dc19 88-14893
CIP

British Library Cataloguing in Publication Data

The USSR and Latin America: a developing relationship.
1. Latin America. Foreign relations with Soviet Union 2. Soviet Union. Foreign relations with Latin America
I. Mujal-Leon, Eusebio
327'.098
ISBN 0-04-445165-2

Printed in Great Britain
at the University Press, Cambridge

Contents

List of Tables

Foreword

The Center of International Studies is very pleased to have sponsored *The USSR and Latin American*, conceived and edited by Professor Eusebio Mujal-León. This volume emerged from the Tinker Foundation's determination to train scholars who would have expertise in both Soviet and Latin American affairs and to contribute to policy-relevant knowledge in Soviet-Latin American relations.

Mujal-León and his colleagues have admirably explored Soviet perspectives on and policies towards Latin America. Along the way, they have inquired into perceptions of the Soviet Union's role in the area. This study reflects broadly on the Soviet-Latin American connection. It shows how Soviet relations with Latin America have expanded, focusing more on countries and less on relations between parties. It explores the impact of the Cuban Revolution on the Soviet Union and on Soviet-Latin American relations. Indeed, the Cuban Revolution and the installation of a communist regime in Cuba fundamentally altered the Soviet-Latin American nexus and the role of Communist parties in Latin American countries. Few of the experts contributing to the present work ignore the Cuban connection to Soviet-Latin American relations.

As Mujal-León himself points out in the Introduction, no uniformity of views emerges. As he also states, however, there is a coherence that often eludes edited works. The authors met in conferences where interactions could occur and individual views could be tested. Princeton University's Center of International Studies is proud to have provided the context in which some of these discussions took place and in which Mujal-León conceived the framework for this enterprise. The result is especially gratifying: a major scholarly work that is sure to make an impact on thinking about Soviet-Latin American relations.

Professor Mujal-León's own acknowledgments recognize the central role of the Tinker Foundation and its President, Ms. Martha Muse. I should like to express my personal thanks to the Foundation and

Ms. Muse and to acknowledge Eusebio Mujal-León's contribution as a contributing author and editor of *The USSR and Latin America*. He and his colleagues have furthered our knowledge on a subject of growing interest and importance. The scholarly and policy-making communities are reflected in the contributors to this volume. Both communities are in debt to the Tinker Foundation, Professor Mujal-León, and his colleagues for conceiving of this study and seeing it through to completion.

Henry Bienen
Princeton University
July 12, 1988

Acknowledgments

This volume is the product of a two-year research and study project sponsored by the Tinker Foundation and prepared under the auspices of the Center of International Studies at Princeton University. To this rather formal recognition I should like to add a special and heartfelt thanks to three people without whose assistance and support this book would never have seen the light of day. Martha Twitchell Muse, President of the Tinker Foundation, provided the initial impulse for the project and, with characteristic energy and vision, remained resolute in her support of it. Henry Bienen and Cyril Black, respectively the present and former directors of the Center of International Studies, gave generously of their time and personified the hospitable and collegial atmosphere of the Center.

The contributors to this volume benefited from the opportunity they had to exchange views and ideas about their chapters during two meetings hosted by the Center of International Studies in February and October 1986. Also in attendance at the latter session were Bruce Bagley, Cole Blasier, Margaret Daly Hayes, James MacAdams, Daniel Papp, Jorge Perez-López, and Ilya Prizel, whose comments and suggestions on the volume and individual chapters proved very helpful. On a sad note, the other contributors and the editor wish to extend their condolences to the family of Morris Rothenberg whose untimely death deprived us of a valued colleague and friend.

I should also like to thank Peter Clement, Thane Gustafson, Brian Lattell, and Ann-Sofie Nilsson for their helpful comments and suggestions, and John Webb for his research assistance.

A final word of thanks are also in order to Margarita Balmaceda of Princeton University for providing research and logistical assistance during the two years the editor was in residence at Princeton University, to Maritheresa Frain of Georgetown University for her help with editing and typing, and to Gladys Starkey and the staff of the Center of International Studies for their many kindnesses.

Introduction

Eusebio Mujal-León

How important is Latin America to the Soviet Union? How has its significance increased over the last three decades? What are the instruments which the Soviet Union has employed in its relations with Latin America? How effective have these instruments been in helping the USSR establish and extend its presence and influence in the region? With which countries has the Soviet Union established its most successful relationships? Is Cuba an economic burden or an imperial asset to the Soviet Union? What role do Cuba and other Soviet allies play in extending Soviet interests in Latin America? To consider these questions, to provide frameworks for their analysis, and to offer at least partial responses to these interrogatories are the aims of this collective volume. The authors are well-known specialists. There are Latin Americanists and Sovietologists, Latin Americans and North Americans in the group. They have come together in this volume with the aim of presenting a thorough and up to date assessment of the nature and dimensions of the Soviet Union's relations with Latin America. Their intention, however, is to provide more than just a chronicle of contemporary reality. They also offer a historical perspective on their subjects, one that demonstrates those patterns of continuity and change in Soviet behavior and attitudes—as well as in the Latin American response—which might provide clues about future trends in the USSR's relationship with Latin America.

Like most edited volumes, this one contains a plurality of perspectives and emphases. This characteristic may be considered a particular source of strength given the complexity of the subject at hand. Not only are there many dimensions to Soviet-Latin American relations, but these are in turn related to the broader questions of East-West perspectives which the authors bring to this collection should only enhance its analytical qualities. The authors and editor have worked closely from the very inception of this project in order to enhance its coherence and organization.

* * * * *

Prior to 1959, Latin America was a region of very low priority for the USSR. As in other parts of the world, since the 1920s the Soviet Union had followed a two-track policy of pursuing state-to-state relations while also emphasizing its support for revolution and solidarity with native Communist parties. Neither policy was particularly successful. Efforts to develop political and trade relations with larger countries such as Argentina and Brazil generally foundered, undercut by Soviet support for the Communist parties' occasional revolutionary thrusts (an example was the 1935 revolt which Luis Carlos Prestes led in Brazil) and by the corresponding distrust regional elites felt toward the Soviet Union. Only during and immediately after World War II did the Soviet Union break its diplomatic and trade neglect of Latin America, but these advances were soon lost in the context of the Cold War.

At the time, the Soviet Union relied on Communist parties as its principal instruments in the region, but with few exceptions (as in Chile, Uruguay, and Venezuela, for example, where they gained national influence through their presence in the labor movement) they never became imposing political actors in their own right. Thoroughly Stalinized by the late 1920s, they loyally followed the zigs and zags of Comintern policy, losing most of their national credibility as they became appendages of Soviet foreign policy. The failure of Communist-led insurrections in El Salvador (1932) and Brazil (1935) signalled an end to the Communist parties' overt revolutionary engagement. From the mid-1930s on, Communist parties pursued the so-called "four class alliance" strategy. Through its emphasis on interclass collaboration, the strategy both implied and justified the postponement of any socialist revolution for Latin America. If it brought the Communists such occasional perquisites as participation in the government or increased influence in the labor movement it also weakened whatever claims they could make to revolutionary vanguard status. Such was the case in Cuba during Fulgencio Batista's first constitutional term in power from 1940 to 1944.

Latin America is distant geographically and culturally from the Soviet Union. It had provided little fertile ground either for Communist parties or Soviet diplomatic and trade activity. The Soviet Union can therefore be forgiven if other concerns and areas attracted its attention through the 1950s. A version of "geographic fatalism" led the USSR to presume Latin America was firmly under United States control. Nikita Krushchev did not even include Latin America in his February 1956 proposal for a Third World "zone of peace."

The Cuban Revolution profoundly changed Soviet perspectives on Latin America. Fidel Castro's consolidation of power, despite vigorous U.S. opposition, demonstrated that there existed real limits to the exercise of American power in the region. His unpredictable evolution toward Marxism-Leninism took Soviet leaders by surprise, but it also engaged them inextricably in Latin American affairs. Not all the consequences of the Soviet-Cuban relationship were favorable to Moscow, especially at the beginning. Admittedly, the emplacement of Soviet missiles in Cuba in mid-1962 had not been Castro's idea (indeed, Krushchev had neither asked him for his opinion then nor when he withdrew them in October), but their withdrawal had also embarrassed the Soviet Union and underscored its military weakness relative to the United States. Castro was also an expensive and highly idiosyncratic ally. During the 1960s difficulties with him were legion. He abhorred central planning or any other economic mechanism which either circumscribed his personal power or frustrated his drive to create a "new socialist man." He projected himself and his Cuba as the new vanguard of the international revolutionary movement. His support for guerrilla movements throughout Latin America during the 1960s split and weakened the region's Communist parties, some of whom were also actively engaged in armed struggle. It also hindered the development of broader Soviet-Latin American diplomatic and trade relations.

But if there were disadvantages which accrued to the Soviet Union from its Cuban link after 1959, over time these diminished. Reeling under the combined weight of domestic economic failures, the defeat of guerrilla movements (including Ernesto "Che" Guevara's death in Bolivia), and growing Soviet economic pressure, Castro moved toward rapprochement with the Soviet Union in the late 1960s. He endorsed the August 1968 Warsaw Pact invasion of Czechoslovakia, not least because he hoped to infer or encourage a Soviet defense guarantee for Cuba. As Soviet-Cuban friction subsided, military ties intensified and the island became a major Soviet naval base and reconnaissance outpost. Foreign policy coordination between the two countries increased during the early 1970s. Cuba assumed an increasingly important role in Soviet strategy toward Latin America, becoming both an interpreter of Latin American reality for the USSR and its interlocutor with extreme left groups in the region. The dissolution of the Portuguese empire in Southern Africa after 1974 provided further concrete opportunities for joint action. Thereafter, Cuba became the USSR's privileged partner in Africa, dispatching large troop contingents first to Angola in support of the Marxist Popular Movement for the Liberation of Angola (MPLA) and then to Ethiopia to be used against Somalia and the Eritrean insurgents. During the 1970s, too, Castro became the Soviet Union's premier spokesman and defender in the Nonaligned Movement.

The Cuban Revolution increased Soviet interest in Latin America and provided the USSR with its first ally and client in the region. There can be little doubt that it has also had an important impact on the politics and foreign relations of Latin America. Among its many dimensions, the Cuban Revolution has a nationalist and forcibly anti-U.S. component which transcends both Castro's personality and the ideology on which his regime relies for its legitimacy. Just as it led numerous Latin Americans who were neither sympathetic to Castro nor to his alignment with the Soviet Union to applaud his capacity to confront the United States, so the Cuban Revolution both presaged and encouraged what might have developed in any case: a new wave of nationalism in Latin America.

The "new" Latin American nationalism was new more in terms of plausibility than in desire. Since independence, Latin American countries had stood in the shadow of the "Colossus of the North," their relations with the United States forged in a crucible where admiration and resentment had become indissolubly linked. Anti-americanism had already found expression in the nineteenth century (as some of Simón Bolívar and José Martí's writings attest), and it intensified in this century as the United States dramatically increased its wealth and power. By the late 1940s, the Monroe Doctrine was at last reality: no extracontinental power had an active presence in Latin America, and the United States had become both architect and guarantor of the interamerican security system. However, as would occur elsewhere in the world, American preponderance was not to last, and within three decades the United States confronted a more competitive environment.

The emergence of the "new" Latin American nationalism coincided with and ain some ways reinforced the shift from bipolarity to multipolarity in the international system. Evident by the early 1970s, this trend had several characteristics. Alongside the resurgence of Western Europe and Japan as rivals for political and economic influence in the Western camp, there was the impact several Third World countries—the People's Republic of China and the oil-producing states, for example—now had on the international system. By this time, too, the USSR had achieved an imperfect but nevertheless effective parity with the United States. This the age of detente confirmed. Paradoxically, the interpretation the Soviet leadership gave to detente also encouraged the USSR to pursue an aggressive Third World policy. For the United States, mired first in the Vietnam War and then in the constitutional crisis provoked by Watergate, the late 1960s and early 1970s were also a period of transition. The rise of isolationist sentiment and the erosion of national self-confidence accompanied the discovery of limits to American power.

Eventually these changes would have profound effects on relations between the United States and Latin America, but in the 1960s and early 1970s their impact was felt slowly and uncertainly. At one level, as in Giovanni Lampedusa's *The Leopard*, the more things changed, the more they stayed the same. The United States retained its ethnocentric and paternalistic outlook toward Latin America. That there was growing effervescence in Latin America, with the radicalization of important sectors linked to the Catholic Church and the military, was duly noted by Nelson Rockefeller in his 1969 report, but with American attention focused on Vietnam, there was neither the time nor the will for great initiatives toward Latin America. The Nixon-Ford administrations combined "benign neglect" and a policy of reliance on "regional influentials" to deal with the situation.

Latin American countries, on the other hand, viewed the prospects for greater autonomy with anticipation. All wanted to increase their room for maneuver vis-à-vis the United States, and the larger countries (Argentina, Brazil, Mexico, and Venezuela) harbored their own regional and sub-regional power ambitions. The result was more assertive foreign policies and initiatives which focused on the recovery of sovereignty over national mineral resources. Whatever the motive, nationalist initiatives struck a profound and deeply popular vein. Already in the mid-1960s, the U.S.-backed Christian Democratic government of Eduardo Frei (1964–1970) had carried out partial nationalizations of American-owned copper companies. Led by the "progressive" military regime in Peru, the Andean Pact countries enacted laws restricting foreign investment and also nationalized a number of American-owned companies later in the decade. Venezuela, too, nationalized its oil industry. Even conservative, anti-Communist military governments in Argentina and Brazil partook of this sentiment. Relations with the United States came under strain in the mid-1970s when these countries purchased nuclear power plants from West Germany. If the rift widened a few years later when the Carter administration intensified its criticism of human rights violations in those countries, it culminated when both countries flaunted the U.S.-decreed embargo on trade with the Soviet Union after the invasion of Afghanistan.

The changing complexion of U.S.-Latin American relations and the corresponding efforts many countries in the region undertook to reduce their economic and political dependence on the United States provided the Soviet Union with an opening in which to expand its influence and presence. Paradoxically the well-known Soviet dispute with Cuba over its efforts to topple incumbent governments made it easier for the USSR to develop political and economic relations with many countries.

Soviet policy toward Latin America in the late 1960s and early 1970s operated along two tracks. One focused on expanding "normal" diplomatic and trade relations. During this period, the Soviet Union established diplomatic relations with democratic governments in Colombia, Costa Rica, and Venezuela as well as with military-led ones in Bolivia, Ecuador, and Peru. Trade with Argentian and Brazil also expanded. Mexico provided an additional target of opportunity for the Soviet Union, but in this case the political dimension prevailed over the economic one. A 1975 agreement with the Council for Mutual Economic Assistance (CMEA) did not increase Soviet-Mexican trade significantly, but by stoutly refusing to join the U.S.-sponsored trade embargo against Cuba, Mexico thwarted the policy of political and trade isolation aimed at Castro.

The second track aimed at consolidating a more lasting, structural relationship with leftist governments in Cuba, Peru, and Chile. The most visible advance came in Soviet relations with Cuba. Although problems persisted, these could not obviate the advantages which the USSR gained from the new, consolidated relationship. Peru and Chile also drew Soviet attention. Peru had had scant dealings with the Soviet Union until a military government headed by General Juan Velasco Alvarado had taken power in 1968. As Rubén Berríos documents in his chapter, the USSR responded quickly to Peruvian requests for economic and military aid, providing nearly $500 million worth of arms between 1973 and 1980 as well as sizeable economic credits.

Underscoring the dangers of dealing with radical militaries in the Third World, however, those sympathetic to the Soviet Union could not prevent a turn to more conservative officers in 1974. The shift transformed the Soviet-Peruvian relationship. On the one hand, the USSR continued to furnish arms and spare parts and to train Peruvian air force officers; economic assistance projects remained in place; and a $900 million debt insured a long-term economic relationship. But overall relations with Peru changed to a more "ordinary" state-to-state status.

In Chile, Salvador Allende's victory at the head of the *Unidad Popular* coalition had confirmed the validity of the *vía pacífica,* which the Soviet Union and the Chilean Communist Party (PCCh) had vigorously defended. Nevertheless, as Edmé Domínguez and Robert Evanson argue in their chapters, the Soviet Union was keenly aware of the Allende government's weaknesses: Allende had won the presidency with only a plurality, bitter factional disputes raged within his Socialist Party, its relations with the Communists were problematic, as were, too, Chilean relations with the United States. Accordingly, the Soviet Union pursued a much more low-key effort than in Peru, providing some economic aid, but not in the quantities some UP members had hoped. Eschewing the instrument of military aid, the Soviet Union relied instead on the PCCh as its primary instrument for exerting political influence. Neither its economic nor political investment survived the September 1973 military coup.

The late 1960s and early 1970s thus presented a checkered balance sheet for the Soviet Union in Latin America. On the one hand, relations with Cuba had been consolidated, and Cuba would soon assume a role as a Third World power. The Cuban connection, moreover, would prove useful in the next decade, first in Africa and later in Central America. Michael Manley's rise to power in Jamaica (his People's National Party gained a narrow parliamentary majority in the 1972 election) had also been a positive development in the Caribbean. Not only did it lessen Cuba's isolation and pave the way for increased Jamaican trade with the Soviet Union, but it encouraged the rise of left wing nationalist sentiment in the English-speaking Caribbean. Soviet diplomatic and trade relations also expanded. But two significant opportunities—in Peru and Chile—had been missed. The USSR established a long-term economic presence in Peru, but its hopes for expanded influence did not materialize. Chile proved a worse disaster, even if in Augusto Pinochet the Soviet Union was given a whipping boy for its propaganda. The rise of conservative military dictatorships in South America, whose path to power had often been paved by the "infantile leftism" of the extreme left, demonstrated anti-Communism was still a strong reflex in the region. As the Nixon administration had shown in Chile, moreover, the United States was still able and willing to intervene where its interests appeared threatened.

* * * * *

Active elsewhere and with few evident opportunities in the region, the Soviet Union did not again focus much attention on Latin America until the late 1970s, this time under more favorable circumstances. New opportunities for the expansion of commercial and diplomatic relations looked. Many countries in the region confronted an economic crisis of growing magnitude. Spurred by the 1973 and 1979 oil price hikes, inflation had become endemic, provoking low and even negative growth rates. A dramatic decline in the price of agricultural foodstuffs and many raw materials aggravated the trade imbalance and underscore the need for alternative markets and financial resources. From a political point of view, the decline and eventual demise of military authoritarian regimes in South America opened, among other things, new perspectives for leftist forces. In Grenada and Nicaragua, revolutionary movements would take power in 1979 and their impact would be felt throughout the Caribbean Basin. U.S. support for Great Britain during the 1982 Falklands/Malvinas War, on the other hand, reinforced the view among many Latin Americans that the U.S. only referred to hemispheric solidarity or to interamerican security when it suited its purposes.

The Soviet Union's reentry onto the Latin American scene in the 980s responded both to the USSR's consolidated global power status and to the expanded opportunities it found in the region as a whole. With respect to South American countries, and perhaps also Mexico, those opportunities came mostly in the sphere of state-to-state relations and reflected Latin American elites' active efforts to reduce economic and political dependence on the United States. With respect to Central America and the Caribbean, the logic of Soviet (and Cuban) involvement focused less on traditional diplomatic and economic relations, and more on the prospects for rapid advances by radical, anti-American groups.

Several developments underscored the increased importance the Soviet Union attached to Latin America in the 1980s.

The Consolidation of the Soviet-Cuban Relationship

A long history of controversy and polemics shadows relations between Cuba and the Soviet Union, and even today it is important to remember that the interests and objectives of the two countries often overlap and coincide, but they are not identical. Nevertheless, after their first joint actions in Africa in the mid-1970s, the two countries developed a strong and symbiotic partnership in foreign policy. As the chapters by Jorge Domínguez and the one by Peter Clement and Raymond Duncan clearly demonstrate, Cuba has been assigned a crucial role in Soviet policy. When the Soviet Union has not wished to become directly or publicly involved, as in providing arms to Nicaragua and Grenada or in helping to organize their military and security forces, Cuba and other bloc allies have been ready to shoulder the burden. Castro and Cuba have drawn several benefits from these roles, among them a massive infusion of Soviet arms (totalling nearly $3 billion for 1981–84)[1] and the opportunity to confirm the Cuban regime's enduring commitment to "proletarian internationalism."

The Soviet-Cuban partnership has also meant closer economic ties between the two countries. The dimensions of the economic relationship are laid out in Carmelo Mesa-Lago and Fernando Gil's chapter in this volume. They convincingly demonstrate that Cuba has become increasingly dependent on, and vulnerable to, the USSR and bloc countries. In 1986 more than 80 percent of Cuba's trade was with CMEA countries and the cumulative Cuban debt to the Soviet Union reached $7.8 billion.

Consolidation of the Sandinista National Liberation Front (FSLN)

The Nicaraguan experience has provided Moscow with the opportunity to test (and, if successful, to expand on) the margins of U.S. tolerance for revolutionary movements which achieve power in Latin America. The Soviet Union has been low-key in its support of the *Sandinistas*. Moscow did not establish diplomatic relations with Managua until nearly a year after the FSLN took power, and it has relied on Cuba, the German Democratic Republic, Bulgaria, and even Libya to furnish Nicaragua with economic and military aid, and to assist Managua in reorganizing its military and security forces. Beginning in 1980, the Communist Party of the Soviet Union (CPSU) signed party-to-party agreements with FSLN similar to those in force with such other Third World parties as the COWEP in Ethiopia, but there is little if any evidence that it encouraged the Sandinistas to flaunt their "Leninist" convictions. Probably quite the contrary, since to have done so would have jeopardized Nicaragua's relations with many Western and Nonaligned countries as well as compromised the FSLN's status as an "observer" to meetings of the Socialist International. Through 1987, Soviet spokesmen had pointedly failed to extend any security guarantees to Nicaragua. As Clement and Duncan note in their chapter, the first direct military shipment to Nicaragua did not arrive until November 1984 with the delivery of MI-24 helicopter gunships.

Ideological Rapprochement between Pro-Soviet Communist Parties and the Revolutionary

Cuba and the Soviet Union had engaged in bitter ideological polemics during the 1960s. Castro argued for an aggressive strategy in the Third World, with reliance on the armed struggle and assumption of the revolutionary vanguard role by insurgent guerrillas. By contrast, the Soviet Union had emphasized the possibilities for the "peaceful path" and identified the Communist parties as the proper vanguard. The Soviet emphasis on developing state-to-state relations in Latin America and their advocacy of a "collaborationist" strategy by the Communist parties in the region, the Cubans charged, smacked of treason against revolutionary principles.

There matters stood through the 1960s and into the early 1970s. Castro's rapprochement with the Soviet Union after 1968 did not resolve the issue. It had simply been shelved. The September 1973 military coup in Chile marked the first stage in what became the ideological reconciliation between Castro and the Soviet Union—between the revolutionary left and the Communist parties—which would be consummated after the *Sandinista* victory in July 1979. Thus, as Edmé Domíngues shows in her chapter, Soviet and Chilean analysts may not have abandoned the *vía pacífica* model after 1973, but they modified it significantly by placing special emphasis on the need to grasp control of the state and its armed forces during the "transition to socialism."

The *Sandinista* victory in July 1979 helped forge a unified Soviet-Cuban perspective on what the political and social strategies of the revolutionary left in Latin America should be. To the satisfaction of the Cubans, the point about the need for armed struggle and the incapacity of traditional Communist parties (the pro-Soviet Nicaraguan Socialist Party or PSN, for example) to lead a revolutionary thrust had been made. In the wake of the Nicaraguan revolution, joint action between extreme left groups and Communist parties in revolutionary fronts, which espoused a two-track policy of armed struggle while pursuing negotiations with incumbent governments, became the order of the day in Guatemala, Honduras, and El Salvador, as well as in Chile. But if the Soviet Union now acquiesced to the use of violent methods in certain countries, they could also take satisfaction from the counsel which the Cubans now gave the *Sandinistas* of not moving too far, too fast, and all that this implied about the dwindling prospects for attaining immediate socialism. Indeed, as Cuban vice prime minister Carlos Rafael Rodríguez declared in March 1986, "There are many objective possibilities which call forth socialism [in Latin America]; however, subjectively we are not ready for it."[2]

Enhancement of Soviet Diplomatic and Trade Relations with Latin America

Twenty-five years ago, the Soviet Union had diplomatic and trade relations with only four countries in Latin America; by the late-1980s, it had exchanged diplomatic representatives and traded with nearly every Latin American country. Although the USSR's overall trade statistics with Latin America are not impressive—if one excludes Cuba, less than one percent of the region's total exports went to the Soviet Union—it has nevertheless developed significant economic relations with Argentina, Brazil, and Peru.

Trade with Argentina reached a peak in 1980–81 when Soviet purchases of grain accounted for nearly $5 billion, but even in 1984–85 it still surpassed $1.3 billion. In January 1986, the two countries signed another five-year grain agreement, with the understanding that Argentina would increase its purchase of Soviet goods. The Soviet Union, however, has not viewed Argentina simply as an important supplier of grain. Moscow also has in mind possible future access to Argentinian ports and opportunities available for bilateral cooperation in exploring the ample mineral resources of the Argentine continental shelf. As Aldo Vacs notes in his chapter, Brazil has also emerged as an important Soviet trade partner, with exports and imports of $402 and $153 million respectively in 1984. In exchange for raw materials and some manufactured goods, the Soviet Union exports oil to Brazil. Despite the constraints imposed because their economies are not especially complementary, Brazil and the USSR have engaged in several joint and "triangular" ventures, the latter in Angola, Ethiopia, and Peru. For its part, Peru has been a major Soviet arms client since the early 1970s with purchases totalling $900 million by 1980. Peru's debt with CMEA countries, Rubén Berríos notes in his chapter, had risen above $700 million by 1985. Soviet relations with Mexico have also been upgraded. This process, Brian Latell explains in Chapter 10, began under the presidencies of Luis Echevarría and José López Portillo, and it has deepened in the 1980s.

Paralleling these Soviet efforts to develop economic linkages with the larger Latin American countries have been similar initiatives on the political front. Especially since Mikhail Gorbachev became CPSU secretary general in 1985, there has been a special effort to upgrade political ties. The foreign ministers of Argentina, Brazil and Mexico have all travelled to Moscow, as did Argentine president Raúl Alfonsín in October 1987. For his part, Edvard Shevardnardze visited Argentina, Brazil, Mexico, and Uruguay in late 1987, becoming the first Soviet foreign minister to travel extensively in Latin America. From the USSR's perspective, more than polite exchanges have been involved, however. As Politburo member Aleksandr Yakovlev wrote in November 1986, "[o]ne must suppose that in the historically foreseeable future, the centrifugal trend—toward the growth of interimperialist contradictions and the further splintering of the centripetal capitalist world of the postwar decades—will actively resist the centripetal forces."[3] From this perspective, because the larger Latin American countries are locked in a politically and economically competitive relationship with the United States, they are viewed as increasingly more open to Soviet initiatives with respect to a number of issues ranging from disarmament to economic development.

* * * * *

The present volume approaches Soviet-Latin American relations from a multiple perspective. Its contributors aim to elucidate the way the region fits into Soviet global concerns and the degree to which the USSR has been successful in employing various instruments in pursuit of its objectives in Latin America.

Part I of this volume examines Soviet and United States perceptions of Latin America and of how this region fits into their overall global competition. Opening the discussion are chapters by David Albright and Elizabeth Valkenier which examine how Latin America fits into the Soviet Union's Third World strategy. Complementing these efforts is Richard Millett's contribution—"An Unclear Menace: U.S. Perceptions of Soviet Strategy in Latin America"—which analyzes the way U.S. elites have viewed and reacted to Soviet policy with respect to Latin America.

Part II focuses on those instruments (parties, countries, and economic relations) which the Soviet Union has employed in pursuit of its objectives in Latin America. Edmé Domínguez's chapter, for example, explores the evolving relationship between the CPSU and its Latin American counterparts. The next two chapters examine the nature and dimensions of the Soviet relationship with its principal Latin American ally, Cuba. The first, by Carmelo Mesa-Lago and Fernando Gil examines the economic parameters of the relationship, while Jorge Domínguez's chapter focuses on political dimensions. Contributions by Michael Radu ("Eastern Europe and Latin America") and Robert K. Evanson ("Soviet Trade Relations with Latin America") complete the discussion in Part II of this volume. Radu's contribution examines the goals and policies of Eastern European states in Latin America, while in his chapter, Evanson reviews Soviet economic and military trade relations with Latin America during the last two decades, with a view to identifying those circumstances where the USSR has used the trade lever to extend its political influence.

The last section examines the Soviet relationship with Latin America from the perspective of the USSR's policies toward a number of countries and subregions. The chapters—with Brian Latell writing on Mexico, Peter Clement and Raymond Duncan on Central America, Rubén Berríos on Peru, and Aldo Vacs on Argentina and Brazil—consider Soviet, and to a certain extent Cuban, efforts to forge political and economic links with these states and/or with left wing political movements active in these countries. Following a historical introduction, each chapter analyzes the major turning points in relations with the Soviet Union and evaluates the reasons for the expansion of contacts at either the official or informal level.

NOTES

1 The information may be found in Pamela Falk, *Cuban Foreign Policy: Caribbean Tempest* (Waltham, MA: Lexington Books, 1985), p. 136.
2 Carlos Rafael Rodríguez, "La oportunidad que no podemos rehusar," *América Latina*, 8 (1986), p. 8.
3 Aleksandr Yakovlev, "Interimperialist Contradictions—The Contemporary Context," *Kommunist*, 16 (November 1986).

I

Latin America in Soviet Third World Strategy

1

Latin America in Soviet Third World Strategy: The Political Dimension

David E. Albright

Since the end of the 1950s, Latin America has constituted a distinct entity, not simply a segment of the Third World in the eyes of the Soviet elite. Nevertheless, Moscow's broad political perspectives with respect to the Third World affect the policy that it devises toward Latin America. The situation in Latin America, to be sure, helps to shape these perspectives, yet it is by no means the sole determinant of them. Indeed, historically it has had a fairly limited impact on them. Therefore, this chapter will analyze Soviet policy toward the region within the framework of the USSR's overall political approach toward the Third World. It will focus on the interrelationship in three major areas: the geopolitical priority that Moscow attaches to the region, the goals that Soviet leaders seek to achieve there, and the method and means whereby they propose to pursue these objectives.

The results of this interrelationship, however, can vary across time to the extent that Moscow sees fit to modify its general outlook toward the Third World. Thus any meaningful treatment of the outcome of the linkage in the 1980s needs to be put in historical context. The discussion here, then, will look at each of the three areas in terms of continuities and changes between the present and the past.

David E. Albright

GEOPOLITICAL PRIORITY

The exact priority that the USSR gives to Latin America has always depended on two separate judgments by Soviet leaders. One is the significance of the Third World at large in world politics; the other involves the relative weight to be accorded to Latin America in comparison with other parts of the Third World.

The Third World

The Third World as a whole has occupied a major place in the Soviet perspective of global affairs since the 1950s. To be sure, it has never seriously challenged either Europe or East Asia for Moscow's attention. Europe, after all, had spawned the chief threats to the USSR prior to the end of World War II; moreover, it has constituted the key arena of U.S.-Soviet competition throughout the postwar period. East Asia, too, had generated substantial anxiety on the part of Soviet leaders before 1945 as a consequence of Japan's invasion and subsequent occupation of Manchuria in 1931, and Moscow's concern about the region has grown greatly during the postwar years. Not only did the Korean War of the 1950s result in a long-term U.S. military presence on the peninsula, but the early 1960s also brought a split between China and the USSR that soon became fraught with security implications. In the wake of the split, Mao Zedong revived Chinese complaints about treaties that had transferred large chunks of Chinese territory to the Russian Empire beginning in the seventeenth century. About the same time, Beijing succeeded in producing its first nuclear weapon. The Sino-American and Sino-Japanese rapprochements of the 1970s even raised the specter of an anti-Soviet coalition involving the United States, China, and Japan.

Nonetheless, the USSR has paid considerable attention to the Third World from the latter half of the 1950s on. According to Moscow, the peoples of the Third World wish to cast off the "fetters" of Western "imperialism" that have long bound them. True, the old forms of Western colonialism have been fading as more and more Third World countries have gained formal independence, but the "imperialists" still strive to retain their dominance there. To achieve this end, they merely employ different means—notably those of an economic character. Thus, the struggle for "national liberation" the argument goes on, weakens Western "imperialism" and thereby renders the international correlation of forces more favorable to the socialist camp. The national liberation movement in the Third World, then, represents at least an objective ally of the USSR.[1]

By the 1980s, however, the precise value that the USSR assigned to the Third World in international affairs had declined markedly from that evident in the late 1950s and early 1960s. The shift reflected a revised Soviet assessment of the extent to which the USSR could work with Third World states for common purposes. By the mid-1960s, Moscow had already discarded all hopes for the quick emergence of fellow communist regimes in the vast bulk of Third World countries, but it had continued to discern enough mutual identification with many of them to see possibilities for worthwhile cooperation on a variety of key issues. On this basis, for example, it depicted the USSR as the "natural ally" of the Nonaligned Movement in the 1970s.[2] Yet as early as 1981, a Soviet analyst observed bluntly: "One apparently has to bear in mind that in their approach to all international questions the developing countries are guided first and foremost by their own national interests, as they understand them. Indira Gandhi said that India does not adhere to a pro-Soviet or anti-American stand, India only adheres to a pro-India stand."[3] Subsequently, other Soviet spokesmen have made abundantly clear that many of the positions of even the most "progressive" Third World states left much to be desired from the USSR's perspective.[4]

Such a development has inevitably affected the standing of Latin America on Moscow's overall list of geopolitical priorities. At the same time, ironically, the region's relative position on the list with respect to other portions of the Third World appears to be higher in the 1980s than it has been at any previous juncture.

Latin America within the Third World

From the beginnings of heightened Soviet interest in the Third World in the 1950s, Latin America's standing in Soviet geopolitical thinking about the Third World has reflected the interplay of several factors. In a direct sense, Latin America is the region of the world least important to the USSR. It lies far from Soviet shores, contains no strong Soviet rivals in the international arena, and serves as neither a source of vital resources nor a key trading partner for the USSR. Yet the region possesses attributes that make it of substantial indirect concern to Moscow. It constitutes the "backyard" of the United States—not only a recognized global power, but also the USSR's chief rival in world affairs. In such a light, the status of the U.S. relationship with Latin America has a decided impact on the region's significance from Moscow's viewpoint. This is particularly true because Soviet leaders have regarded, and still regard, adversities for the United States as gains for the USSR in international affairs.[5] When, therefore, Moscow has discerned a reduction in the degree of U.S. control of Latin America to be either in progress or possible, this consideration has figured in its geopolitical calculations. The exact weight that Soviet leaders have assigned to such a development—and to trying to promote or exploit it—has depended on their judgments about the inherent opportunities currently available to the USSR in other parts of the Third World. These judgments, just as those about the extent of U.S. dominance of Latin America, have varied over time.

Not surprisingly, the precise geopolitical priority that Moscow has accorded to Latin America within the Third World has shifted over the years. Never, of course, has Latin America claimed the top spot in Soviet thinking. This ranking has gone to a variety of entities since the mid-1950s. First, Moscow initially bestowed it on Africa and Asia as a whole, then on those countries throughout the Third World that had embarked on a "noncapitalist" path, and finally on those states—largely in Africa—where a transition to "scientific socialism" in the foreseeable future appeared genuinely possible to Soviet analysts. Since the mid-1960s, Soviet leaders have consistently conferred it on the southern rimlands of the USSR, that is from South Asia in the east around to North Africa in the west, in the areas forming a broad arc to the south of the Soviet borders.[6] These regions have obvious strategic importance to the USSR, for they constitute its "soft underbelly."

Nonetheless, Latin America on occasion has moved upward as well as downward on the USSR's ladder of geopolitical concerns. Of perhaps greater consequence here, each time that the region has risen on the ladder, it has attained a higher place than it had reached previously, and each time that it has dropped, it has retained a position above that of all preceding low points. Thus, the increased importance that the USSR has attached to Latin America within the Third World in the 1980s represents merely an extension of a general historical trend. This trend has been derived fundamentally from Soviet assessments of the escalating severity of U.S. problems in the region.

LATE 1950s TO LATE 1960s

Latin America first attracted serious Soviet attention at the end of the 1950s. Since the 1920s, however, Moscow had promoted the formation of and maintained relations with communist parties in various countries of the region. Yet Soviet leaders had seen few indications that these activities were producing promising results.[7] In the early 1950s, too, Moscow had briefly thought that it might have found another opening wedge into Latin America. It vocally backed and even clandestinely supplied some arms to the leftist and anti-U.S. Arbenz government in Guatemala in 1953–54. The ouster of this government with U.S. assistance in 1954, however, convinced Soviet leaders that internal and international conditions in Latin America remained essentially unfavorable for the survival of such regimes or for any real expansion of the USSR's role in the region. Not only did conservative land-holding classes still dominate societies throughout the region, but conservative militaries continued to serve as the final arbiters of political authority, regardless of whether they held the formal reins of power or not. In foreign affairs, moreover, both of these groups evinced an anti-Communist and pro-American orientation. To top things off, the United States gave every sign that it was prepared to act decisively to prevent any breaches of the Monroe Doctrine.[8] Accordingly, Moscow focused on former Western colonies in Asia and Africa, whose leaders evinced greater ambivalence toward the West and a desire to have dealings with the USSR.

It was Fidel Castro's advent to power in 1959 and the mounting tensions between his regime and the United States that produced the new Soviet interest in Latin America.[9] Moscow watched with growing approval Castro's public evolution from "nationalist" in January 1959 to "socialist" in April 1961 to "Marxist-Leninist" in December 1981 in reaction to these tensions. The USSR also applauded Castro's victory over the Bay of Pigs invasion by Cuban exiles supported by the United States—an accomplishment which suggested that he might hang onto power even in the face of sharp U.S. opposition.

During the 1959–62 period, the USSR manifested increasing enthusiasm for Cuba in a variety of concrete ways. These began with the signing of a trade pact with Havana in February 1960, and three months later, the USSR reestablished diplomatic relations with the Caribbean state. Soon Moscow was providing military backing as well. Ultimately, of course, Nikita Khrushchev decided to ship missiles to the island.

Moscow did not, however, view Cuba in isolation from the rest of Latin America. Rather, it tended to look upon developments in Cuba as an indication that the region *in toto* might be undergoing fundamental changes. The fervor that Castro stirred among leftists and even straightforward nationalists in other Latin American countries reinforced this inclination.

Hence, even though Cuba was the only state in Latin America to qualify as one of the primary concerns of the USSR in the Third World, in the early 1960s the entire region assumed a place along with Asia and Africa as a venue in which Moscow believed it could successfully carry out wooing efforts. The most visible sign came in an institutional form when Soviet leaders established a Latin American Institute within the USSR Academy of Sciences in 1961. Other evidence of a less tangible sort cropped up as well. For example, Soviet analysts in the early 1960s began to speak of the "national liberation movement" as a tricontinental phenomenon—embracing Asia, Africa, and Latin America. It should be stressed, however, that even with their enhanced stature the countries of the region (aside from Cuba) remained comparatively minor targets of Soviet courtship.

The Cuban missile crisis of October 1962 and its aftermath dashed Soviet optimism about conditions in Latin America. Not only did the United States once again demonstrate a willingness to act unilaterally to protect its perceived interests in the region, but all of the Latin American states except Mexico either approved or eventually yielded to U.S. pressure to endorse a quarantine of Cuba. Furthermore, the leftist, anti-American elements of the region who continued to identify with Castro proved incapable of winning power anywhere. Inevitably, then, Latin America as a whole again became a distant also-ran to Asia and Africa in Moscow's geopolitical considerations.

Nevertheless, the region did not revert to the virtual cipher that it had been in Soviet eyes prior to the rise of Castro. Two factors kept it from doing so. First and foremost, Castro remained in authority in Cuba, and his persisting need for Soviet economic and military assistance in the face of U.S. hostility assured the USSR of a base of operations in Latin America, although Soviet-Cuban relations continued to be fairly prickly until the late 1960s.[10] Second, after the formal Sino-Soviet split in 1963, Beijing attempted to gain the loyalties of the Latin American communist parties. When it had little luck in this regard, it promoted the formation of alternative bodies sympathetic to it ideologically.[11]

LATE 1960s TO CLOSE OF 1970s

The late 1960s and early 1970s witnessed another improvement in Latin America's standing in Soviet geopolitical calculations. During this period, the region became a major secondary target of Soviet interest in the Third World. Although the persisting conflict in Southeast Asia unmistakably rendered that region the chief concern of Moscow (after the southern rimlands of the USSR), Latin America appeared to follow fairly closely thereafter.

A symbolic indication of the region's new importance from Moscow's perspective was the inauguration in 1969 of *Latinskaia Amerika*, the first Soviet journal to deal exclusively with Latin America. By the fall of 1971, as prominent a Soviet personage as Boris Ponomarev, the head of the International Department of the CPSU, was declaring that "the upsurge of the revolutionary movement on the Latin American continent" had "tremendous significance for the world revolutionary movement."[12]

A number of things contributed to this development.[13] Beginning in the late 1960s, there was a visible decline in Pan-Americanism. Perhaps more important, the number of the governments in the region that Soviet leaders deemed "progressive" was growing, especially in South America,[14] and these governments found themselves increasingly at odds with the United States over such issues as control of natural resources. Finally, the blossoming of detente between the USSR and the United States gave Soviet leaders increased confidence that they could exploit the new opportunities they discerned in Latin America without precipitating direct U.S. intervention.[15]

Together, these considerations convinced Moscow that a new stage in U.S. interaction with Latin America had arrived. The U.S. position in the region was visibly eroding in many places, although principally in areas geographically remote from North America; moreover, Washington confronted increased constraints on what it could do to stop the erosion.

This time, Latin America's elevated ranking in Soviet geopolitical thinking lasted a little longer than it had in the early 1960s, but by the mid-1970s the region's place in Moscow's geopolitical priorities had again fallen. The reasons for the decline were multiple. After the U.S. encouraged the overthrow of Salvador Allende's government in Chile in September 1973,[16] Soviet leaders concluded that they had overestimated the decline of both U.S. will and influence in Latin America.[17]

Soon after the ouster of the Allende government, events elsewhere in the Third World furnished Soviet leaders with opportunities more attractive than those to be found in Latin America. Specifically, the military coup in Lisbon in April 1974, the subsequent collapse of the Portuguese empire in Africa, and the Angolan civil war of 1975–76 yielded significant new openings for the USSR in sub-Saharan Africa. Last, yet in no sense least, U.S.-Soviet detente began to unravel in 1974–75. Of special relevance here, the Soviet-Cuban role in installing the MPLA in authority in Luanda aroused great ire in Washington. Thus, success in Africa sharply curtailed what the USSR could do in Latin America without arousing U.S. suspicions and even provoking a confrontation that would be difficult to handle in such a distant milieu.

Despite its reduced status in Soviet geopolitical calculations after the mid-1970s, Latin America did not occupy as low a spot as it had after the 1962 Cuban missile crisis. Manifestations of discontent with the United States continued to mount in many quarters of the region. These were especially evident in the economic realm and particularly over the negative U.S. response to Third World proposals for the establishment of a New International Economic Order. Furthermore, there were some signs of a leftward drift and a greater receptivity to ties with the USSR and other Communist countries even in areas thought critical to the United States—namely, the Caribbean and Central America. Michael Manley's Jamaica constituted the most prominent example. By the late 1970s, then, Moscow seems to have regarded Latin America as an area of interest about on par with Southeast Asia, where the Indochina war had just terminated.

THE 1980s

A third rise in the geopolitical merit that Soviet leaders accorded Latin America commenced during the last few months of the 1970s. By early 1981, no less a figure than Leonid Brezhnev, the general secretary of the CPSU, was stressing that "the states of Latin America...are playing a more important role" in international affairs.[18] As of the mid-1980s, the region appeared to occupy a position immediately below the southern rimlands of the USSR in Moscow's geopolitical assessments.[19]

This general development was triggered by the New Jewel Movement's seizure of power in Grenada in March 1979 and especially the revolution in Nicaragua the following July. From the very outset

Soviet commentators spoke of events in Nicaragua as a sign that significant weaknesses now existed in the most vital part of the U.S. "strategic rear."[20] Moreover, regardless of their individual (and diverse) views as to the merits of a resort to arms elsewhere in Latin America, they typically depicted the Nicaraguan revolution as the "beginning of a new stage in the struggle on the scale of the entire continent."[21]

As the 1980s progressed, several other considerations strengthened Moscow's conviction that the ability of the United States to keep its "backyard" quiet and submissive had decreased dramatically. Among these were the civil war in El Salvador, the ire of Latin American governments at U.S. backing of Great Britain in the Falklands/Malvinas War in mid-1982, and the discontent of the major debtor countries in the region over the policies of the U.S. government and U.S. banks on the debt repayment question. Soviet observers hailed all of these things as further evidence of the breakdown of the old interamerican system under U.S. aegis.[22]

The U.S. invasion of Grenada in October 1983, it is true, reminded Soviet leaders that the United States still possessed formidable capacities for shaping the situation in Latin America.[23] Nevertheless, the broad consensus reached at a Soviet symposium sponsored by the journal *Latinskaia Amerika* in the early 1980s continued to prevail in the late 1980s. According to this view, Latin American states had assumed "a more important role in world affairs," and their foreign policies contained "an anti-imperialist element" that could "restrict the sphere of imperialism's freedom of movement" in the global arena, and "complicate the achievement of its strategic and tactical goals on a global scale, in Latin America, and in other parts of the world."[24]

OBJECTIVES

Since the 1950, Soviet objectives in Latin America have flowed fundamentally from broad purposes that Moscow has defined with respect to the Third World as a whole, but Latin America's peculiarities have produced a few distinctive features in Soviet application of these general aims to the region.[25] The broad purposes have been medium-term operational goals whose attainment Soviet leaders have regarded as essential for the pursuit of more ambitious aims in the Third

World. Although Moscow has rarely, if ever, stated these purposes explicitly, they are fairly easily discerned from Soviet words and deeds.

The mix of general purposes has remained basically the same since the mid-1960s, and the individual objectives themselves all antedate that period.[26] This mix includes establishing a lasting presence throughout the Third World; gaining a voice in the affairs of every Third World region; and weakening Western and Chinese influence in the Third World.

Creating an Enduring Presence

Since the late 1950s, the USSR has maintained that it is a global power. To be sure, Moscow softpedaled this claim after the Soviet confrontation with the United States during the 1962 Cuban missile crisis, but it did not forsake it. On the contrary, Nikita Khrushchev's successors, after carrying out a substantial military buildup in the 1960s, accorded it new prominence in the early 1970s. It soon became a common feature of Soviet policy pronouncements.[27]

Global-power status, however, does not emerge from divine right or the consent of the world community; rather, it must be self-asserted, self-achieved, and self-sustained. No less important, a superpower does not automatically qualify as a global power. The attributes of a global power go beyond the possession of large stocks of nuclear weapons and the means to deliver them. Such a country must be able to demonstrate global reach. This, in turn, usually requires not just intermittent forays into distant regions, but a sustained presence in those regions.[28] Thus, Moscow has long viewed the building up of a permanent Soviet presence throughout the Third World as critical to its credibility as a global power, and it has clearly shown a determination to bring about such a condition. In the case of Latin America specifically, for example, the number of states with which the USSR carried on formal diplomatic relations rose from three in 1959 to 16 in the mid-1980s.[29]

Soviet expansion in the economic realm provides even more telling evidence of the changing relationship with Latin America. Over the years, the most dramatic increase in Soviet economic involvement in the region has been, of course, in Cuba. Prior to 1960, the USSR had minimal economic ties with the island, but by the mid-1980s Moscow was supplying Havana with more that $4 billion a year in economic aid—roughly one-quarter of Cuba's gross national product. By the mid-1980s, too, there were some 7,000 Soviet economic advisers in the country.[30]

Soviet economic relations with other states in the region have grown substantially as well. As late as 1965, the USSR's trade turnover with these countries amounted to just $160 million; however, by 1981–85 it had jumped to an annual average of more than $3 billion,[31] Brazil and Argentina accounting for the bulk of the sum. In 1960, the Soviets had engaged in commerce with only 4 states in the region; by the 1980s, the figure exceeded 20.[32] Soviet economic credits and grants to Latin American countries other than Cuba rose from $30 million in 1955–64 to nearly $1.1 billion in 1980–84. The largest portion of the latter figure went to Nicaragua, but Argentina, Bolivia, Brazil, Ecuador, and Peru obtained significant amounts as well.[33]

Soviet military undertakings in Latin America, however, have afforded perhaps the most revealing testimony demonstrating the desire to establish a lasting presence in the region. Moscow has expanded its military ties with Cuba enormously since 1960: by the mid-1980s, the USSR's military contingent amounted to a 2,800-man combat brigade, 2,800 military advisers, and an additional 2,100 technicians at the Lourdes electronic intelligence facility. Since 1969, the Soviet navy has deployed task forces to Cuba and the Caribbean 24 times and for a number of years the Soviet air force has maintained long-range naval reconnaissance aircraft on the island. In the 1981–84 period alone, Moscow furnished the Havana government with nearly $3 billion in military aid.[34]

Elsewhere in the region, the USSR has been unable to forge military links even remotely comparable to those with Cuba, but these relations are still noteworthy. Prior to 1975, the USSR had supplied a grand total of $30 million in arms to Latin American states other than Cuba. In 1975–79, however, Peru received $650 million worth of Soviet weapons and equipment,[35] and after the Nicaraguan revolution in 1979, Moscow began to ship arms to the new *Sandinista* government. By 1985, these shipments amounted to about $240 million in value.[36] Before the U.S. invasion of Grenada in 1983, the New Jewel Movement government there obtained Soviet weapons and equipment worth nearly 20 million rubles (roughly $25 million) under the terms of three secret military agreements signed with the USSR in the early 1980s.[37] In addition, there is considerable evidence that Moscow has furnished some arms to insurgents in El Salvador, Guatemala, and Chile in the 1980s.[38]

Winning a Say in Regional Affairs

As already mentioned, Soviet leaders have long contended that the USSR is a global power and have striven to substantiate its global reach. Yet they have also recognized that an extensive presence abroad does not alone entitle the USSR to global-power status. The USSR also must truly make its weight felt around the world. An understanding of this reality has clearly underscored comments like that of former USSR foreign minister Andrei Gromyko in 1971 when he said that "today there is no question of any significance which can be decided without the Soviet Union or in opposition to it."[39] Consequently, Moscow has assiduously sought to influence events in all corners of the globe.

Manifestations of a Soviet wish to have an impact on the affairs of Latin America have abounded over the years, as a few highlights will suffice to illustrate. In the early 1960s, for example, Moscow tried to persuade Latin American governments not to cut their economic and diplomatic ties with Cuba. Again, after the U.S. invasion of the Dominican Republic in 1965, the USSR encouraged Latin American countries to take Washington to task for violating the provision of the Charter of the Organization of American States forbidding unilateral interventions. In the early 1970s, Soviet leaders prodded Latin American governments to refrain from involvement in U.S.-sponsored efforts to bring economic pressure to bear on Salvador Allende's Chile, and they promoted the "normalization" of Cuba's relations with other Latin American countries. With the triumph of the Nicaraguan revolutionary forces in 1979, Moscow endorsed the armed struggles of insurgent movements in such states as El Salvador and Guatemala and extended some military aid to them. Three years later, during the Falklands/Malvinas War, the USSR supported Argentina. As Washington's commitment to the anti-*Sandinista* Nicaraguan rebels grew in the 1980s, Soviet leaders provided Managua with increased weapons and equipment, but they also backed the attempts of the Contadora group of Latin American countries (Mexico, Colombia, Venezuela, and Panama) to resolve the interstate tensions in Central America peacefully.

Undermining Western Influence

From the earliest days of major Soviet involvement in the Third World in the 1950s, Moscow has perceived itself in a competition with the West for sway there. It has viewed this competition as basically a zero-sum game, in which advances for one side represent losses for the other.[40] In such a light, growth of the role of the USSR in the Third World is inextricably linked to decrease of Western influence there.

To be sure, a school of thought has emerged in the Soviet hierarchy in the 1980s, as we shall see later, that foresees the possibility of East-West cooperation on some matters of mutual concern with regard to the Third World. Yet not even this moderate approach anticipates any easing of the fundamental competition between the two sides. If anything, it looks for an intensification of the competition in certain respects, especially in the political and ideological realms.

Although Soviet leaders in the 1980s continue to want to reduce the West's role in the Third World, they no longer deem a rapid Western departure from there to be desirable. They have come to believe that, at least in an economic sense, the USSR could not fill the vacuum that would ensue.[41] Thus, both conservative and liberal Soviet analysts now counsel Third World states not to shun Western capital but to attract it by establishing rules that, while not harming local interests, offer foreign investors advantages.[42]

To Moscow, weakening Western sway in Latin America has largely meant restricting the U.S. role there. Several kinds of Soviet behavior over the years have attested to the USSR's unrelenting dedication to this end. Perhaps the most obvious has been Moscow's development of substantial ties with self-proclaimed Marxist governments whose policies have put them at odds with Washington. The Castro government in Cuba, the Allende government in Chile during 1970–73, the Bishop government in Grenada during 1979–83, and the *Sandinista* government in Nicaragua since 1979 afford the primary illustrations. Soviet leaders have also actively supported Marxist-dominated forces seeking to oust pro-American governments from power. The "liberation movements" in El Salvador and Guatemala provide the most outstanding examples of recent years, but other cases in the past typically involved Soviet political and economic aid rather than military assistance. In addition, Moscow has sought to cooperate with a large number of circles that have expressed unhappiness with the United States for one reason or another. The potpourri has included the military regimes in Brazil and Argentina during the late 1970s and early 1980s as well as the left-leaning governments of Michael Manley in Jamaica in the 1970s and Forbes Burnham in Guyana in the 1970s and 1980s.

As elsewhere in the Third World, however, the USSR has for some time now refrained from attempts to curtail U.S. influence in Latin

America by offering to replace the United States as an economic partner in the short term. For instance, Moscow extended only $240 million in economic assistance to the Allende government in Chile in 1970–73.[43] While it has proved somewhat more generous to the *Sandinista* government in Nicaragua (Soviet credits to Managua had amounted to more than $570 million by the end of 1984), it has left no room for misunderstanding about its unwillingness to accept the burden of "another Cuba."[44]

Furthermore, since the early 1960s the USSR has imposed another limitation on its efforts to weaken the U.S. position in Latin America, a limitation which has not been evident in its actions in other parts of the Third World. Specifically, it has carefully avoided military involvement in the region that Washington would construe as "offensive" in character: in late 1962, Nikita Khrushchev withdrew the intermediate-range missiles that he had sought to install in Cuba, and since then Soviet leaders have not tried to repeat his gambit. Moscow apparently offered some arms to the Allende government in Chile, but these seem to have been of a sort useful only for domestic purposes. In any event, Allende rejected the offer.[45] During the 1980s, the USSR has heeded U.S. warnings not to supply "offensive" MiG-21s to Nicaragua—even though Nicaraguan pilots reportedly have received training in Bulgaria to fly such planes and have continued to hone their skills in Cuba.[46]

Minimizing the Chinese Role

Since the early 1960s, and especially since the open rift between Moscow and Beijing in 1963, the USSR has regarded China as a threat to its drive to establish itself as the chief patron of the "national liberation movement" in the Third World. Sino-Soviet tensions, it is true, have eased since mid-1982, but China has continued to demonstrate that it has no intention of deferring to the USSR in the Third World. In the fall of 1982, Hu Yaobang, then general secretary of the Chinese Communist Party (CCP), declared that China followed "an independent foreign policy"; it "never attaches itself to any big power or group of powers, and never yields to pressure from any big power." Then he went on to assert that "socialist China belongs to the Third World," for it has "experienced the same sufferings as most other Third World countries, and...is faced with similar problems and tasks."[47] More telling still, China has in low-key fashion stepped up its own undertakings in the

Third World—even with respect to states fairly closely aligned with the USSR.[48] It is hardly surprising, then, that although Moscow no longer virulently attacks Chinese policy in the Third World as it has in previous years, Soviet commentaries still betray a strong sense that China poses a challenge to the USSR there.[49]

The exact nature of the threat China presents to the USSR in the Third World has altered since the mid-1970s, however. In approaching the Third World, China has abandoned its earlier effort to cloak itself in the mantle of a militant revolutionary power; now it highlights its commitment to economic development and to policies that ensure such development. This stance creates difficulties for Moscow—especially in view of the economic successes China has registered in the 1980s.[50] These successes render the Chinese economic model potentially appealing, and China itself is seen as a desirable economic partner from the standpoint of the many Third World states that have been experiencing major economic problems during the 1980s. Moreover, they stand in stark contrast to the faltering performance of the Soviet economy since the mid-1970s.[51]

Until the early 1980, Soviet leaders had not demonstrated much concern about curbing Chinese influence in Latin America, except for a brief period during the first half of the 1960s. During that period, Beijing strove to break Moscow's hold on the allegiance of the existing Latin American communist parties. When this effort failed, China then encouraged the formation of rival parties dedicated to a Maoist ideological outlook and alignment with Beijing. From the Soviet standpoint, this Chinese challenge began to recede in the mid-1960s after Cuba rejected Beijing's courtship and elected to promote an alternative revolutionary path to that advocated by Mao Zedong. But it did not pass entirely until later in the decade, when Cuba moved solidly into the Soviet camp and Chinese leaders became preoccupied with internal matters during the Great Proletarian Cultural Revolution.[52] By the early 1970s, Chinese interest in Latin America had revived, and active Sino-Soviet rivalry in the region resumed.[53] Yet not until the early 1980s did the competition again cause worry in Moscow. At that juncture, Beijing embarked on a major expansion of its undertakings in Latin America, as part of an attempt both to identify more closely with the Third World and to strike a balanced policy toward the USSR and the United States.[54]

This increased Chinese attention to Latin America has produced particular unease in Moscow because Soviet leaders reckon that China could emerge as a formidable adversary of the USSR in the region. What might give China such stature, in Soviet perceptions, is not the relative attractiveness of the Chinese economic model in comparison with the Soviet model, for the Chinese model, *per se,* clearly has a distinctly limited appeal in the region. Instead, it is China's new image as a highly vocal champion of economic development and of pragmatic pursuit of this end, as well as Beijing's enthusiasm about international trade and other forms of international economic cooperation that is seen as a threat. Such attributes, Soviet leaders calculate, could evoke a sufficiently positive response from the region to afford China substantial influence there.

Interrelationship of Goals

Moscow has not established any discernible hierarchy with respect to these four objectives. Often, it has managed to pursue all or a number of them simultaneously, for they have been essentially complementary in character. Yet from time to time the ends have conflicted, and Soviet leaders have failed to resolve the resulting policy dilemmas uniformly in every case.

A concrete illustration will drive home the point. After anti-Communist, pro-U.S. military elements in Brazil ousted the left-leaning and incipiently anti-U.S. government of João Goulart in 1964, Moscow opted to maintain its presence in the country rather than to try to reduce Washington's influence by promoting efforts to unseat the new rulers. In fact, Soviet-Brazilian ties expanded modestly over the remainder of the 1960s. The USSR followed a similar course in Jamaica when "capitalist-oriented" and pro-U.S. Edward Seaga defeated "socialist-oriented" and pro-Cuban Michael Manley in national elections there in 1980. However, Soviet choices in these instances contrasted sharply with the Soviet decision regarding Chile after the overthrow of the Marxist and anti-U.S. Allende government in 1973. Not only did the USSR eschew all dealings with the anti-Communist, pro-U.S. military elements that had taken power, but it even supported armed opposition to the new Pinochet regime.

Prior to the early 1970s, it is true, there did tend to be some systematic linkage in Soviet minds among the objectives. Specifically, Moscow seemed to believe that reduction of Western influence and curtailment of China's role in Third World areas in general would result in a major Soviet presence there and give the USSR a big voice in the affairs of the various regions.[55] During the 1970s, however, Soviet leaders arrived at a more complex understanding on the matter: the relationship, they concluded, could work both ways. By the outset of the 1980s, for instance, two Soviet commentators were describing "the growing contacts between the Latin American countries and the socialist community states" as "an important factor reducing Latin America's dependence on the USA." In elaboration, they contended that "in increasing the number of their trade, economic, and political partners, the Latin American states are strengthening their international positions and acquiring greater opportunities for conducting a more equal dialogue with Washington, this in turn, creating the conditions for greater independence in world affairs as a whole."[56] Moscow even appeared to foresee that the predominant linkage among the objectives might turn out to be the reverse of what had been anticipated in the 1950s and 1960s. A prominent Soviet Third World analyst, for instance, maintained in the late 1970s that "imperialist states have lost the possibility of suppressing other nations by armed force, a possibility that was unrestricted in the past when capitalism was an all-embracing system." He stressed that "origination and consolidation of the world socialist system deprived the imperialist states of their monopoly position as the sole source" of weapons and military material as well as "loans, credits,...scientific and technical know-how and expert advice for the young independent countries."[57]

METHODS AND MEANS

Over the years, the method and means whereby the USSR has sought to accomplish the foregoing goals in the Latin American setting have altered on several occasions, and it is impossible to understand the Soviet approach in the 1980s without an appreciation of the nature of this evolution. Here, "method" refers to the conception of the course to be followed, and "means" to the resources to be employed and the concrete steps to be taken to realize the conception. The former has two key aspects: the particular entities to which the USSR has decided to devote its primary attention and the type of relationship that it hopes to fashion with them. The principal features of the latter are the instruments upon which Moscow plans to rely and the posture that it intends to assume toward the West in the region.

Changes in the method and the means that Moscow has prescribed with regard to Latin America, however, have grown essentially out of modification in the method and the means that Moscow has endorsed for working toward its ends in the Third World at large. In part, the latter changes have reflected alterations in circumstances in the Third World, yet they have also stemmed from revisions in Soviet perceptions of the Third World and lessons that Soviet leaders have drawn from their dealings with it.

In looking at the linkage between the method and the means that Moscow has devised for attaining broad Soviet objectives in the Third World, and the method and the means by which Soviet leaders have attempted to further these same general purposes in Latin America, it is useful to frame the discussion in terms of historical phases. Three basic stages are relevant here: the late 1950s to the mid-1960s, the mid-1960s to the end of the 1970s, and the 1980s.

Even though major Soviet interaction with parts of the area now known as the Third World did begin in the mid-1950s, the late 1950s constitute the logical starting point for the present analysis for two reasons. First, Moscow, as already noted, was relatively slow to conclude that changes with profound implications for the international system were taking place throughout the entire Third World. Specifically, not until the close of the 1950s did Soviet leaders come to believe that U.S. "hegemony" in Latin America, which they deemed to be the last bastion of Western domination in the Third World, was significantly eroding.

Second, this shift in Soviet assessment coincided roughly with important developments on the world scene that reshaped the broad context in which the USSR worked out its methods and means for the entire Third World. Toward the end of 1957, the USSR successfully launched both an intercontinental ballistic missile and an artificial earth satellite. Prior to these events, Moscow had regarded the correlation of global forces as favoring the United States and its allies, so Soviet leaders had viewed the Third World from an essentially "defensive" standpoint. This is, they had looked upon association with Third World countries and especially the so-called "neutralist" countries of the Third World as a means of buttressing the USSR's position against any possible Western onslaught. Not only had Moscow endeavored to establish relations with these states on the basis of principles of "peaceful coexistence" that involved tolerance for differences of political systems and noninterference in the internal affairs of one another, but it had also tried to enlist their support in establishing regional "zones of peace." After the two launchings, however, Soviet leaders judged that a situation of mutual military deterrence prevailed between East and West, and they commenced to handle the Third World from a more forward perspective, treating it as an arena for pursuing the global-power aspirations of the USSR.[58]

Late 1950s to Mid-1960s

This period was a highly complicated one, for neither the method nor the means that the USSR embraced—and especially the former—remained constant. Nevertheless, the period did have a coherence that justifies dealing with it as a single unit. This derived from the revolutionary optimism that pervaded Soviet thinking about the Third World throughout the years in question.

Vladimir Lenin's theory of imperialism had conditioned the Soviet elite to believe that the collapse of colonialism would open up possibilities for fairly rapid transitions to "scientific socialism" in former colonial territories; thus, to Soviet analysts the proliferation of new states in Third World areas suggested that a revolutionary tide would soon engulf these areas.[59] Hand in hand with this revolutionary optimism went a key calculation. Apparently assuming that Communist regimes in the Third World would establish close ties with Moscow, Soviet leaders judged that the rise of such governments there would redound to the USSR's advantage in international affairs. Not even the public Sino-Soviet rift in 1963 induced them to revise this assessment before the mid-1960s. Moscow's revolutionary optimism greatly affected the nature of the method and the means that the USSR employed during this entire time frame. It had a particularly strong impact on what entities Soviet leaders designated as objects of interest and how they tried to associate the USSR with those entities.

TARGETS OF INTEREST AND RELATIONSHIPS DESIRED

As in previous years, the USSR continued to display a wish for normal diplomatic, economic, and cultural relations with any state in the Third World willing to establish such ties. In Latin America, indeed, Moscow directed a large share of its activities toward the creation of these kinds of links, with the main recipients of its overtures being Argentina, Mexico, Brazil, and Chile.[60]

Yet the principal objects for courtship that Moscow identified in the Third World shifted.[61] Earlier in the 1950s, Soviet leaders had focused on states that expressed a dedication to "neutralism" or "nonalignment" in their foreign policies. Now Moscow turned its attention primarily to those countries that espoused a commitment to a "noncapitalist" internal path, although it plainly presumed that a "progressive" domestic course would result in a "progressive" stance in foreign affairs.

From the outset, the USSR deemed that the "bourgeois-nationalist" leaders in power in virtually all of these "noncapitalist" countries were capable of launching initial "progressive" reforms but would balk at carrying out deep-seated social and economic transformations. Nevertheless, Soviet leaders anticipated that the revolutionary process, once set in motion, would quickly bring to the fore orthodox Communists ready to undertake the total restructuring of their societies. Under such circumstances, Moscow felt, the USSR need only maintain close contacts with these states and bide its time.

However, events in various countries soon raised doubts about this appraisal. In places like the United Arab Republic, local Communists found themselves under severe attack from the ruling elements. Elsewhere, the genuineness of such elements, commitment to any "noncapitalist" measures came into serious question.

Consequently, by early 1961 Moscow had narrowed the definition of the USSR's chief targets of concern in the Third World to states that were demonstrably taking steps of a "noncapitalist" nature. Furthermore, it now urged left wing forces within these states to adopt a more assertive posture toward local ruling elements—one which mixed "alliance" and "struggle." Specifically, it encouraged them to set up a "national-democratic" front with the authorities in their countries, if one did not already exist. Wherever possible, this would involve some leftist participation in the decisions of government. At the same time, according to the Soviet advice, left wing forces in the Third World should push to deepen the internal transformations in their countries because they would thereby strengthen their links with the masses and position themselves to capitalize on further radicalization of politics there.

As time passed, misgivings emerged about the merits of even such a revised Soviet perspective. Marxist-Leninist forces in the vast majority of noncapitalist states remained weak. In fact, such forces did not exist at all in a number of the countries, particularly in Africa. On the other hand, several radical Third World leaders had begun to voice approval of "scientific socialism" and were introducing substantial changes in the economic and social life of their states.

By the end of 1963, therefore, Moscow had once again decided to narrow its list of principal targets in the Third World. It would henceforth concentrate on the relatively small number of countries with rulers that it believed had long-range revolutionary potential. In the Soviet assessment, these leaders, depicted as "revolutionary democrats," might embrace Marxism-Leninism and move to implement it in their states. While doing so, the argument went on, they would set up true Communist parties to consolidate their new orders. The USSR, for its part, could further such a development by playing the role of international mentor.

The best illustration of Moscow's application to Latin America of its preferred method of pursuing its ends in the Third World—and of all of that method's mutations during the late 1950s and early 1960s—involves Soviet behavior toward Cuba. Early on, Moscow perceived post-Batista Cuba as travelling on some type of "noncapitalist" road, and its handling of the state conformed to the shifting Soviet perspective on how to approach countries of this sort throughout the Third World.[62]

At the beginning, Soviet leaders granted that the Cuban revolution seemed more radical than any that had preceded it in Latin America, but they had major doubts about Fidel Castro, especially because he insisted that he rather than the local Communist party (the *Partido Socialista Popular*—PSP) should chart the course of revolution. Thus, they attempted to enhance the role of PSP in the unfolding situation by championing unity of "all democratic and progressive elements" in Cuba.

During the latter part of 1960, the USSR switched to another tack. In Moscow's view, Castro had by now become sufficiently "progressive"—adopting a strong stance against the United States, a radical domestic program, and a positive attitude toward the PSP—to justify close cooperation with him, but Soviet leaders envisioned that this cooperation would take place within a framework of "alliance" and "struggle," even if "struggle" had to be muted in view of Castro's sensitivities. They intended that the PSP would work within the regime to push the revolution further leftward and to entrench itself in positions of authority, thereby laying the groundwork for its eventual (though not immediate) assumption of power.

With Castro's embrace of "socialism" in early 1961, his absorption of the PSP into his Revolutionary Integrated Organization in the summer of that year, and his pronouncement the following December that he was a "Marxist-Leninist," the USSR decided to drop the "struggle" aspect of its formula for dealing with Cuba. That is, it opted to accept Castro at face value as a "Marxist-Leninist" and to provide the "education" necessary to deepen his understanding of "scientific socialism." This development, incidentally, predated by a year and a half official Soviet endorsement of the notion that the USSR could promote transitions to "true socialism" in the Third World countries by aligning itself with "revolutionary democrats" there. Obviously, then, the broad Soviet prescription did not shape the USSR's response to Castro; rather, the Soviet experience with Cuba inspired Moscow to search for other Castros in the Third World. It should be noted, however, that Moscow and Havana continued to engage in bitter polemics until the end of the 1960s over such issues as what constituted a revolutionary vanguard, what was the proper Marxist-Leninist road for acquiring power, and the best means of transforming a country into a "socialist" state.[63]

INSTRUMENTS

Throughout the later 1950s and early 1960s, Soviet leaders used a mix of political, economic, and military tools to implement their designated method for achieving their goals in the Third World, but two aspects of this mix deserve highlighting. First, the weight that Moscow attached to existing Communist parties of the Third World in its undertakings there decreased somewhat in the early 1960s.[64] (An extended analysis of Soviet attitudes toward the Latin American Communist parties since the 1950s may be found in the chapter by Edmé Domínguez in this volume.) Prior to then local Communist parties of the Third World had figured integrally in the method to which Soviet leaders had committed themselves. Indeed, the revolutionary transformations that Moscow envisioned for Third World countries entailed the ultimate rise to power of these parties. However, the Soviet decision to endorse the revolutionary capabilities of Third World rulers who professed an attraction to "scientific socialism" even though they did not belong to an organized Communist party altered the situation. This decision created a potential conflict of interests for Moscow in places where Communist parties had formed previously but a local ruler insisted that he should head any vanguard body within his domain. To resolve the problem, Moscow counseled established Communist parties in such areas to dissolve and to instruct their members to join revolutionary organizations under the aegis of local rulers. In Cuba, for example, this was the course that it urged upon the PSP.

Second, and perhaps of more overall consequence, Soviet leaders plainly regarded economic instruments as the principal tools at their disposal. During the early years, Soviet officials touted the USSR's ability to furnish economic aid to Third World countries to help them consolidate their political independence from the West, and Moscow attributed this ability to the Soviet model of development. According to Soviet spokesmen, Russia had lagged behind the West economically and technologically at the time of the Great October Revolution in 1917, but Russia's embrace of socialism had allowed it to close the gap in relatively short order. Indeed the Soviet Union was now on the verge of surpassing the West in both respects.[65] As the 1960s wore on, to be sure, it became increasingly apparent that the USSR's rate of economic growth was falling, that the state faced other major economic problems, and that the heady expectations of previous years about how rapidly its economic performance would overtake that of the West had been overly optimistic. Under such circumstances, Moscow saw no alternative but to downplay the Soviet model. Nonetheless, it persisted in proclaiming the virtues of Soviet economic assistance for Third World countries.

Available figures on Soviet aid to the Third World during the period bear out the USSR's stress on economic instruments. In 1956–64, Soviet military deliveries to Third World states (including Cuba) totaled about $6 billion, while Moscow's economic commitments to these states only amounted to roughly $5 billion. Yet of the nearly 30 countries to which the USSR provided some form of assistance, the vast bulk garnered more economic credits than supplies of arms and equipment. Indonesia, Iraq, and Syria appear to be the primary exceptions, and in all three cases Soviet military deliveries greatly outweighed Soviet economic commitments.[66]

As for Latin America specifically, there is no question about the predominance of economic aid. Aside from Cuba, countries of the region got $30 million in economic credits and no supplies of arms and equipment from the USSR in 1956–63.[67] Cuba obtained more than $2 billion in Soviet economic help of various types in 1961–67 and it received about $750 million in Soviet military deliveries in the same time frame.[68]

POSTURE TOWARD THE WEST

In keeping with its emphasis on economic instruments, the USSR assumed a highly conflictual but nonconfrontational stance toward the West in the Third World during the years in question. It did seek to draw Third World states into the socialist camp—and thereby enhance its own position in the Third World—yet it endeavored to do so through the attraction of its own economic and technological accomplishments and its claim to represent the wave of the future. Moreover, although Nikita Khrushchev championed national liberation movements and defined "wars of national liberation" as "just," he nevertheless expressed a preference for the "peaceful path" to socialism. He held to this line even in the face of strong criticism from the Chinese.[69]

The Soviet posture toward the United States in Latin America conformed fundamentally to such a stance. Moscow tried hard to avoid direct confrontation with Washington in this distant milieu. Khrushchev did grossly miscalculate the likely U.S. response when he tried to put intermediate-range missiles in Cuba in 1962 (he seems to have believed that the Kennedy administration would not move to counter this action), but he backed away from a military showdown over the issue.[70] Throughout the period, Moscow also defended the Latin American Communist parties that had opted for a "peaceful road" to power.[71]

Mid-1960s to Close of 1970s

Events of the mid-1960s brought on a new era in the method and means whereby the USSR pursued its purposes in the Third World at large. As a consequence of the ousters of "revolutionary-democratic" rulers in states like Ghana and Mali, Moscow reassessed conditions in the Third World. This reappraisal resulted in two key conclusions. First, existing "revolutionary-democratic" leaders in the Third World evinced such severe faults that they would probably never preside over transitions to "scientific socialism" in their states. Second—as mentioned above—the USSR could not count on the rapid emergence in the Third World of Communist regimes that would look to it as a natural ally. Indeed, the revolutionary process in Third World areas was in all likelihood going to be protracted, and probably few, if any, countries there would undergo "genuinely socialist" transformations in the foreseeable future.[72]

The latter judgment remained the underlying premise upon which the USSR operated in the Third World until the late 1970s. Not even the emergence in the mid–1970s of a number of Third World rulers that verbally embraced Marxism-Leninism and actually set up parties modeled along Communist lines persuaded Moscow to alter its position. The USSR applauded the "progressiveness" of these radical rulers, and it categorized them as "revolutionary democrats." Yet Soviet spokesmen took great pains to point out that these "revolutionary democrats" lacked a proper understanding of Marxism-Leninism. Furthermore, Moscow described the parties that they had founded as "vanguard parties of a new type," and explicitly distinguished such parties from Communist parties.[73]

This new premise triggered a revision in the method that Moscow employed to try to achieve Soviet ends in the Third World at large, and Latin America in particular. The change involved both the objects of Soviet courtship and the nature of the relationship that Moscow hoped to build with them.

TARGETS OF INTEREST

Soviet leaders decided that it made little sense to worry about which forces in the Third World had real revolutionary potential if circumstances there were not generally conducive to revolution in the near or even the medium term. Rather, the USSR should concentrate on identifying forces with whom association would advance Soviet purposes at the moment.

As one criterion for picking out such forces, Moscow fixed upon geopolitical merit. For instance, as in the past it opted to attach the highest priority to constructing ties with those states that form the southern rimlands of the USSR. It also elected to woo countries of recognized consequence—whether because of size, economic prowess, political influence, or whatever—in distant regions. Furthermore, in singling out such countries, it paid no heed to ideological orientation. Among the states that it selected for special wooing, for example, was Nigeria, unquestionably a "capitalist-oriented" country.[74]

However, Soviet leaders believed that the USSR would gain the most advantages from close links with entities that exhibited a measure of ideological affinity with it, particularly states of "socialist orientation."

Moscow regarded such states as favorably disposed to the USSR's initiatives and stances on many foreign policy issues.[75]

Soviet undertakings in Latin America during the years at issue by and large followed these broad guidelines. There were, it is true, some elements of continuity with the recent past. Cuba, which the USSR has recognized as a full-fledged member of the "socialist camp" by no later than 1963, still received a major portion of the attention that Moscow devoted to the region. Between 1968 and 1976 alone, for instance, the USSR furnished nearly $6 billion in various economic aid packages to the Havana government. From 1968 through the end of the 1970s, it shipped more than $1.5 billion in weapons and equipment to Cuba as well.[76] Moscow also continued to woo all Latin American governments disposed to enter into traditional diplomatic, economic, and cultural relations with the USSR—even the governments of "capitalist-oriented" states like Venezuela, Ecuador, Colombia, and Costa Rica.[77]

Yet the USSR directed the lion's share of its energies toward two groups of countries. The first of these consisted of the big regional powers, namely, Argentina, Brazil, and Mexico. The second included states that Moscow classified as "socialist-oriented" or otherwise "progressive" in character. Among these were Chile under Salvador Allende, Peru under Juan Velasco Alvarado, Guyana under Forbes Burnham, and Jamaica under Michael Manley.

TYPE OF RELATIONSHIP SOUGHT

If the USSR could not in the foreseeable future rely on bonds of "proletarian internationalism" to ensure itself a lasting position in the Third World countries that it has designated as primary objects of courtship, Moscow saw plainly that some other way of satisfying this requirement was essential. Events in states like Ghana and Mali had highlighted the folly of banking simply on relations with current ruling elements, no matter how "progressive" such elements might be. Even "progressive" governments might fall because of the instability endemic to Third World areas, and their successors might be unsympathetic or outrightly hostile to the USSR.[78] Under such circumstances, the USSR could well lose whatever position it had established in the countries concerned.

The solution to this dilemma, Moscow concluded, lay in fashioning long-term structural links with those states upon which the USSR chose to focus attention. Mutually beneficial links of this sort, Soviet leaders felt, would give whatever forces controlled the governments of these states an incentive to retain close ties with the USSR. In this sense, such links would help to insulate Soviet relations with individual states from the vagaries of political turnovers.[79]

The long-term structural relationship that Moscow originally had in mind was an international economic division of labor. That is, Third World countries would produce goods to sell to the USSR, and vice versa. (See Elizabeth Valkenier's chapter in this book for additional treatment of Soviet outlook on the subject.) According to the Soviet view, a good foundation for this type of trade partnership already existed in some cases because of a complementarity in items for export. Where it did not, an astute use of Soviet economic aid could remedy that situation. In other words, the USSR could furnish the financing, technical advice, and equipment for economic projects that would turn out goods for the Soviet market when completed.[80] At the outset, Moscow seems to have envisioned this commercial exchange as involving essentially items of a nonmilitary character, but as the years passed, it showed increasing inclination to include arms among its assets for purchase by Third World states.

Developments in the 1970s, however, caused a modification in Soviet thinking about the kind of long-term structural relationship that it should seek to effect. The mounting difficulties that the Soviet economy was experiencing reduced the chances that the USSR would be able to forge a meaningful international economic division of labor with most Third World states. At the same time, the rising number of self-styled Marxist-Leninist regimes in the Third World suggested to Moscow another sort of structural relationship that it might foster, i.e., joint collaboration with radical Third World governments in constructing institutions that would enable these governments to entrench themselves in power. This would entail cooperating in building a party apparatus, in establishing or strengthening intelligence and security services, in training military personnel, and the like. By the late 1970s, the USSR was devoting a substantial part of its energies to creating this type of structural relationship.[81]

In Latin America, the USSR expended some effort on trying to tighten its "proletarian-internationalist" links with Cuba,[82] and a lesser amount on creating normal diplomatic, economic, and cultural relations with a variety of other states. It concentrated, however, on working out long-term structural relationships with the two groups of countries that constituted its prime targets in the region. Neither of these groups qualified as the most advanced "progressive" states of the Third World in Soviet eyes, so the sort of relationship that Moscow endeavored to fashion in both cases was the above outlined international economic division of labor.

To take the large regional powers first, by the close of the 1970s the USSR had extended more that $250 million in economic credits to Argentina and $90 million to Brazil to further economic interaction with them. More significant, Moscow did its utmost throughout the years in question to expand Soviet trade with these two countries, even accepting large trade deficits for the time being in order to strengthen the ties. The average annual trade turnover between the USSR and Argentina increased from $60 million in 1965–69 to $330 million in 1975–79; that between the USSR and Brazil rose from $50 million to $324 million during the same period. In attempting to create structural economic ties with Mexico, the USSR went so far as to approve the signing in 1975 of a formal agreement of cooperation between the Council of Mutual Economic Assistance and Mexico. Not even such a mechanism, however, produced satisfactory results from the Soviet standpoint. In only one year of the entire period did the USSR's trade turnover with Mexico exceed $20 million.[83]

Constructing mutually beneficial economic ties with the "socialist-oriented" or otherwise "progressive" Latin American states posed greater difficulties for Moscow than building such links with the major regional powers. After all, the "progressive" states had smaller economies and produced fewer items for export than did the larger ones. Nonetheless, Moscow unmistakably made an attempt with regard to the "progressive" countries. During Allende's tenure in office in Chile, for example, the USSR committed itself to provide $240 million in economic assistance to the state, and its trade turnover with the country grew from nothing to about $10 million a year. With respect to Peru, Moscow offered the Lima government $25 million in economic credits; moreover, the USSR's trade turnover there jumped from less than $1 million a year on the average in 1965–69 to an annual average of more than $52 million in 1975–79. In part to compensate for the unfavorable balance here, the USSR agreed to supply weapons and equipment to the Andean country, and by the end of the 1970s, it had delivered $685 million worth of arms to Peru. Soviet trade turnover with Guyana also went up from virtually nothing in 1965–69 to an annual average of more than $7 million in 1975–79. In the case of Jamaica, Moscow proffered $30 million in economic credits, and the trade turnover increased from nothing in 1965–69 to almost $12 million a year on the average in 1975–79.[84]

INSTRUMENTS

The late 1960s and 1970s witnessed several consequential changes in the mix of tools to which Moscow resorted in the implementation of its defined method of attaining its goals in the Third World. To begin with, Third World Communist parties figured much less prominently in Soviet dealings with the Third World than had been the case in the immediately preceding years. If Marxist-Leninist transformations were not in the offing in at least most Third World states as Moscow obviously calculated, then the USSR was going to have to try to further its purposes within the prevailing noncommunist milieu of the Third World. Local Communist parties had limited relevance to such endeavors. Indeed, these parties could even wind up being liabilities to the USSR, for close identification with them could antagonize Third World rulers and render these rulers unreceptive to Soviet overtures. Despite Moscow's downgrading of Third World Communist parties as instruments, however, it did still invest substantial time and energy in attempting to ensure their allegiance.[85]

The new Soviet assessment of Communist parties was especially evident in Latin America. Only in the case of Chile—particularly during the Salvador Allende's Popular Unity government—did a local Communist party play a significant role in the USSR's undertaking in the region.

Second, certain of the Soviet government's fellow Communist regimes acquired enhanced stature as tools in Moscow's eyes. These included the governments of some of the USSR's Warsaw Pact allies in Eastern Europe (such as the German Democratic Republic), but the chief member of the group was the Cuban government. The Soviet-Cuban relationship continued to be a complicated one, and Fidel Castro certainly did not become a stooge of Moscow. (For detailed analysis of Soviet-Cuban interaction see the chapter by Jorge Domínguez in this book.) Nevertheless, by the mid-1970s Cuba was cooperating closely with the USSR in military interventions in African conflicts, first in the Angolan civil war and then in fighting between Ethiopia and Somalia in the Ogaden.

Moscow's increased esteem for Cuba as an instrument was not as manifest in the Latin American setting, where fewer opportunities existed for the USSR to employ Cuba usefully. Yet Moscow did plainly count on Cuba for links with ultra-left and guerrilla movements in the region. In the mid-1970s, for example, the USSR seems largely to have ceded to Cuba what it regarded as the minor task of forging contracts with Nicaragua's Sandinist National Liberation Front.[86]

Finally, Moscow's preferred type of instruments shifted from economic to military tools. Because of the initial Soviet emphasis on constructing an international economic division of labor with Third World states, economic instruments remained the key tools upon which the USSR relied at the outset of the period. Military deliveries to Third World countries did still surpass economic commitments, with the former running to about $8.5 billion as compared with roughly $7 billion for the latter in 1965–74. Yet, as in earlier years, a few states—in this instance Egypt, Iraq, Syria, Libya, India, and Algeria—had large imbalances, so the great majority of the 40 plus recipients of economic credits got more economic aid than supplies of arms. Trade statistics provide additional testimony of Moscow's primary concern with economic instruments. In 1965, the USSR had a trade turnover of approximately $1.7 billion with the Third World as a whole; by 1975, the figure was nearing $7 billion.[87]

The situation was much the same with respect to Latin America. Specifically, Soviet economic credits to states in the region aside from Cuba amounted to $595 million, as compared with $30 million in deliveries of weapons and equipment. The USSR's trade turnover with these countries rose from $160 million in 1965 to almost $1.3 billion in 1975. Not even the inclusion of Cuba alters the picture. The less than $200 million in arms supplies that Havana obtained from Moscow during 1965–74 paled beside the nearly $4.25 billion in different kinds of economic help that Cuba received from the USSR in 1968–74.[88]

During the 1970s, however, the Soviet outlook altered, and military instruments emerged as the main tools that Moscow used. Comparative statistics on economic commitments and military deliveries afford the most telling evidence. During 1975–79, the economic credits that the USSR extended to Third World states increased by about a third, to roughly $9.5 million, but Soviet arms deliveries to these states nearly tripled, escalating to more than $24 billion. Moreover, of the 30 Third World countries that garnered Soviet economic credits during 1975–79, only 12 got more economic assistance than they did deliveries of weapons and equipment.[89] The USSR also employed its own military power more extensively in the Third World than it had in preceding years. Its behavior in the Angolan civil war in 1974–76, in the conflict between Ethiopia and Somalia in the Ogaden in 1977–78, and in Afghanistan in 1979 provide the most dramatic examples.

This change in the priorities that Moscow attached to kinds of instruments for dealing with the Third World seems to have had at least limited impact on Soviet undertakings in Latin America, although this was not nearly so pronounced as elsewhere. In value terms, the balance between economic commitments and arms deliveries did tip in favor of the latter in the case of states other than Cuba. During 1975–79, Soviet supplies of weapons and equipment reached $650 million, while Soviet economic credits totaled only $420 million. Yet this comparison is somewhat distorting in that all of the military deliveries went to Peru. In courting other noncommunist states in the region, the USSR persisted in resorting primarily to economic instruments.

Perhaps the most important way in which the new Soviet preference of instruments manifested itself in Latin America had to do with Moscow's strategy for revolution. Throughout the 1960s and well into the 1970s, Moscow had touted the "peaceful road" as the best route to power for Communist parties in the region. From the mid-1970s on, however, it evinced growing skepticism that revolutionary forces in some parts of Latin America could triumph without engaging in an armed struggle. After Allende's overthrow in Chile, Soviet leaders publicly faulted the Chilean Communist party for not having prepared for a possible turn to violence to sustain revolutionary momentum in the country. Subsequently, Moscow appears to have endorsed Cuban initiatives to help the FSLN in Nicaragua wage a more effective guerrilla war, although Soviet leaders clearly misjudged the near-term prospects for the success of this armed effort. Then in the wake of the FSLN's triumph in July 1979, the USSR unmistakably sanctioned the adoption of a guerrilla-warfare line by the Communist Party of El Salvador.[90] Nonetheless, the USSR continued to champion the "peaceful path" as the desirable course in many contexts—even in conservative, military-controlled states like Brazil and Argentina.[91]

POSTURE TOWARD THE WEST

In conjunction with the new stress on military instruments, the USSR took a more confrontational stance toward the West in the Third World than it had assumed before. It thrust itself fairly directly into the conflicts in Angola and the horn of Africa in the mid-1970s despite U.S. involvements and concerns in both areas, and when faced with what it viewed as an intolerable situation in Afghanistan, it sent its military forces marching across the borders in an unprecedented breach of the principles of "peaceful coexistence." To be sure, Moscow plainly banked that the Vietnam syndrome would keep the United States virtually immobilized during these ventures. Nevertheless, the episodes revealed a Soviet readiness to accept a higher degree of risking a head-on clash with the West than had previously been evident.

This tendency to approach the West in a more confrontational manner in the Third World as a whole had only a limited effect on Soviet activities in Latin America. According to Moscow's geopolitical calculations, the United States still retained dominance in the region, especially in Central America and the Caribbean; therefore, caution was in order. At the same time, the willingness of Soviet leaders to recognize armed struggle as proper revolutionary strategy in places like Nicaragua did heighten the Soviet challenge to the United States in Latin America to some degree.

Schools of Thought in the 1980s

The 1980s have brought shifts in the USSR's method and means of pursuing its ends in the Third World, and Latin America in particular, that are more complex than any preceding changes. The additional complexity has stemmed from two factors. First, there has been a proliferation of schools of thought within the Soviet hierarchy about the most suitable method and means, and second, the top Soviet leadership has failed to embrace the views of a single school exclusively. Although disagreements about the best method and means have existed almost constantly among the Soviet elite since the early 1960s, the basic positions on the subject were previously few in number. Moreover, in the past the top leadership always threw the weight of its authority behind one of them.[92]

Because of this complexity, it is imperative to begin with an examination of the Soviet method and means in the 1980s with an analysis of the prescriptions that have emerged on the issue during the decade. There are basically four of these, each with advocates at or near the center of power in the USSR.[93] The four represent varying responses to the evolving situation in the Third World, but they also reflect differing perceptions of what Third World realities are. The discussion here will refer to the individual schools as the "socialist-orientation," the "pro-military," the "national-capitalism," and the "economic interdependence" perspectives.

THE "SOCIALIST-ORIENTATION" PERSPECTIVE

Adherents of this outlook favor a method and means similar to the method and the means that the USSR employed in the last half of the 1970s. They maintain, to begin with, that Moscow should concentrate largely on courting states of "socialist orientation" in the Third World, and particularly "revolutionary democracies" which have established "vanguard parties" of a "new type." Underlying this position is a set of assessments about trends in the Third World. Proponents of this viewpoint insist that a gradual process of radicalization is going forward in Third World areas; these areas, despite some zigs and zags, are bypassing capitalism and moving directly toward socialism. In the eyes of these observers, not only have the ranks of the "socialist-oriented" states in the Third World grown, but the emergence of ruling "revolutionary-democratic" parties of a "vanguard" kind in such countries as the People's Democratic Republic of Yemen, Angola, Mozambique, and Ethiopia testifies to a deepening of the Third World revolutionary process. As this revolutionary process continues to intensify, the estimate goes on, the number of "socialist-oriented" countries will increase still further, the circle of "vanguard" parties will expand, and some of these parties will effect transitions to full-fledged Communist parties, although a reversal of path cannot be ruled out in all cases.

Partisans of this line in the 1980s, it is true, have been much more willing to admit than were its supporters in the 1970s that existing "revolutionary-democratic" regimes with "vanguard" parties have deficiencies. For instance, they charge that most of these regimes have not steadfastly carried out socialist measures; in fact, they sometimes even say that the regimes have as yet failed to advance farther on the path to socialism than the Russian populists did in the mid-1800s.[94] They also upbraid these Third World governments for vacillation in foreign affairs. Still, representatives of this school of thought have not discarded the premise that the Third World is marching inexorably toward socialism and in the process is going to bypass capitalism. To these observers, therefore, the current "socialist-oriented" governments, whatever their faults, constitute the wave of the future and the best available allies for the USSR in the Third World at present.

In keeping with the group's stress on Soviet links with "revolutionary-democratic" regimes with "vanguard" parties, its members urge that the USSR try to build long-term structural relationships with the states over which these regimes preside. They appear to accept the unlikelihood that the USSR can manage in the near future to work out an international economic division of labor with the countries concerned, but they hold that with patience and perseverance Moscow can create lasting ties with these countries by helping the existing governments put down firm roots in local soil.

As for instruments, those who subscribe to this position see virtue in using "socialist" forces of various strips to bolster—and even to enlarge the number of—Third World "revolutionary-democratic" regimes, especially regimes with "vanguard" parties. These forces range from straightforwardly Communist elements to "socialist-oriented" entities, and they include the governments of the East European states and Cuba, as well as nonruling groups in the Third World.

No less important, the champions of this vision of method and means lean toward primary reliance on nonmilitary tools. They do not, to be sure, contest the value of military instruments. On the contrary, they have approved Soviet use of military force to ensure the survival of "revolutionary-democratic" governments with "vanguard" parties, and they have underscored the role that military assistance has played in the forging of close Soviet ties with such regimes. Yet their vision of a long-term structural relationship with these governments implicitly pushes them toward emphasis on nonmilitary instruments, especially political ones.

With respect to the precise posture that the USSR should adopt toward the West in the Third World, the backers of this outlook seem to endorse the approach of the late 1970s, but in a selective way. They evince a readiness to risk confrontation with the West where ruling "revolutionary-democratic" parties of a "vanguard" type in the Third World are concerned. For example, they have blessed large-scale Soviet military aid to parties of this type faced with strong challenges from local opposition elements—no matter what support the opposition elements have enjoyed from abroad. Yet the members of the group shy away from military confrontation with the West in contexts involving other forces in the Third World. They do, however, appear to foresee that Soviet relations with the West in such instances will always be contentious in nature.

Among the most visible formulators and defenders of this school of thought has been Rostislav Ul'ianovsky, a deputy director of the International Department of the CPSU from the 1960s until the end of 1986 and still an associate of the African Institute of the USSR Academy of Sciences. He received substantial assistance in both regards from Anatolii Gromyko, head of the African Institute and son of Andrei Gromyko, until recently chairman of the Presidium of the USSR Supreme Soviet and previously USSR foreign minister. Both Grigorii Romanov, until 1985 a CPSU Politburo member and a leading rival of Mikhail Gorbachev, and Boris Ponomarev, prior to early 1986 a CPSU secretary and head of its International Department as well as an alternate member of the Politburo, also openly associated themselves with the "socialist-orientation" viewpoint before they departed from office, but neither ever figured as prominently in the elaboration of it as Ul'ianovsky and Anatolii Gromyko have.[95]

THE PRO-MILITARY PERSPECTIVE

Exponents of this position hold that in the Third World the USSR should devote its energies primarily to military regimes—particularly those of a radical character. A high percent of Third World governments, they stress, are either under military rule or at least dominated by military elements; furthermore, a substantial number of these governments display a resolve to effect major social transformations in their countries and a willingness to enter into close relations with the USSR.

Proponents of this line of argument do concede that in the abstract a "vanguard" party might constitute not only a more satisfactory vehicle for carrying out social change, but also would be a more reliable ally for the USSR than military regimes. They note, however, that "vanguard" parties have not yet emerged in most Third World states controlled by militaries. Nor do they see this situation changing in the years immediately ahead in that many militaries in power in the Third World see "vanguard" parties as potential competitors for political control. Even where militaries have tolerated the formation of "vanguard" parties, advocates of this viewpoint go on, the armed forces remain the key institutions shaping the destinies of their countries. If they decide to act in opposition to local "vanguard" parties, or to do away with such parties altogether, these parties do not have the mass base and the access to instruments of violence required to meet such challenges effectively. Hence, those committed to the outlook conclude, ties with Third World militaries, and especially radical militaries, afford the USSR the greatest opportunities available to encourage a deepening of the revolutionary process in the Third World and to enhance the Soviet role there.

Support for creating long-term structural relations with states in which militaries, and particularly radical militaries, are preeminent flows naturally from the group's rationale for focusing on such countries, but the structural links that the group envisions differ from those that Moscow championed in the preceding period. This school of thought discounts the possibility of bringing about an international economic division of labor between the USSR and these states, and it plays down the notion of helping in the foundation and strengthening of nonmilitary institutions there. Instead, it presses for cooperation that will render the countries at issue dependent on the USSR in a military sense.

As for instruments and posture toward the West in the Third World, partisans of the "pro-military" position appear to find much about the Soviet means of the late 1970s basically acceptable. They do, it is true, assign even less value to Communist parties of the Third World as tools than Moscow did in the 1970s, although they do not treat such parties as utterly worthless. At the same time, the group's proposed efforts to woo military-based regimes and to make these regimes highly dependent on the USSR militarily imply an inclination to rely heavily on military instruments. They also suggest a propensity to see value in East European countries and particularly Cuba as military surrogates for the USSR. Finally, they tend to indicate a willingness to involve the USSR in military strife in the Third World, even if such involvement leads to a clash with the West.

Public articulation of this viewpoint has come principally from military quarters. The "pro-military" school originated in the mid-1970s, and although it received open endorsement from at least some lower-level civilians at that time, it enjoyed support largely in military circles even then. During the late 1970s, moreover, all overt civilian backing disappeared. In fact, the line of argument itself appeared to vanish entirely from Soviet thinking for several years.[96] When it resurfaced in 1982, it never regained any public civilian endorsement. Among the military defenders of this line in the 1980s, however, has been Colonel E. Rybkin, long a leading figure in the shaping of Soviet military doctrine and strategy.[97]

THE "NATIONAL-CAPITALISM" PERSPECTIVE

Champions of this vision of method and means identify a much more varied set of Third World candidates for courtship than Moscow did throughout the 1970s. Their eclecticism stems from fairly complicated calculations. In the group's judgments, the vast majority of Third World states have now chosen the path of development that they are going to follow, and the bulk of them have opted for the capitalist, or at least a nonsocialist, path. Thus, most Third World countries will probably pass through a capitalist or nonsocialist phase of development before embarking on a socialist course. This prospect means that "socialist-oriented" countries will in all likelihood remain in the minority in the Third World for the indefinite future. Furthermore, from the standpoint of the subscribers to this outlook, the states that have adopted a "socialist orientation" have disturbing faults. Even the most "progressive" of these states—the "revolutionary democracies" with "vanguard" parties—have displayed a less than steadfast desire to implement far-reaching social transformations internally and have vacillated in their foreign policies. As a consequence, they have substantial deficiencies as Soviet allies. Under all of these circumstances, adherents of this school of thought insist, the USSR needs to diversify its relationships in the Third World.

Diversification of ties is not only imperative but also possible, the group suggests. The objective bases for it lie in "contradictions" between Third World "capitalist-oriented" states and the West that the USSR can exploit. Perhaps the most important of these "contradictions" have economic roots. In the opinions of these Soviet commentators, the rulers of many "capitalist-oriented" Third World countries want to develop a "nationalist" type of capitalism in their domains, while the "imperialist" Western powers strive to foster a "dependent" form of capitalism there. "Contradictions" of a strictly political and ideological nature exist as well. According to backers of this perspective, commitment to Islam coupled with resistance to Westernization can produce tensions between a "capitalist-oriented" Third World state and the Western powers.

Advocates of this viewpoint believe that the USSR has little chance of constructing long-term structural links with the great bulk of the states that they themselves consider targets for wooing. Not only does the USSR patently lack the capabilities to create an international economic division of labor with such a large number of countries, but the vast majority of these states show no wish for heavy Soviet involvement in efforts to solidify their governments.

Therefore, members of the group accept the probability that there will be divergences of interests over time between the USSR and many countries that they pinpoint for attention. Nevertheless, as they see things, eclecticism in defining potential allies will tend to offset this difficulty, for profitable relations with a large and varied circle of states will reduce the impact that a setback in any one of these states can have on overall Soviet fortunes in the Third World. The sheer volume of ties, in short, will help to insulate the Soviet position.

Concerning instruments, proponents of this outlook seem to regard both Third World Communist parties and the governments of Communist states like the German Democratic Republic and Cuba as of quite limited utility under current conditions. To these Soviet analysts, such entities, and particularly the Communist governments, may have substantial merit as tools in Soviet courtship of "socialist-oriented" movements and regimes in the Third World, but movements and regimes of this sort will probably remain a relatively minor force in the Third World for the foreseeable future. Furthermore, neither Third World Communist parties nor the government of the USSR's fellow Communist states have the kind of image among "nonsocialist-oriented" parties and ruling elements in the Third World that can help the USSR much in wooing such parties and elements.

The group also plainly weights specific instruments differently than Moscow did in the late 1970s. Although the group gives no sign of rejecting military tools to forge links with the diverse states upon which it focuses, the type of opportunities that it discerns for building these ties prompts it to emphasize other instruments. Economic tools play a prominent role in its calculations. Yet because such instruments are in short supply at present, the group places primary stress on political tools.

In downplaying military instruments, the "national-capitalism" school appears to endorse a less confrontational stance toward the West in the Third World than the USSR took in the last half of the 1970s. Nevertheless, it still seems to favor a highly conflictual approach toward the West there. The bases upon which it proposes to construct relations with a wide range of Third World countries are varied types of anti-Western sentiment, and it anticipates fashioning and/or strengthening ties by fanning such sentiment.

The front ranks of the shapers and exponents of this vision of method and means have included Karen Brutents, a deputy director of the International Department of the CPSU since the mid-1970s. Another key figure in both respects has been Evgenii Primakov, until early 1986 the head of the Institute of Oriental Studies of the USSR Academy of Sciences and now director of the Academy's Institute of World Economy and International Relations.[98]

THE "ECONOMIC INTERDEPENDENCE" PERSPECTIVE

Like the preceding group of Soviet observers, espousers of this line of argument set forth an eclectic list of targets of interest in the Third World, but their rationale for doing so differs greatly from the one advanced by partisans of the "national-capitalism" viewpoint. The "economic interdependence" school of thought maintains that strong incentives have developed in "capitalist-oriented" as well as "socialist-oriented" states to intensify relations with the USSR. These are largely economic in nature. Most countries in the Third World, the subscribers to the position note, have to date chalked up poor records of economic performance. Not only have they been slipping farther and father behind the advanced industrial powers, but they have even failed to achieve significant economic growth in absolute terms. Thus, according to the assessment, leaders of these diverse states are seeking ways to improve their local economic situations, and they are prepared to expand their dealings with the USSR substantially in pursuit of this goal.

Proponents of the outlook go on to contend that the USSR has the wherewithal to take advantage of this opportunity. To be sure, the USSR has economic troubles of its own, members of the group implicitly admit, and it does not possess the resources to solve the economic problems of Third World countries. But, they insist, these deficiencies do not really matter. The only way of overcoming Third World economic woes anyway is through the working out of a coherent world system of economic interdependence. Within such a system, the USSR could play a key part that would enable it to build up links with a broad spectrum of countries, not to mention strengthening its own domestic economy.

The system that the champions of this perspective foresee has several features. First, the industrialized states of the West would produce goods of high technological sophistication for sale to the USSR and other members of the Soviet bloc. The USSR and its allies, in turn, would manufacture items of a lower level of technological sophistication for export to Third World countries. This last category of states would devote its energies, at least at the outset, to producing minerals and raw materials for sale to both the Western powers and the Soviet bloc. By specializing in such output, they would develop the requisite skills and surpluses to diversify their economies, beginning with labor-intensive food and processing industries. This projected system, it should be underscored, entails no meaningful distinctions between "capitalist-oriented" and "socialist-oriented" countries in the Third World.

Supporters of this line urge the creation of a long-term structural relationship with Third World states that they deem to be worthwhile objects for courtship, but their notion of the relationship does not conform to either of the two versions that Moscow endorsed in the previous period. The conception of such a relationship that gained predominance in the late 1970s stressed mutual cooperation with regimes of designated countries in establishing and/or bolstering their institutions of control, but the vision of it here focuses on the fashioning of economic ties. Unlike the earlier idea of constructing an international economic division of labor, however, the current perception entails economic links that solidify in a multilateral context. The notion of an international economic division of labor posited an essentially bilateral arrangement. That is, the USSR would help build projects that would then produce for the Soviet market. The present conception of the relationship anticipates that economic ties will flourish in a broader setting in which other actors have major roles to perform.

With respect to instruments, commentators of this persuasion seem to see relatively little merit in either Third World Communist parties or existing Communist regimes as tools. The group's preoccupation with enhancing the economic interdependence of the Third World and the Soviet bloc disposes it to esteem as instruments any entity that can help the USSR further this end. Third World Communist parties, however, lack such a capacity. So, by and large, do Communist governments in economically less advanced countries like Cuba and Vietnam. The regimes of the more industrialized countries of Eastern Europe have some capabilities to assist in the process, but these are not extensive.

More significant, adherents of the viewpoint clearly rank the general types of tools available to the USSR in an order that contrasts sharply with Moscow's preferences of the late 1970s. Although the group does not reject the use of military instruments out of hand, the character of the opportunities that it discerns in the Third World dictates a heavy stress on economic tools. Even political instruments become decidedly secondary in such a light. This emphasis also distinguishes the group from the "national-capitalism" enthusiasts.

Promoters of this vision of method and means favor a much less conflictual posture toward the West in the Third World than the USSR took in the 1970s or than any of the other current schools of thought advocate. These observers appear to assume that competition between the USSR and the Western powers will continue in the Third World, but they do not anticipate that this competition will necessarily result in military clashes or political strife. On the contrary, they foresee the possibility of Soviet-Western cooperation in certain instances. For example, they sanction close Soviet trade ties with the West, and they contemplate a situation where both the West and the USSR will purchase the minerals and raw materials that Third World states will have to sell as these states attempt to develop economically.

Although no eminent political figures have visibly had a key hand in formulating this basic outlook, several have publicly associated themselves with it. Among these have been Vadim Zagladin, until 1986 the sole first deputy head of the International Department of the CPSU and now a personal advisor to Mikhail Gorbachev; N. N. Inozemtsev, until his death in 1982 the director of the Institute of World Economy and International Relations of the USSR Academy of Sciences as well as a member of the CPSU Central Committee; and Georgii Arbatov, director of the Institute for the Study of the United States and Canada of the USSR Academy of Sciences and also a member of the CPSU Central Committee.[99]

Soviet Behavior in the 1980s

As noted already, the Soviet leadership has not officially embraced any of the four fundamental Soviet schools of thought of desirable method and means in the Third World. Whether this state of affairs reflects conscious choice on the part of the leadership, inability of the leadership to reach a consensus on a particular viewpoint, or diffusion of decision-making power within the Soviet foreign-policy establishment is beyond the scope of the discussion here.[100] What matters in the present context is the situation's impact on Soviet behavior in the Third World overall, and in Latin America more particularly. This has been twofold. First, although the method and the means that have shaped

Moscow's activities in the Third World have had most in common with the method and the means championed by the "national-capitalism" school of thought, Soviet behavior has embodied elements of other perspectives as well. Second, the exact mixture of elements of the four lines has varied from region to region.[101]

In the 1980s, then, the methods and the means that the USSR has employed in Latin America have displayed a substantial degree of distinctiveness. For this reason, the ensuing analysis will focus on the precise amalgam of the four viewpoints that has characterized Soviet dealings with the region.

TARGETS OF INTEREST

In accordance with the urgings of the partisans of the "national-capitalism" and "economic interdependence" outlooks, the USSR has focused on wooing "nonsocialist-oriented" entities in Latin America. For instance, Moscow has worked harder than ever before to intensify its relations with large "capitalist-oriented" states like Brazil, Argentia, and Mexico. Some concrete aspects of its undertakings with respect to Brazil will drive home the point. In the early 1980s, Soviet leaders began to dispatch parliamentary delegations to Brazil and to entertain similar Brazilian delegations in the Soviet Union. Representatives of the USSR Supreme Soviet traveled to Brazil in April 1980, July 1982, May 1984, and March 1985, and members of the National Congress of Brazil made official trips to the USSR in December 1980, December 1983, and July 1986. In May 1984, Soviet officials in Moscow marked another milestone by receiving the governors of the Brazilian states of Amazonas and Pará. Then in December 1985, Brazilian Foreign Minister Olavo Setúbal spent several days in Moscow consulting with Soviet leaders. Never previously had a Brazilian foreign minister visited the USSR. In February 1987, Soviet Deputy Foreign Minister Viktor Komplektov arrived in Brazil to lay the groundwork for a reciprocal visit later in the year by Soviet Foreign Minister Eduard Shevardnadze.[102]

Moscow has also stepped up its courtship of a number of smaller "capitalist-oriented" countries to which it was already paying some heed—notably, Peru, Colombia, Venezuela, and Panama. A few highlights of recent Soviet overtures to Panama will indicate the degree of the efforts. Karen Brutents, a deputy chief of the International Department of the CPSU, conferred with the president of Panama, in

Panama City in December 1984, and Arnold Ryuytel, a deputy chairman of the USSR Supreme Soviet Presidium, did the same in May 1986. More revealing still, Soviet media in July 1986 sympathetically reported the charges of General Manuel Antonio Noriega, head of Panama's National Guard and the *de facto* strongman of the country, that the United States was plotting to prevent Panama from assuming full control of the Panama Canal in 2000. In doing so, they glossed over the fact that Noreiga was responding to U.S. accusations that he was involved in the drug traffic to the United States.[103] In March 1987, officials of the USSR welcomed to Moscow a Panamanian parliamentary delegation led by Octavio Díaz, president of the Legislative Assembly. During this group's stay, Soviet representatives broached the possibility of establishing formal diplomatic ties and instituting Aeroflot links with Panama.[104]

With regard to several other smaller "capitalist-oriented" states, Moscow has shown a clear resolve to open up new contacts or to revive those that had languished in the 1970s. Uruguay provides a good illustration. After the restoration of civilian rule there in 1985, the USSR took a variety of steps to signal its good intentions toward the new government headed by Julio María Sanguinetti. By August 1986, Soviet leaders were receiving a Uruguayan foreign minister in Moscow for the first time. A few weeks later, Karen Brutents arrived in Montevideo to participate in the celebrations of the 150th anniversary of the ruling Colorado Party. In February 1987, USSR deputy foreign minister Komplektov journeyed to Uruguay for consultations about, among other things, a visit to Moscow by President Sanguinetti during the summer of 1987.[105]

Particularly striking was the reaction of the USSR to the 1980 electoral defeat in Jamaica of the "socialist-oriented" People's National Party of Michael Manley by the "capitalist-oriented" Jamaica Labor Party of Edward Seaga. Soviet-Jamaican ties did not suffer. If anything, they grew stronger. In 1983, the USSR committed itself to furnish another $10 million in economic aid to the Kingston government, and the annual average of trade turnover between the two countries jumped from about $12 million in 1975–79 to nearly $30 million in 1980–84.[106] Moreover, regular discussions on such matters as the agenda for U.N. General Assembly sessions and bilateral relations continued to take place.[107]

In line with the counsel of subscribers to the "revolutionary-democratic" viewpoint, however, the USSR has persisted, too, in pursuing close links with "progressive" and especially "socialist-oriented" forces in Latin America. The most salient objects of courtship in this category have been the self-styled Marxist-Leninist regimes in Nicaragua and (until October 1983) Grenada.

At no juncture has Moscow shown a desire to become as involved with either Nicaragua or Grenada as it has been with Cuba since the 1960s, but it has still proved ready to provide a sizable amount of its resources to them. Prior to the turmoil within the New Jewel Movement that resulted in U.S. intervention in Grenada in October 1983, the USSR had furnished more than $10 million in economic credits to the small Caribbean state, and as pointed out earlier, it had agreed to supply arms valued at almost 20 million rubles (about $25 million) to the Bishop government. A substantial portion of these arms had already reached the island by the time of the U.S. invasion.[108] During 1980–84, Moscow pledged to Nicaragua about $575 million in economic aid, and by 1985 it had delivered about $240 worth of weapons and equipment to the Central American country, including a number of Mi-24/HIND D attack helicopters and other items of a more advanced technology. Along with this economic aid and military hardware to Nicaragua went Soviet economic and military technicians. By the close of 1984, Soviet and East European economic advisers in the state totaled 475, and in 1985 there were 50–70 Soviet military advisers there.[109]

The depth of the USSR's political dialogue with the two countries affords an even more telling gauge of Soviet interest in them than the exact resources that the USSR has channeled to them. Such interaction has been particularly intense in the case of Nicaragua. A brief summary of the visits to Moscow by top FSLN leaders during the early 1980s will give some sense of the extent of the contacts. Interior Minister Tomás Borge, Defense Minister Humberto Ortega, Minister of Planning Henry Ruiz, and junta member Moisés Hassan commenced the treks in March 1980. Humberto Ortega returned to Moscow in November 1981; so did Borge in September 1982 and Ruiz in February 1983. Daniel Ortega, the head of the ruling junta, traveled to the USSR for the first time in May 1982 and then went back in November 1982 and March 1983. Jaime Wheelock, Minister of Agriculture, Cattle Development and Agrarian Reform, was in Moscow in December 1982 and July 1983, and Bayardo Arce, head of the Sandinista Political Commission, journeyed to the USSR in June 1983.

Despite Moscow's preoccupation during this period with "progressive" forces in power in places like Nicaragua and Grenada, the USSR has paid considerable attention as well to some "progressive" nonruling elements. In the wake of the Nicaraguan revolution of 1979, Moscow became convinced that certain other states in Latin America might be ripe for armed takeovers. It singled out El Salvador, Honduras, Guatemala, and Chile in this regard. However, for takeovers actually to occur in these countries, it believed, united fronts encompassing a broad spectrum of "progressive" forces dedicated to armed struggle had to form.[110] Consequently, it attempted to promote the organization and consolidation of such fronts. By the mid-1980s, however, Soviet optimism about the immediate prospects for armed victories in at least the Central American states had waned,[111] but the rudimentary foundations of the sort of fronts that Moscow had envisioned had taken shape in El Salvador (the Farabundo Martí National Liberation Front), Guatemala (Guatemalan National Revolutionary Unity), Honduras (the National Patriotic Front), and Chile (the Manuel Rodríguez Patriotic Front). Each enjoyed Soviet recognition and backing.

NATURE OF RELATIONSHIP DESIRED

With respect to the "nonsocialist-oriented" countries, Moscow has essentially seemed to accept the judgment of the "national-capitalism" perspective that only nonstructural, potentially short-term ties are feasible under existing circumstances. Certainly, Soviet leaders have betrayed no illusions about the willingness of the governments of any of the states to collaborate closely with the USSR to shore up their own domestic positions.

Economic data do leave room for arguing that Moscow has retained some hope of forging a meaningful international economic division of labor with a few states—principally Argentina and Brazil.[112] During 1980–84, Soviet commitments of economic aid to Argentina and Brazil totaled $65 million and $70 million respectively. More critical, the USSR's annual average trade turnover with each has run much higher in the 1980s than it did in the 1970s: that with Argentina exceeded $2 billion in 1980–84, as compared with $330 million in 1975–79; that with Brazil topped $680 million in 1980–84, as compared with about $325 million in 1975–79.

Yet other evidence indicates that Moscow had more pressing reasons for increasing trade with the two countries during the early 1980s than simply to create an international division of labor with them. Not only did Soviet exports to the two states stay quite low even when Soviet imports soared, but there was also a downward trend in trade turnover with Argentina after 1980 and with Brazil after 1983. Such signs suggest that the rise in trade turnover had primarily to do with specific Soviet needs—especially of food and grain.

In the case of "socialist-oriented" countries, Moscow has followed the prescriptions of the "revolutionary-democratic" school of thought. It has worked to establish structural links with these states by collaborating with their avowedly Marxist-Leninist regimes in building institutions to enable the regimes to survive. Yet the USSR has preferred to keep a low profile in such endeavors. Although it has provided much general advice and logistical support for undertakings of this sort, Moscow has depended on its allies, notably Cuba, to supply the manpower required. Cuba, for its own reasons as well as at Soviet instigation, has shouldered this responsibility. By late 1983, the more than 780 Cubans in Grenada included 43 with the armed forces, and of the 7,500 Cubans present in Nicaragua at the end of 1984, some 3,000 were military or security personnel attached to the armed forces or to internal security and intelligence organizations.[113]

To be sure, Soviet use of surrogates, and especially Cuba, to help fashion the desired structural ties has had drawbacks. Fidel Castro has not always seen eye to eye with Moscow about how to proceed, and he has sometimes gone his own way.[114] On balance, however, Soviet leaders seem to believe that cooperation with Cuba in such contexts has more positive than negative features—particularly in light of the perceived need to restrict direct Soviet involvement in areas like Central America and the Caribbean.

As long as "progressive" united fronts in places like El Salvador, Guatemala, Honduras, and Chile remain merely seekers of power, Soviet efforts to construct any kind of structural relationship with them can only be tentative. Nonetheless, the USSR has shown some inclination to develop the kind of links that proponents of the "pro-military" line favor. That is, it seems to have tried to render these organizations militarily dependent on them by functioning as their chief supplier of weapons and equipment, although the precise levels of its arms shipments to them are unknown.[115]

INSTRUMENTS

The tools that the USSR has employed in Latin America in the 1980s have differed according to the general type of situation that it has confronted. Moscow has unquestionably distinguished between contexts in which a substantial degree of political radicalization has occurred recently or has seemed possible within a finite period of time and contexts in which such a radicalization has appeared remote at best.

In the former cases, Soviet leaders have heeded the advice of the exponents of the "revolutionary-democratic" outlook and, to a lesser extent, the "pro-military" one. To help them exert influence on the broad united fronts that they have deemed essential in states like El Salvador, Guatemala, Honduras, and Chile, they have pressed local Communist parties to become key components of these fronts.[116] Similarly, Moscow has displayed additional interest in using governments of other Communist states, and particularly Cuba, as tools for dealing with both ruling and nonruling revolutionary elements in Latin America. Cuba has at times served as an intermediary in the USSR's relations with the guerrilla movements in most of the countries at issue here,[117] and as already mentioned, it has performed important roles in the USSR's efforts to cooperate with the self-proclaimed Marxist-Leninist governments in Grenada and Nicaragua to consolidate their power.

As for the relative weight that Soviet leaders have assigned to broad types of instruments here, military tools have plainly enjoyed top priority in Moscow's undertakings regarding united fronts engaged in armed struggle, and military instruments have also acquired new significance in Moscow's handling of its relations with "revolutionary democracies" like Grenada and Nicaragua. As noted previously, the USSR had promised the New Jewel Movement regime in Grenada about $25 million in arms and a little more than $10 million in economic aid before that regime fell in late 1983. By 1985, Moscow had delivered to Managua about $240 million of weapons and equipment, while Soviet extensions of economic credits amounted to $575 million in 1980–84. Yet especially with respect to Nicaragua, the USSR has put primary stress on political tools, as the intensity of the political contacts referred to above attests.

Where Soviet leaders have discerned no prospects for radicalization, they have relied basically on the instruments championed by the "national-capitalism" and "economic interdependence" schools of persuasion, but the perspectives of the former group have clearly had the greater impact on the precise selection. Local Communist parties and the governments of Communist states like Cuba, it should be underscored, have figured little in Soviet activities toward such countries. Of far more consequence, Moscow has tended to favor economic tools over military ones here. During 1980–84, the USSR made economic commitments totaling more than $500 million to nonradical states, while it provided only $400 million in arms to them in 1981–85. More critically, the economic aid in 1980–84 went to seven individual recipients, but just two states got Soviet military deliveries in 1981–85.[118] Finally, the USSR's trade turnover with nonradical countries rose from about $860 million a year on the average in 1975–79, to an annual average of roughly $25 billion in 1980–84.[119]

For all the value that Moscow has attached to economic instruments in these instances, however, it has seen the most virtue in political ones. As data already presented show, Soviet leaders have devoted great effort to expanding the range and frequency of political interaction with "capitalist-oriented" states. This interaction has now come to entail everything from exchanges of top-ranking political figures to the staging of mass cultural exhibitions.

POSTURE TOWARD THE UNITED STATES

The stance of the USSR toward the United States in Latin America has conformed to a large degree to that recommended by the "national-capitalism" enthusiasts. That is, Moscow has not eschewed conflict, but it has attempted to avoid confrontation. For example, it has tried to exploit for its own purposes the "contradictions" between Latin American countries and the United States on such issues as the Falkland/Malvinas Islands, the Latin American debt crisis, and the clash between Nicaragua and its neighbors in Central America.[120] At the same time, it has sent military aid to the insurgents in El Salvador and even to the Bishop government in Grenada through friendly powers like Cuba and Nicaragua in order to reduce the risk of a military response by Washington.[121] U.S. military intervention in Grenada in 1983 highlighted for Soviet leaders the need for caution in such situations.

Nonetheless, the position of the "revolutionary-democratic" school of thought on the matter appears to have affected the Soviet posture insofar as it relates to "progressive" and especially "revolutionary-democratic" forces. At least through the early 1980s, Moscow seemed to perceive new revolutionary opportunities in Latin American states like El Salvador, and it encouraged insurgents there to try to capitalize on such openings.[122] It has also furnished increasingly sophisticated arms to the Sandinista government in Nicaragua,[123] although it has carefully refrained from providing items that the United States has made plain would strain its tolerance. In both of these respects, the USSR has manifested a greater willingness to challenge the United States than it evinced even in the late 1970s.

PROSPECTS

How stable is the Soviet policy toward Latin America that has emerged in the 1980s? If any changes in its broad framework loom on the near horizon, what form might they take?

Neither the geopolitical priority that Moscow assigns to Latin America in world affairs nor the general goals that it pursues in the region seem likely to alter much in the foreseeable future. Unfavorable conditions in many portions of the Third World and Mikhail Gorbachev's ambitious domestic agenda together will probably discourage any significant upsurge in Soviet interest in the Third World at large at least through the early 1990s; at the same time, Moscow displays no inclination whatsoever to withdraw from involvement there. The ranking that Moscow accords to Latin America among Third World regions, of course, could fall, as it has at specific junctures in the past. If the situation in Southern Africa, for instance, reached the boiling point, that area might again assume more importance in Soviet eyes than Latin America enjoys. Yet the ongoing disintegration of the old social and political order in Latin America and the widespread wish there to chart paths in foreign policy independent of the United States appear to ensure that the region will retain a fairly high spot on the USSR's list of Third World priorities. Individual objectives that Moscow has been trying to achieve in Latin America in the 1980s date from the late 1950s, and the precise mix of these objectives has not changed since the mid-1960s. Therefore, it is exceedingly doubtful that they will undergo modifications of a major kind in the years immediately ahead.

How enduring the method and the means by which the USSR seeks to accomplish its ends in Latin America will prove to be is much more debatable. The discontinuities in Soviet methods and means since the 1950s suggest that important shifts will eventually take place in the methods and means of the 1980s, but the speed at which the shifts will come, as well as their nature, will depend on several factors, a key one of which will be the results the method and the means of the 1980s yield. In prior years the USSR suffered a number of severe setbacks in the Third World, and these triggered changes in the method and the means whereby Moscow endeavored to achieve its purposes there. Such reversals could occur again. From an outsider's standpoint, it is true, the Soviet method and means of the 1980s in Latin America seem better attuned to regional realities than have those of any earlier period. Nevertheless, the situation in Latin America and many other Third World regions has become volatile, and this volatility makes it impossible to rule out developments that could entail new Soviet setbacks. A good illustration of a development with such potential impact would be the collapse of the *Sandinista* government in Nicaragua.

Another influence will be how much diversity persists within the Soviet hierarchy on the subject of method and means. Unless there continue to be three or more fundamental Soviet outlooks on the issue, the method and the means that Moscow actually employs in Latin America will probably lose some of the complexity that they have exhibited in the 1980s. By the late 1980s, indeed, the underpinnings of two of the outlooks had already eroded somewhat, for criticism of the performances of even the most radical forces in power in the Third World was flowing from every quarter in the USSR.[124] This disillusionment could reach the point where the "socialist-orientation" and "pro-military" perspectives simply vanish from the scene.

In such an event, which of the two remaining schools of thought would exercise sole or predominant sway on Soviet behavior in Latin America? On the record of the 1980s, the "national-capitalism" viewpoint would seem to have a distinct edge over the "economic interdependence" one, but some blend of the two might emerge even if the "national-capitalism" school turned out to have the primary impact.

The last major consideration will be whether the Soviet leadership continues to refrain from endorsing a single vision of method and means as the official line. Since assuming the CPSU general secretaryship, Gorbachev has shown no inclination to do otherwise, despite his emphasis on "new thinking" in foreign as well as internal affairs; nor is there visible reason to anticipate a switch in his position in the future. Moreover, he appears likely to retain his job at least until the early 1990s, even though many of his programs have stirred up significant domestic opposition.[125] At the time of writing, the disaffected groups differed greatly among themselves on issues, and they had not managed to find either a platform or a personality around which to coalesce.

Perhaps one person who might attempt to bring about a coherent and consistent Soviet stance on methods and means in the Third World is Anatolii Dobrynin, who was head of the CPSU International Department until late 1988, subsequently becoming a personal aide to Gorbachev and assuming responsibility for relations with nonruling Communist parties. As noted previously, the upper ranks of the International Department contained representatives of three of the basic outlooks on method and means during the final years of Boris Ponomarev's tenure as chief. Whether such diversity would be tolerated—or, more crucial, can be eliminated—still remains to be seen. What was beyond doubt was his commitment not only to playing an important role himself in formulating Soviet foreign policy but also to making the International Department the key body for coordinating foreign policy implementation. For example, he increased the number of first deputy chiefs of the International Department to two and filled the new post with a former first deputy minister of foreign affairs. He also drew into the Department—presumably as head of a sector dealing with arms control—a lieutenant general who previously served as the Soviet commissioner at the Standing Consultative Commission (for U.S.-Soviet arms control discussions).

Were Dobrynin to try to establish such a Soviet position on method and means, its nature is hard to forecast. In light of Dobrynin's "Americanist" background, and especially his role for a quarter of a century as Soviet ambassador to the United States, one might assume that he would lean toward the "economic interdependence" school of thought, and some of his early public statements after he took over his new job tended to reflect the arguments of this school. Yet other pronouncements he has made seemed to mix elements of the "national-capitalism" and "economic interdependence" viewpoints.[126]

On balance, the chances of drastic alterations of the USSR's method and means in Latin America, and the Third World more broadly, appear reasonably slim for the immediate future. This assessment, to be sure, does not preclude some adjustments in the method and means. Perhaps the most likely of these in Latin America would be increased Soviet implementation of features of the "national-capitalism" perspective. If the foregoing judgments are accurate, then well into the early 1990s the Soviet approach to Latin America will not vary much from that of the early and mid-1980s.

NOTES

1 The views expressed in this chapter are the author's and do not necessarily reflect those of the U.S. government or the U.S. Air Force. For a recent authoritative restatement of this viewpoint, see V. V. Zagladin, ed., *Mezhdunarodnoe kommunisticheskoe dvizhenie* (Moscow: Politizdat, 1984).

2 On the change in Soviet outlook in the mid-1960s, see Robert Legvold, *Soviet Policy in West Africa* (Cambridge, MA: Harvard University Press, 1970), chapters 7–8; Roger E. Kanet, ed., *The Soviet Union and the Developing Countries* (Baltimore: The Johns Hopkins University Press, 1974); Richard Lowenthal, "Soviet 'Counter-imperialism,'" *Problems of Communism*, 25:6 (November 1976) 52–63; David E. Albright, "Moscow's African Policy of the 1970s," in Albright, ed., *Communism in Africa* (Bloomington: Indiana University Press, 1980), pp. 37–52; also see his *The Dilemmas of Courtship: The Soviet Union, China, and the Third World*, forthcoming, chapter 6.

For a good illustration of Moscow's efforts to portray the USSR and the nonaligned movement as "natural allies," see the message of General Secretary Leonid Brezhnev to the Algiers summit meeting of the Nonaligned Movement in 1973. The text is in Foreign Broadcast Information Service, *Daily Report: Soviet Union* (hereafter FBIS-SOV), September 5, 1973.

3 Y. Alimov, "The Newly-Free Countries in World Politics," *International Affairs*, 9 (September 1981) p. 23.

4 For authoritative examples, see Boris Ponomarev, "Real'nyi sotsializm: osvobodivshiesia strany," *Slovo lektora*, 3 (March 1984) pp. 13–19; Karen Brutents, "Dvizhenie neprisoedineniia v sovremennom mire," *Mirovaia ekonomika i mezhdunarodnye otnosheniia*, 5 (May 1984) pp. 26–41; Evgenii Primakov's summary of the discussion of an international research group, "Anti-War Potential of the National Liberation Forces," *World Marxist Review*, 4 (April 1985) pp. 90–97.

5 Even Soviet observers who have foreseen some possibilities for cooperation between the United States and the USSR in the global arena have not anticipated that such cooperation would end competition between the two powers, and they have held that losses for one side in this continuing rivalry would constitute advances for the other. For perhaps the most explicit statement of this position, see G. A. Arbatov, *The War of Ideas in Contemporary International Relations* (Moscow: Progress Publishers, 1973). It is also reflected in V. V. Zagladin and I. T. Frolov, *Global'nye problemy sovremennosti: nauchnye i sotsial'nye aspekty* (Moscow: Mezhdunarodnye otnosheniia, 1981); N. N. Inozemtsev, ed., *Global'nye problemy sovremennosti* (Moscow: Mysl', 1981).

6 For more extended discussion, see Albright, "Moscow's African Policy of the 1970s," pp. 37–49 and "The Middle East and Africa in Recent Soviet Policy," in Roger E. Kanet, ed., *Soviet Foreign Policy in the 1980s* (New York: Praeger, 1982), pp. 287–88.

7 On the history of the Latin American Communist parties and Soviet relations with them prior to the late 1950s, see Robert J. Alexander, *Communism in Latin America* (New Brunswick: Rutgers University Press, 1957), and *Trotskyism in Latin America* (Stanford: Hoover Institution Press, 1973); Rollie E. Poppino, *International Communism in Latin America: A History of the Movement, 1917–1963* (New York: Free Press, 1964); Stephen Clissold, ed., *Soviet Relations with Latin America, 1918–1968: A Documentary Survey* (London: Oxford University Press, 1970); Luis E. Aguilar, ed., *Marxism in Latin America* (Philadelphia: Temple University Press, 1978).

8 On events in Guatemala and the Soviet response, see Clissold, *Soviet Relations with Latin America, 1918–1968*, pp. 40–41, 226–30; Herbert S. Dinerstein, *The Making of a*

Missile Crisis: October 1962 (Baltimore: The Johns Hopkins University Press, 1976), chapter 1. For treatment of the general Soviet outlook on Latin America before 1959, see Jacques Levesque, *The USSR and the Cuban Revolution: Soviet Ideological and Strategic Perspectives, 1959–77* (New York: Praeger, 1977), Introduction; Edward Gonzalez, *Cuba Under Castro: The Limits of Charisma* (Boston: Houghton Mifflin, 1974), pp. 121–22.

9 For relevant discussion, see Dinerstein, *The Making of a Missile Crisis*; Levesque, *The USSR and the Cuban Revolution*; J. Gregory Oswald and Anthony J. Strover, *The Soviet Union and Latin America* (New York: Praeger, 1970); Cole Blasier, *The Giant's Rival: The USSR and Latin America* (Pittsburgh: University of Pittsburgh Press, 1983); W. Raymond Duncan, *The Soviet Union and Cuba: Interests and Influence* (New York: Praeger, 1985); Tad Szulc, *Fidel: A Critical Portrait* (New York: William Morrow and Company, 1986), especially part IV.

10 See, for instance, Levesque, *The USSR and the Cuban Revolution*; Blasier, *The Giant's Rival*, chapter 5; Duncan, *The Soviet Union and Cuba*, chapters 4 and 5; Szulc, *Fidel: A Critical Portrait*, parts IV and V; D. Bruce Jackson, *Castro, the Kremlin, and Communism in Latin America* (Baltimore: The Johns Hopkins University Press, 1969).

11 See, for example, Duncan, *The Soviet Union and Cuba*, pp. 40–83; Jackson, *Castro, the Kremlin, and Communism in Latin America*; Szulc, *Fidel: A Critical Portrait*, particularly part V.

12 "Aktual'nye problemy teorii mirovogo revoliutsionnogo protsessa," *Kommunist*, 15 (October 1971), p. 62.

13 For more extended treatment of these, see Abraham F. Lowenthal, "The United States and Latin America: Ending the Hegemonic Presumption," *Foreign Affairs*, 55:1 (October 1976), pp. 199–213; Robert S. Leiken, *Soviet Strategy in Latin America*, Washington Papers No. 93 (New York: Praeger for the Center for Strategic and International Studies, Georgetown University, 1982), chapter 1; William H. Luers, "The Soviets and Latin America: A Three Decade U.S. Policy Tangle," *Washington Quarterly*, 7:1 (Winter 1984), pp. 3–26; Brasier, *The Giant's Rival*, chapters 2 and 6; Duncan, *The Soviet Union and Cuba*, pp. 88–97.

14 By the mid-1960s, as already mentioned, Moscow had abandoned hope that Communist regimes would emerge in the foreseeable future in at least most Third World states that opted for a "noncapitalist" path, but it still regarded relations with "progressive" countries of the Third World as likely to pay the greatest dividends for the USSR in international affairs. For a succinct summary of this perspective, see N. I. Gavrilov and G. B. Starushenki, eds., *Afrika: problemy sotsialisticheskoi orientatsii* (Moscow: Nauka, 1976), p. 419.

15 See, for instance, the discussion of U.S. policy toward Chile in I. Lavretskii, *Sal'vador Al'ende* (Moscow: "Molodaia Gvardiia," 1974).

16 For an exhaustive look at U.S. involvement in the situation, see Paul E. Sigmund, *The Overthrow of Allende and the Politics of Chile, 1964–1976* (Pittsburgh: University of Pittsburgh Press, 1977).

17 Soviet postmortems on Allende's downfall attested to this revised outlook. For representative discussions of the Allende government's overthrow and its implications, see the contributions on the topic in *Latinskaias Amerika*, 5–6 (September–October and November–December 1974) and 1–2 (January–February and March–April 1975); A. I. Sobolev, "Revoliutsiia i kontr-revoliutsiia: opyt Chili i problemy klassovoi bor'by," *Rabochii klass i sovremennyi mir*, 2 (March–April 1974) pp. 12–22; I. N. Zorina and Iu. F. Kariakin, "Politicheskaia khronika chiliiskoi revoliutsii," *ibid.*, parts I and II, 4–5 (July–August and September–October 1974), pp. 143–160, 132–150; M. O. Karamanov, "Opyt Chili i revoliutsionnyi protsess," *ibid.*, 6 (November–December 1974), p. 131 ff.

18 Speech to the 26th CPSU Congress in February 1981, as published in *Pravda*, February 24, 1981.

19 Mikhail Gorbachev's report to the 27th CPSU Congress in February 1986, for instance, spoke of a number of crises in the Third World that needed attention. It listed them in the following order: the Middle East, Central America, and Southern Africa. See *Pravda*, February 26, 1986.

20 See, for example, *Sovetskaia Rossiia*, July 20, 1979; *Izvestiia*, July 29, 1979.

21 The quotation is from B. I. Koval', "Revoliutsiia—dlitel'nyi istoricheskii protsess," *Latinskaia Amerika*, 3 (March 1980), p. 12.

22 For a representative Soviet commentary along these lines, see the talk in the series "Topical Problems of International Life" by Aleksandr Baryshev, Radio Moscow Domestic Service in Russian, March 3, 1983, in FBIS-SOV, March 4, 1983, pp. K1–4.

23 Quite revealing in this regard, Moscow soon took pains to increase the ambiguity of its commitment to the Sandinista government in Nicaragua, and the USSR placed heightened emphasis on the efforts launched by Mexican President José López Portillo in February 1982 to produce a negotiated political settlement of the conflicts in Central America. See, for instance, Peter Clement, "Moscow and Nicaragua: Two Sides of Soviet Policy," *Comparative Strategy*, 5:1 (1985), pp. 75–91.

24 The full report of the symposium appears under the title "Latinskaia Amerika: vneshniaia politika i ekonomicheskaia zavisimost'," in *Latinskaia Amerika*, 8–10 (August–October 1981).

25 For treatment of the relevance to other Third World regions of the ends discussed in this section, see Albright, "The Middle East and Africa in Recent Soviet Policy," and his *Soviet Policy Toward Africa Revised*, Significant issues Series, Center for Strategic and International Studies, 9:6 (1981).

26 The major difference in Soviet goals before the mid-1960s has to do with a commitment on Moscow's part to promote near-term transitions to "scientific socialism" in at least some Third World countries.

27 For a recent illustration, see the report of former USSR Foreign Minister Andrei Gromyko to the USSR Supreme Soviet session on June 16, 1983, "The International Situation and the Foreign Policy of the Soviet Union," *New Times*, 26 (June 1983), p. 32.

28 For elaboration of these points, see Vernon V. Aspaturian, "Soviet Global Power and the Correlation of Forces," *Problems of Communism*, 29:3 (May–June 1980), pp. 1–18.

29 U.S. Department of State, Bureau of Public Affairs, *Soviet Activities in Latin America and the Caribbean*, Current Policy 669 (Washington, D.C.: Government Printing Office, 1985), p. 3.

30 These are estimates of the U.S. intelligence community. See *ibid.*, p. 2; U.S. Central Intelligence Agency, *The Cuban Economy: A Statistical Review*, ALA 84–10052 (Washington, D.C.: Government Printing Office, 1984), p. 40.

31 U.S. Central Intelligence Agency, *Communist Aid Activities in Non-Communist Less Developed Countries, 1979 and 1954–79*, ER 80-10318U (Washington, D.C.: Government Printing Office, 1980), p. 24; International Monetary Fund, *Direction of Trade Statistics Yearbook 1986* (Washington, D.C.: Government Printing Office, 1986), p. 395. The yearly average for 1981–85 was calculated by the author of the basis of data in the latter source.

32 See the annual volumes of *Vneshniaia torgovlia SSSR* (Moscow: Izdatel'stvo "Mezhdunarodnye Otnosheniia").

33 U.S. Central Intelligence Agency, *Communist Aid Activities in Non-Communist Less Developed Countries*, p. 7; U.S. Department of State, *Warsaw Pact Economic Aid to Non-Communist LDCs, 1984* (Washington, D.C.: Government Printing Office, May 1986), p. 13. The total for 1980–84 was arrived at by the author from information in the second source.

34 U.S. Department of State, *Soviet Activities in Latin America and the Caribbean*, p. 2;

U.S. Department of State and Department of Defense, *The Soviet-Cuban Connection in Central America and the Caribbean* (Washington, D.C.: Government Printing Office, 1985), p. 3.

35 U.S. Central Intelligence Agency, *Communist Aid Activities in Non-Communist Less Developed Countries*, p. 14; U.S. Arms Control and Disarmament Agency, *World Military Expenditures and Arms Transfers 1970–79* (Washington, D.C.: 1982), p. 129.

36 *Soviet Military Power 1986* (Washington, D.C.: Government Printing Office, 1986), pp. 130–31.

37 See Documents 13, 14, and 15 in *Grenada Documents: An Overview and Selection* (Washington, D.C.: Department of State and Department of Defense, 1984).

38 See U.S. Department of State, *Communist Interference in El Salvador*, Special Report 80 (Washington, D.C.: Government Printing Office, 1981), and *Soviet Activities in Latin America and the Caribbean*, pp. 4–5; U.S. Department of State and Department of Defense, *The Soviet-Cuban Connection in Central America and the Caribbean*, pp. 31–5, and *The Challenge to Democracy in Central America* (Washington, D.C.: Government Printing Office, 1986), *passim*, *Washington Times*, December 12, 1986. As Raymond Duncan warns (*The Soviet Union and Cuba*, chapter 6), the claims put forth in these materials concerning the degree of Soviet involvement with the insurgents in El Salvador need to be approached with caution; nonetheless, it is hard to dismiss as utterly meaningless the basic intelligence out of which these claims grow.

39 *Pravda*, April 4, 1971.

40 For a recent authoritative statement of this perspective in direct reference to Latin America, see M.F. Gornov, "Latinskaia Amerika: usilenie bor'by protiv imperialisma i oligarkhii, za demokratiiu i sotsial'nyi progress," *Latinskaia Amerika*, 7 (July 1982), p. 22. "Gornov" appears to be a pseudonym of M.F. Kudachkin, head of the Latin America sector of the International Department of the CPSU. For evidence on this score, see Jerry F. Hough, *The Struggle for the Third World: Soviet Debates and American Options* (Washington, D.C.: Brookings, 1986), p. 173, fn. 90.

41 Speech of General Secretary Yurii Andropov to the plenary session of the CPSU Central Committee on June 15, 1983, in *Pravda*, June 16, 1983.

42 For a good, detailed analysis of Soviet writings on Third World development, see Elizabeth Kridl Valkenier, *The Soviet Union and the Third World: An Economic Bind* (New York: Praeger, 1983). Also see her chapter in this volume.

43 U.S. Central Intelligence Agency, *Communist Aid Activities in Non-Communist Less Developed Countries*, pp. 19–42.

44 On Soviet economic aid to Nicaragua, see *Warsaw Pact Economic Aid to Non-Communist LDCs, 1984*, p. 13; Andropov's speech to the plenary session of the CPSU, June 15, 1983; and Ponomarev, "Real'nyi sotsialism osvobodivshiesia strany," lay out in no uncertain terms the circumscribed nature of the USSR's economic commitment to states like Nicaragua.

45 Sigmund, *The Overthrow of Allende and the Politics of Chile, 1964–1976*, p. 194.

46 U.S. Department of State and Department of Defense, *The Soviet-Cuban Connection in Central America and the Caribbean*, pp. 27–28; Edward González, "The Cuban and Soviet Challenge in the Caribbean Basin," *Orbis*, (Spring 1985), pp. 88–89.

47 Report to the 12th CCP Congress in September 1982, "Create a New Situation in All Fields of Socialist Modernization," *Beijing Review*, 37 (September 13, 1982), p. 29.

48 For illustrative purposes, see the chapters on "China and Africa" in the annual volumes of Colin Legum, ed., *Africa Contemporary Record* (London: Holmes and Meier) for the 1980s. Evidence of a more broad-ranged type may be found in "Aid to Foreign Countries," *Beijing Review*, 11 (March 17, 1986), p. 28.

49 A typical commentary by a Soviet observer prior to 1982 is Y. Semyonov, "Peking and the National Liberation Movement," *International Affairs*, 1 (January 1980), pp. 29–39. For a representative one that has appeared since 1982, see I. Alexeyev and F. Nikolayev, "Some Trends in PRC Policy," *ibid.*, 12 (December 1984), especially p. 39.

50 See, for example, A. Doak Barnett, "Ten Years After Mao," *Foreign Affairs*, 65:1 (Fall 1986), pp. 37–65.

51 U.S. Central Intelligence Agency, *Handbook of Economic Statistics, 1982*, CPAS 82-10006 (Washington, D.C.: Government Printing Office 1982), pp. 68–69, and *Handbook of the Nations*, Fifth Edition (Detroit: Gale Research Co., 1985), p. 211; Boris Rumor, "Realities of Gorbachev's Economic Program," *Problems of Communism* 35:3 (May–June 1986), pp. 20–31; Seweryn Bialer, *The Soviet Paradox: External Expansion, Internal Decline* (New York: Knopf, 1986).

52 For accounts of Sino-Soviet competition during these years, see Jackson, *Castro, the Kremlin and Communism in Latin America*; Duncan, *The Soviet Union and Cuba*, chapters 2 and 3; Szulc, *Fidel: A Critical Portrait*, particularly part V.

53 See, for instance, Cecil Johnson, "China and Latin America: New Ties and Tactics," *Problems of Communism* 21:4 (July–August 1972), pp. 53–66.

54 For indications of the scope of Chinese initiatives in Latin America in the 1980s, see *Beijing Review*, 1 (January 6, 1986), pp. 11 and 43, and 11 (March 17, 1986), p. 29; Bridgetown CANA (Caribbean News Agency) in English, July 7, 1986, in Foreign Broadcast Information Service, *Daily Report: Latin America* (hereafter FBIS-LAM), July 8, 1986, p. 16; *Jornal de Brasilia*, January 29, 1987; *O Globo* (Rio de Janeiro), March 27, 1987, p. 29.

55 For particularly revealing insights into this perspective, see K. Brutents, "The Regenerated East," *New Times*, 45 (November 1958), pp. 5–7.

56 V. Lunin and P. Yakovlev, "Washington's Latin American Policy," *International Affairs*, 3 (March 1980), p. 21.

57 Y. Primakov, "Neo-colonialism: Essence, Forms, Limits," *ibid.*, 11 (November 1978), p. 66.

58 For further discussion, with sources, see Albright, "Moscow's African Policy of the 1970s," pp. 37–38.

59 For a retrospective Soviet critique of this view with respect to Africa, see K. Brutents, "African Revolution: Gains and Problems," *International Affairs*, 1 (January 1967), p. 21.

60 For details of Soviet interaction with Latin American countries aside from Cuba during the years in question, see Clissold, *Soviet Relations with Latin America, 1918–1968*, pp. 172–252; Blasier, *The Giant's Rival*, pp. 23–49.

61 The ensuing analysis draws upon Richard Lowenthal, "On 'National Democracy': Its Function in Communist Policy," *Survey*, 47 (April 1963), pp. 119–34; Uri Ra'anan, "Moscow and the Third World," *Problems of Communism*, 14:1 (January–February 1965), pp. 22–37; Legvold, *Soviet Policy in West Africa*, chapters 2–7; Albright, "Moscow's African Policy of the 1970s," pp. 38–40, and *The Dilemmas of Courtship*, chapter 2, 4, and 6.

62 On Soviet-Cuban relations during the period, see, for example, Dinerstein, *The Making of a Missile Crisis*; Gonzalez, *Cuba Under Castro*; Levesque, *The USSR and the Cuban Revolution*; Duncan, *The Soviet Union and Cuba*; Szulc, *Fidel: A Critical Portrait*, part IV; Jorge I. Domínguez, *Cuba: Order and Revolution* (Cambridge, MA: Belknap Press of Harvard University Press, 1978), pp. 149–65.

63 In addition to the sources cited in the preceding note, see Jackson, *Castro, the Kremlin, and Latin America*, and part V of Szulc's *Fidel: A Critical Portrait*.

64 For relevant discussion with sources, see Albright "Vanguard Parties and Revolutionary Change in the Third World: The Soviet Perspective and Its Implications," a forthcoming Policy Paper in International Affairs from the Institute of International Studies, University of California, Berkeley.

65 See, for instance, Nikita Khrushchev's address to the graduates of Soviet military academies on November 14, 1958, in *Pravda*, November 15, 1958, and his report to the 21st CPSU Congress in January–February 1959, in Leo Gruilow, ed., *Current Soviet Policies III: The Documentary Record of the Extraordinary 21st Congress of the*

Communist Party of the Soviet Union (New York: Columbia University Press, 1960), p. 55.

66 The sum for economic aid was arrived at by the author on the basis of data in U.S. Central Intelligence Agency, *Communist Aid Activities in Non-Communist Less Developed Countries*, p. 7, and *The Cuban Economy: A Statistical Review, 1968–1976* (Washington, D.C.: Government Printing Office, 1976), p. 14. That for military deliveries was derived from estimates in U.S. Central Intelligence Agency, *Communist Aid Activities in Non-Communist Less Developed Countries*, p. 14; U.S. Arms Control and Disarmament Agency, *World Military Expenditures and Arms Transfers, 1965–1974* (Washington, D.C.: Government Printing Office, 1976), pp. 74–6; *The International Transfer of Conventional Arms*, A Report to Congress by the U.S. Arms Control and Disarmament Agency (Washington, D.C.: Government Printing Office, 1973), pp. A-8 through A-10 and A-13 through A-14.

On the recipients of economic credits from the USSR and rough estimates of the Soviet commitments to them, see U.S. Department of State, Bureau of Intelligence and Research, *The Communist Economic Offensive Through 1964*, Research Memorandum RSB-65 (Washington, D.C.: Government Printing Office, 1965). Unclassified sources contain only incomplete information about Soviet supplies of arms and equipment to individual Third World states during 1956–64, but that information is sufficient to sustain the judgments in the text. See Leo Tansky, "Soviet Foreign Aid: Scope, Direction, and Trends," in U.S. Congress, Joint Economic Committee, *Soviet Economic Prospects for the Seventies* (Washington, D.C.: Government Printing Office, 1973), p. 772; *The International Transfer of Conventional Arms*, pp. A-8 through A-10 and A-13 through A-14.

67 U.S. Central Intelligence Agency, *Communist Aid Activities in Non-Communist Less Developed Countries*, pp. 7, 14; U.S. Arms Control and Disarmament Agency, *World Military Expenditures and Arms Transfers, 1965–1974*, p. 76.

68 U.S. Central Intelligence Agency, *The Cuban Economy*, p. 14; *The International Transfer of Conventional Arms*, pp. A-8 and A-12.

69 For more detailed discussion, see Mark N. Katz, *The Third World in Soviet Military Thought* (Baltimore: The Johns Hopkins University Press, 1982), chapter 1.

70 An excellent analysis of Khrushchev's behavior toward the United States in the Latin American context in the early 1960s may be found in Dinerstein, *The Making of a Missile Crisis*.

71 See, for instance, Jackson, *Castro, the Kremlin, and Communism in Latin America*; Katz, *The Third World in Soviet Military Thought*, chapter 1; Duncan, *The Soviet Union and Cuba*, chapters 2 and 3.

72 For documentation, see, for example, Legvold, *Soviet Policy in West Africa*, chapters 7–8; Albright, "Moscow's African Policy of the 1970s," p. 40, and *Dilemmas of Courtship*, chapter 6.

73 For elaboration, with sources, see Albright, "The Middle East and Africa in Recent Soviet Policy," pp. 296–97, and his "Vanguard Parties in the Third World," in Walter Laqueur, ed., *The Pattern of Soviet Conduct in the Third World* (New York: Praeger, 1983), pp. 208–25.

74 On this general aspect of the Soviet perspective, see Fritz Ermarth, "The Soviet Union in the Third World, Purpose in Search of Power," *Annals of the American Academy of Political and Social Sciences*, 386 (November 1969), pp. 31–40; Kanet, *The Soviet Union and the Developing Countries*; Lowenthal, "Soviet 'Counterimperalism'"; Albright, "Moscow's African Policy of the 1970s," pp. 40–48.

75 See, for instance, Gavrilov and Starvshenko, eds., *Afrika: problemy sotsialisticheskoi orientatsii*.

76 On economic assistance, see U.S. Central Intelligence Agency, *The Cuban Economy*, p. 14. For arms deliveries, see U.S. Arms Control and Disarmament Agency, *World Military Expenditures and Arms Transfers, 1970–1979*, p. 129.

77 For more extended discussion of the USSR's relations with these states and the ones cited in the next paragraph, see Blaiser, *The Giant's Rival*, particularly chapter 2.

78 For an authoritative statement to this effect, see V. Solodovnikov and N. Gavrilov, "Africa: Tendencies of Non-Capitalist Development," *International Affairs*, 1 (January 1967), p. 33. Solodovnikov at that time served as the director of the African Institute of the USSR Academy of Sciences.

79 For more extended treatment of Soviet attitudes regarding long-term structural links with Third World countries, see Lowenthal, "Soviet 'Counterimperialism'," and the "Epilogue" in his *Model or Ally? The Communist Powers and the Developing Countries* (New York: Oxford University Press, 1977), pp. 359–76.

80 See Valkenier, *The Soviet Union and the Third World*, pp. 11–12; Lowenthal, "Soviet 'Counterimperialism'" and "Epilogue" to *Model or Ally?*

81 For more details regarding such Soviet efforts, see, for instance, Albright, *The USSR and Sub-Saharan Africa in the 1980s*, Washington Paper 101 (New York: Praeger for the Center for Strategic and International Studies, Georgetown University, 1983), pp. 12–17.

82 See Jackson, *Castro, the Kremlin, and Latin America*; Gonzalez, *Cuba Under Castro*; Levesque, *The USSR and the Cuban Revolution*; Duncan, *The Soviet Union and Cuba*; Szulc, *Fidel: A Critical Portrait*, part V; Domínguez, *Cuba: Order and Revolution*, pp. 149–65.

83 The economic aid figures were compiled by the author on the basis of information in U.S. Central Intelligence Agency, *Communist Aid Activities in Non-Communist Less Developed Countries*, pp. 7, 19; U.S. Department of State, *Warsaw Pact Economic Aid to Non-Communist LDCs, 1984*, p. 13. Those on trade turnover were calculated by the author in light of data in International Monetary Fund and International Bank for Reconstruction and Development, *Direction of Trade*, Annual for 1964–68, p. 385, and Annual for 1968–72, p. 367; International Monetary Fund, *Direction of Trade Statistics Yearbook 1981*, p. 388.

84 On economic assistance and trade turnover totals, see the sources cited in footnote 83. The sum for deliveries of weapons and equipment to Peru was arrived at by the author on the basis of information in U.S. Arms Control and Disarmament Agency, *World Military Expenditures and Arms Transfers, 1965–1974*, p. 76, and U.S. Arms Control and Disarmament Agency, *World Military Expenditures and Arms Transfers, 1970–1979*, p. 129.

85 With respect to Soviet efforts to assure the loyalty of these parties, see, for instance, Kevin Devlin, "The Interplay Drama," *Problems of Communism*, 24:4 (July–August 1975), pp. 18–34.

86 See, for example, Duncan, *The Soviet Union and Cuba*, chapter 6.

87 The discussion of economic aid derives from data in U.S. Central Intelligence Agency, *Communist Aid to the Less Developed Countries of the Free World, 1976*, ER 77-10296 (Washington, D.C., August 1977), pp. 11–13, and *Communist Aid Activities in Non-Communist Less Developed Countries*, pp. 7, 18–20; U.S. Department of State, *Warsaw Pact Economic Aid to Non-Communist LDCs, 1984*, pp. 12–13. That on military deliveries is based upon information in U.S. Arms Control and Disarmament Agency, *World Military Expenditures and Arms Transfers, 1965–1974*, pp. 74–6. The trade turnover figures come from data in U.S. Central Intelligence Agency, *Communist Aid Activities in Non-Communist Less Developed Countries*, p. 24. Unless otherwise noted, the statistics in the ensuing paragraphs stem from these sources.

88 On Soviet assistance to Cuba, see U.S. Central Intelligence Agency, *The Cuban Economy*, p. 14; U.S. Arms Control and Disarmament Agency *World Military Expenditures and Arms Transfers, 1965–1974*, p. 76.

89 For information on Soviet supplies of arms to Third World states in 1975–79, see U.S. Arms Control and Disarmament Agency, *World Military Expenditures and Arms Transfers, 1970–1979*, pp. 127–30.

90 For purposes of illustration, see Boris Ponomarev, "The World Situation and the Revolutionary Process," *World Marxist Review*, 6 (June 1974), pp. 10–11; Duncan, *The Soviet Union and Cuba*, chapter 6; the speech of Salvadoran Communist Party leader Shafik Jorge Handal published in *Kommunist*, 17 (November 1980), especially p. 103.

91 See the chapter by Aldo C. Vacs in this volume for details and documentation.

92 For relevant discussion and sources, see Ra'anan, "Moscow and the Third World"; Legvold, *Soviet Policy in West Africa*; Albright, *The Dilemmas of Courtship*, chapters 4 and 6; Albright, "Vanguard Parties and Revolutionary Change in the Third World: The Soviet Perspective."

93 For extensive treatment of the evidence that four alternative policy outlooks have been set forth, see Albright "Vanguard Parties and Revolutionary Change in the Third World: The Soviet Perspective and Its Implications." It should be acknowledged here that the question of how to interpret the debates about the Third World that have cropped up in the open Soviet literature in the 1980s has stirred much controversy among Western analysts. The vast majority of these analysts agree that the debates do have policy implications, but beyond that point the consensus vanishes. Some contend that the disagreements apparent on a substantial number of issues attest to the existence of many schools of thought in the Soviet hierarchy about desirable Soviet policy toward the Third World. Hough, *The Struggle for the Third World*, affords the classic illustration, and Daniel S. Papp, *Soviet Perceptions of the Developing World in the 1980s: The Ideological Basis* (Lexington: Lexington Books, 1985), seems to lean in the same direction. Other analysts suggest that it is possible to identify in the debates a few broad tendencies or preferences with respect to policy, and they link these tendencies or preferences to generational factors. See, for example, Valkenier, *The Soviet Union and the Third World*, especially chapter 5. The present writer, in contrast, holds that not all of the debates offer equal insight into policy inclinations: historically the debate most relevant to policy has concerned the relationship between vanguard parties and revolutionary change in the Third World. The number of fundamental stances on this matter has increased in the 1980s but remains confined to four.

94 See, for instance, R. Ul'ianovskii, "O national'noi i revoliutsion noi de mokratti, puti evoliutsii," *Narody Azii i Afriki*, 2 (1984), pp. 9–18.

95 For insights into Ul'ianovsky's position, see his *Sovremennye problemy Azii i Afriki* (Moscow: Nauka, 1978); "O stranakh sotialisticheskoi orientatsii," *Kommunist*, 11 (July 1979), pp. 114–123; "Dvadtsatyi vek i natsional'no-osvoboditel'noe dvizhenie," *Narody Azii i Afriki*, 2 (1980), pp. 2–9; "Ograblenie pod maskoi 'vazimozavisimosti,'" *Kommunist*, 16 (November 1981), pp. 76–87; "O natsional'noi i revoliutsion noi demokratii: puti evoliutsii"; "O revoliutsionnoi demokratii, ee gosudarstve i politicheskoi sisteme," *Voprosy filosofii*, 4 (1984); *Pobedy i trudnosti natsional'no-osvoboditel'nogo bor'by* (Moscow: Politizdat, 1985). For a sample of Gromyko's published commentaries, see his "Aktual'nye problemy noveishei istorii razvivaiush chikhsia stran," *Kommunist*, 4 (March 1979), pp. 117–24; "Socialist Orientation in Africa," *International Affairs*, 9 (September 1979), pp. 95–104; "Aktual'nye problemy sovremennoi Afriki," *Kommunist*, 2 (1980); "The Imperialist Threat to Africa," *International Affairs*, 7 (July 1981), pp. 47–53; "Afrika segodnia," *Kommunist*, 13 (September 1982), pp. 81–90. On Romanov and Ponomarev, see, for instance, the former's speech of September 7, 1984, at the founding congress of the Workers' Party of Ethiopia, as published in *Pravda*, September 9, 1984, and the latter's article "Real'nyi sotsializm: osvobodivshiesia strany."

96 For more detailed discussion of the emergence and fate of the school of thought in the 1970s, see Katz, *The Third World in Soviet Military Thought*, pp. 81–83, 104–05.

97 See, for example, his "Armiia v politicheskoi sisteme razvitogo sotsializma," *Voennó-istoricheskii szhurnal*, 8 (August 1982), and "Osnovy ucheniia o voine i armii," *Kommunist vooruzhennykh sil*, 5 (March 1983), pp. 88–91.

98 For representative writings of Brutents, see his article in *Pravda*, February 10, 1978; "Neokolonializm na poroge 80-kh godov; 'modernizatsiia' strategii," *Aziia i Afrika segodnia*, 6 (June 1979), pp. 72–84; *Osvobodivshiesia strany v 70-e godvy* (Moscow Politicheskaia literatura, 1979); article in *Pravda*, February 2, 1982; "Osvobodivshiesia strany v nachale 80-kh godov," *Kommunist*, 3 (February 1984) pp. 102–13; article in *Pravda*, January 10, 1986. Regarding Primakov, see his "Nekotorye problemy razvivaiushchikhsia stran," *Narody Azii i Afriki*, 5 (1980), pp. 15–28; "Zakon neravonomernosti razvitiia i istoricheskie sud'by osvobodivshikhsia stran," *Mirovaia ekonomika i mezhdunarodnye otnosheniia*, 12 (December 1980), pp. 28–47; *Vostok posle krakha kolonial'noi sistemy* (Moscow: Nauka, 1982).

99 See, for example, Zagladin and Frolov, *Global'nye problemy sovremennosti*; Zagladin, "Sotsializm i global'nye problemy sovremennosti," *Politicheskoe samoobrazovanie*, 9 (September 1986), pp. 13–22; Inozemtsev, *Global'nye problemy sovremennosti*; address of Georgii Arbatov to the 26th annual convention of the International Studies Association in Washington, D.C., on March 6, 1985, and published in *International Studies Newsletter*, 12:4 (May 1985), pp. 1–5.

100 Even though this is not the place to develop the argument, it is perhaps worth remarking briefly that the weight of the evidence suggests that all three factors have been contributory.

101 The differences in Soviet handling of Latin America and Soviet behavior toward Africa will suffice for purposes of illustration. Compare the picture set forth below with that presented in Albright, *Soviet Policy Toward Africa Revisited*.

102 For these and other Soviet activities, see V. Vanin, "Soviet-Brazilian Relations Keep Developing," *International Affairs*, 2 (February 1986), pp. 37–40; Brasilia Radio Nacional da Amazonia Network in Portuguese, July 4, 1986, and February 3, 1987, in FBIS-LAM, July 8, 1986: pp. D1–2, and February 4, 1987:D/1.

103 See, for example, Moscow Tass in English, July 21, 1986, in FBIS-SOV, July 22, 1986: p.K2.

104 *La Prensa* (Panama City), March 6, 1987.

105 *El Día* (Montevideo), February 8, 1987.

106 The figure for economic assistance comes from U.S. Department of State, *Warsaw Pact Economic Aid to Non-Communist LDCs, 1984*, p. 13, while the figures for average yearly trade turnover during the two time frames were calculated by the author on the basis of data in International Monetary Fund, *Direction of Trade Statistics Yearbook* for 1981 (p. 388) and 1986 (p. 395).

107 See, for instance, *Izvestiia*, September 1, 1986.

108 On economic commitments, see U.S. Department of State, *Warsaw Pact Economic Aid to Non-Communist LDCs, 1984*, p. 13. Regarding the arms uncovered by U.S. troops in 1983, see Jiri and Virginia Valenta, "Leninism in Grenada," in Jiri Valenta and Herbert J. Ellison, eds., *Grenada and Soviet/Cuban Policy: Internal Crisis and U.S./OECS Intervention* (Boulder: Westview Press, 1986), p. 18.

109 The figures concerning economic credits and economic technicians may be found in U.S. Department of State, *Warsaw Pact Economic Aid to Non-Communist LDCs, 1984*, pp. 13, 16. On the types of weapons supplied and Soviet military advisers, see U.S. Department of State and Department of Defense, *The Soviet-Cuban Connection in Central America and the Caribbean*, pp. 24, 27–28, and *The Challenge to Democracy in Central America*, pp. 20–21; *Soviet Military Power 1986*, pp. 130–31.

110 This basic line constituted the dominant position at the roundtable discussion reported in the first three issues of *Latinskaia Amerika* in 1980, and a similar perspective soon prevailed in Soviet media generally. For further analysis, see Mark N. Katz, "The Soviet-Cuban Connection," *International Security*, 8:1 (Summer

1983), pp. 89–93; Morris Rothenberg, "Latin America in Soviet Eyes," *Problems of Communism*, 32:5 (September–October 1983), pp. 11–14; González, "The Cuban and Soviet Challenge to the Caribbean Basin," pp. 80–82.

111 Highly indicative was the positive, if cautious, Soviet reaction to the inauguration of Christian Democrat Marco Vincio Cerezo as president of Guatemala in January 1986 (see, for instance, *Pravda*, January 17, 1986). By February 1987, Moscow had even dispatched its ambassador in Costa Rica to Guatemala City to explore the possibility of resuming diplomatic relations with Guatemala (Guatemala City Radio Television in Spanish, February 27, 1987, in FBIS-LAM, March 2, 1987; pp. P2–3). Viktor Volsky, director of the Latin American Institute of the USSR Academy of Sciences, addressed the subject of general revolutionary outlook fairly directly in an interview published in *La Razón* (Buenos Aires), November 21, 1986, p. 8.

112 The ensuing discussion draws upon information in U.S. Department of State, *Warsaw Pact Economic Aid to Non-Communist LDCs, 1984*, p. 13; International Monetary Fund, *Direction of Trade Statistics Yearbook* for 1981 (p. 388) and 1986 (p. 393). The figures for average yearly trade turnover were arrived at by the author.

113 *The New York Times*, October 31, 1983; U.S. Department of State and Department of Defense, *The Soviet-Cuban Connection in Central America and the Caribbean*, p. 27; *Soviet Military Power 1986*, p. 130.

114 For elaboration of this point, see Duncan, *The Soviet Union and Cuba*, chapter 6.

115 Much controversy surrounds the question of the extent of Soviet military ties to these various fronts, and it is impossible to resolve this definitively on the basis of information in open sources. Strong indications exist, however, that the USSR has supplied at minimum a large share of the arms acquired by the fronts but has striven to mask this role by funneling the arms through intermediaries like Cuba and Nicaragua. See, for instance, U.S. State Department, *Soviet Activities in Latin America and the Caribbean*, pp. 4–5; U.S. Department of State and Department of Defense, *The Soviet-Cuban Connection in Central America and the Caribbean*, pp. 33–35, and *The Challenge to Democracy in Central America*, *passim*; U.S. Department of State, *"Revolution Beyond Our Borders": Sandinista Intervention in Central America*, Special Report 132 (Washington, D.C., 1985), *passim*; *Washington Times*, December 12, 1986.

116 In early 1982, for instance, the USSR called publicly for the unity of all Guatemalan revolutionary forces, including the local Communist party (the Partido Guatemalteco del Trabajo—PGT). See Radio Moscow in Spanish to Latin America, February 12, 1982, in FBIS-SOV, February 23, 1982: pp. K3–4.

117 See, for example, U.S. Department of State and Department of Defense, *The Soviet-Cuban Connection in Central America and the Caribbean*, pp. 33–35, and *The Challenge to Democracy in Central America*, *passim*; U.S. Department of State, *Soviet Activities in Latin America and the Caribbean*, pp. 4–5, and *"Revolution Beyond Our Borders," passim*.

118 On economic commitments, see U.S. Department of State, *Warsaw Pact Economic Aid to Non-Communist LDCs, 1984*, p. 13; for deliveries of weapons and equipment, see U.S. Arms Control and Disarmament Agency, *World Military Expenditures and Arms Transfers, 1986* (Washington, D.C., April 1987), p. 145.

119 The yearly averages for the two periods were calculated by the author in light of data in International Monetary Fund, *Direction of Trade Statistics Yearbook* for 1981 (p. 388) and 1986 (p. 395).

120 For a typical illustration, see the joint communique issued by Dante Mario Caputo, Argentina's minister of foreign affairs and religion, and E. A. Shevardnadze, the USSR's minister of foreign affairs, *Pravda*, February 2, 1986.

121 See the sources cited in footnote 117 plus Documents 13, 14, and 15 in *Grenada Documents*.

122 See, for example, *Izvestiia*, January 6, 1981.

123 See the issues for 1982–83 through 1985–86 of *The Military Balance*, published in London by the International Institute for Strategic Studies; International Institute

for Strategic Studies, *Strategic Survey, 1985–1986* (London, 1986), p. 202; U.S. Department of State and Department of Defense, *The Soviet-Cuban Connection in Central America and the Caribbean*, pp. 21–28, and *The Challenge to Democracy in Central America*, pp. 20–21.

124 Ul'ianovsky, "O natsional'noi i revoliutsionnoi demokratii: puti evoliutsii," is illustrative of the trend, for Ul'ianovsky, one of the prime architects of the "socialist-orientation" perspective, had not hitherto subjected "revolutionary democrats" to attack.

125 For acknowledgment by Gorbachev himself that this opposition exists even within the CPSU Central Committee, see his speech to the 20th Komsomol Congress, as carried by Moscow Television Service in Russian, April 16, 1987, and translated in FBIS-SOV, April 17, 1987, p. R5.

126 Compare his speech on disarmament issues to Soviet scientists in May 1986, in *Moscow News*, 23 (1986), p. 5–6, and his article on "Glavnaia sotsial'naia sila sovremennosti," *Kommunist*, 16 (November 1986), pp. 15–25.

2

Soviet Economic Strategy in Latin America

Elizabeth Kridl Valkenier

In Lenin's writing on imperialism the Soviets had ready at hand the theoretical justification and guidance to exploit the economic grievances of the colonial and semi-colonial peoples, but not until well after the end of World War II did Moscow avail itself of the opportunities. In the interwar period the struggling USSR had conducted trade with its independent neighbors to the south—Iran, Afghanistan, Turkey—and had even given them some economic assistance. It also traded with Latin America and set up an Armtorg office in Buenos Aires in 1925. But, given the widespread fear of Communist subversion, as well as Moscow's inability to reinforce its political goals with economic incentives, these *ad hoc* activities were never coordinated in a purposeful anti-Western strategy.

Only after Stalin's death did the new leadership embark on a serious challenge to the West in the Third World. Hence, this chapter examines policies since 1953, first reviewing the evolution of Soviet thinking about international economics and relating it to Moscow's over-all strategies in the Third World and in Latin America. Next, changing patterns in Soviet economic policies are discussed. The concluding sections outline the emergent strategies evident in Gorbachev's Russia and the prospects for their success.

Perforce, the discussion of theory deals more with the Third World as a whole than with Latin America, for the larger view determines and explains Soviet regional activities. Latin America's place in the general theoretical constructs is significant for a further reason. To the extent that Soviet economic theory and strategy have become less systemic—i.e., more pragmatic and flexible—the Latin American experience and example have played an important role in the Soviet learning process.

Soviet Views on the International Economy and the Third World

During Khrushchev's ascendancy Soviet aid and trade policies became a major component of a bold offensive against the West that was based on shrewd and optimistic calculations about the West's vulnerabilities, the Third World's needs, and Soviet capabilities. What Marxism-Leninism had to say about international economics merely reinforced these assumptions. The Soviets then saw the world as divided into two opposed and competing economic systems (two separate capitalist and socialist markets, in fact). Furthermore, they saw imperialism, the highest and last stage of capitalism, as dependent for its survival on the markets and the resources of the colonial and newly independent countries. As seen from Moscow, imperial rule had brought nothing but backwardness and exploitation in the past; in the future, it had only more of the same to offer. By contrast, in the words of the 1961 Party program—the best source for Soviet world views under Khrushchev—"the world socialist system...offered the peoples of the newly free countries the prospects of national renascence, of ending age-long backwardness and poverty, and achieving economic independence."[1]

Given the divided international economy, what was the place of Third World states in this scheme of things? Khrushchev's Party program classified them as "belonging neither to the system of imperialist states, nor to the system of socialist states." Although the document conceded that they had not yet "broken free from the world capitalist economy," they were said to occupy "a special place in it," the obvious assumption being that with the unpromising future of the one system, the new nations would gravitate toward the other. Accordingly, policies during the first decade of the USSR's active entry into the Third World were centered on facilitating that transition and on reaping rewards from the change in the world balance of forces that it would bring about.

The direction of transition was taken for granted. Khrushchev's Russia recognized and treated the developing countries (or the national liberation movements) as one of the three basic revolutionary forces with an important role to play in "undermining the foundations of imperialism," to use the felicitous wording of the Party program. The Soviets then expected, preached, and fostered a continuing revolutionary process in Asia, Africa, and Latin America. Political independence, they held, was incomplete; it had to be extended by further struggle to attain economic liberation and genuine sovereignty.

In this period the Marxist development model and Soviet aid-trade policies were geared to incite and to support economic liberation. In its final, full form it would entail not merely breaking dependent relations with capitalist powers abroad but also eradicating capitalist relations at home. Capitalism in all its forms and manifestations offered, in the words of Khrushchev's program, nothing but "suffering to the people." Hence the only path to alleviating the situation lay through undertaking a "noncapitalist path of development." In general, this alternate, socialist development model was based on the USSR's experience of rapid industrialization during the early Five Year Plans and the impressive transformation of the Soviet Asian periphery with the aid of the center. It advocated the following policies: restricting or ousting foreign investment, limiting local private enterprise, building up the public sector, import-substitution industrialization, a fairly radical land reform—all accompanied by expanded economic ties with the Soviet bloc as well as with other developing nations.[2]

In tandem with such advice went confident offers of Soviet economic support. Typical of Soviet self-assurance in those days were the 1961 program's assertions that the CPSU "regards it as its international duty to assist peoples who have set out to win and strengthen their national independence." The immediate aim of Soviet economic activities was not necessarily to displace the West in Third World markets but to discredit Western policies by offering more "generous" socialist terms and to undercut the Western presence by fostering noncapitalist institutions and central planning. Thus, it was not the size of Soviet credits or loans that was crucial, but their political aim. Moscow made it a point to take up large development projects that were turned down by the West (the case with the Aswan High Dam in Egypt and with the Bhilai steel plant in India). Soviet credits carried much lower interest rates (2 percent or 2.5 percent), and the USSR was willing to accept traditional exports rather than hard currency in repayment. Moreover, the USSR made much of the fact that the projects it financed became full property of the developing country.

How did Latin America fit into this general scheme? Here, one has to distinguish between Soviet theory and practice. As far as theory was concerned, the Soviets regarded Latin America as an integral part of the Third World; they drew no distinctions. The fact that most Asian and African states had achieved independence only after World War II, whereas that process had taken place in Latin America some 150 years earlier, caused no problems. Moscow saw all three regions as playing the same role of the "world countryside," exploited by the industrial West. The need for economic liberation gave these disparate political entities—so vastly different in size, history, and development levels—a common character and destiny.

Specialists at the Latin American Institute of the Soviet Academy of Sciences, set up in 1961, were obliged to parrot the generalizations framed by the 1961 program. Accordingly, they wrote tomes about the growing realization on the continent that capitalism offered no answers and that various local problems could be solved only through noncapitalist development.[3] The example of Cuba, in those days, furnished proof to Soviet policy makers and specialists alike that other nations in Latin America could also win complete emancipation from the political domination and economic exploitation of the imperialist powers.[4]

Although Soviet theory during the Khrushchev period insisted on grouping Latin America with the rest of the Third World, it should be noted that Soviet economic policies in the region were much more in tune with the realities of its higher development level. Whereas in Asia and Africa the USSR concentrated on aid loans and economic assistance, in Latin America it granted commercial credits and was busy with fostering trade.

Despite the more openly commercial nature of Soviet economic activities in Latin America, the geopolitical motivation was as evident here as elsewhere in the Third World. Trade contacts often served as preliminary steps to establishing formal diplomatic relations and to legitimizing the Soviet presence in Latin America, demonstrating in the process that the USSR was an accepted member of the international community. Similarly, trade loans could have a political purpose. For example, credits to the national oil company in Argentina were not solely intended to increase sales of Soviet machinery. They were also meant to undermine the power of American monopolies. Visits by trade delegations gave the Soviets a chance to criticize American behavior and policies. For one, Anastas Mikoyan availed himself of this opportunity when speaking to Mexican audiences at the opening of the Soviet exhibit in November 1959. He expounded on how the USSR sought "no profit at the expense of others"; how it helped to build industry, offered easy repayment terms, furnished technical design free of charge; how Soviet specialists worked as advisers, not as directors; and he taunted the U.S. to change its terms of assistance.[5]

Substantial changes occurred in Soviet economic thinking and strategy after Khrushchev's ouster in October 1964. The ambitious and extreme views devised by Nikita Sergeevich, and by those who shared his optimistic faith in neo-Leninist categories, were scaled down and replaced by more moderate analysis and more pragmatic policies. Since Khrushchev's impulsive and costly economic approach to the Third World contributed in part to his dismissal, less "generous" programs were instituted by the Brezhnev leadership almost from the outset. Later, other events—the rise of East-West trade, the appearance of petro-dollars, the oil crises, and mounting economic problems in the USSR—led to the formulation of different interpretations of international economics and of a new economic strategy in the Third World. Official rhetoric did not cease preaching economic liberation (as the emotional appeal of that slogan remained most useful for Soviet diplomacy), but substantive economic analysis and actual policies were more intent on fostering economic relations beneficial to the USSR.

Revision of the basic doctrine on international economics, redefinition of Soviet obligations to the Third World, and a new development model testified to the post-Khrushchev interests and policies. In the early 1970s, the Stalinist theory of two separate and competing world markets was quietly shelved. Instead, the Soviets acknowledged and accepted the existence of a single world market encompassing its socialist and capitalist components. The new doctrine was needed to legitimize the growing East-West trade, and at first it was not interpreted as affecting Soviet-Third World trade. For a while, Moscow tried to maintain that it sought to create a socialist International Division of Labor (IDL) with the South based on special, never well-defined (but largely political) principles. By the late 1970s the fiction about one set of rules in one segment of international trade and of a different set elsewhere was abandoned, and the Russians began to talk about a world-wide IDL based on comparative advantage, pretty much jettisoning the former systemic labels.[6]

A decisive redefinition of Soviet obligations to the South had already taken place at the 23rd CPSU Congress in 1966. There, Brezhnev asserted that buildup of the Soviet economy was the "chief international duty" of the USSR and thanked "our foreign friends" for having agreed that the "successful building of communism in the Soviet Union contributes the main support for their revolutionary struggle."[7]

With this reformulation the Soviets became less shrill in advocating systemic solutions and far more concerned that Third World countries pursue economic policies that were viable for their own sake locally as well as beneficial to the USSR. Soviet specialists developed a sober respect for the sequential nature of development in which capitalist forms of ownership and capitalist work habits fulfilled economically (even if historically limited) functions. A mixed economic model replaced the noncapitalist model. As for foreign economic relations, here the Soviets stopped advocating liberation through import-substitution, industrialization, and other forms of severance. Instead, they came to recognize that reliance on traditional production would best contribute to an effective functioning and utilization of the IDL. In view of the Soviet recognition of a single world market in the early 1970s and of global interdependence by the early 1980s, the production of raw materials by the developing countries acquired a new meaning—even respectability.

The direction of evolving theory under Brezhnev was unmistakable. How did it affect Soviet views on Latin America? The question should be turned around for, as already said, Soviet experience in and observation of Latin America contributed to the new thinking about economic development and the diverse conditions in the Third World. In brief, the realities of Latin America helped undermine the Khrushchev-era theories about the unity of the developing nations and capitalism's role in these regions. Or to phrase it in Soviet jargon, they helped formulate a more up-to-date political economy of the Third World.

Academic specialists on general theory had suggested already in 1965 that Latin America should not be classified together with Asia and Africa.[8] More specifically, they argued that the obligatory schema of non-capitalist development did not fit the Latin American situation. By 1968 no less an authority than Viktor Volsky, who succeeded S. Mikhailov as director of the Latin America Institute, wrote that capitalism had developed to far more mature levels in Latin America than elsewhere in the Third World. Moreover, he went on, "It is quite late for these countries to proceed along the non-capitalist path of development. One can only speak about the possibility of destroying capitalism."[9]

Admitting the existence of mature capitalism in Latin America raised a host of related problems for which the existing theory had no answers. In particular, given the predatory nature of imperialism, how was it possible to attain such a high level of development, and what did all this portend for the future? The most pertinent questioning and debates—in the sense that they touched on both Soviet economic and political strategies—concerned the issue of dependency. As the discussions developed, it became evident that the more moderate interpretations of the economic standing of Latin America tended to substantiate arguments for a less confrontational Soviet foreign policy on that continent.

After Khrushchev's ouster, the crude dependency theory (namely, that so long as a developing country stayed in the capitalist world market it would remain an economically dependent, exploited producer of raw materials) was replaced with a more sophisticated version, which to a large extent rose out of debates on Latin America. The revised views on dependency admitted that development could nevertheless occur and, indeed, had taken place. Initially (until the mid-1970s) this advance was labeled "dependent" capitalism. The definition acknowledged that substantial economic growth was possible but always within the limits of a subservient relationship to the capitalist centers.[10]

By the end of the 1970s the chipping away at the dependency theory had proceeded much further. Viktor Sheinis, a specialist at the Institute of World Economy and International Relations (IMEMO), began to argue that the more advanced Latin American nations (as well as India) had attained middle levels of capitalist development, akin to those of Portugal and Southern Italy. This new concept met with vociferous objections from the conservative experts, including persons with important Party positions. Prominent among them was Rostislav Ul'ianovsky, deputy head of the International Department of the Central Committee, who opposed any modification in theory that conceded the possibility of self-sustaining or self-defining economic growth in any part of the Third World.[11] But other experts, with credentials almost as impressive as Ul'ianovsky's, supported and built on the Sheinis line. Academician Evgenii Primakov, director of the Oriental Institute and an economist by training, advanced the proposition that there were two types of dependency. In addition to the classic "asymmetric" dependency with its exploitation and inequality, there now existed an ordinary dependency affecting all countries—the most developed as well as the least—because of the global nature of economic relations. The ordinary dependency did not cripple; hence many newly independent countries had been able to reach sufficient levels of technological development to become and to act as "sub-imperialist" islands on the world market.[12]

In a similar vein, Karen Brutents, the second deputy chief of the International Department and an expert on both the Near East and Latin America, drew the distinction between "national" and "dependent" capitalism in the Third World. Whereas the latter nurtured and perpetuated the neocolonial relationships, the former promoted genuine economic development, eroding the historic exploitation. Significantly, already at that time and consistently since then, Brutents has argued that the USSR should cultivate both normal state-to-state relations and commercial ties with the larger, stable countries of the region, the unspoken assumption being that backing the weak radical states was unrewarding both diplomatically and economically. In other words, rather than count on undermining or destroying capitalism in Latin America, as Viktor Volsky had suggested in 1968, the USSR should learn to deal with the fact of its existence just as it had in East-West relations.[13]

Altogether, during the last five years of Brezhnev's rule the theoretical picture was in disarray. Once the old dogmas were tampered with, there was no stopping the revisions, each spurred on by the Latin American and other anomalies. From about 1978 on, many specialists were discussing interdependence more than dependency, the advanced levels of many developing countries more than the backwardness of others.[14] The polemic surfaced not only in the academic journals but also on the pages of the Party press—in *Pravda* and *Kommunist*. However, the top leadership, though not discouraging the experts' departures from the accepted dogma, never legitimized new concepts such as the single world market, interdependence, and the diversity of the Third World by either openly discussing the reality of facts or promulgating some sort of an updated version of Marxism encompassing these new developments in international economics.[15]

Attempts to adjust theory to reality were made during Andropov's brief tenure and have been vigorously pursued under Gorbachev since he became general secretary in March 1985. The resulting revisions were incorporated into the new Party program, made public in October 1985 and adopted at the 27th Party Congress in February–March 1986. And Gorbachev's report to the Congress went much farther in some ways than the program itself in sketching a new vision of international economic relations.

The new program, replacing the 1961 Party charter, no longer reads like a Communist Manifesto for a Third World ready to turn toward socialism. In fact, the program devotes most attention to building socialism in the USSR, not to theorizing about the balance of forces in the world shifting in favor of the USSR. It does contain separate, though very short sections on Soviet relations with the "liberated" and the "capitalist" countries, thus still categorizing the Third World as a distinct grouping in the international community. Among the liberated countries, it distinguishes states with "socialist orientation" from those which are "travelling the capitalist road," but makes no prognosis about the political future of either grouping beyond emphasizing that each state chooses its own system. The program does not treat the economic and other grievances of the liberated countries against the imperialist states as a motor force in history or as contributing to general progress. Quite explicitly the USSR no longer regards support of all Third World strivings as its bound "international duty." Moreover, the program delivers a short, pointed lecture on economic policies to the radical states: "Every people create the material and technical base...for building the new society mainly through their own efforts." And to cap the point, it specifies that the USSR will assist them only "to the extent of its ability."[16]

The text on the Third World is skimpy and restrained. It takes on much more meaning not only when compared with the effusive optimism of Khrushchev's times, but also when read in conjunction with Gorbachev's report to the Congress (as well as with the subsequent writings of the foremost specialists in academic and Party journals). Gorbachev's report conveys new inflections on imperialism, moderate solutions for the economic problems of the Third World, and an unprecedented articulation of world-wide economic interdependence.[17] Altogether, important revisions in Marxist political economy, suggested by various academic experts during Brezhnev's last years, found legitimation during the 27th Party Congress.

Although still denouncing imperialist exploitation at length, Gorbachev put the traditional argument in a framework that differed from that of his predecessors. Instead of arguing that imperialist policies drew the developing countries closer to the USSR, he stressed that the economic behavior of the capitalist powers was the cause of many conflicts in Asia, Africa, and Latin America. In other words, instead of being a source of revolutionary progress or helping tilt the balance of forces in favor of socialism, the economic deprivations of the developing countries were a source of international instability.

The resolution of the South's grievances against the Northern industrial powers which Gorbachev proposed was low-keyed. For example, he did not call on the Third World to cancel its debts unilaterally, but urged a "fair" and presumably negotiated solution, warning that otherwise the situation "is fraught with grave socio-economic and political consequences for international relations." Taken in sum, he did not speak of ousting the capitalist powers from the Third World, but urged the West to resort to "cooperation on an equitable basis" in its dealings with less developed countries (LDCs).

Most remarkably, he used the concluding section of his report on the international situation not to underscore the systemic differences and competition between the capitalist powers and the Socialist bloc, but to talk about the forces that were creating an "integral world" (*tselostnyi mir*), a concept that could be seen as a notable advance over the "single world market" principle formulated by academic specialists in the 1970s. "The realistic dialectic of present-day development consists in a combination of competition and confrontation between the two systems and in the growing tendency toward interdependence of the countries of the world community."

Gorbachev's approach to the economic problems of the Third World implies a new and different strategy. It sets aside the theme of economic liberation under conditions of competition between the two systems in favor of cooperation or coexistence of all members of the world community. This approach—as already mentioned—accords with and builds on the concepts of a single world market and global interdependence that became current under Brezhnev. But, for the first time, the Soviet leader proposes certain departures in foreign policy that are in keeping with these precepts. Here, it is instructive to note that Gorbachev's code of conduct for the superpowers in the Third World is consistent with these new perceptions of international economics. He has proposed that every permanent member of the U.N. Security Council undertake "strictly to observe the principle of non-interference, non-use of force or threat of force in relations with countries [of Asia, Africa and Latin America], and not draw them into military blocs." Gorbachev's formulation differs significantly from Brezhnev's by not endorsing the economic grievances of the LDCs. It omits Brezhnev's ritual mention of "full recognition of these states' sovereignty over their natural resources...and support for their efforts to eliminate remnants of colonialism."[18]

Changing Patterns in Soviet Economic Policies

As already mentioned, Soviet economic policies in Latin America during the Khrushchev period did not dovetail with the general theoretical constructs about Soviet obligations to the Third World and differed from Soviet practice elsewhere. In Latin America, the USSR was busy with promoting trade, not with providing aid projects. Rather than finance showy development schemes, the USSR organized trade fairs—the first was held in Argentina in 1955, the second in Mexico in 1958.[19] Similarly, Soviet terms were less concessional and more commercial. Except for Cuba, where they were concessional, Soviet commercial credits carried the high interest rate of four percent, almost double the rate charged in Asia and Africa.

The aim of the Soviet trade drive was to sell machinery. Several assumptions underlay that goal. First, the Soviets foresaw a good market, given the higher development levels in most countries; second, they also expected to benefit from resentment of U.S. domination and counted on doing business with the "independent-minded" state sector, which per Marxist definition was supposed to be eager to ease out American capital.

The results of the trade drive were not impressive, however. Undoubtedly, increased imports of coffee, sugar, and tropical fruit helped ease the lot of Soviet consumers. But hopes for huge sales of machinery did not materialize. On the whole, the USSR was able to make the best inroads on Latin American markets by offering oil in exchange for local food products and raw materials. Altogether, despite optimistic expectations and considerable effort, statistics for 1955–64 show no dramatic rise in trade.

During the Brezhnev years, the gap between ideology and practice narrowed. Soviet theory now admitted that the aim of socialist economic relations was to strengthen the USSR, not to help the economic liberation of the LDCs. In keeping with this aim Moscow found more efficient ways to promote machinery sales in Latin America: its policies became better integrated with the national development plans of partners and better suited to Soviet capacities. The Soviets must have also taken into account the fact that detente with the U.S. and the flourishing East-West trade would remove some political barriers to trading with the Communist bloc.

The 1970s were marked by a renewed effort to expand economic ties, the introduction of more flexible credit policies, and a more selective choice of remunerative fields.[20] In 1975 the USSR had formal trade agreements with 20 states, as against 4 in 1964; by 1979, 15 Latin American countries had received credits from the Soviet bloc, double the number of the decade before. Ties were no longer limited to the largest states like Brazil and Argentina, but were extended to smaller countries, like Costa Rica and Jamaica.

The granting of open-ended export-financing credits at the time of signing long-term trade agreements replaced the earlier practice of short-term credits for the purchase of specified quantities and types of Soviet machinery or equipment. For example, in 1977 $200 million were allocated for Colombia's power development (the Alto Sinua hydropower project) under the terms of the trade agreement signed in 1975 which provided 10-year credits. This more flexible policy allowed Moscow to become involved in the ambitious development projects and to bid in fields where Soviet equipment was competitive on the world market—or in which the USSR had its own needs. The former was the case with Soviet credits for hydroelectric projects (by 1979, about one half of the $1 billion in credits was earmarked for power development in Argentina, Brazil, Colombia, and Uruguay); the latter, where the Soviet Union offered to help develop mining industries. Here, Soviet credits for Bolivia's tin mines furnish a good example. Having helped to construct a large tin volatization plant at Potosí, Moscow offered to increase its tin purchases. By 1978, the USSR had become Bolivia's third most important customer after the United States and Great Britain. In addition to dovetailing its export potential with local development plans, the USSR was also able to promote certain pet projects of its own. This was especially characteristic of Soviet offers to Mexico, Peru, and Argentina to develop or start a local fishing industry. Obviously, the USSR is not motivated simply by the economic benefits to be gained from access to the region. The strategic-military advantages—such as proximity to U.S. territory or missile-testing grounds and spying or surveillance facilities—are an equally important factor.

Attempts at multilateralization were another example of innovation. They were undertaken on several levels. The Council of Mutual Economic Assistance negotiated a cooperation agreement with Mexico in 1975 that was ratified the following year. In 1978, the USSR arranged a convenient oil deal, whereby Moscow supplied Venezuela's customers in Europe in exchange for Venezuelan crude shipped to Cuba. Finally, in Bolivia, the USSR started negotiating for a joint venture with a West German firm to build a lead and a silver smelter with Soviet technology.[21]

As a result, Soviet trade with Latin America during 1968-1978 increased substantially. It shot up from 3 percent of Soviet-Third World nonmilitary trade to 11 percent. Nevertheless, certain serious problems plagued Soviet-Latin American exchanges that did not arise in the rest of the Third World, with which Soviet trade also increased substantially during the 1970s.[22]

Trade with Latin America showed a persistent and large deficit at a time when Moscow had a surplus with Asia and the Near East that enabled it to pile up hard currency earnings. Soviet credits remained underutilized—with only about 25 percent being drawn upon. Obviously, unlike elsewhere, Soviet machinery and equipment failed to gain acceptance on the Latin American markets and a high proportion of Soviet exports continued to be in raw materials. Trade remained concentrated with three or four large partners. Moreover, it experienced wide fluctuations from year to year. Finally, although Latin America's share in Soviet-Third World trade kept growing, the Soviet share in Latin American trade remained almost stationary, amounting to less than two percent by 1980.[23]

Economic Strategies in the Post-Brezhnev Era

Thus the post-Brezhnev leadership inherited an uneven situation. The 1970s were a success in terms of acquiring more trade partners, of broadening areas and methods of cooperation. But the USSR was unable to establish viable exchanges in terms of either stability or content. This was the picture in the early 1980s when changed economic circumstances in the USSR, as well as in Latin America, created additional strains and posed new problems. As a result, the future of Soviet economic strategy—in both its commercial and its political aspects—looks far from bright. At the same time, the current plans for Latin America, given their design and Moscow's capacity to implement them, pose less of a threat to the U.S. than in the past.

The present-day goals of Soviet economic policies in Latin America are amply clear: to intensify and render more workable the business-minded policies instituted under Brezhnev. In the late 1980s we are witnessing yet another trade drive. This time it is prompted by declining growth rates in the USSR and the determination of the new leadership to stem this decline through modernization not only of Soviet industry, but also of the structure of foreign trade. Though the basic economic motivation remains similar to what came to prevail under Brezhnev, the political framework in which the drive is cast is different. As indicated above, Gorbachev, unlike Brezhnev, has signaled a willingness to keep systemic economic competition in the Third World out of Soviet foreign policy, i.e., not to play the "economic liberation" card.

In line with that departure, Gorbachev's speeches on foreign economic relations avoid ideological jargon and deal forthrightly with Soviet needs and plans. He has stressed repeatedly that Soviet foreign trade must be built on "principles of mutual benefit"; he has avoided commitment to generous support of the developing countries, and has urged a "closer look at the state of our foreign economic relations."[24] The same tone pervades the outline of the Twelfth Five Year Plan (1986–1990). Reporting on the plan to the 27th Party Congress, Nikolai Ryzhkov, chairman of the Council of Ministers and the Kremlin's top spokesman on economics, stressed that foreign trade should make a tangible and growing contribution to the development of Soviet economy mainly through increased machinery exports.[25]

Several departures suggest how serious the Soviets are about infusing their Latin American trade with new life and vigor. One of the best indications of the Soviet resolve, as well as of its dimensions, was the convocation of the 39th CMEA session in Havana in October 1984—the first meeting to be held outside Eastern Europe. In addition to observers from Nicaragua and Mexico, it was attended by Enrique Iglesias, then secretary general of the Economic Commission for Latin America (ECLA), and by a representative of the Latin American Economic System (SELA). At the same time, the USSR is again organizing trade fairs on the continent and offering seminars to explain the intricacies of trading with socialist countries.

The drive for more and broader contacts is reinforced by new forms of activity. What is now favored by the Soviets as facilitating more dynamic exchanges departs from traditional "socialist" methods.[26] For one, the Soviets are reaching out beyond the state sector. Binational chambers of commerce have existed since the mid-1970s with Argentina, Brazil, Peru, Colombia, and Mexico, but the current drive centers on activating these institutions. Moreover, private firms are being encouraged to set up offices in Moscow. The Soviets also show considerable interest in promoting joint ventures with private Latin American firms. By 1985, there were 38 mixed companies operated by Latin American business and Eastern bloc associations. But the USSR participated in only two—the rest were the product of East

European efforts, where nations have not felt constrained by Marxist strictures against investment when doing business abroad. Moscow is now ready to sidestep ideology and wants to set up joint ventures with Latin American entrepreneurs not only in their homelands, but in other, third countries, as well. Similarly, the Russians are willing to cooperate with Western firms in forming consortiums or in joint bidding and joint projects.[27]

In addition, the USSR is ready to expand what an outsider might term "capitalist" activities of its own. A Soviet tractor assembly plant and a watch assembly plant have been in existence since 1974 in Mexico and Panama respectively. To save on labor and transportation costs, Moscow would like to organize similar projects elsewhere. Setting up consulting firms and finding other ways of realizing returns of Soviet licenses and technology is another topic under discussion. There is even mention of forming joint-stock companies. The new pragmatism regarding forms of economic cooperation is demonstrated by the positive response of the USSR to Mexico's opening up its petrochemical industry to private and foreign investors.[28]

The USSR is addressing its own economic needs with greater forthrightness in other ways as well. It openly insists on a *quid pro quo*. In the past, in order to entice Latin American states into trade deals, the USSR would oblige itself to devote a certain percentage of its imports to local manufactured products. At present, the reverse is in evidence. In order to balance trade, the Soviet Union demands that Latin American states undertake to increase their imports of Soviet machinery. For example, in Argentina a certain portion of Soviet food imports is financed by a counter purchase of Soviet equipment.[29] In a similar vein, Moscow is offering cooperation, design services, or machinery in fields that are not immediately directed toward "industrialization" or "economic liberation" of the Latin American partners. Soviet concentration on hydroelectric power and on mining, evident in the 1970s, has been expanded to include geological surveys and prospecting, and there are now land reclamation and improvement projects—all offering prospects for production of raw materials and food items needed by the USSR.

In the effort to overcome the Latin Americans' lack of familiarity with and aversion to Soviet equipment and technology, the USSR has greatly expanded its training facilities. Whereas in 1965 there were 935 scholarship students from Latin America in the Soviet Union, by 1984 their number had climbed to 8,140, of whom about 1,500 came from Nicaragua.[30] It is not known how many of these studied engineering and other technical subjects. But significantly, the current Soviet expectation is that upon returning home these students will serve Soviet commercial interests—a hope that I first heard expressed by Soviet economists only in 1985.

Prospects for Soviet Economic Strategy

The direction and substance of this recent Soviet economic drive are pretty evident. But what are the prospects? The Soviets are basing their plans not only on their own needs, but also on a certain reading of the situation in Latin America. They calculate that the debt crisis, the rising tide of protectionism, and other difficulties will force Latin American nations to diversify their economic ties. Thirty years earlier, Moscow based its expectations mainly on political calculations, namely resistance to Yankee imperialism, today it expects to reap benefits from the economic crisis affecting the area. Such an analysis breeds assurance and explains why the current-day Soviet specialized commentary discusses so candidly what is wrong with Latin American economic behavior vis-à-vis the USSR and why Soviet trade negotiators are pushing hard bargains.[31] Nevertheless, an outside observer has to conclude that these plans, predicated largely on Soviet needs and Latin America's plight, do not seem to be realistic. They ignore a number of economic and political obstacles.

To begin with, Gorbachev's Russia seems to underestimate the extent and degree of American *interests* in this hemisphere, as distinct from *controls*. Soviet expectations do not take into account the efforts that American and Latin American businesses, banks, and governments will make to resolve the debt crisis. A visit to Moscow may inspire President Alfonsín to state that Argentina wants to display and practice "ideological pluralism in [its] commercial ties."[32] But such claims should be seen in the proper light. The web of the existing interdependencies is much too great to permit an outside and unfamiliar force simply to step in and reap excessive advantage.

Soviet plans assume a complementarity between the Soviet and Latin American economies. If the expectations of flourishing exchanges of Soviet machinery for Latin American raw materials did not materialize 30 years ago, they are less likely to do so now when countries like Brazil have joined the ranks of the newly industrialized countries and are competitors of the Soviet bloc on world markets. Aside from a lack of complementarity, the quality of products each side supplies the other is not appreciated. The Latin Americans complain about the low level of Soviet technology, and the Soviets reciprocate with critical remarks about the quality of Latin American products. Americans have been alarmed by the size of Soviet purchases of Argentinian grain, but have not noticed that Moscow was dissatisfied with the quality control and sent several inspection teams to Buenos Aires to remedy the situation.

The Soviet Union is unlikely to obtain optimal results so long as it does not adopt more flexible and remunerative institutional forms and ignore the issue of Latin American manufactures. Substantive discussion in Soviet professional literature of the opportunities that economic advances of countries like Brazil or Mexico could open for imports of middle-level technology is only starting.[33] As yet, there are no signs of Soviet plans to expand imports of manufactured goods from Latin America. But as far as the Latin Americans are concerned, they also want a *quid pro quo* and expect the USSR to purchase more of their industrial production. One round of Soviet-Brazilian trade negotiations foundered in May 1985 when the Soviet team wanted to purchase only iron ore, while the Brazilian side insisted on selling steel products as well. Thus, when the Brazilian foreign minister went to Moscow in December 1985, he insisted that the extension of agreements for the purchase of Soviet machinery be accompanied by a Soviet commitment to buy Brazilian manufactures to cover 50 percent of the total value of the deal.[34] Such bargaining indicates that economic difficulties will not force Latin Americans to capitulate to Soviet demands.

Success of the more pragmatic and flexible policies depends on the future of economic reforms in the USSR itself. In August 1986 the Gorbachev leadership took fairly serious steps to reorganize the administration of foreign trade. The powers of the Foreign Trade Ministry were curbed, and some 20 industrial ministries as well as 70 large enterprises received the right to negotiate and operate directly with foreign partners. The change, which took effect on January 1, 1987, is aimed at increasing economic efficiency through autonomy and through profit-sharing.[35] In part the new procedures are meant to facilitate deals with the private sector, to which the Soviets are so eagerly reaching out.[36] It is still too early to speculate on the extent or the course of Soviet reforms or about their effect on Soviet economic performance abroad. It should be kept in mind, however, that Gorbachev does not have a free hand; he faces considerable ideological and bureaucratic opposition to excessive tampering with the old system.

Finally, this new round of the Soviet economic offensive is being launched at a time of severe financial crisis and deep cutbacks in the ambitious development programs in Latin America. Conversely, it is being undertaken by a Soviet Union that is experiencing both an economic slowdown and a shortage of convertible currency. Moscow's offers of barter deals as a way to increase trade and to circumvent its financial constraints have not met with a favorable response in Latin America.

All these factors do not forecast a cloudless future. In the meantime, statistics in no way indicate any substantial expansion of trade. By the end of 1986 there were no dramatic breakthroughs or changes. At present, Moscow's total turnover with the area (Cuba excepted) is less than Soviet trade with Japan.

The political atmospherics attendant on Gorbachev's plans are not in the USSR's favor either. This aspect cannot be overlooked, for no matter how pragmatically intended, the economic policies of a superpower do carry political implications that directly or indirectly reinforce or weaken the country's diplomacy.

To the extent that Soviet economic strategy carries a political purpose, it is still to redraw the economic map of the world. But today, three decades after Khrushchev's grandiose intentions, its aim is no longer to replace the existing networks with a socialist model, but instead offers to include the USSR as an equal partner in trade on an interdependent world market.

The present-day Soviet version of the New International Economic Order (NIEO) diverges from that of the Group of 77. The Soviets now urge a general "democratization" of international economic relations—meaning the removal of various trade barriers, especially those affecting East-West trade—so that *all* countries would have an equal chance to engage in world trade. Hence Gorbachev's proposal at the 27th Party Congress for the convocation of an international economic conference on this topic. The Soviet plan is a far cry from the developing countries' visions and needs, which are predicated on concessional and preferential arrangements for the LDCs, not on equal treatment for all. The developing countries are well aware of the Soviet "defection" from their ranks and keep nudging the USSR to back their cause. The radical states, no matter whether they belong to the Socialist bloc or not, call on the USSR to back their one-sided solutions. Fidel Castro—heavily indebted to the USSR—proposes to solve the debt crisis through unilateral cancellation, and has convened an international conference on this issue at Havana. By contrast, as already noted, Gorbachev has urged a solution that is "fair to all" in his report to the 27th Congress.[37] States that are not closely allied to or dependent on the USSR may be more diplomatic, but they also manage to convey criticism of the current Soviet policies on NIEO issues. Thus, the Mexican deputy minister of foreign trade, speaking before the 39th session of CMEA in Havana, said pointedly that the "traditional" support shown by the Socialist states for the Group of 77 should be rendered more "effective and substantive."[38]

The current Soviet version of IDL does not correspond to the wishes and needs of the developing countries either. As mentioned, plans for the expansion of trade are predicated on increased sales of Soviet machinery and technology in return for raw materials either in short supply or too expensive to produce in the USSR. Basically, the Soviets expect the Third World to keep on fueling the industries of the more advanced nations. To the extent that the Soviets recognize, on a practical level, that Brazil and Mexico have joined the ranks of the newly industrialized countries, they want to enlist them in setting up joint projects in third countries (i.e., to help the USSR penetrate other markets). The Soviets do not propose to change their own production or allocation plans to allow for greater utilization of this potential in the USSR. It is significant that the Soviets no longer enthusiastically endorse various Latin American regional cooperation plans, since such policies tend to strengthen the bargaining power of the Latin states and counter the Soviet aim of removing various barriers to the free flow of goods and services.[39] For similar reasons the *dependencia* school now meets with considerable criticism, since it negates the notions of interdependence and of international trade being the prime mover of economic development for the less advanced countries, and for the first time the current research plans of the Latin American Institute include "a critical analysis of contemporary economic thought in Latin America."[40]

The Soviet development model, as exemplified by Cuba and Nicaragua, cannot be attractive to other states on the continent. Since the USSR now insists on "beneficial" ties, it has not supported in either country any of the deep structural changes in the economy once so readily advocated under the slogan of economic liberation. Because of Soviet pressure in the late 1960s, Cuba had to scrap its ambitious industrialization plans (modeled on the Soviet experience of the early 1930s) for a crash program in sugar production. The country's subsequent integration into CMEA has resulted in various hallmarks of dependency—monoculture, concentration, trade of partners, and undiversified sources of capital and technology—but now under a different systemic label. Undoubtedly social services have improved in Cuba, but not labor productivity or growth rates. Interestingly enough, the same pattern of supporting those branches of the economy that are deemed to produce mutually advantageous ties are now emerging in Soviet-Nicaraguan ties. The USSR supports projects in agriculture, textile and mining industries, and geological prospecting and fishing—areas which do not necessarily lead to a transformation of the Nicaraguan economy. The same pattern of integrating Nicaragua into an international division of labor convenient to the USSR is in evidence.[41]

The original development model that had once impressed the Third World has lost its appeal in Soviet eyes as well. Right after the Sandinista revolution, before American pressures pushed Nicaragua closer to the Eastern bloc, Soviet advice was to retain and cultivate economic pluralism. Moscow urged Managua to preserve and nurture the private sector so that it could participate in reconstruction and development.[42] Similarly, the Soviets expected Nicaragua to conduct its trade with (and seek assistance from) the U.S., the other Latin American countries, Western Europe, and the Eastern bloc in more or less equal shares.[43]

Finally, the Third World no longer considers Soviet economic assistance as adequate. Fed up with Soviet attempts to gain mileage through rhetoric rather than through actual aid, the LDCs have stopped granting the socialist countries any special dispensation, and at the IV UNCTAD meeting in 1976 asked that all the industrially developed nations, no matter what their system, give the same percentage of their gross national product—0.7 percent—in economic assistance. Rather than increase its assistance, the USSR resorted in 1982 to publishing differently compiled figures (adding the underdeveloped members of the bloc—Cuba, Vietnam, and Cambodia to the independent Third World nations). The problem, however, remains. At the 39th CMEA session in Havana, the Nicaraguan delegate's pleas for hard currency loans bespoke not just pressure from Western creditors, but a Soviet refusal to assist as well.[44] The absence of a so-called "socialist solidarity," as demonstrated by the USSR's reluctance to extend itself on behalf of an ally/client, must have struck other Latin American delegates, whom Moscow was so eager and proud to have attend.

CONCLUSION

There are two ways to interpret the implications of current Soviet economic strategies in Latin America: either as economic opportunism or as economic fatalism. At first glance, the facts cited in this chapter seem to argue for opportunism. Without incurring any excessive burdens or obligations, the USSR expects to reap the benefits of a "free rider" in three areas. After all, Moscow is now quite candid about its unwillingness and inability to underwrite radical (but weak) clients and potential allies, whom it advises to survive with the help of the nonsocialist West and the rest of the continent. It would like to concentrate on conducting remunerative trade with the larger, economically viable states without, however, making appropriate adjustments to their actual development levels. Last, it tries to press for changes in international trade practices that would benefit the USSR more than the Third World countries.

But beneath the surface of these undeniable facts, one can detect what I would term economic fatalism, which has long-term political implications of quite a different sort. This brand of fatalism assumes more significance when one takes into account that geographic realism (or fatalism) now prevails in Soviet views on the prospects for radical change in Latin America. When one recalls how 30 years ago the Cuban revolution was hailed in the USSR as having put a stop to "geographic pessimism"—i.e., acceptance of U.S. domination—on the continent, it is ironic to discover that the Soviets do not now dismiss American hegemony with such facile phrases. The captured Grenada documents show that the Soviets would put off entreaties of the New Jewel Movement for more support and recognition with the argument that Grenada was "very small" and "very distant".[45] One does not have to search in such obscure sources to find the same sober respect for geographic realities. During the May 1982 visit of Daniel Ortega, Brezhnev also referred to the "vast oceanic expanse" separating the Western Hemisphere from the USSR.[46]

The observable trend that the USSR no longer hopes and tries to undermine or disrupt the ties that connect Latin America to the American and world markets indicates not so much opportunism, but a coming to terms with the economic weakness of the Soviet bloc and the economic power of the U.S. and the West. Soviet impotence dictates accepting American or capitalist hegemony in Latin America and operating within that framework. On the economic level, these facts necessitate conducting commercially motivated trade within the existing system. On the diplomatic level, the same facts mean acceptance of definite limits to what anti-Americanism can accomplish in Latin America.[47]

Gorbachev has been urging his countrymen to give up "wishful thinking" (read: a simplistically optimistic, Marxist-Leninist analysis of world trends), and to start confronting the often uncomfortable realities. The current trend in Soviet economic policies in Latin America would indicate attempts to come to terms with the situation as it is, rather than to exploit it to America's disadvantage. On balance, no matter whether it is the actual Soviet aim and intention, this is the reading that Latin American states are bound to give to current Soviet policies. And in the long run, after all, the success of Soviet economic strategies, whatever they are, depends as much, if not more, on the reactions and receptivity of Latin America as on plans concocted in Moscow.

Notes

1 *Programme of the Communist Party of the Soviet Union* (Moscow: Foreign Languages Publishing House, 1961), p. 43. For another good source, consult Otto Kuusinen, ed., *Fundamental of Marxism-Leninism*, 2nd ed., (Moscow: Foreign Languages Publishing House, 1963).

2 See Charles Wilber, *The Soviet Model and the Underdeveloped Countries* (Chapel Hill: University of North Carolina Press, 1969); appropriate sections in Stephen Clarkson, *The Soviet Theory of Development: India and the Third World in Marxist-Leninist Scholarship* (Toronto: University of Toronto Press, 1978); and Elizabeth Kridl Valkenier, *The Soviet Union and the Third World: An Economic Bind* (New York: Praeger, 1983).

3 The writings of S. S. Mikhailov, the first director of the Institute, are a good example of the stereotyped thinking. See his "Latin America: Time of Change," *New Times*, 12 (March 25, 1964) pp. 6–9, as well as the monograph by the Institute's second director, V. V. Volsky, *Latinskaia Amerika: neft' i nezavisimost'* (Moscow: Mysl, 1964).

4 See report on Latin American problems covened by the Latin American Institute, *International Affairs*, 8 (August 1964), pp. 93–97.

5 Text of speech, *New Times*, 50 (December 1959), pp. 33–35.

6 For a more detailed discussion of changes in the three fields, see Valkenier, *The Soviet Union and the Third World*.

7 Brezhnev's report, *Pravda*, March 30, 1966, pp. 2–3.

8 G. Dadashev, "Marksistskaia politicheskaia ekonomiia i razvivaiushchiesia strany," *Mirovaia ekonomika i mezhdunarodnye otnosheniia*, 2 (February 1965), pp. 84–90 [Hereafter cited as MEMO]. S. Tiul'panov, "Osnovnye problemy politekonomii razvivayushchikhsia stran," *ibid.*, 9 (September 1965), pp. 70–76.

9 *Agrarnyi vopros i voprosy osvoboditel'nogo dvizheniia v stranakh Latinskoi Ameriki* (Moscow: Nauka, 1968), p. 9. Similar arguments about capitalism having taken strong roots in Latin America appeared in V. L. Tiagunenko, ed., *Klassy i klassovaia bor'ba v razvivaiushchikhsia stranakh*. iii, (*Vybor puti*) (Moscow: Mysl', 1968), pp. 342–71, volume meant to present the new, post-Khrushchev interpretation.

10 For the fullest treatment of dependent capitalism, see *Razvivaiushchiesia strany: zakonomernosti, tendentsii, perspektivy* (Moscow: Nauka, 1974)—a collective volume produced by IMEMO and intended to correct the one-dimensional interpretations still prevalent at the start of the decade. See also B. Koval', S. Semenov, and A. Shulgovsky, *Revoliutsionnye protsessy v Latinskoi Amerike* (Moscow: Nauka, 1974). Jerry Hough relates disputes regarding "dependent" capitalism to revolutionary tactics, "The Evolving Soviet Debate on Latin America," *Latin American Research Review*, 16:1 (1981), pp. 124–43.

11 V. Sheinis, "Strany srednego kapitalizma," *MEMO*, 9 (September, 1977), pp. 105–24. The concept was subject to acrimonious disputes at an academic conference reported in *Latinskaia Amerika*, 1 (January–February 1979), pp. 53–100. [Hereafter cited as *LA*].

12 E. Primakov, "Nekotorye problemy razvivaiushchikhsia stran," *Kommunist*, 11 (July 1978), pp. 81–91. See also his, "Zakon neravnomernosti razvitiia i istoricheskie sud'by osvobodivshikhsia stran," *MEMO* 12 (December 1980), pp. 28–47.

13 K. Brutents, *Osvobodivshiesia strany v 70-e gody* (Moscow: Politicheskaia Literatura, 1979). See also his "Sovetskii Soiuz i osvobodivshiesia strany," *Pravda*, February 2, 1982, pp. 4–5.

14 The distinction between the petro-dollar wealth and the more solid advances of Latin American states was always kept clear.

15 Probably the single most significant ideological reformulation related to the economic situation in the Third World made during Brezhnev's last years was to upgrade "backwardness" to a "global problem" category and to cease regarding it as a consequence of imperialism.

16 Text of the CPSU Program, Foreign Broadcast Information Service-Soviet Union Daily Report (FBIS-SOV), October 28, 1985, p. 24.

17 Text of Gorbachev's report, FBIS-SOV, February 26, 1986, especially pp. 7–8.

18 Gorbachev's proposal was made during Rajiv Gandhi's visit, *Pravda*, May 22, 1985, p. 2. For Brezhnev's proposal see, *Pravda*, April 28, 1981, p. 2.

19 For an informative general account of Soviet trade policies, see Cole Blasier, *The Giant's Rival: The USSR and Latin America* (Pittsburgh: University of Pittsburgh Press, 1983) and *Strany SEV i Latinskaia Amerika* (Moscow: Nauka, 1976). See also, Marshall Goldman, *Soviet Foreign Aid* (New York: Praeger, 1967).

20 Facts cited in this section are taken from the Soviet foreign trade monthly, *Vneshniaia torgovlia* (also published in English translation, *Foreign Trade*) and from the annual volumes published either by the State Department or the CIA and entitled variously as *Communist Aid to Less Developed Countries*. For a more general description, see Orah Cooper, "Soviet Economic Aid to the Third World," in Joint Economic Committee, *Soviet Economy in a New Perspective* (Washington, D.C.: Government Printing Office, 1976).

21 All the long-term trade agreements that the USSR signed with the major European countries in the late 1970s contained clauses for joint cooperation in third countries. Moscow hoped to be able to expand East-West trade and cooperation into the developing countries.

22 For a fair summary of the Soviet view of the problems affecting exchanges with Latin America see, N. Zinoviev, "Soviet Economic Links with Latin America," *International Affairs*, 1 (January 1981), pp. 100–07.

23 Of course, if one looks at Soviet economic activities in Latin America mainly as an effort to diminish the American presence, one can cite another set of figures

to justify another set of conclusions. By the end of the 1970s, less than 33 percent of Latin American exports went to the U.S., a decline from 50 percent 2 decades before. Robert Leiken, "Soviet Strategy in Latin America," *The Washington Papers*, 93 (New York: Praeger, 1982), pp. 3–4.

24 See Gorbachev's speech at the April 23, 1985, CC plenum. Text in *Vneshniai torgovlia*, 6 (June 1985) p. 1. Hereafter cited as *VT*.

25 FBIS-SOV, March 5, 1986, pp. 23–25. Interest in this export is now even more urgent, as the USSR plans to replace and renovate half of its industrial plant. Good use can be made of outdated machinery by exporting it to the Third World.

26 In some respects this was true of the various changes made after Khrushchev's ouster. But in the 1970s, these forms were represented in a political garb and as still being a challenge to the capitalist methods. At present the new forms are not only more intensive, they also tend to be described in terms of economic feasibility.

27 The paragraphs are based on the following sources: A. Olshany, "Sotrudnichestvo s gosudarstvami Latinskoi Ameriki," *Ekonomicheskoe sotrudnichestvo stran chlenov SEV*, 3 (March, 1985), pp. 63–67; G. Kuznetsova, A. Manenok, "Sovetsko-argentinskie torgovo-ekonomicheskie otnosheniia," *VT*, 3 (March 1986) pp. 23–25; and A. I. Bel'chuk, ed., *SSSR-razvivaiushchiesia strany: torgovo-ekonomicheskie otnosheniya* (Moscow: Mezhdunarodnye Otnosheniia, 1985), chapter 2, pp. 49–135.

28 See the Mexican report on the results of the 4th meeting of the Mixed Soviet-Mexican Economic Commission in Moscow when the Soviet side showed interest in investing and requested additional information. Foreign Broadcast Information Service-Latin America Daily Report (FBIS-LAM), Oct. 27, 1986, p. M2.

29 See G. Kuznetsova, A. Manenok, "Sovetsko-argentinskie torgovo-ekonomicheskie otnosheniya."

30 National Foreign Assessment Center, *Communist Aid Activities in Non-Communist Less Developed Countries, 1979 and 1954–79* (Washington, D.C.: CIA, 1980), p. 11; U.S. Department of State, *Warsaw Pact Economic Aid to Non-Communist LDCs*, 1984 (Washington, D.C.: Government Printing Office, 1986), pp. 6, 17.

31 For the best article with detailed criticism see, N.V. Zinov'ev and L.L. Klochkovsky, "K novym rebezham vo vzaimnoi torgovle," *LA*, 4 (April 1985), pp. 7–19.

32 FBIS-LAM, October 27, 1986, p. B1.

33 See A. Vlasov, "Novye aspekty gotovykh izdelii," *Ekonomicheskie Nauki*, 7 (July 1985), pp. 62–68.

34 FBIS-SOV, May 30, 1985, p. D1; FBIS-SOV, December 9, 1985, p. D1.

35 Patrick Cockburn, "Moscow Carries out Foreign Trade Shakeup," *Financial Times*, September 4, 1986; Serge Schmemann, "Kremlin Eases Rules on Trade," *The New York Times*, September 25, 1986. These reforms have produced a favorable response in Latin America. See President Alfonsín's report on his visit to Moscow during which expansion of Soviet-Argentine economic ties was discussed. FBIS-LAM, October 21, 1986, p. B1.

36 See the April 7, 1986 issue of *CACEX informacão semanal* outlining the structure of the Soviet foreign trade establishment, as well as negotiating procedures and preferences that used to obtain before the recent reforms. The account is very skeptical about chances of any dynamic exchanges, especially about prospects for barter trade. It also makes the point that the Soviets are much less flexible than the East Europeans and that this inflexibility creates more barriers than do Western restrictions.

37 There was another angle to Castro's move. The Havana meeting was convened in late 1985, that is on the eve of the scheduled negotiations on repayment of the huge Cuban debt to the USSR which had been postponed until 1986. Not surprisingly, the Soviet media almost ignored Castro's venture. For figures on Cuban debt to the USSR see Mesa-Lago in this volume.

38 *Ekonomicheskoe sotrudnichestvo stran chlenov SEV,* 1 (January 1985), p. 46.

39 See N. Zinov'ev, *Latinskaia Amerika: regional'noe sotrudnichestvo i problemy razvitiya* (Moscow: Progress, 1983). It is the second, substantially revised, version of a book published in 1977, which dealt with regional cooperation in terms of economic independence.

40 D. Volsky, "Osnovnye napravleniia izucheniia Latinskoi Ameriki," *Nova i noveishaia istoriia,* 2 (April 1986), p. 27. Some publications of the Institute were critical of radical economic thought in the past. But arguments of this type were not the central theme of any one monograph, nor were they ever before singled out in research plans.

41 See, "SSSR-Nikaragua: sotrudnichestvo rasshiraetsia," *VT,* 6 (June 1986), pp. 12–13.

42 *World Marxist Review,* 6 (June 1981), p. 40.

43 See the round-table discussion in *Latinskaia Amerika* on the meaning and the future course of the Nicaraguan revolution, issues 2,3 (February, March 1980), especially Sergo Mikoyan's summary in the March issue.

44 *Ekonomicheskoe sotrudnichestvo stran chlenov SEV,* p. 36. For facts on Soviet aid to and trade with Nicaragua, see P. Clement's and W. R. Duncan's contribution to this volume.

45 Maurice Bishop, "Line of March for the Party" (Sept. 13, 1982), reprinted in J. Valenta, H. J. Ellison, eds., *Grenada and Soviet/Cuban Policy* (Boulder, CO: Westview, 1985), pp. 301–02.

46 TASS, May 4, 1982, quoted in Peter Clement, "Moscow and Nicaragua: Two Sides of Soviet Policy," *Comparative Strategy,* 1 (1985), p. 80.

47 For a good example of this type of thinking at the higher echelons see, Karen Brutents' article on the Malvinas crisis in *Latin America: Studies by Soviet Scholars,* 3, (1984), pp. 123–48. For a good example of academic analysis consult the writings of Irina Zorina.

3

An Unclear Menace: U.S. Perceptions of Soviet Strategy in Latin America

Richard L. Millett

Both the 1985 movie, *Red Dawn*, and the 1987 ABC television miniseries, *Amerika*, portrayed a Soviet takeover of the United States with Communist troops from Latin American nations. Such a scenario would have been unimaginable a few years earlier, but its appearance in these mid-1980s productions underlines how much popular perceptions of both the actual and the potential extent of Soviet influence in Latin America have increased in recent years. Part of this is due to the conflicts in Nicaragua and El Salvador and the U.S. intervention in Grenada, part to incessant efforts by the Reagan administration to portray turmoil in the hemisphere as a product of Soviet influences and actions, and part to the actual increase in Soviet interests and activities in the region over the past decade.[1]

While the current level of preoccupation, both actual and rhetorical, over the activities of the USSR in Latin America is perhaps higher than at any previous time, the concern is by no means new. It dates back at least to the establishment of diplomatic relations between Mexico and the Soviet Union in 1924.

The issue of "international Communism" in Latin America reared its head numerous times during the late 1920s and 1930s, but it never became a major concern in the United States. Preoccupied first with the Great Depression and later by the coming of war in Europe, the United States government subordinated whatever concerns it may have had in this sphere to its desires to avoid intervention and to promote hemispheric unity. In 1932, Communist involvement in an abortive rebellion in El Salvador led the Hoover administration to dispatch naval vessels there, but this did not alter its refusal to recognize the existing government.[2]

The administration of Franklin D. Roosevelt was even more reluctant to intervene directly in Latin America. His administration proclaimed a "Good Neighbor Policy" for the Western Hemisphere, abandoning Theodore Roosevelt's Corollary to the Monroe Doctrine which had asserted the right of the U.S. to intervene in Latin America to end instability, promote debt collection, and preclude increased regional involvement by extra-hemispheric nations. When a group of American businessmen in Cuba tried to complain to Ambassador Sumner Welles about growing Communist influence in the labor movement, Welles dismissed their concerns, attributing labor problems to the national political climate.[3] Again, when Mexico expropriated American oil properties in 1938, the oil companies raised the specter of Communist influence and Senator Styles Bridges of New Hampshire charged the Roosevelt administration with "encourag[ing] and even conniv[ing] at the establishment of Communism in Mexico."[4] The administration, however, was more concerned about Mexico selling its oil to Nazi Germany than it was with any potential Soviet influence and accordingly concentrated its efforts on promoting a negotiated settlement.

Concerns over Communist influence in the Hemisphere were at a low ebb during World War II, in part because of the wartime alliance with the Soviet Union. In Chile, the formation in 1938 of a Popular Front cabinet, which included ministers from the Communist party, failed to elicit serious concern. Neither, initially, did the 1944 revolutions in Guatemala and El Salvador which toppled long-standing, pro-American dictators. The influence of the Cold War on U.S. relations with Latin America became obvious during the 1947 Inter-American Conference on the Maintenance of Continental Peace and Security, popularly known as the Rio Conference. The United States had repeatedly postponed this meeting because of ongoing disputes with Juan Domíngo Perón's administration in Argentina, but by 1947 fears of Soviet influence outweighed concerns over the pro-fascist nature of Perón's government. At Rio, the United States created the first peacetime military alliance in its history, a pact whose prime purpose was to provide a military framework for opposing Communist expansion in the Western Hemisphere.[5]

The anti-Communist orientation of U.S. policy became more explicit during the 1948 International Conference of American States held in Bogotá, Colombia. Prior to the Conference, the State Department's Policy Planning staff recommended that anti-Communist measures within the interamerican system draw on the following principles:

(a) International Communism at the present time must be regarded as the tool of the Kremlin, which the latter utilizes to advance Russian imperialistic designs and to supplant democracy throughout the world with a totalitarian police state system that suppresses human rights and civil liberties;
(b) International Communism, consequently, is a direct and major threat to the national security of the United States and to that of all the American Republics;
(c) This threat, at the present time, is a potential rather than an immediately serious one in Latin America generally, but preventive measures should be taken to minimize it before it becomes more dangerous.[6]

While the Conference was meeting in Bogotá, a massive urban riot broke out, sparked by the murder of the popular socialist political figure, Jorge Gaitán.[7] The building where the Conference was being held was destroyed, but the meeting itself continued at U.S. insistence. The United States professed to see the hand of international Communism in the riots, with Secretary of State George Marshall declaring that "revolutionary movements here were not confined to Colombia, but had world-wide implications," and later charging that the riots were part of a plan not only to sabotage the Conference, but also to disrupt the European Recovery Program and the upcoming Italian elections.[8]

This view of the Bogotá riots as somehow related to a world-wide Communist conspiracy eminating from Moscow has generally been discredited by later historical analysis, but it reflects the emerging mentality of the U.S. government with regard to Soviet influence in Latin America. At the Bogotá Conference, no single nation was identified as especially vulnerable to such influences, but in the years following the meeting, American concerns increasingly focused on Guatemala.

The American public paid little attention to the Communist threat in Latin America during the 1940s. The academic community also ignored the subject.[9] Developments in Guatemala in the early 1950s, however, began to change this pattern.

Concerns over growing Communist influence in Guatemala had begun under the Truman administration. Suspicions multiplied when Colonel Jacobo Arbenz became President in 1951 and began a major program of agrarian reform. During the early 1950s, American press coverage of Guatemala increased steadily, with most stories both voicing concerns over Communist influences and expressing sympathy for the United Fruit Company, the source of much of the negative publicity surrounding Guatemala. By the end of 1952, the State Department was investigating ways to pressure Guatemala to move against the Communist party which was collaborating in the Arbenz government. Implementation of such policies, however, was left to the incoming Eisenhower administration.[10]

Both the Truman and Eisenhower administrations assumed that Communist activities anywhere in the hemisphere were directly controlled by the Soviet Union, a point of view which accurately reflected the aims—if not always the abilities—of the Soviet Union under Stalin. In the words of State Department Latin American expert Thomas Mann, "Communists the world over [are] agents of Soviet imperialism."[11] Thus, any Communist influence in Guatemala provided an opening for the Soviet Union and posed a potential threat to American security.

Eisenhower's secretary of state, John Foster Dulles, and his brother, CIA Director Allen Dulles, were more than willing to increase pressure on Guatemala. By August 1953, the CIA was preparing a covert operation to oust Arbenz,[12] and from then until the CIA-sponsored exile invasion in June 1954, there was an intensive propaganda campaign designed to portray Guatemala as little more than a puppet of the Kremlin. This provoked acrimonious exchanges between the United States and Guatemala in international fora such as the United Nations and the Organization of American States (OAS). Under strong pressure from the United States, and without mentioning Guatemala by name, the March 1954 OAS Conference in Caracas adopted a resolution characterizing the "activities of the international Communist movement as constituting intervention in American affairs," and added that "the domination or control of the political institutions of any American State by the international Communist movement . . . would constitute a threat to the sovereignty and political independence of the American States." Guatemala voted against the Caracas declaration and charged the United States, before the U.N. Security Council, with attempting to overthrow its government. Such public attacks on U.S. policy by a small, Third World nation were virtually unprecedented and served to harden administration perceptions of Soviet influence, especially when the USSR took the floor in the U.N. to support the Guatemalan position.[13]

A 1954 attempt by the Arbenz government, which had been under a U.S. arms embargo since 1949, to secure arms from Eastern Europe provided Washington with what was seen as conclusive evidence of Soviet influence in Guatemala. The success of the June 1954 exile invasion was viewed as a victory over the Soviets and a rebuff of their designs on the Western Hemisphere. Secretary of State Dulles, in a nationwide radio address, declared that the Soviet Union "chose Guatemala as a spot which it could turn into an official base from which to breed subversion which would extend to other American republics. The intrusion of Soviet despotism was, of course, a direct challenge to our Monroe Doctrine,"[14] At that time, most of the media supported this view. Conservative journalists such as Daniel James devoted considerable effort to chronicling both the alleged threat and the U.S. response to it.[15] Much of the academic community subscribed to the administration's view, albeit with some dissent from the prevailing wisdom.[16]

With the fall of the Arbenz regime, official U.S. concern about Soviet activities in Latin America receded. Administration officials evidently believed that direct Soviet involvement in the hemisphere was now unlikely. Meanwhile, as official American concerns during the late 1950s focused on other areas of the world and on the race for outer space where the Soviets were achieving some embarrassing successes, academics began to show the first signs of serious, scholarly interest in the subject of Soviet policy toward Latin America.[17]

The 1959 victory of Fidel Castro in Cuba renewed concern over Soviet influence in Latin America and ultimately shattered the comfortable assumptions about the ability of the United States to maintain unchallenged hegemony in the region. The Soviets were uninvolved in Castro's victory and the Cuban Communist Party (then known as the Popular Socialist Party) was a late convert to the cause. Nevertheless, Communist and, ultimately, Soviet influence in Cuba increased steadily during the last two years of the Eisenhower administration, producing a crisis for U.S. policy.

In June 1959, Cuba concluded a trade agreement with the Soviet Union, but waited until the following May to establish diplomatic relations. Three months earlier, however, in an event unprecedented in the history of the smaller nations of the Caribbean Basin, Soviet Deputy Premier Anastas Mikoyan paid an official visit to Havana. This visit galvanized U.S. concerns. The following month, President Eisenhower authorized the CIA to begin preparations for a covert operation to oust Castro.[18]

By mid-1960, the Cuban issue had become a direct point of conflict between the United States and the USSR, with Nikita Khrushchev declaring the Monroe Doctrine dead and threatening the United States with missiles if there was a U.S. military intervention in Cuba. Eisenhower responded that the Soviet leader's remarks revealed his determination to make Cuba serve the objectives of the USSR. He added that the United States would never accept a communist regime in the Western Hemisphere, and the State Department, in a memo to the Inter-American Peace Commission, charged that Castro was in open league with the USSR and China.[19] Khrushchev's public embrace of Castro and their joint attacks on U.S. policies at the U.N. General Assembly meeting in September 1960 strengthened perceptions of a Cuban-Soviet alliance. In October, the Eisenhower administration placed an embargo on all trade with Cuba (except food and medicine) and in January, a few days before Eisenhower left office, the United States broke diplomatic relations. Throughout this period, preparations for an exile invasion progressed steadily.

The inauguration of President John F. Kennedy produced no discernible change in policy, and the exile invasion was launched in April 1961 with disastrous results. In the aftermath of the Bay of Pigs fiasco, an ongoing debate developed within the United States as to whether Castro had deliberately led his nation into an alliance with the Soviet Union, or whether he had been pushed into dependence by aggressive, insensitive U.S. policies. The general consensus was that the impetus for the ties had come from Castro rather than from the USSR.[20]

The evolution of events in Cuba also set off a debate over how best to respond to the increased Soviet presence in—and threat to—the hemisphere. U.S. policy concentrated on preventing future Cubas, on isolating Castro, and on strengthening the political, economic, and military structures elsewhere in Latin America. One result was an ongoing effort to expel Cuba from hemispheric organizations and to persuade other nations to break all ties with Castro. The Kennedy administration developed the Alliance for Progress, an ambitious effort to link economic development with political and social reform, to aid existing regimes, encourage progress towards more democratic governments and reduce the chances of future Castro-style revolutions in the hemisphere. Military assistance was also increased, with greater emphasis placed on counterinsurgency training and on civic action programs.[21] While the Kennedy administration continued to talk about eliminating the Soviet beachhead in Cuba, the policy pursued actually represented an extension of the containment doctrine to the Western Hemisphere.

The October 1962 Cuban missile crisis produced a direct U.S.-USSR confrontation. The Kennedy administration believed that the principal Soviet objective in placing missiles in Cuba was to alter the global balance of power, rather than to advance Soviet objectives in the Western Hemisphere specifically.[22] In the negotiations leading to a resolution of the crisis, Cuba was virtually excluded. Ultimately, and over Castro's protests, the Soviet Union withdrew the missiles, obtaining in return a vague U.S. commitment not to invade Cuba "if all offensive weapons are removed from Cuba and kept out of the hemisphere in the future under adequate verification and safeguards and if Cuba is not used for the export of aggressive Communist purposes."[23] At the time, this was perceived as a major American victory, but some analysts have since contended it made the U.S. "the guarantor of Cuba's Communist government" without effectively limiting Soviet use of the island.[24]

The missile crisis strained Cuban-Soviet ties and encouraged Castro to promote revolution throughout the hemisphere in defiance of Soviet efforts to establish "peaceful coexistence." Combined with the Sino-Soviet split, these developments led most government and academic analysts to modify or abandon the traditional view of a monolithic Communist movement and to analyze Latin American communism, Cuban initiatives, and Soviet policies toward the region as separate, albeit interrelated problems.[25] In early 1963, Assistant Secretary of State Edwin M. Martin devoted the bulk of a statement on "Communist Subversion in the Western Hemisphere" to an analysis of Cuban activities. He noted, "The Soviets undoubtedly regard Latin America as an area offering unusual possibilities, but they themselves have been cautious in their tactics, except where special opportunities have developed, as in the case of Cuba.[26]

This change in official perceptions of Soviet intentions was virtually complete by the time of the 1965 crisis in the Dominican Republic. In his messages and pronouncements justifying the dispatch of American forces to that nation, President Lyndon Johnson never mentioned the

Soviet Union. Instead, he blamed the conflict on "Communist leaders, many of them trained in Cuba," and declared that he would not permit "the establishment of another Communist government in the Western Hemisphere."[27]

The Dominican intervention and the failure of Cuban-sponsored insurgent movements in Venezuela and Bolivia, combined with growing U.S. preoccupation over events in Southeast Asia, led to a decline of official interest in and concern over Soviet activities in the Western Hemisphere. For their part, academic analyses of Cuban-Soviet relations stressed divergences between the two countries.[28]

Shortly after taking office in 1969, President Richard Nixon dispatched Governor Nelson Rockefeller on a fact finding trip to Latin America. The mission encountered considerable hostility and criticism, but Rockefeller attributed this more to U.S. neglect and severe socioeconomic problems than to any Soviet influence or Communist subversion. The *Rockefeller Report* gave overwhelming emphasis to economic and social problems, stressing the need for a clearer, more consistent U.S. policy and greater attention to these issues at higher levels of government. The brief section on subversion concentrated on the threat from Cuba, concluding that "the opinion in the United States that communism is no longer a serious factor in the Western Hemisphere is thoroughly wrong." The Report noted the visit of Soviet warships to Havana and linked the USSR to Castro's activities. Otherwise, however, it virtually ignored the Soviet Union.[29]

During the late 1960s and early 1970s, the Soviets steadily expanded their diplomatic and trade ties with Latin America and increased their naval activities in the Caribbean. These efforts attracted only limited U.S. attention, although an apparent Soviet project to establish a submarine base in Cuba in 1970 did produce a sharp official reaction (after which the Soviets backed off).[30] The Nixon and Ford administrations, absorbed by Vietnam, preoccupied with Watergate, and concerned with the maintenance of detente, focused little attention on Latin America, much less to the implications of the growing Soviet presence in the region.

While official and public concern over Soviet activities seemed limited through the late 1960s and into the early 1970s, academic attention grew steadily. In a pioneering 1967 effort Herbert Dinerstein argued that Soviet policy in Latin America was seeking to "isolate the United States and end its influence," but concluded that in the wake of the Cuban missile crisis, Soviet objectives had become "more limited and more realistic."[31]

Dinerstein's work was followed by numerous scholarly treatments of Soviet policies toward Latin America. A documentary history of Soviet views of the region, two edited volumes, two articles in *Orbis*, a lengthy study of Latin America's place in the Cold War, and a volume on China's Latin American policies all appeared in the early 1970s.[32] There was considerable convergence in the treatment of Soviet policies in these studies. Emphasis was placed on the expanded Soviet presence, on the cautious and opportunistic nature of Soviet policy, on the divisions between the USSR and China and the difficulties of managing ties with Cuba, and on the lessened Soviet control over the increasingly fragmented Communist parties of the region. Most of the authors also found significant tensions between the ideological component of Soviet policy and the need to advance Russian national interests, tensions which were generally resolved in favor of national interests.

There were, nevertheless, significant differences in the conclusions drawn by these authors. J. Gregory Oswald took the most sanguine view of Soviet activities. He asserted that "far from trying to foment revolution, the Soviet leaders, in line with their gradualist policy, are actually doing their best to exert a moderating and restraining influence on Latin American Communist parties." Oswald concluded that "the subversive activities of earlier decades do not presently form part of Soviet policy toward Latin America."[33] While not going nearly this far, State Department official Wayne Smith stressed the restraining factors on Soviet actions. These included the higher priority given to relations with the U.S., the Cuban experience which demonstrated "just how expensive—and thankless—the support of an underdeveloped ally can be," and the peculiar situation of Latin America which made it less receptive to Communist ideology than other Third World areas. "[R]ather than ideological objectives," Smith concluded, "Soviet aims more accurately reflect traditional great-power strivings for political advantage. Moscow does not seek to replace the existing governments with Communist ones (at least in the near term). It aims to undercut the U.S. position and to increase its own political stock with existing governments."[34] For his part, W. Raymond Duncan stressed expanded Soviet ties in the region, especially in the economic field, and concluded "Soviet-Latin American relations contained new opportunities for Moscow." The "decreased threat from Cuba toward Latin American governments," he noted, "improves Moscow's image and reduces the limited sense of United States-Latin American unity created by the common external threat."[35]

United States opposition to the government of President Salvador Allende in Chile, at the head of a coalition which included the Communist party, was the most prominent issue in U.S.–Latin American relations in the early 1970s. Fear of another Cuba in the hemisphere which could serve as a further instrument of Soviet policy was a major factor in the Nixon administration's determination to dislodge Allende, but concern for U.S. economic interests was also a factor. Soviet support for Allende was restrained—perhaps in the hope of averting a hostile U.S. reaction—consisting largely of public statements of support accompanied by very limited economic assistance and credits.[36] The Nixon administration, however, was concerned with the potential rather than the actual extent of Soviet influence and accordingly supported the efforts that led to the regime's fall in September 1973. Democrats such as Senators George McGovern and Frank Church, and defenders of the Kennedy-Johnson policies such as Senator Henry Jackson raised some protests over the Chilean policy and, after Nixon left office, it became the subject of congressional investigations. Much of this, however, was in the post-Watergate context of suspicion towards, and even rejection of, involvement by the United States in the internal affairs of other nations.

The Chilean experience reinforced Nixon administration perceptions of the cautious, opportunistic nature of Soviet policies and the relatively low level of the Soviet threat. In his public statements during a six-nation Latin American trip in February 1976, Secretary of State Henry Kissinger stressed economic issues and never mentioned Cuba or the Soviet Union.[37]

Official concern over the expanded Soviet presence in Latin America remained muted during the Ford administration, but conservatives showed signs of growing concern. Two volumes published in the mid-1970s reflected this view. Writing in 1974, James D. Theberge warned that "Moscow is banking on strategic parity (a better correlation of world forces) and East-West detente to create a political climate in Latin America that favors the radicalization of its politics, disintegration of the interamerican system, greater independence from the United States, the elimination of American ownership of strategic raw materials and energy reserves and closer ties with the Soviet Union."[38] Theberge devoted special attention to Soviet espionage operations and to the presence of Soviet naval vessels in the Caribbean, but concluded that "Soviet policy aims at extending its influence without provoking a head-on clash with the United States and adversely affecting the far from smooth course of detente."[39]

The following year, Leon Gouré and Morris Rothenberg argued that "the Soviet Union is investing increasing resources to expand its influence in Latin America and to reinforce trends which are inimical to U.S. interests."[40] They emphasized Soviet controls over Cuba, expanded economic and diplomatic ties with the area (notably major arms sales to Peru), and new efforts to promote ties with "progressive military regimes." These expanded contacts were used by the USSR to reinforce its "struggle against U.S. domination and as a deliberate act of defiance of the U.S."[41]

If the warnings of Theberge, Gouré, Rothenberg, and others had little effect on the Ford administration, they had even less influence after Jimmy Carter's inauguration. President Carter expanded the policy of detente to include limited contacts with Cuba. In Latin America, human rights rather than anti-Communism was made the centerpiece of U.S. policy, and warnings about the Soviet-Cuban menace received scant attention. In an address to the OAS delivered shortly after taking office, President Carter made no mention of the Soviet Union and, in the case of Cuba, concentrated on his desire to improve relations.[42]

The issue of Soviet and Cuban influence emerged during the debates over the ratification of the 1977 Panama Canal Treaties. Opponents of the treaties tried to raise the issue of Soviet-Cuban ties with Panama, charging that its ruler, General Omar Torrijos, had links with Communists and was even allowing Soviet aircraft to use Panamanian facilities.[43] The Carter administration rejected such charges, as did the government of Panama, and the issue largely disappeared once the treaties were ratified.

The outbreak of civil conflict in Nicaragua in 1978 provided another opportunity for conservatives to charge the Carter administration with ignoring Cuban-Soviet activities in the hemisphere. Even some Democratic congressmen, such as John Murphy of New York and Larry Wilson of Texas, joined in these charges. The Carter administration generally downplayed the role of Cuba and the Soviet Union in Nicaragua until June 1979 when, on the eve of an emergency OAS meeting on the Nicaraguan situation, it released charges of a major escalation in Cuban support for the *Sandinista* rebels. Conservatives used these declarations to support their attacks on the *Sandinistas*, but when the OAS rejected the U.S. proposal for sending a peacekeeping force to Nicaragua, Carter rejected unilateral intervention.[44]

At that point the Carter administration still perceived the risk of Communist influence in Nicaragua as less costly than the domestic and international costs of direct action designed to forestall a *Sandinista* victory.[45] Caught between its opposition to intervention and its commitment to human rights, the administration was unable to formulate an effective policy to avert its own worst-case scenario—the triumph of Marxist-Leninist guerrillas in Nicaragua.

The *Sandinista* victory occurred in an international context marked by the breakdown of detente. The Soviet invasion of Afghanistan and the downfall of the Shah of Iran's pro-American government set the tone for the general debate on U.S.-Soviet relations. Events in Nicaragua, for their part, reignited the nearly dormant debate over Soviet actions and intentions in the Western Hemisphere. The expanded Cuban role in Africa during the 1970s and the concomitant expansion of Soviet military ties with Cuba, as well as the establishment of a pro-Cuban government in Grenada and the rising tide of civil conflict in El Salvador, provided additional fuel for this controversy. The Cuban issue produced the first response from the Carter administration. Evidence of an expanded Soviet presence had been accumulating for some time,[46] and in September 1979, President Carter charged a Soviet combat brigade had been stationed in Cuba. He found this development "unacceptable." Eventually, the administration accepted Soviet descriptions of this force as a training unit, but from that point on, and particularly as Cuba became more engaged with Nicaragua and with providing support to guerrilla groups elsewhere, efforts to normalize relations with Cuba were essentially frozen.[47]

As conditions in Central America deteriorated, U.S. policy in Latin America emerged as an issue in the 1980 elections. The Republican platform denounced the policies of the Carter administration, deplored the growth of Communist influence, and called for stern measures to deal with the breaking Central American situation, including a suspension of aid to Nicaragua.[48] For Republican presidential candidate Ronald Reagan, the Caribbean was "rapidly becoming a Communist lake in what should be an American pond," and throughout the campaign he denounced the growth of Soviet influence in the region.[49] The theme was taken up by other Republican candidates and by the conservative press, which ran editorials warning that Cuban and Soviet-backed Communists were taking over Central America and the Caribbean.[50]

In the months following Reagan's victory, it became clear that the statements on Latin America were not simply campaign rhetoric. Latin American specialists associated with the Reagan campaign, known as The Committee of Santa Fe, declared that attacks on Latin American governments by "domestic revolutionary groups assisted by the Soviet-Cuban axis, must be understood not just as a threat to some alleged oligarchy, but as a threat to the security of the United States," and urged a U.S. policy aimed at "the exclusion of communism from the Americas."[51] This tone was paralleled in January 1981 by the Reagan administration's future U.N. Ambassador, Jeane Kirkpatrick, who blamed the Carter administration for the fall of Somoza and the installation of a Cuban-Soviet backed regime in Nicaragua.[52]

On February 23, 1981 the Reagan administration opened its campaign against what it perceived as the Cuban-Soviet sponsored threat to Central America by releasing several hundred pages of documents detailing external support to the Salvadoran insurgents, many of which concerned visits by the head of El Salvador's Moscow-line Communist party, Shafik Jorge Handal, to Moscow and several Eastern European nations.[53] At his March 6 press conference, President Reagan accused the Soviet Union of "exporting terrorism and guerrilla war to El Salvador,"[54] and on April 24, Secretary of State Alexander Haig expanded on this theme, declaring that the United States could not allow the government of El Salvador to "be overthrown by armed intervention supported by Moscow or its surrogates."[55] The campaign to link the Soviet Union and Cuba to the conflict in El Salvador encountered skepticism among Democrats, journalists, and academics.[56] By 1982, the issue was becoming increasingly partisan with perceptions of the Soviet threat in El Salvador closely connected to an individual's degree of support for or opposition to administration policies.[57]

The effort to link the Soviet Union to events in El Salvador continued throughout the President's first term, but the campaign reached a crescendo in early 1983, during the debate over military assistance to El Salvador. The President, Secretary of Defense Caspar Weinberger, and Secretary of State George Shultz were all involved in this effort, Weinberger charging that the Salvadorean guerrillas were "supplied by the Soviet Union and resupplied."[58] By mid-1983, however, both the administration and the public's attention had begun to shift from El Salvador to Nicaragua and, briefly, to Grenada.

The October 26, 1983 U.S. intervention in Grenada opened a new chapter in the debate over Soviet policy and intentions. The documents captured during this operation shed new light on Soviet relations with revolutionary regimes and Marxist parties in the Third World. The documents seemed to support charges of aggressive Soviet involvement in the Caribbean Basin. The Reagan administration moved rapidly to make them public. Disputes soon arose, however, over the motives and goals of the Soviet involvement in Grenada, and the impact of the intervention on future Soviet actions. Soviet specialists joined with

Latin American and Caribbean specialists in this debate, a development which indicated the growing interest of the former in Soviet activities in Latin America. Supporters of the intervention usually accepted the President's contention that "we got there just in time," because Grenada was being converted into a base for Soviet and Cuban operations throughout the region. They argued that the invasion had an inhibiting effect on future Soviet actions in the region, had strained Soviet ties with Cuba, Nicaragua, and Suriname, and would reduce the prospects for success for Marxist-Leninist parties throughout the Caribbean Basin. Critics disputed the extent to which Soviet involvement in Grenada has aimed at influencing events beyond that island. Instead, they emphasized it was the New Jewel Movement which had strived to gain Soviet support in the face of the USSR's reluctance to undertake such commitments. More generally, they downplayed any lasting impact from the Grenada intervention on the USSR's actions in the Third World.[59]

Even while troops were landing in Grenada, the focus of U.S. attention had been shifting toward Nicaragua. Revelations of covert U.S. activities against that nation, including the arming and training of the insurgent groups known as the *contras* and the mining of Nicaraguan harbors, had unleashed a new debate over U.S. policy in Central America. In an effort to gain support for his position, the President appointed a National Bipartisan Commission on Central America, headed by former Secretary of State Henry Kissinger. In its final report, the Commission declared that the United States must "bar the Soviet Union from consolidating, either directly or through Cuba, a hostile foothold on the American continents in order to advance its strategic purposes." In the 1970s, the Commission argued, Soviet policy had shifted "toward a more adventurous approach, including support for armed struggle in Central America." The USSR was now "pursuing a strategy of progressively greater involvement in the Western Hemisphere." This effort, portrayed as low risk, inexpensive, and with a high potential for Soviet gains, aimed to "end the unchallenged U.S. preeminence within the hemisphere and possibly to see other Cubas established, to divert U.S. attention and resources, . . . to complicate our relations with Western Europe, and to burnish the Soviet Union's image as a revolutionary state." Efforts to counter Soviet policies in the region would be "a significant concern for years to come," since "the United States cannot accept Soviet military engagement in Central America and the Caribbean beyond what we reluctantly tolerate in Cuba." The Commission saw "little promise in negotiating with the

Soviet Union over Central America," and noted "The United States cannot eliminate all Soviet political involvement and influence within Central America and the Caribbean." Nevertheless, the Commission argued, the U.S. "must curb Soviet military activity in the hemisphere," while "reduc[ing] Soviet opportunities and increas[ing] the incentives for others to abstain from forging ties with Moscow that damage U.S. and regional interests."[60]

The Commission's report failed to end the debate over Central American policy. The issue intensified during President Reagan's November 1984 reelection campaign, with administration charges that the Soviets were shipping advanced combat aircraft to Nicaragua. While this charge ultimately proved unfounded, the issue of increased Soviet military assistance to Nicaragua (for details, see the chapter by Peter Clement and Raymond Duncan) became a key element in administration efforts to secure funding for the *contras*. A major instrument in this was a "White Paper" entitled *The Soviet-Cuban Connection in Central America and the Caribbean*, issued by the Defense and State Departments in early 1985. This document branded Cuba, Nicaragua, and the Soviet Union as "the principal threats to democracy in Central America," and concluded, "the Soviet Union hopes to force the United States to divert attention and military resources to an area that has not been a serious security concern." The document described Cuba as "the key Soviet proxy" and Nicaragua as an important complement to Cuba in the Soviet strategy to increase pressure on the United States in the Caribbean Basin."[61]

On February 28, 1985, the House of Representatives held hearings on "Soviet Posture in the Western Hemisphere." In opening the hearings, Congressman Michael Barnes, a critic of *contra* aid, observed that "the Congress needs to have a detailed understanding of the nature and scope of the Soviet presence in the hemisphere," in an effort to have the United States "deal more effectively to prevent the expansion of Soviet influence."[62]

Responding to this request, Deputy Assistant Secretary of State James Michel made a distinction "between Soviet activities in recent years in the Caribbean Basin and Soviet activities in South America." In South America, Michel testified, Soviet activities were largely overt, while in the Caribbean Basin "they have encouraged insurgency in nonMarxist regimes." In the Basin, he said, "the Soviets prefer to use Cuba as a surrogate . . . and keep a low profile themselves." Michel stressed that he was "not suggesting an identity between the two, but a convergence of actions that would not be possible without Soviet economic and military support for Cuba." Deputy Assistant Secretary of Defense Nestor D. Sánchez also testified, stressing Soviet military aid to Nicaragua and arguing that "Soviet and Cuban objectives in this region are complementary."[63]

Two scholars, Jiri Valenta and Carl Jacobsen, also testified at the time. Valenta cited the Grenada documents as evidence of "the increasing sophistication of Soviet methods in furthering Third World strategic objectives," and concluded that the U.S. intervention in Grenada "was only a temporary setback for Soviet and Cuban policies." On Nicaragua, Valenta concluded that there were tactical differences between the USSR and Cuba: "[T]he Cubans are concerned with circumscribing the Nicaraguan conflict in order to exclude U.S. participation, whereas the Russians would probably like to see direct American military engagement, even though this might bring down the Sandinistas." But he warned against "exaggerating the differences between Moscow and Havana," because of Cuba's dependence on Soviet support. Jacobsen was more cautious. He argued that the Soviet Union was "moving back to its traditional and preferred emphasis on improved relations with South American regimes." In Central America, the Soviets had reduced their emphasis on revolution and "switched to narrow state-to-state support for the *Sandinista* regime." According to Jacobsen, "Moscow concedes that Washington's right to intervene in Nicaragua is the same basic security right that she invoked in Afghanistan," and, in the event of intervention "the Soviet response will be restricted to solidarity and full political support."[64]

The testimony of Valenta and Jacobsen reflected the increasing involvement of academics in the analysis of Soviet policies towards Latin America. More studies of this subject were produced during the first 6 years of the Reagan administration than in the previous 50 years. Increased interest was by no means confined to academics: columnists and political analysts across the political spectrum began to deal with Soviet and Cuban involvement in the hemisphere. All three commercial networks and the Public Broadcasting Service devoted time to examining the subject, although television found it easier to deal with Cuban rather than Soviet activities. Political lobbies on the left and right produced a variety of films, defending or debunking the Reagan administration's claims of Soviet-Cuban responsibility for instability in the Caribbean Basin.

The parameters of the debate over Soviet policy in Latin America remained basically unchanged into 1987. Each time the issue of *contra* funding arose in the Congress, the administration revived the issue.

In a March 16, 1986 address to the nation, President Reagan pushed the rhetoric to new heights. He proclaimed that "using Nicaragua as a base, the Soviets and Cubans can become the dominant power in the crucial corridor between North and South America. Established there, they will be in a position to threaten the Panama Canal, interdict our vital Caribbean sealanes, and, ultimately, move against Mexico."[65] Opponents of funding responded that such rhetoric was exaggerated. Indeed, they claimed, aid to the *contras* exacerbated rather than reduced the threats of which the administration warned.

The proliferation of writings on Soviet policy towards Latin America during the 1970s and 1980s has produced its own set of problems. Evaluating these perceptions of Soviet policy in Latin America is complex and difficult, although there are major areas of continuity and general consensus in American perceptions. Virtually all analysts agree that Latin America was an area of relatively low priority for the Soviets, but its priority has risen in recent years. There is a continuing consensus that the Soviet approach has been cautious, opportunistic, and heavily constrained by perceptions of what might be the U.S. response. There is broad, ongoing agreement that the Soviets encounter serious obstacles and dilemmas in their dealings with Latin America and that there is constant tension between the ideological dimension of Soviet policy and the interests of the Soviet state, a conflict which is most frequently resolved in favor of state interests. Further, there is general agreement that Communist parties in the region are both objects and instruments of Soviet policy, but they are often weak or face stiff competition from ultra-left groups. The proliferation of Marxist-Leninist parties and factions produced by the Sino-Soviet split and conflicts over peaceful versus violent roads to power have made for a more unmanageable situation. While economic difficulties and the high cost of maintaining Cuba also act as limiting factors, the most basic and continuing constraint is the region's distance from the USSR and its proximity to the United States.

There is even some continuity and consensus in perceptions of Soviet goals in Latin America. Most writings acknowledge that Soviet policies reflect superpower rivalry and thus an effort to increase the USSR's presence in the region in order to weaken U.S. influence and divert American attention away from areas where the Soviet Union has greater direct concerns. Most authors agree that nationalism, resentment of past American policies, present levels of U.S. economic and political influence, and a lack of negative experiences with the USSR all work to Soviet advantage, facilitating efforts to brand the USSR as a defender of national sovereignty and the United States as the prime menace in that area.

There is also a consensus that increased Soviet activity in Latin America, and the lessened American ability to exclude such influence, reflect basic changes in the wider world of superpower competition. The Soviet achievement of nuclear parity is a major factor in this equation. So, too, has been the American experience in Vietnam and the subsequent decline in the United States' ability to control events in the Third World and in the American public's willingness to support the use of force in efforts to influence conflicts in other nations. A growing sense of Latin American identification with the Nonaligned Movement and with the Third World on economic issues has also reduced the U.S. ability to resist Soviet influence in Latin America. Resentment over American policy in the Falklands/Malvinas conflict has further eroded U.S. influence. As a result of these factors, public perceptions as to what constitutes unacceptable activities by the Soviet Union in Latin America have been notably reduced since 1960, and the ability of any administration to create a consensus on this question has declined.

Beyond these broad areas of consensus, however, there are major areas of disagreement. One ongoing area of dispute refers to the nature and significance of the contemporary Cuban-Soviet relationship. The Reagan administration has characterized Cuba as a Soviet surrogate, emphasizing the utility of Cuba as a base for Soviet military and intelligence operations.[66] While avoiding characterization of Cuba as a puppet, some academics lend support to this position. Edward González, for example, describes Cuba as "a client state of the Soviet Union," and further argues that "Cuban and Soviet interest in the Caribbean Basin have been congruent in recent years primarily because of the expansionist surge in Soviet global policy and the emergence of new targets of opportunity in the Basin itself."[67] Robert Leiken also argues for a growing convergence of Soviet and Cuban policies and interests in the Caribbean Basin, declaring "the role of Cuba is crucial to Soviet Latin American strategy, and that Moscow has given Castro "Soviet blessings to fish in troubled waters." Leiken devotes special emphasis to Cuba's role as an instrument of Soviet policies in Nicaragua and to the threat posed to American shipping lanes by the combined Soviet-Cuban naval presence in the Caribbean.[68] For his part, David Ronfeldt also emphasizes the potential military threat from what he describes as "fortress Cuba," and calls for a U.S. effort to "de-Sovietize Cuba, or at least to contain and diminish its close military collaboration with the USSR."[69]

In contrast, Cole Blasier argues that "Cuba's primary utility to the Soviet Union is political. The strategic advantages Cuba offers are offset by its exposed and not easily defensible location near Florida."[70] Blasier stresses differences between Soviet and Cuban policies, the extent to which "U.S. errors" rather than Soviet policies account for Cuban successes, and the high costs to the Soviets of involvement in Cuba.[71] Similar arguments have been presented by William LeoGrande and Wayne S. Smith.[72]

Elements of both preceding positions may be found in the writings of Jorge I. Domínguez, Robert Pastor, and W. Raymond Duncan. Domínguez has argued that Cuban actions have "served to radicalize Soviet foreign policy," noting "it is the Soviet Union, not Cuba that has changed its policy towards support of revolutions in the Third World as a means of bringing Marxist-Leninist regimes to power." Domínguez believes that the Cuban-Soviet alliance is not necessarily permanent, and "as the threats of overthrow and war recede, the conditions might emerge for more independent policies by Cuba . . . with regard to the Soviet Union."[73] Pastor stresses the unique character of the Soviet-Cuban relationship and contends "Soviet strategy has to be much more ambivalent than Cuban strategy." He concludes, "[T]he Soviets do not tell the Cubans what to do, but they let the Cubans know what they cannot do and the Cubans accept that."[74] Duncan has long emphasized the problems for the Soviet leadership in dealing with Castro and points of divergence on such key issues as policies toward Nicaragua and reaction to the intervention in Grenada. But he acknowledges the importance of Cuba as a facilitator of Soviet arms shipments to regional revolutionaries, the threat posed by the Soviet military presence in the island, and the limits which dependence on the USSR place on Cuba's freedom of action. For Duncan, there is no doubt that "Soviet-Cuban ties will experience some ups and downs in the future," but Gorbachev "will probably still consider Cuba a useful investment."[75]

Soviet policy in Central America and the Caribbean has generated numerous conflicting interpretations. Issues include the extent to which the Soviet Union is involved in and/or responsible for conflicts in the region, the actual and potential military threat posed by the Soviet presence, the degree of Soviet interest in acquiring additional military bases in the Basin, and the nature of interactions between the Soviet Union and Marxist regimes in the region.

Some analysts have emphasized the geostrategic dimension of Soviet policy and the USSR's willingness to support insurgencies.[76] Jiri Valenta has argued that military-security objectives are primary in the formulation of Soviet policies. Others, like Cole Blasier, minimize both Soviet involvement in Central America's insurgencies and the degree to which Nicaragua is allied with the Soviet Union. Blasier explains the growing Soviet role in Nicaragua as "largely a product of U.S. hostility," and views of Soviet objectives in Central America as "more political than strategic or military." On the issue of military bases, Blasier believes that "it is unlikely that the Soviets would deploy any significant forces into such a vulnerable area far from their home bases. The acquisition of basing facilities in the Caribbean would not alter this unfavorable balance."[77]

Another group of analysts (Leiken, Duncan, and the late Morris Rothenberg) have adopted positions between those of the Valentas and Blasier on this issue. Duncan argues that "to identify Soviet foreign policy as the central source of the Caribbean Basin turmoil is to credit the USSR with more control over events than it actually posessed." While acknowledging the increased Soviet activity in the area, he sees few concrete advantages for the USSR in Nicaragua. For him, "the Soviet quest for new footholds will be offset by continuing limits to Moscow's influence."[78] Leiken similarly emphasizes Soviet efforts to support insurgencies, but also stresses the limits on Soviet influence and the cautious nature of their approach.[79] Rothenberg also saw "a variety of constraints on Moscow's commitment and the directness of its involvement in the region." His writings portray Moscow's prime objectives in Central America as political, its approach as cautious and its commitments as limited.[80]

Soviet involvement in South America has been given much less attention and, as a result, has generated little controversy in the United States. There is a consensus that "Moscow's interest in the major South American countries stems from its own economic needs as well as from a desire to reduce American influence in the region and increase its own."[81]

The reasons for conflicting perceptions of Soviet policies are varied. Political and ideological differences are an obvious factor. In the case of members of the Reagan administration or their Democratic opponents, it is often difficult to separate rhetoric designed for political effect from actual perceptions of Soviet policy. Newspaper columnists, editorial writers, and even some academics are also influenced by these factors—at times appearing more interested in influencing the debate on U.S. policy towards Central America than in carefully analyzing Soviet goals and actions.

There are also wide divergences on these issues between those who study the Soviet Union and those whose primary concern is Latin America. William Luers has pointed out that:

> Latin Americanists are often influenced by the Latin left, severely critical of the U.S. government and . . . sympathetic to and supportive of Latin criticism of the United States . . . . They tend to be idealistic about the U.S. ability and desire to shape events. . . .
>
> Russian-East European specialists tend to be critical of the Soviet Union, communism and revolution . . . .
>
> The Soviet specialists tend to think of Latin America as a minor side show in U.S. foreign policy. To the Latin Americanists, the region is of major importance to the United States . . . . Therefore, the Soviet and Latin American specialists tend at times to reinforce each other's low tolerance for discussing seriously the Soviet threat in the Caribbean Basin.[82]

Many of those who write and speak on the subject know little about the Soviet Union and/or the Caribbean Basin. At times they lack the language skills necessary to do original research. One result is a tendency to see both the Soviet Union and the nations of the region as monolithic actors and to neglect points of internal division, and in this respect Jerry Hough's article on "The Evolving Soviet Debate on Latin America," represents a valuable contribution toward bridging the gap.[83]

Perceptions of the Soviet threat are often based on unstated, unclear, or even contradictory assumptions of what constitute U.S. interests in the region. There are unstated assumptions about the extent to which any Marxist regime, regardless of its ties to the USSR, serves Soviet interests, and the extent to which ideological considerations make efforts by such regimes to subvert their neighbors more or less inevitable. Finally, many writers assume that U.S.-Soviet rivalry is basically a zero-sum game, with any gain for one side an automatic loss for the other. At the very least, this assumption demands further testing and evidence.

Both the past history and current state of U.S. perceptions of Soviet policy toward Latin America warrant much greater study. A host of questions remain to be examined, including the ways in which Latin Americans strive to shape and take advantage of U.S. perceptions of a Soviet threat, and the extent to which Soviet activity reinforces or weakens the U.S. commitment to the region. The changes introduced by the new leadership in Russia and by whatever administration takes office in the United States in 1989 will insure that the subject of U.S.

perceptions of Soviet policy in Latin America will continue to be a dynamic and open area of inquiry.

While perceptions of Soviet policies remain clouded and conflictive, a few things are clear. The simple answers and broad consensus of the early 1950s are gone forever. Soviet policy has become a major factor in hemispheric realities and efforts to interpret and respond to it will become increasingly important. Hopefully, Soviet and Latin American specialists can learn from each other, narrowing the gap described by William Luers and working together to form clearer understandings of their own areas. Such cooperation could contribute to a better informed, more rational public debate on U.S. policy and could make that policy more effective and less divisive.

Notes

1 For details on the increase in Soviet interest see the chapter in this volume by David Albright.

2 See Martin Schmitz, "Non-Recognition of El Salvador: The Failure of a Policy," unpublished M.A. thesis, Southern Illinois University at Edwardsville, 1968.

3 Irwin F. Gellman, *Roosevelt and Batista: Good Neighbor Diplomacy in Cuba, 1933–1945* (Albuquerque: University of New Mexico Press, 1973), p. 35.

4 Quoted in David Cronin, *Josephus Daniels in Mexico* (Madison: University of Wisconsin Press, 1960), p. 232.

5 J. Lloyd Mecham, *The United States and Inter-American Security, 1889–1960* (Austin: University of Texas Press, 1961), pp. 278–86.

6 Paper prepared for the Policy Planning Staff, March 22, 1948, in *Foreign Relations of the United States, 1948*, 9 (Washington D.C.: Government Printing Office, 1972), pp. 198–99.

7 See Vernon Lee Fluharty, *Dance of the Millions: Military Rule and the Social Revolution in Colombia, 1930–1956* (Pittsburgh: University of Pittsburgh Press, 1957), pp. 99–105.

8 The Secretary of State to the Acting Secretary of State, April 10, 1948, and the Ambassador in Colombia (Beaulac) to the Acting Secretary of State, April 12, 1948, in *Foreign Relations of the United States, 1948*, 9, pp. 39–43.

9 Neither of the two classic works on U.S.-Latin American relations, Samuel Flagg Bemis, *The Latin American Policy of the United States* (New York: Harcourt, Brace, Jovanovich, 1973) or Dexter Perkins, *A History of the Monroe Doctrine*, 2nd ed., rev. (Boston: Little Brown, 1955), even mentions Communism or the Soviet Union. Graham H. Stuart, *Latin America and the United States*, 5th ed., rev. (New York: Appleton-Century-Crofts, 1955), also omitted these subjects in his previous editions, but does add a brief discussion of the Bogotá Conference and the 1954 Guatemalan crisis to his 1955 edition.

10 Richard H. Immerman, *The CIA in Guatemala* (Austin: University of Texas Press, 1982), pp. 82–122.

11 *Ibid.*, p. 103.

12 Stephen Schlesinger and Stephen Kinzer, *Bitter Fruit* (Garden City: Doubleday & Co., 1981), p. 108.

13 Immerman, pp. 168–72.
14 John Foster Dulles, "International Communism in Guatemala," *Department of State Bulletin*, 31 (July 12, 1954), p. 43.
15 Daniel James, *Red Design for the Americas* (New York: John Day, 1954).
16 Robert J. Alexander, "Guatemalan Communists," *Canadian Forum*, 34 (July 1954), pp. 81–83.
17 See, for example, Robert J. Alexander, *Communism in Latin America* (New Brunswick, N.J.: Rutgers University Press, 1957); Robert L. Allen, *Soviet Influence in Latin America: The Role of Economic Relations* (Washington D.C.: Public Affairs Press, 1959); and Cole Blasier, "The Cuban and Chilean Communist Parties, Instruments of Soviet Policy, 1935–1948, unpublished Ph.D. dissertation, Columbia University, 1955.
18 Peter Wyden, *Bay of Pigs* (New York: Simon & Schuster, 1979), pp. 19–25.
19 *New York Times*, July 10, 1960, p. 1; July 13, 1960, p. 1; August 8, 1960, p. 1.
20 Literature on this subject is prolific. For the conspiracy theory see Daniel James, *Cuba: The First Soviet Satellite in the Americas* (New York: Avon Books, 1961). The opposite view is represented by Herbert L. Matthews, *The Cuban Story* (New York: G. Braziller, 1961).
21 For a critique of these policies see Willard F. Barber and C. Neale Ronning, *Internal Security and Military Power* (Columbus: Ohio State University Press, 1966), and Jerome Levinson and Juan de Onis, *The Alliance that Lost Its Way* (Chicago: Quadrangle Books, 1970).
22 Even Cuban specialists generally adopted this view. See Jaime Suchlicki, *Cuba: From Columbus to Castro* (New York: Charles Scribner's Sons, 1974), p. 190; Hugh Thomas, *Cuba: Pursuit of Freedom* (New York: Harper & Row, 1971), pp. 1387–94. For recent documentation on Kennedy administration attitudes see "White House Tapes and Minutes of the Cuban Missile Crisis, *International Security*, 10 (Summer 1985), pp. 164–203.
23 Department of State, "U.S. Arrangements with the Soviet Union Regarding Cuba," *Inter-American Economic Affairs*, 25 (Spring 1971), pp. 92–94.
24 Jeane J. Kirkpatrick, *Kennedy, Khrushchev, and the Sandinistas* (Miami: Cuban-American National Foundation, 1985), pp. 6–7.
25 In 1962, Dorothy Dillon, *International Communism and Latin America* (Gainesville: University of Florida Press, 1962), still treated Latin American communism as largely an extension of Soviet policy, arguing on p. 41 that "the Soviet Union is taking a firmer hand in directing Communist activities in Latin America." This view was much less pronounced in later publications such as Rollie Poppino, *International Communism in Latin America, 1917–1963* (Glencoe, IL.: The Free Press of Glencoe, 1964), or Karl M. Schmitt, *Communism in Mexico* (Austin: University of Texas Press, 1965).
26 Assistant Secretary of State Edwin M. Martin, "Communist Subversion in the Western Hemisphere," *Foreign Affairs Outlines* (March 1963), pp. 1–2.
27 President Lyndon B. Johnson, "Purposes of the U.S. Intervention," Transcript of Nationwide Broadcast, May 2, 1965, published in *Documents on American Foreign Relations, 1965* (New York: Harper & Row, 1966), pp. 961–65. Subsequent studies of the intervention, such as Abraham Lowenthal, *The Dominican Intervention* (Cambridge: Harvard University Press, 1972), generally omit any mention of the Soviet Union.
28 In a 1968 article, Desmond O. Wilson Jr. stressed the disadvantages to the Soviet Union of its commitment to Cuba. Wilson saw the Soviet involvement in Cuba as not "necessarily detrimental to U.S. worldwide interests" and viewed the commitment to the island "as a constraint of some magnitude on Soviet behavior." Desmond P. Wilson Jr., "Strategic Projections and Policy Options in the Soviet-Cuban Relationship," *Orbis*, 12 (Summer 1968), pp. 504–17. The following year, Cuba scholar D. Bruce Jackson wrote about the "indefinite continuation of the Soviet-Cuban divergence over Latin American revolutionary strategy," because "Soviet

reasons incline them toward caution even where slim chances for revolutionary success might exist; Cuba's reasons produce an inclination to keep insurgencies going now, even if the longer run chances for revolution are thereby jeopardized." D. Bruce Jackson, *Castro, The Kremlin, and Communism in Latin America* (Baltimore: The Johns Hopkins University Press, 1969), pp. 154–55.

29 *The Rockefeller Report on the Americas* (New York: Quadrangle Books, 1969), pp. 34–35.

30 Wayne S. Smith, "Soviet Policy and Ideological Formulations for Latin America," *Orbis*, 15 (Winter 1972), pp. 1124–26.

31 Herbert S. Dinerstein, "Soviet Policy in Latin America," *American Political Science Review*, 6 (March 1967), pp. 80–90.

32 Robert G. Carlton, ed., *Soviet Images of Contemporary Latin America, 1916–1968* (Austin: University of Texas Press, 1970); J. Gregory Oswald and Anthony J. Stroyer, eds., *The Soviet Union and Latin America* (New York: Praeger, 1970); Donald L. Herman, ed., *The Communist Tide in Latin America* (Austin: University of Texas Press, 1972); W. Raymond Duncan, "Soviet Policy in Latin America Since Khruschev," *Orbis*, 15 (Summer 1971), pp. 643–69; Smith, "Soviet Policy," 1122–46; F. Parkinson, *Latin America, the Cold War, and the World Powers* (Beverly Hills: Sage Publications, 1974); Cecil Johnson, *Communist China and Latin America, 1959–1967* (New York: Columbia University Press, 1970).

33 J. Gregory Oswald, "Postscript," Oswald and Stroyer, pp. 187–88.

34 Smith, "Soviet Policy," pp. 1126–29, 1143.

35 Duncan, "Soviet Policy in Latin America Since Khruschev," pp. 668–69.

36 Parkinson, *Latin America*, pp. 238–40.

37 Department of State, *Major Statements on Latin America by Secretary of State Henry Kissinger: Made During His Visits to Venezuela, Peru, Brazil, Colombia and Costa Rica, February, 1976* (Washington, D.C.: Department of State, 1976).

38 James D. Theberge, *The Soviet Presence in Latin America* (New York: Crane Russak, 1974), p. 93.

39 *Ibid.*, pp. 26–36, 67–73, and 90.

40 Leon Gouré and Morris Rothenberg, *Soviet Penetration of Latin America* (Miami: University of Miami Press, 1975), p. 1.

41 *Ibid.*, p. 195.

42 President Jimmy Carter, "The United States and Latin America," *Speech Before the Permanent Council of the Organization of American States, April 14, 1977* (Department of State Press Release). This pattern appears in other 1977 statements such as Assistant Secretary of State Terence A. Todman's July 21, 1977 speech to the State Department's Media Seminar on U.S.-Latin American Relations.

43 For example, see the exchange between the State Department's Director of the Office of Cuban Affairs, Wayne Smith, and Congressman Robert Lagomarsino, April 5, 1978, in U.S. Congress, House Committee on International Relations, *Impact of Cuban-Soviet Ties on the Western Hemisphere, Hearings before the Subcommittee on Inter-American Affairs, Committee on International Relations*, 95th Congress, 2nd Session, 1978, pp. 74–75.

44 William LeoGrande, "The U.S. and the Revolution," in *Nicaragua in Revolution*, ed. Thomas Walker (New York: Praeger, 1982), p. 69; U.S. Congress, House Committee on Foreign Affairs, *U.S. Policy Towards Nicaragua, Hearings before the Subcommittee on Inter-American Affairs of the Committee on Foreign Affairs*, 96th Congress, 1st session.

45 For details on the Carter administration's thinking on this subject see Robert A. Pastor, *Condemned to Repetition: The United States and Nicaragua* (Princeton: Princeton University Press, 1988), chapters 8 and 9.

46 See the March 14–15, 1978 testimony of several Defense Intelligence Agency officials in *Impact of Cuban-Soviet Ties in the Western Hemisphere*, pp. 3–50.

47 Alfred Stepan, "The United States and Latin America," *Foreign Affairs*, 58:3 (1980), pp. 685–86.

48 Republican Party, *1980 Platform*, pp. 68–69.

49 Quoted in Ronnie Dugger, *On Reagan: The Man and His Presidency* (New York: McGraw-Hill, 1983), p. 360. See also candidate Reagan's remarks on the September, 1980 NBC TV White Paper, "The Castro Connection."

50 See for example "Communists Devouring Latin America," *St. Louis Globe Democrat*, October 27, 1980, p. 16.

51 The Committee of Santa Fe, *A New Inter-American Policy* (Washington D.C.: Council for Inter-American Security, 1980).

52 Jeane Kirkpatrick, "U.S. Security and Latin America," *Commentary*, 71:1 (January 1981), pp. 29–40.

53 Department of State, *Communist Interference in El Salvador* (Washington D.C.: Department of State, 1981).

54 "Statement of President Ronald Reagan at his March 6, 1981 Press Conference," *Public Papers of the President: Ronald Reagan, 1981* (Washington D.C.: Government Printing Office, 1982), p. 207.

55 "Address by Secretary of State Alexander Haig before the American Society of Newspaper Editors," in *El Salvador: Central America in the New Cold War*, Marvin E. Gettleman et.al., eds. (New York: Grove Press, 1981), pp. 8–9.

56 For a summary of the critiques see Raymond Bonner, *Weakness and Deceit: U.S. Policy and El Salvador* (New York: Times Books, 1984), pp. 256–57. A more scholarly critique is Cole Blasier, "The Soviet Union," in *Confronting Revolution: Security through Diplomacy in Central America*, Morris J. Blachman, William M. LeoGrande, and Kenneth Sharpe, eds. (New York: Pantheon Books, 1986), pp. 264–65.

57 This was already apparent in late 1981. See U.S. Congress, House Committee on Foreign Affairs, *U.S. Policy Options in El Salvador, Hearings and Markups before the Committee on Foreign Affairs and its Subcommittee on Inter-American Affairs*, 97th Congress, 1st session, 1981. Also see the 1982 "Transcript of a Department of State Press Briefing on U.S. Policy in Central America," in *American Foreign Policy, 1982: Current Documents* (Washington D.C.: Government Printing Office, 1985), pp. 1418–25.

58 Quoted in Bonner, *Weakness and Deceit*, p. 268.

59 The best selection of views, albeit with some conservative bias, is *Grenada and Soviet-Cuban Policy*, Jiri Valenta and Herbert J. Ellison, eds. (Boulder, CO: Westview Press, 1986). See also the Fall 1983 issue of *Caribbean Review*, p. 12. For a reasoned critique of U.S. policy toward Grenada see Robert Pastor, "Does the United States Push Revolutions to Cuba? The Case of Grenada," *Journal of Inter-American Studies and World Affairs*, 28:1 (Spring 1986), pp. 1–34. For the administration's view on Soviet involvement, see *Grenada: A Preliminary Report* (Washington: Departments of State and of Defense, 1983). For contrasting political interpretations, see William F. Buckley Jr., "Missing the Point of Grenada," *National Review* (November 25, 1983), p. 1504; and J. Bryan Hehir, "The Case of Grenada," *Commonweal* (December 16, 1983), p. 681.

60 *Report of the National Bipartisan Commission on Central America* (Washington D.C.: Department of State, 1984), pp. 122–23.

61 Departments of State and of Defense, *The Soviet-Cuban Connection in Central America and the Caribbean* (Washington D.C.: Government Printing Office, 1985), pp. 1–28.

62 U.S. Congress, House Committee on Foreign Affairs, *Soviet Posture in the Western Hemisphere, Hearings before the Subcommittee on Western Hemisphere Affairs of the House Committee on Foreign Affairs*, 99th Congress, 1st session, 1985, p. 1.

63 *Ibid.*, pp. 2–23.

64 *Ibid.*, pp. 58–64, 48–53.

65 President Ronald Reagan, "Address to the Nation on Central America and U.S. Security," *Current Policy*, 805 (Department of State, 1986).

66 Department of State and Department of Defense, *The Soviet–Cuban Connection*, pp. 3–12.

67 Edward González, "Cuba and the Soviet Union in the Caribbean Basin: Interests, Objectives and Capabilities," unpublished paper delivered at the conference on Central America and the Caribbean in the 1980s, Claremont-McKenna College, December 10–11, 1984, pp. 1–2.

68 Robert S. Leiken, *Soviet Strategy in Latin America* (New York: Praeger, 1982), pp. 61–65, 77–81, 102.

69 David Ronfeldt, *Geopolitics, Security and U.S. Strategy in the Caribbean Basin* (Santa Monica: Rand Corp., 1983), pp. 37, 45.

70 Cole Blasier, *The Giant's Rival: The USSR and Latin America* (Pittsburgh: University of Pittsburgh Press, 1983), p. 137.

71 In addition to *The Giant's Rival*, see Cole Blasier, "The Soviet Union," p. 269, and his untitled contribution in U.S. Congress, Senate Committee on Foreign Relations, *Perceptions: Relations Between the United States and the Soviet Union* (Washington D.C.: Government Printing Office, 1979), pp. 230–32.

72 See William LeoGrande, "Cuba," in *Confronting Revolution*, pp. 229–55; Wayne S. Smith, "Dateline Havana: Myopic Diplomacy," *Foreign Policy*, 48 (Fall 1982), pp. 157–74.

73 Jorge I. Domínguez, "It Won't Go Away: Cuba on the U.S. Foreign Policy Agenda," *International Security*, 8 (Summer 1983), pp. 114, 128; Domínguez "Latin America," in *East-West Tensions in the Third World*, Marshall D. Shulman, ed. (New York: W. F. Norton & Co. 1986), pp. 62–63.

74 Robert A. Pastor, "Cuban and the Soviet Union: Does Cuba Act Alone?," in *The New Cuban Presence in the Caribbean*, Barry B. Levine, ed. (Boulder, CO.: Westview Press, 1983), pp. 203, 207.

75 W. Raymond Duncan, "Castro and Gorbachev: Politics of Accommodation," *Problems of Communist*, 25 (March–April 1986), p. 56. See also Duncan, "Soviet Interests in Latin America," *Journal of Inter-American Studies and World Affairs*, 26 (May 1984), pp. 175–80.

76 Jiri Valenta, "Soviet Strategy in the Caribbean Basin," *United States Naval Institute Proceedings*, 108 (May 1982), p. 170. Jiri and Virginia Valenta, "Soviet Strategy in the Caribbean Basin," in *Confrontation in the Caribbean Basin*, Alan Adelman and Reid Reading, eds. (Pittsburgh: University of Pittsburgh Press, 1984), pp. 242, 258, 265.

77 Cole Blasier, "Comment," in *Confrontation in the Caribbean Basin*, pp. 268–74; Blasier, *The Giant's Rival*, pp. 93–94; Blasier, "The Soviet Union," pp. 268–70.

78 Duncan, "Soviet Interests in Latin America," pp.175, 191–94.

79 Robert Leiken, "The USSR and Central America," in *Central America and the Western Alliance*, Joseph Cirincione, ed. (New York: Holmes & Meier, 1985), pp. 163–67; Leiken, *Soviet Strategy*, pp. 73–88.

80 Morris Rothenberg, "The Soviets and Central America," in *Central America: Anatomy of Conflict*, Robert Leiken, ed. (New York: Pergamon, 1984), pp. 131–47; Rothenberg, "Latin America in Soviet Eyes," *Problems of Communism*, 22 (September–October, 1983), pp. 1–18.

81 Juan M. del Aguila, "The Soviet Union in South America," unpublished paper delivered at the Workshop on Soviet-Third World Security Relations, University of Illinois, September 25–27, 1986, p. 7.

82 William H. Luers, "The Soviets and Latin America: A Three Decade U.S. Policy Tangle," 7:1 *Washington Quarterly* (Winter 1984), p. 8.

83 Jerry F. Hough, "The Evolving Soviet Debate on Latin America," *Latin American Research Review*, 16:1 (1981), pp. 124–39.

II

Soviet Perspectives on Latin America

4

The Latin American Communist Movement: Realities and Relations with the Soviet Union

Edmé Domínguez

INTRODUCTION

Soviet behavior toward the external world has always been conditioned by two factors; one pragmatic, the other ideological. The pragmatic one, characterized by the need to survive and to have relations with other states, has led the Soviet Union to adopt a foreign policy very similar to the one followed by other states. The ideological factor, whose aim of expanding socialism worldwide, has made the Soviet leadership encourage and support Communist parties, not only as instruments for this expansion, but as auxiliaries for the pursuit of the Soviet state interests.

There are many ways to approach the Soviet Union's links with the Latin American Communist movement or, for that matter, with any Communist movement in the world. It may be approached from the classical perspective which emphasizes Soviet use of these movements for subversive purposes within individual countries or for general ideological as well as pragmatic purposes. These Communist parties may otherwise be viewed as pursuing their own interest within their respective societies, with only a formal link to the Soviet Union. Alternatively, these parties may be seen as engaged in contradictory tasks, seeking a significant role within their society, while at the same time maintaining a close relationship with the international Communist movement from which they draw a certain international identity and support.

Reality, however, is often more complex than theoretical models. In this chapter, we have tried to adapt our model as much as possible to the dynamics of the relationship we are trying to understand. That is why we have focused on the relationship between the Soviet and Latin American Communist parties as a complex one from both points of view. The Soviet viewpoint is contradictory. It portrays links with the Communist movement as fulfilling a very important ideological role in providing internal and external legitimacy to the Soviet state. On the other hand, there is also a competing need to use the Communist movement as an instrument for Soviet foreign policy interests. The Communist parties, too, face a variant on this contradiction; they wish to attain a certain level of effectiveness within their countries (that is, making a revolution), but they also seek links to the Soviet Union and the international Communist movement. These relations and contradictions manifest themselves in quite different ways, depending on the time frame and the country involved. In some cases these contradictions even tend to disappear, as apparently opposed objectives complement each other. In sum, as we shall see, the Soviet Union cannot be viewed as pursuing only one sort of interest in Latin America, nor can the Communist parties be appreciated as being completely foreign to the general forces at work in their countries either.

HISTORICAL ANTECEDENTS: PHASES

The expansion of the world Communist movement came as a consequence of the triumph of the Russian Revolution and of the Soviet Union's isolation from the rest of the world. As their hopes for further revolutions in Europe were frustrated, and as they faced the need to break the blockade organized by the Western powers, the Bolsheviks turned their attention to the colonial areas. Their debates about the strategy and tactics the liberation movements should follow in these areas focused on two alternatives: whether to privilege the anti-imperialist character of the struggle by supporting the local bourgeoisie, or to encourage more radical and socialist goals by organizing peasants and workers against their national bourgeoisie.[1]

The Communist Parties Emerge in Latin America

Since its birth and through the 1970s, the Communist movement in Latin America has gone through three phases: (a) the revolutionary period from the 1920s until 1935 (during these years, we see valuable intellectual Marxist analysts such as José Carlos Mariátegui in Peru and important revolutionary experiences such as the Salvadoran insurrection); (b) the Stalinist period, from 1935 through the late 1950s (when Soviet Marxist interpretations became the rule and the "four-class alliance" scheme was applied to Latin America); and (c) the second revolutionary period opened by the Cuban Revolution in 1959 (during which all previous schemata were revised and questioned by groups within and outside the existing Communist parties).

First Revolutionary Period: 1920–1935

Although not very interested in the revolutionary potential of Latin America, the Comintern had acknowledged Latin America beginning in 1921 within two documents: "About the Revolution in America" and "Appeal to the Working Class in the Two Americas."[2] According to these, the Latin American countries had to go through an agrarian, anti-imperialist and anti-capitalist struggle; that is, a process of uninterrupted revolution leading from underdevelopment to proletarian dictatorship. These views found an echo on the Latin American side, with such leaders and intellectuals as Julio Antonio Mella and José Carlos Mariátegui arguing the revolution in Latin America had to be socialist and anti-capitalist, without any long "bourgeois-democratic" phase.

After 1921, however, the Comintern had abandoned its radicalism and begun to insist on the need for a "bourgeois-democratic" phase in all underdeveloped countries.[3] This shift coincided with the emergence of a new set of cadres, trained in the tradition of obedience to the Comintern's instructions and identified with Stalin, who assumed leadership positions in the newly-founded parties. One typical example of this sort of leader was Victor Codovilla in Argentina, who in 1926 had already led the Argentine Communist party (PCA) to approve a resolution condemning Trotskyism and expressing its solidarity with the group headed by Stalin within the leadership of the Communist Party of the Soviet Union (CPSU).

During the Sixth Congress of the Comintern (1928), in which a new radical line was to be approved, the presence of Latin America within the international Communist movement was acknowledged. The Brazilian and the Mexican representatives gave speeches in the opening ceremony, and at the end of the meeting seven Latin American delegates were elected to the Executive Committee of the Comintern.[4] A year later the South American Secretariat of the Comintern was organized, and Codovilla became one of its members.

The new Comintern line equated Social Democrats with fascists ("social-fascism") and identified most of the Latin American governments existing at that moment as "national-fascist." However, Codovilla admitted that in Latin America revolution would have to go through different phases, including the "bourgeois-democratic."[5]

The new turn in the Comintern policy took the Latin American parties by surprise. Most of the Communist parties on the continent followed the new line, at least rhetorically, but others put into practice the new line, either encouraged or inspired by the Comintern. This was true in the case of both the Sandino movement in Nicaragua in the early 1930s and the Salvadorean insurrection of 1932.

With Augusto Sandino in Nicaragua, the Comintern accepted the principle of nonideological collaboration," as its main goal was to profit from the anti-imperialist character of the movement. They also gave his movement direct assistance, dispatching two cadres, Carlos Aponte from Venezuela and Augusto Farabundo Martí, who became important assistants to Sandino's high command. Aponte had mainly military functions (he became Lieutenant Colonel in the Sandino Army), while Martí had political responsibilities, trying to influence Sandino to develop a more revolutionary profile for his movement. The relationship, however, lasted only two years (from June 1928 to April 1930), and apparently, Sandino resisted Martí's attempts to radicalize the movement.

As a whole, the Comintern's policy toward Sandino's movement in Nicaragua is a typical example of the transition from a line supporting all liberation movements because of their anti-imperialist character to another line which tried to radicalize these movements within the "struggle against all reformist" trends. The Comintern never understood

Sandino's mentality and contradictions, nor his country's situation. As a result, the hero the Comintern had helped to become known all over the world became the "traitor" they condemned for not having pursued his struggle into a more "revolutionary phase."

The Comintern's policy in El Salvador was completely different. The circumstances there were also different, and by this time the Comintern's turn to the left had been clearly defined. The organization which became more involved in this case was not the Anti-imperialist League, but rather the International Red Aid or *Socorro Rojo Internacional* (SIR).[6] In contrast to Nicaragua, social contradictions in El Salvador predominated over anti-imperialist feelings among the population, with 30 rich families controlling a country with the highest population density in Central America. It was an area in which the proletarianization of the countryside was quite advanced.

Drawing its cadres mainly from the skilled trades and university circles, the Communist Party of El Salvador (PCES) had emerged during the 1920s. By 1932, in the wake of a military coup and unclear election results the PCES participated/led an almost spontaneous insurrection. It failed, and the PCES' main cadres, including Martí, were imprisoned and executed as a bloody repression (between 10,000 and 30,000 victims) put an end to the rebellion.[7]

During this radical period, other Latin American Communist parties pursued sectarian policies. In Chile, the PCCh refused any alliance with other parties opposing the Carlos Ibañes dictatorship, a decision which provoked several internal divisions and prevented the party from supporting the brief Socialist Republic of 1932, while in Cuba the communists attacked the civilian government that had replaced the dictator Gerardo Machado accusing it of "fascism."

Throughout this period, the Comintern's goals were not intended to provoke revolutionary changes, but rather to exploit local anti-imperialist feelings in an effort to weaken U.S. and British efforts to control Latin American markets. Moreover, the Comintern's leadership, firmly under Stalin's control after 1929, was suspicious of any indigenous organizations' capacity (including the local Communist parties) to undertake any real revolutionary enterprise by themselves. In any case, the Comintern now considered any such eventuality as remote given U.S. influence in Latin America.

Closure of this revolutionary phase and the opening of the "Popular Front" period came with the Brazilian insurrection of 1935. The insurrection (discussed in the chapter by Aldo Vacs) was supposed to have the support of a front organization (the *Aliança Libertadora Nacional,* or

ALN) whose reformist program aimed to attract the support of the "national bourgeoisie."[8] Planned mainly as a military operation, the rebellion failed. With little mass support, it had been quickly and easily suppressed. The experience had a long-lasting negative impact on relations between the military and the Communist party in Brazil. On a continental scale, however, it opened the way for the "broad alliance" policy initiated by Latin American Communist parties.

The Popular Front: 1935–1948

During the 7th Comintern Congress in 1935, the Comintern leadership criticized the Latin American Communist parties for their "lack of criteria" regarding the distinction between enemies and allies in the anti-fascist struggle.[9] That is to say, the "radical" experiences were condemned, even though the Comintern itself had encouraged their actions. In line with the Soviet Union's search for alliances with the Western powers, the Latin American Communists parties were instructed to form "four-class alliances" (joining workers, peasants, petite bourgeoisie, and "national bourgeoisie") in order to accomplish "national and democratic tasks." This strategy, originally elaborated by Stalin for application in China, was eventually applied to all the "colonial and semi-colonial territories." It aimed to eliminate Western countries' suspicions regarding "Soviet inspired" rebellions in their colonial domains.

The result was a rather "economistic" interpretation of Marxism-Leninism; through this policy of alliances, the Latin American Communist parties would struggle for immediate and moderate demands rather than for revolutionary goals. Abandoning their earlier isolationist policy, the Communist parties turned to the pursuit of alliances, in most cases with conservative groups (provided these were anti-fascist). During this period, the "Stalinization" of Latin American Communist parties was finally consolidated (by which we mean the constitution of a leading bureaucratic hierarchy linked in an ideological and political way to the Soviet leadership and to its foreign policy "zigzags").

In Peru, for example, the Communist Party (PCP), having failed to forge an alliance with the *Alianza Popular Revolucionaria American* (APRA), joined the liberal oligarchic parties in a "democratic front." The situation was similar in Colombia, where the Communists supported the right wing of the Liberal Party. In Mexico the Communists helped to build a powerful confederation of trade unions in 1936 (the *Confederación de Trabajadores Mexicanos,* or CTM) whose leadership would shortly thereafter seek to eliminate all Communist influence within its ranks. In 1939, moreover, the Communists refused to support the left wing of the Mexican *Partido Revolucionario Institucional* (PRI), backing instead the conservative candidate, Avila Camacho. In 1939, the Cuban Communists supported Fulgencio Batista, who had overthrown the legally elected civilian government, because of his promises to collaborate with the United States in their anti-fascist policy.[10]

The only case where the local Communist party actually carried out a "front policy," as it was understood in Europe, was Chile in 1938. The PCCh joined the Socialists and some other center-left groups to elect Pedro Aguirre Cerda to the presidency under a program to encourage independent development of national capital. This popular front lasted in varying forms through 1947, finally disappearing during the Cold War years. During 1935–36, the "popular front" policy had an anti-imperialist dimension which would eventually fade during the war years. The Communist parties' close dependence on Soviet foreign policy would eventually create problems for them; the 1939–41 Nazi-Soviet Non-Aggression Pact required a reassessment of the "fascist threat." Some Communist parties solved this by adopting a policy of neutrality toward Nazi Germany. Others, like the Communist Party of Argentina (PCA), went all the way, referring to "Yankee imperialism" as the main enemy and justifying fascism as a movement somehow representative of "mass aspirations."[11]

The Cold War: 1948–1959

With the onset of the Cold War, the Latin American Communist parties found themselves increasingly isolated from their previous allies; thereupon they returned to their earlier emphasis on anti-imperialism. Nevertheless, they continued to regard the "four-class" alliance strategy as the way to accomplish a "national-democratic" revolution in Latin America. One example of this approach was *Partido Guatemalteco de los Trabajadores'* (PGT) relationship with the Arbenz government during 1951–1954. The PGT collaborated with the Arbenz government in order to accomplish democratic reforms (agrarian reform, nationalizations, etc.). The PGT's program called for a "democratic, anti-feudal national revolution" which was to have, like the 1935 insurrection in

Brazil, the "national-bourgeoisie's" support against the oligarchy. As in Brazil, this support never materialized and the counterrevolutionary movement headed by Castillo Armas took the PGT by surprise. In their "post-coup" analyses, Communist leaders admitted they had overestimated the "national bourgeoisie's" independence and the army's loyalty, but they still claimed that only "national-democratic" changes could be applied in Guatemala.[12]

After Stalin's death in March 1953, and with the enunciation of Khrushchev's new doctrine of "peaceful coexistence," there emerged a new period of search for alliances by the Latin American Communist parties. They offered their support to the democratic governments that succeeded some of the fallen dictatorships, as in Argentina with Arturo Frondizi and in Brazil with Kubitschek. These moves coincided with Khrushchev's attempt to establish friendly relations with progressive regimes in Third World countries. During this period, the younger generations' disenchantment with the Communist party's ability to provoke revolution led them to seek more radical paths. One of the results of this radicalization was the Cuban Revolution. Paralleling these trends was a new intellectual current on the left: some Latin American intellectuals came to the conclusion that Latin America did not have economic conditions similar to those of Europe prior to the French Revolution. According to them, feudal conditions did not exist in Latin America. Capitalism was already well rooted here, although with special characteristics that Europe had never known; consequently, no "democratic-bourgeois" phase was needed before the transition to socialism.[13]

From the Cuban Revolution to the 1970s

The Cuban Revolution opened a new period in Latin American history, not only for its consequences regarding the East-West conflict, but also for the challenge it posed to the traditional Communist parties and to Soviet perspectives on revolutionary strategy in Latin America. As mentioned earlier in this volume, Fidel Castro's "26th of July Movement" not only lacked the support of the Communist PSP, but was actually opposed by it. Only in 1958, at the final phase of the struggle, did the PSP finally join the movement, helping to coordinate the urban insurrection through its influence within organized labor. During the first two years of Castro's rule, there were points of convergence between the "26th of July Movement" and the PSP, since each needed the other and both believed in making progressive reforms, not revolutionary changes, for the short term.

The Soviet Union and the Latin American Communist parties shared in this assessment. For the Soviet Union, the Cuban Revolution meant the definitive incorporation of Latin America into the "liberation struggles" of the Third World. For the Latin American Communist parties, it opened new opportunities for forming "broad fronts of solidarity" with Cuba and for strengthening their domestic-front policy. However, the quick radicalization of the Cuban Revolution provoked a rupture with both these traditional methods and with the classical, gradual approach to revolution followed by most of the Latin American Communist parties. The Cuban radicalization also affected the Soviet schemata of analysis for Latin America, which was in some ways even more conservative than the ones employed by the Communist parties themselves. At the time, as David Albright notes in Chapter 1, Soviet specialists had created such concepts as "national" and "revolutionary democracy." The first term described the qualities of a "national bourgeois" regime that implemented social reforms.The concept of "revolutionary democracy" referred to the more radical regimes (led by the army, for example) which undertook a "noncapitalist" way of development." This conceptual innovation served to justify, from an ideological viewpoint, Khrushchev's "charm offensive" towards these new types of regimes.[14]

Both of these new concepts sacrificed the role of local Communist parties and, in the case of the "national democracy," did so in favor of the "national bourgeoisie." Many Latin American Communist parties objected to this scheme, as for example, the Uruguayan Communists who argued that in Latin America the national bourgeoisie was completely reactionary.

When the Cuban leadership decided to jump over these models and move directly into "socialist construction," the entire Soviet theoretical and political framework fell to pieces. The result was multiple debates over the prospects for armed struggle, the vanguard role of the Communist parties, and the stages leading to socialism. Most Soviet analysts opposed the application of the Cuban revolution's methods to seize power and to undertake a rapid transition to socialism elsewhere in Latin America. Others, however, thought there were conditions similar to Cuba in other countries. Still a third group recommended a combination of methods.[15]

These debates reflected the mixed feelings, even the disarray, with which the Latin American Communist parties confronted the wave of radicalization provoked by the Cuban revolution. Some, like the Venezuelan Communist Party or the PGT in Guatemala, organized their own "armed wings" in the form of guerrillas. However, most Communist parties refused to accept violent methods and attacked radical groups ready to follow the Cuban example. Such was the case of the Revolutionary Left Movement (MIR) in Chile and the National Army (ELN) in Peru or the *Sandinista* National Liberation Front in Nicaragua.

Confronted with this situation, the Soviet Union sought to mediate an agreement during the second Latin American Communist parties conference in Havana in 1964. This was particularly urgent in view of the Chinese challenge, which also threatened to provoke new fragmentations within the left. The agreement reached permitted some parties (Venezuela, Colombia, Honduras, Peru, and Haiti) to form guerrilla fronts, while others (Chile, Argentina, and Uruguay) could continue with legal or semi-legal tactics.[16]

The 1964 agreement proved short-lived. By 1965, the Venezuelan Communists had begun to review their guerrilla strategy in light of the poor results it had yielded. Similar developments elsewhere made the Cubans denounce the Communist parties for their ineffectiveness, bureaucracy, and lack of wholehearted engagement in guerrilla struggle. Compounding the issue, Cuba also began to have serious frictions with the Soviet Union. The outcome of the missile crisis, Soviet criticisms of Cuba's internal policies, the purge of the Aníbal Escalante faction within the PSP and Soviet overtures to Latin American governments all reflected the Cuban-Soviet problems.

These conflicts produced a very radical Cuban foreign policy. The Cuban government organized first the Tricontinental Conference (gathering "national liberation" movements from the three continents) in 1966, and then the *Organización Latinoamericana de Solidaridad* Conference (OLAS) in 1967, to which very few Communist parties were invited (with the exception of the Costa Rican, Salvadoran and Uruguyan parties). During these meetings, there were sharp attacks on the Soviet Union and the Latin American Communist parties. Indeed, the Cuban strategy was to create a new, continental revolutionary vanguard to displace the traditional Communist parties.

By 1968–70, as discussed in the chapters by Carmelo Mesa-Lago and Fernando Gil and Jorge Domínguez, the contradictions between Cuba, the Latin American Communist parties, and the Soviet Union had begun to lose their sharpness. The guerrilla movements had failed nearly everywhere on the continent, and especially suffered a setback in Bolivia with Ché Guevara's death. Cuba's economic problems were also growing as a result of discreet Soviet pressure. Feeling isolated ideologically, politically, and economically, the Cuban leadership gave way, and their approval of the Soviet invasion of Czechoslovakia was in this way symbolic. However, underlying such approval was a request for a "similar" Soviet protection for distant countries like Cuba or Vietnam in case of necessity.

At the 1969 International Communist Conference in Moscow, the Cuban party delegation sharply criticized the principal general resolution, saying it was a mistake to recognize the Communist parties in Latin America as the only revolutionary vanguard. They argued that there was a danger of "democratic seduction" by trusting in Latin American governments' reformist potential. Moreover, the struggle for socialism (not for peace) should be the main goal for the international Communist movement.[17] These criticisms symbolized the conditions under which Cuba reentered the international Communist movement; there was an acceptance of certain rules, but also a basic questioning of certain principles.

Despite its rapprochement with the Soviet Union, after 1968 Cuba still maintained close and discreet links to such groups as the Tupamaros in Uruguay, the ALN and MR 8 (Movimiento Revolucionario 8 de Octŏbre) in Brazil, or the MIR in Chile. These groups belonged to the "second Castroist wave" which had moved from the countryside to the cities; they had been seriously decimated by the mid-1970s. Of these, the only significant one to survive was the FSLN in Nicaragua.[18]

Whatever these ideological and political divergences, the Soviet-Cuban reconciliation was quite developed by 1970. This also meant a rapprochement between the Cuban Communist party and its Latin American counterparts, although these relations never attained the level they had had at the beginning of the 1960s. One salutory consequence of this new-found harmony was an end to the process of factionalism and fragmentation within the Communist parties themselves. Here, too, Chinese actions played a role as a "catalyzer" in overcoming animosities.

THE 1970s: THE COMMUNIST PARTY'S APPRAISAL OF THE CONTINENTAL SITUATION

Soviet analyses, as well as those elaborated by the Communist parties in the early 1970s, were very optimistic regarding the possibilities for advance by the left in Latin America. Popular fronts with Communist participation had gained force in Uruguay, Bolivia, Peru, Panama, Argentina, and Chile, and progressive reforms had been undertaken by military regimes in both Bolivia and Peru. Moreover, in 1970 the Popular Unity government led by Salvador Allende had come to power in Chile.

The overall situation led the secretary general of the Uruguayan Communist Party (PCU), Rodney Arismendi, to claim that the objective factors for revolutionary change were already present, especially economic and political crisis in a situation of dependent capitalism and feudal backwardness. However, Arismendi admitted, the "subjective factors," that is, political organization, were still missing. He also discussed the program of the revolution to come; as before, it would be a "democratic, agrarian, anti-imperialist, and (as a novelty) anti-capitalist." It would contain democratic transformations which, in the second phase would become socialist. Regarding the form of struggle, Arismendi insisted on the need to analyze on a case by case basis whether to choose between peaceful or violent means. Historically, dominant classes had never left power willingly. Therefore, revolutionaries should be prepared to use both peaceful and violent methods (which did not necessarily mean armed struggle) to destroy the bourgeois state and its repressive bureaucratic machine—to have revolution without insurrection and to destroy the bureaucratic-military apparatus. For Arismendi, the Chilean revolution would show if it were possible to bring about the change without general violence.[19]

These thoughts and concerns were shared by most Communist parties, as well as by Soviet specialists on Latin America. All of them thought the new era of peaceful coexistence between the superpowers provided real opportunities for social change in Latin America whether in Peru with its "patriotic military" or in Chile with the Popular Unity (UP) government. Different points of view emerged, however, regarding the success of these new experiences.

In the case of the military regime in Peru, Soviet specialists examined the social origin of the military cadres engaged in the process of reform. For A. Shulgovsky, it was a question of social class background and of social consciousness that made some military cadres develop a "patriotic nationalism" eager to fight backwardness, corruption, and social injustice. For Shulgovsky, the army's modernization and the policies adopted by the U.S. against these regimes had also contributed to their nationalistic ideology. The reforms accomplished by these regimes, however, were not enough. In order to consolidate the changes, these reforms had to be complemented by stronger links with the masses.[20] M. Mirsky, from the Institute of World Economy and International Relations (IMEMO) adopted a different point of view. Having in mind the Egyptian case, he mistrusted the "adventuristic petite bourgeois" mentality of these military leaders. According to him, they could change easily from reformism to fascism.[21]

The Communist parties' own reaction to the progressive military regimes can be seen through the behavior of the two parties most concerned, the PCB in Bolivia and the PCP in Peru. In Bolivia, the PCB first cautiously supported the policy reforms undertaken by the Ovando regime in the late 1960s, despite its "petite bourgeois" origin and "lack of support among the masses,"[22] and then more enthusiastically those of Juan José Torres (1970–71). For the PCB, socialism was attainable so long as the country passed through an anti-imperialist, democratic phase. Mass struggle, it insisted, could take several forms, not just the violent ones, despite what the "terror-anarchistic elements" contended.[23] The Bolivian Communists also agreed with the need for a "popular front," grouping "workers, peasants, middle class sectors, and some factions of the national bourgeoisie."[24] However, the PCB considering itself the only possible vanguard, rejected all cooperation with other leftist groups. In this sense, its attitude had not changed since the 1960s when it had opposed Ché Guevara's failed guerrilla enterprise.

In the case of Peru, the PCP adopted attitudes similar to its Bolivian counterpart. Immediately after the 1968 military coup, the PCP condemned both the takeover itself and the reform projects of the new regime, calling it "nationalist, bourgeois reformist." However, the PCP soon reconsidered this judgment, and approved the new agrarian reform law and the nationalization of some of the American oil companies.[25] Support for the military regime gradually increased even though the PCP insisted, as had the PCB, on the preservation of its role as "vanguard." The military regime's transformations were seen only as the first phase of a long revolutionary project. On the whole, the PCP agreed with Shulgovsky's analyses as to the social basis of the Peruvian military's nationalism and "progressive" consciousness and insisted (as did Shulgovsky) that the Velasco Alvarado regime should organize a more solid and institutional popular support for the transformations to be irreversible.[26]

The PCP's orthodoxy reflected itself as well in its mistrust of the extreme left. Moreover, the PCP blamed these "leftists" groups for Velasco Alvarado's replacement in 1975 by more moderate elements within the army. However, immediately after this replacement, the PCP published a communique in which it welcomed the changes, congratulated the new president and the army for their unity, and called on the people to watch "for new reactionary and imperialist provocations."[27] It is interesting to note that this attitude coincided with the Soviet Union's position toward these changes.

In contrast to its Peruvian and Bolivian counterparts, in Chile the PCCh held a mixture of orthodox and independent views, having developed the "peaceful path" even before the CPSU 20th Congress in 1956. Throughout the 1960s it had maintained a certain neutrality in the dispute between advocates of armed struggle and those behind the peaceful means to power. The PCCh was also a relatively strong party (150,000 members in 1972), with a broad worker base, representing 35 percent of the trade union movement.

From the beginning of the Popular Unity (UP) government (in which it participated), the PCCh distinguished itself from Soviet positions in two key ways: (1) the Chilean experience was peculiar to Chilean conditions and was not a model to be exported; and (2) pluralism within the revolutionary coalition was not a concept to be applied only during the transition process, but *permanently*, even after the revolutionary seizure of power.

Documents from the PCCh's 14th Congress in 1969 argued that although Chile's revolutionary forces aimed at eliminating imperialism and oligarchic power, the first phase of the revolution should not rely on a workers government, but rather on one with a broad social base aiming at both "democratic and socialist transformations."[28] The PCCh also envisioned a strategic alliance with the Socialist Party, with both parties sharing the vanguard duties. The CPSU also seemed to accept this "shared vanguard role," receiving Chilean Socialist Party (PSCh) representatives on the same level as those of the PCCh in Moscow and, in return, sending high level delegations to their respective congresses.[29] The PCCh agreed with most Soviet analysts as to the need to attract the progressive elements of the army and of the Catholic Church. Without the support of these sectors, the PCCh insisted, revolutionary changes would be very difficult. Not surprisingly, the PCCh had an enormous mistrust of the "extreme left" (in this case the MIR), whose violent methods it criticized and categorically rejected. Further, the Communists perceived the MIR's radical demands (not to mention some of the PSCh) as a recipe for disaster.

After the military coup in 1973, Soviet specialists and the leadership of the PCCh analyzed the Popular Unity government's experience and the Communists role in it. The discussion centered around two points: (1) could unity and discipline be maintained within an alliance of such heterogeneous forces?; and (2) what was the proper role for the PCCh as a unifying and vanguard force?

In general, all Soviet specialists agreed that the UP coalition suffered from a lack of unity and discipline. Some of these specialists argued the reason for this was a "dogmatic trend" followed by both left and right extremes within the coalition. The PCCh, for these Soviet observers, had headed the "revolutionary trend," but it had ultimately failed to impose itself.[30] Other Soviet analysts were more critical toward the PCCh. They reproached it for not having assumed the vanguard role. In the opinion of these specialists, the PCCh was the only party within the coalition with the organizational and ideological capability to be a vanguard.[31]

The Central Committee of the PCCh published its own analysis of the UP experience in a 1978 book.[32] This book gathered previous analyses made by party leaders after 1974 and gave a general overview of the party's views on these questions. Often there was lack of agreement, coinciding with the divergence among Soviet analysts. For some of PCCh leaders, the UP government had committed several "leftist mistakes," while for others, these mistakes had been "rightist." Those leaders who thought the UP had been too conservative, criticized it for having been too attached to the peaceful path. For them, the military policy of the UP government had failed by neither democratizing the army (the army's professionalism and respect for the Constitution had been overestimated) nor by preparing popular armed detachments. Others argued there had also been a lack of popular participation (for example, in the distribution of foodstuffs) and that reactionary forces had enjoyed too much freedom to promote their subversive activities.[33] According to other opinions, the UP government had been too inclined to a "leftist" policy, failing to understand that they were facing a "transition" period in which power had not been entirely conquered. Thus, "leftist" currents had promoted hasty changes, such as unjustified nationalizations and had raised popular expectations for social benefits to a level not compatible with the economic situation faced by the movement. For this group the PCCh (and the UP more generally) had failed in its propaganda work among the military. Finally, all these failures related to the lack of a unified economic and political leadership which the party should have provided.[34]

Both Soviet analyses and PCCh's self-criticisms insisted on the lack of a unified leadership and coalition discipline, but it was the Soviet writers who most strongly underlined the PCCh's failure to fulfill its vanguard role. In this regard, Soviet analysts seem to have forgotten that they themselves had supported the PCCh-PSCh alliance and had appeared to understand the kind of concessions the PCCh made to maintain it. President Allende himself was a Socialist, and one can hardly understand how, under conditions of a *coalition* electoral victory, the PCCh could have fulfilled a vanguard role. That Soviet analysts insisted on this reflects their more general efforts to transform the Chilean experience into a model. Thus they insisted on explaining the UP's failure because of the mistakes committed by the protagonists, rather than by the inapplicability of the model itself.[35]

THE 1980s

The Impact of Revolution on Central America and the Caribbean

By the early 1980s, general perspectives for revolution in Latin America were not so grim as they had seemed in the mid-1970s. Revolution in Nicaragua had succeeded in July 1979 against all odds, and the time had come for the Central American Communist parties to revise their tactics and to reflect on the consequences of this revolutionary victory for their own reality. Traditional Soviet analyses of these questions were also to suffer a considerable shake-up following the Nicaraguan events. In this section, we shall try to present the new analyses made by these Communist parties, their theoretical repercussion at the continental level, and the Soviet reactions to them.

NICARAGUA

In Nicaragua, as in Cuba, revolution had been organized and guided by the FSLN, a leftist group formerly rejected by the local Communist party, or PSN (*Partido Socialista Nicaragüense*) as it was known. Moreover, the revolution had been carried out through violent means, by guerrilla warfare and general insurrection, a strategy rejected by the PSN and most of the Communist parties in the region. Events in

Nicaragua, therefore, reawakened the debate over the Latin American revolutionary movement's general strategy and tactics not just among Soviet theoreticians, but within the Communist parties, and for the first time, within groups to their left.

The FSLN was a typical product of the Cuban "first revolutionary wave." Created in 1962 by Carlos Fonseca Amador, by 1975 it had divided into three factions which only became reunified in 1978 in the midst of the insurrectionary campaign and through Cuban mediation.

Needless to say, the FSLN was very critical of the PSN. The latter party had been created during the "Browderist" period at the end of World War II and had always preferred alliance with the most conservative opposition sectors to one with the radical left. Since 1976, however, it had accepted armed struggle as the only way to fight the dictatorship. After the revolutionary victory, one faction of the PSN chose to join the FSLN, while another entered the Revolutionary Patriotic Front, a group of leftist parties supporting the FSLN. However, by 1984–85 the PSN began to criticize the *Sandinistas* for their economic policies, their polemics with the Church, and the drastic "state of emergency" measures. Some of their criticisms, however, referred to the *Sandinista* lack of "revolutionarism" and their "conciliation" with the bourgeoisie.[36]

Because the Nicaraguan experience follows in this domain the same pattern as the Cuban one, it provides us with the possibility to observe the Soviet reactions to this situation. As in the Cuban case, the Nicaraguan revolution came as a surprise to Soviet observers. IMEMO's Yearbook for 1979 presented a brief discussion of the ongoing struggle against Somoza in Nicaragua, giving much greater space to the *Unión Democrática de Liberación* (in which the PSN participated and to the active role played by this party within the labor movement) than to the FSLN. Immediately after the *Sandinistas'* victory, an article in *Kommunist* also stressed the role played by the PSN in the struggle, although it recognized the FSLN's importance as the vanguard of the whole insurrectionary movement.[37]

Notwithstanding these rather orthodox reactions, enthusiasm among Soviet Latin Americanists was enormous, and they started right away discussing the new situation created by the events in Nicaragua. The discussion centered around three general concepts: (1) the way to revolution, armed or peaceful; (2) the unification of the left and the creation of the vanguard; and (3) the program of transformations. The first two concepts were the most polemical. For Sergo Mikoyan, the director of *Latinskaia Amerika,* Nicaragua was part of a historical pattern. There had not been a single revolution in Latin America during the twentieth century carried out through nonviolent means. To him, both the Cuban and the Nicaraguan experiences demonstrated that the "proletarian party" could be replaced by a "new type of vanguard." Such was also the opinion of Kiva Maidanik from IMEMO who went further, emphasizing the importance of the unification of the left (with a unified political direction) and the adoption of a "realistic program."[38]

Other specialists, however, were not so sure about Nicaragua's significance for the rest of the continent. For Shulgovsky, who was with the Latin American Institute (ILA), Nicaragua proved there was a diversity of ways for revolution in Latin America, but not that the same methods could be employed elsewhere in the region. Moreover, he warned of the dangers of an "ultrarevolutionary" phraseology. To I. Bulichev and Y. Koroliov more or less supported these remarks, stressing again the PSN's importance in the urban struggle and the necessity for the FSLN to become a real vanguard, that is to say, to consolidate itself into a party based on "scientific principles."[39] Apparently to this end, the CPSU and FSLN had signed their first agreement in 1980.

Most specialists and observers agreed about the necessity of a "realistic," moderate program which emphasized the mixed economy principles, with reforms not extending beyond democratic transformations in a capitalist context.

EL SALVADOR

The Communist Party of El Salvador (PCES), heir to the revolutionary tradition of the 1932 insurrection, had nearly disappeared after those events, reemerging onto the political scene only in the late 1960s. Successful in developing a trade union presence, the PCES opted for political and electoral rather than violent means of opposition. This choice facilitated the proliferation of groups to the PCES' left which were more inclined to radical solutions in the early 1970s.

Within PCES ranks a heated discussion on the peaceful versus the armed path to power took place in 1973. Both Cayetano Carpio and Roque Dalton, members of the PCES Central Committee, favored an insurrectionary strategy. Their difference of views with the rest of the PCES leadership eventually led them to break with the party and to form separate organizations the *Frentes Populares de Liberación-Farabundo Martí* (FPL-FM) and the *Ejercito Revolucionario del Pueblo* (ERP).[40]

Meanwhile, the PCES went through several electoral alliances with center parties only to come back, given their frustration on the electoral front, to the old argument over strategies. Finally, after the *Sandinista* victory and the brief period of a military revolutionary junta in El Salvador (in which the PCES participated together with other groups to the left and center), the party opted in favor of armed struggle in late 1979.

Clearly enough, the PCES tried to make use of the Sandinista experience, but its actions went beyond a simple revision of tactics. Apparently, the PCES' leadership now felt the need to make a self-criticism of its past attitudes and behavior, as well as those of other Latin American Communist parties. Shafik Jorge Handal, the PCES general secretary, analyzed these issues at the end of 1981,[41] concluding that Latin American Communist parties had been more active in supporting reformist and "progressive" projects headed by the military in Peru or fighting against the ultra-left in Chile, to cite only two examples, than in concentrating on how to attain power. For Handal, the Cuban, Nicaraguan, and Chilean experiences had demonstrated revolution in Latin America to be impossible through peaceful means. Reformist tactics had been and were still useful to "train the masses in the political struggle" (as in El Salvador where the PCES had struggled for eleven years in the electoral front), but they had also been dangerous in the sense of cultivating reformist illusions in the ranks of the party and preventing a flexible approach to strategy.

Another problem Handal discussed was the unification of the left. Traditionally reformist, the Communist parties had difficulties in dealing with others on the left. For Handal, this was due to their failure to understand the structural causes of the "leftist phenomenon." These groups had emerged as a consequence of the 1950s industrialization process with the rise of a new, more qualified (albeit lacking in "class consciousness") working class, and the proliferation of "marginalized sectors" (unemployed, unqualified workers, as well as middle class intellectuals). It was not enough for the Communist parties to fight against these groups ideologically; it was necessary to establish a real dialogue with them—between *equals*—through a joint analysis of the country's realities and cooperation in formulation of the strategy to attain power. This was the PCES objective after 1979, with the immediate goal of creating a new, unified Marxist-Leninist party.[42] Handal's analysis was very provocative. Many orthodox Communist parties and Soviet ideologists would either ignore or reject its validity.

The issues he raised, however, would be discussed at a continental level.

GRENADA

The Nicaraguan revolution was not the only event to have an impact at the regional level. The April 1979 revolution in Grenada, under the leadership of the New Jewel Movement (NJM), was also significant for the left in the Caribbean Basin. The NJM belonged to the "radical left" category despised by so many Communist parties. It had been organized by radical, middle class intellectuals eager to overthrow the Eric Gairy dictatorship and to make social changes in the country. The association of these leaders with Cuba had been almost "casual," almost a reaction against American pressure not to approach Cuba. Moreover, after April 1979, the evolution of Grenada's links with Cuba—and afterwards with the Soviet Union—were in great part a consequence of growing American hostility.

There was certainly a "socialist" project elaborated by NJM leaders, but the movement's transformation into a Communist party and its eagerness to be accepted as such by the Soviet Union was related to its need for aid and protection from the United States. In July 1982, the NJM signed an agreement with the CPSU providing for "an exchange of common experiences," technical "cooperation of party cadres," and the establishment of "concrete plans to carry out this cooperation." Similar agreements were signed with Cuba, Bulgaria, and the German Democratic Republic (GDR). Cadres went to Moscow and Havana for training, and instructors and material were forthcoming from both countries. Apparently, according to the documents captured by the American forces of occupation, the relationship between Grenada and Moscow obeyed more Grenadan requests than Soviet interests. NJM leaders wanted not only to be considered as a fraternal party, but to be *useful* to the Soviet Union by serving as a bridge between it and the Caribbean left. This, NJM leaders thought, might gain them protection against a possible American blow.[43]

However, as with most Communist parties, the NJM was not a homogeneous movement. It had at least two factions, one radical and dogmatic, the other flexible and nationalist. The first one, headed by Bernard Coard, was finally able to establish solid positions among most of the party cadres and the army, although it was quite isolated from the masses. Maurice Bishop, the leader of the nationalist faction, was popular among the people, but he had lost support in the party by 1983. There had been much speculation as to a possible Soviet backing of Coard's anti-Bishop plot, but there is not much evidence to support such a thesis.[44]

In private conversations in Moscow, most Soviet specialists condemned Coard's sectarianism and ambition. Some linked him to CIA machinations, while others pointed to his contacts with Caribbean extreme left groups. However, all analyses agreed on two facts: Bishop's unquestionable popularity and the NJM's failure to attract other than middle class elements.[45]

Grenada's tragic outcome had a definite impact on the revolutionary processes in the region. For one, it made evident the need to close ranks among the revolutionary movements and parties, especially in view of American pressures. It also highlighted the importance of continuous work among the masses, a theme particularly stressed by the Salvadorans and the *Sandinistas.* Finally, it made all these movements reflect on the limits of solidarity from "brother countries" like Cuba or the Soviet Union. The revolutionary process had to defend itself with its own forces, and this underscored the importance of military preparedness. In a different form, the Chilean lessons reemerged after ten years.

The Rest of Latin America: Diversity and Homogeneity

REVISION OF CONCEPTS: RENEWAL OR CONTINUITY?

Central American events provoked divergent reactions within the Latin American Communist movement. The need for a conceptual revision gave way to polemics similar to those in Moscow. A continental conference took place in Havana in 1982 attended by Communist parties and radical left representatives who met to discuss these issues. There was general agreement on such points as the structural nature of the crises that affected the continent, the need for unity within revolutionary movements, the diversity of situations these movements faced in the different countries and, thus, the impossibility to blindly copy revolutionary models.[46]

There were also several points of disagreement, however. Of these, perhaps the most polemical focused on the unification process and the vanguard role. The Chilean MIR, the Guatemalan PGT, the Salvadoran PCES, and the Cuban Communist party insisted on the need to join forces with all groups on the left with the goal of forming a new party capable of becoming the real vanguard of the revolutionary process. The Argentine Communist party stressed the importance of giving priority to the alliance with the "broad democratic forces," including "some important sectors of the national bourgeoisie." For their part, the Communist parties from Uruguay and Venezuela expressed their confidence in the Communist capacity to become natural vanguards of the movement. The Cubans, like the Argentinians, emphasized the need for flexibility, pointing out that revolutionary forces should be open to an alliance with such centrist forces as Social Democracy and progressive Catholics at a certain point of the struggle.

The issue of whether to opt for peaceful or armed forms of struggle also elicited strong debate. The most orthodox parties (Uruguay, Argentina, and Costa Rica) naturally insisted that both paths were still open in many countries. The Cuban Communist party, the MIR, the PCCh, and most leftist groups argued there should be flexibility of tactics in the different phases of the struggle, but insisted arms were *always* needed, whether in the phase of conquering power, or later in defending it.

Soviet reactions to this discussion were not uniform. What may be interpreted as an official CPSU reaction to these debates came in a book entitled *Los partidos comunistas de América Latina: en la lucha por la unidad de las fuerzas anti-imperialistas*.[47] In this book, the authors acknowledge the importance of the Central American revolutionary wave as well as the need for most Communist parties on the continent to revise tactics and accelerate unification processes. However, the alliances the authors recommended were classical alliances with all "progressive forces"—middle classes, Catholics, and even Social Democrats. The "ultra-left" was, as usual, excluded and condemned, in the same way as were other forms of "revisionism," including "Eurocommunism" which was considered a variant of "Trotskyism."

According to the collective authors, the peaceful path to power was still the predominant one in Latin America, and the Communist parties continued to be the *only* vanguard of the revolutionary movement. Once the revolution came to power, the program of transformations should avoid radical measures in the first phase of reform (following the lessons of the Chilean experience). Revolutionary tasks would be primarily anti-imperialist, but anti-capitalist goals would already be planned for later implementation. Probably fearful of radicalism and theoretical innovation, the Soviet analysts ignored the PCES theoretical discussions. Although they mentioned the Salvadoran stress on unifying the left and on the choice of armed struggle, they emphasized its anti-imperialist character.[48]

As is obvious, Soviet orthodoxy did not easily accept radical ideological revisions of strategy. However, Soviet ideologists would have to put up with more than theoretical polemics. The Mexican and Chilean Communist parties, although their experiences were not directly linked to the revisions promoted by Central American events, provide further evidence of the changes in Marxist-Leninist doctrine undertaken to suit different situations.

In 1980, the PCCh put forward, for the first time, a proposition interpreted as a strategic innovation. According to Luis Corvalán, "The people of Chile will have to discover in the struggle the specific forms of expression of the revolutionary and democratic process taking into account the various methods...that could lead to victory."[49] Claiming there was no possibility either for the "liberalization" of the military regime (a new constitution preserving the right for Pinochet to stay in power until 1989 had just been approved) nor for a unification of nonfascist forces (including the *Partido Demócrata Cristiano*, or PDC), the PCCh declared the "right of the people to rebellion." However, according to one of the party's representatives, this right of rebellion did not automatically mean "insurrection," but rather "resistance" to reject any obedience, to "develop dynamic and creative forms of anti-fascist rebellion."[50]

Whatever interpretation is given to these concepts, they meant a real turn in the PCCh's traditional tactics, leading it into an alliance with the "extreme left" (the MIR and the Clodomiro Almeyda faction of the PSCh, or the *Partido Socialista Chileno*), and definitely precluding any agreement with the PDC and other centrist forces.[51] Moreover, an armed group, the Manuel Rodríguez Patriotic Front, active since 1984, claimed responsibility for an assassination attempt against Pinochet in late 1985. The Front has no official links with the PCCh, but many have identified it with the party.

Soviet ideologists and analysts have been very discreet in their reaction to the PCCh's change of tactics. In *Los Partidos Comunistas*, the PCCh's adoption of this new strategy was not even cited, although the authors wrote in an understanding vein about other Communist parties (like the Colombian party which had left open the possibility of using violence).[52] For its part, the Mexican Communist party adopted a much more "legalistic" and "peaceful path to power" attitude in the late

1980s than it had assumed in the previous decades. These developments are discussed in Brian Latell's chapter. Here we might, however, note that, as part of its ideological renewal, the PCM abandoned the notion it was the only possible vanguard of the revolution. Responding to an opening in the Mexican political system, the PCM disappeared in late 1981, merging itself with four other leftist organizations into the newly created *Partido Socialista Unificado de México* (PSUM).

The experiences we have been discussing in this section seem to confirm that the theoretical innovations undertaken by several Latin American Communist parties at the beginning of this decade responded entirely to local conditions. Soviet academic specialists followed these changes with interest, but official Soviet orthodoxy preferred to continue with the old formulas rather than question them.

REACTIONS TO THE NEW SITUATIONS

The situations confronting Communist parties in Latin America at the beginning of the 1980s were quite different from the ones a decade before. Most of Latin America suffered from a deep economic crisis, reflecting the one at the world level. However, the situation in Latin America was also aggravated by the debt problem and the harsh economic conditions the International Monetary Fund (IMF) imposed on these countries. Economic problems increased social unrest, and military dictatorships, unable to handle the situation any longer, gave way in many countries to civilian power. Restoration of democracy, however, did not solve social and economic problems.

The Communist parties in South America adapted their tactics accordingly. We can divide their reactions and attitudes into two groups according to the political scenarios they confronted. For the first group, the passage from clandestinity to legality meant acceptance of the rules imposed by the restoration of democracy and their participation in the electoral arena. For the second group, already facing civil governments for some time, unsolved and aggravating socioeconomic problems made recourse to violence still a potentially valid choice. The exceptions to both these groups were Chile, where the military dictatorship continued in power, and Paraguay, where Alfredo Stroessner, in power for nearly 40 years, has nearly eliminated the local Communist party.

In the first group stand Argentina, Brazil, Uruguay, and to a certain extent, Bolivia. The PCA in Argentina provides an example of the pattern. It contributed to the national chauvinism organized by the military government around the Falklands/Malvinas War and enthusiastically supported the whole enterprise as an "anti-imperialist cause." The party never questioned the motives or honesty of the entire government, arguing instead that there were fascist and democratic factions within the army. This approach permitted the PCA to coexist with the military government, without suffering as much persecution as others on the left. Here, too, as Aldo Vacs and Robert Evanson make clear in their chapters, Argentine economic relations with the Soviet Union played a role. With the transition to democracy in 1983, the PCA recovered its legality and chose, in a new change of tactics, to ally itself with the Peronist party for the elections. Surprised by the Peronists' unexpected defeat, they turned to the left and organized the *Frente del Pueblo Unido* (FREPU) together with the *Movimiento al Socialismo* (MAS), providing "critical" support to the Alfonsín government.[53]

In the second group are the Communist parties of Peru, Ecuador, Colombia and Venezuela. The Peruvian situation became surprisingly favorable for the PCP in the 1980s. As Ruben Berríos notes, following electoral and front tactics, the PCP forged a left coalition, called the *Izquierda Unida* (IU), that became the second political force (receiving 30 percent of the votes in 1983) in the country and the first of such a type and strength in Latin America (nearly as strong as the Popular Unity in Chile in the early 1970s). In 1983, the IU elected its first Communist mayor, and in 1985 the IU contributed to the defeat of Belaunde Terry's conservative government. In its place came the populist, APRA-led government of Alan García.

The PCP faced two problems in the post-1985 situation: to maintain its own identity and program (there were few differences in the kind of reforms it and APRA demanded) and to mark its distance from the ultra-left activities of the *Sendero Luminoso* (Shining Path) guerrillas and other armed groups. In fact, within the PCP opinions differed as to the prospects for dialogue or confrontation with guerrillas, whose tactics were nevertheless totally rejected. The PCP expressed its commitment to democratic pluralism and electoral procedures even though it believed that repression directed against the guerrillas also endangered the security of the left more generally.[54]

In an intermediate situation between the South and Central American problems was the Colombian Communist party (PCC). It chose to support Belisario Betancur's conservative government in its efforts to pacify the extensive guerrilla movement in the country, but at the same time leaving open the possibility of undertaking armed struggle. Moreover, the PCC has maintained a benevolent attitude toward one guerrilla group, the *Fuerzas Armadas Revolucionarias Colombianas* (FARO), which many observers consider to be the PCC's "armed arm." By 1985, the truce with the guerrilla movement implemented by President Betancur had failed owing in part to army pressures. Violence continued, however, and by late 1986 representatives of the *Unión Patriótica* (UP)—a front within which the PCC was active—were being systematically murdered by the paramilitary groups. Political polarization will probably push the PCC toward more radical attitudes in the 1990s.[55]

The 1980s did not bring any significant changes for the orthodox, Communist Party in Venezuela (PCV). Already legal, it continued to strive for an electoral front with other forces of the left, even inviting its "revisionist" rival, the *Movimiento al Socialismo* (MAS), a splinter of the PCV and deeply anti-Soviet, to join with it. The MAS has repeatedly declined such propositions, making the PCV's electoral efforts quite disappointing (only 2 percent of the national vote in 1983). With the death of Gerardo Machado (one of the party founders) in 1983 and the replacement of Jesús Faría as secretary general in 1985, a process of renewal has apparently begun within the PCV leadership. This may have some influence over the party's future orientation. Although committed to peaceful forms of struggle—especially after its costly guerrilla failure in the 1960s—the new secretary general has declared that the adoption of violent tactics would depend on the further exacerbation of social contradictions.[56]

South America does not face as revolutionary a situation as does Central America. On the contrary, the reestablishment of democracy has meant a stabilization process which has limited the impact of the Central American revolutionary wave. However, aggravated socioeconomic problems and already existing patterns of violence may provoke greater social unrest, in which case the Communist parties may shift.

CONTINENTAL REALITIES AND INTERNATIONAL VIEWS

Soviet analyses about the situation in Latin America have generally followed the views of the continent's Communist parties. As we have seen in the case of Chile, such analyses are not monolithic but, as the chapter by David Albright indicates, have developed into several schools of thought. In the same way, the Latin American Communist parties have diverse views about the continental situation. There are coincidences between these views and Soviet schools of thought, and it raises the following question: who has influenced whom? The hypothesis of a mutual feedback seems the most plausible one, given that much of the input for Soviet analyses comes from contacts with the Communist parties and the latter often show great respect for Soviet opinions.

The Communists and the Labor Movement

Historically, the Latin American Communist parties have tried to gain a representation within the labor movement. Sometimes they have succeeded. However, few Communist parties in Latin America had a real influence within the workers movement at the beginning of the 1980s. Some never had it; others, having had it, lost their base in labor during the military dictatorships and only slowly recovered. Perhaps the best example of this latter case is Chile.

The PCCh had been founded by mineworkers in the nitrate zones of northern Chile. From the beginning this gave the party a very broad labor base and a strong influence in the labor movement. Even as early as the 1930s, leaders of the principal national trade unions belonged to the PCCh. During the "popular front" period, the PCCh gained new members among the middle classes, but after 1947 it reverted to its almost entirely proletarian base. By 1971, 65 percent of its members (representing 35 percent of all trade unionists) were workers; 13.6 per cent were peasants. Only 8.1 per cent were intellectuals and 8.9 per cent white-collar workers. This proletarian base accounted, perhaps, for the party's orthodoxy and fidelity to the Soviet Union, as well as for its discipline and loyalty to hierarchical rules and leadership.[57]

However important its influence, the PCCh had to share leadership in labor since the 1930s with another important party, the Socialist PSCh. After 1953, both parties chose to work together within the major Chilean worker confederation, the *Central Unitaria de Trabajadores* (CUT). This PCCh-PSCh alliance served as the model for electoral coalitions at the national level from 1958 to 1970. According to Soviet specialists, the CUT also played an important role during the Allende government "helping to control workers' demands."[58] After the military coup, the

CUT and all other trade unions and parties were dismantled. In more recent years, PCCh members have helped organize the *Coordinación Nacional Sindical* (CNS), a grouping of different worker and shanty-town organizations. The CNS has been quite active in the coordination of several anti-Pinochet demonstrations and other protest activities.

In contrast to the PCCh, the Argentinian Communist party lost all significant influence in the workers' movement after 1943. With Peronism dominant among workers, the PCA recruited most of its membership among the middle classes, white-collar workers, and intellectuals. Consequently, it had difficulty competing with Peronism. In the 1980s, and especially after the Peronist failuire in the 1983 elections, the PCA has been trying again to challenge the Peronists within labor, but without much success.

Both in Bolivia and Peru, the Communists have been influential in the mining sector. In Bolivia, despite its small size, the PCB controlled important positions within the COB (*Confederación Obrera Boliviana*) through 1984. The party's factionalism and its support for the Siles government made it lose most of these positions. In 1985, however, Simón Reyes, one of the COB's main leaders, became the PCB's new secretary general, and it appears that this will reinforce the party's position both among miners and labor generally.[59]

The Mexican experience is quite different compared to those we have described. The PCM never had control of any main branches in the labor movement, although it contributed indirectly to labor's institutionalization within the ruling PRI during the 1930s. The Communists participated in important railway workers' and teachers' strikes in the 1950s, but in a way similar to the PCA, they lost all significant influence within labor after the 1950s.

During the second half of the 1970s and in the 1980s, the PCM became active among university and nuclear industry workers. The PCM's transformation into the *Partido Socialista Unificado de México* (PSUM) extended the newly formed party's influence over some other minor unions. In the countryside, the PCM has helped to organize Indians and peasants in some regions, like Juchitán in the south, where they participated in the successful coalition that won the municipal elections in 1983. Also, in 1982, after the government nationalized the banking system, the PSUM helped to organize the banking workers' trade union. However, all these actions have been marginal in comparison to the predominant control exercised by the PRI within labor.

Elsewhere in Latin America, with the possible exception of Brazil where the PCB controlled some metallurgical unions in the São Paulo region (and historically El Salvador, Cuba, and Nicaragua), Communist influence in organized labor has been quite weak or nonexistent. The trade unions affiliated with the *Congreso Permanente de Unidad Sindical de los Trabajadores de América Latina* (CPUSTAL), the Communist labor movement, are not among the largest and more powerful in Latin America. Also, while concentrating their efforts on the urban worker movements, the Communist parties have nearly totally neglected the rural movements. Generally speaking, peasants and rural workers (also with some exceptions) have been either unorganized or else controlled by the government (as in Mexico), by Catholic organizations, or drawn by extreme left groups into guerrilla movements.

Tentatively, we may conclude that those Communist parties with greatest success in the labor movement are those in which workers have been substantially present as party members. In other countries, the Communists' appeal has been restricted to intellectuals or some middle class sectors. Interestingly enough, where a proletarian base exists within a Communist party, there tends to be a tradition of orthodoxy and conservatism as well as an unquestionable loyalty to the Soviet Union. Such orthodoxy and loyalty, however, have not necessarily been linked to a broad proletarian base or to a strong influence within labor.

The Capitalist Level of Development in Latin America

One of the most interesting Soviet academic debates since the 1970s has revolved around the level of capitalism in Latin America.[60] This discussion has been particularly important, for it sheds light not only on the evolution of Soviet thought, but also on the means and strategy recommended to the revolutionary forces on the continent. It also sheds light on coincidences or disagreements between Soviet specialists and Latin American Communist party ideologues.

Most Soviet specialists have agreed that capitalism has strong roots in Latin America (compared to other regions of the Third World). They also agree in stressing the importance of state capitalism (*gozkapitalism*), as well as the existence of serious structural crises. However, for those specialists linked to the Institute of Latin America (ILA), capitalism in this region is essentially "dependent" on American monopolies and unable, therefore, to attain higher levels of development. According to this group (the "classical dependence" group), the external factor is still clearly predominant over the internal one. In other words, imperialist contradictions hold sway over class contradictions: Latin American capitalism suffers from a "structural crisis" whose only solution is revolution. Nevertheless, given the absence of subjective conditions and the survival of precapitalist forms in these societies, revolution in a socialist sense is still a long way off. Also, according to these specialists, not all military dictatorships are necessarily fascist, and thus Communist parties may approach them in varying ways.

This approach is representative of the most conservative school of thought in the Soviet Union. Not surprisingly, it coincides with (or is inspired by) the views of the most orthodox Communist parties, among these, the PCA (Argentina), the PCB (Bolivia), the PCV (Venezuela), and, up to 1973 at least, the PCCh (Chile). Although their strategies, experiences, and circumstances have been diverse, these Communist parties see dependent capitalism as justifying the priority of anti-imperialist struggle and the implementation of broad alliances in order to realize (most certainly through peaceful means) the bourgeois revolutions these countries missed. The structural crisis, in their view, will last a long time and, as a result, revolutionary forces should focus on democratic and nationalist tasks. For the PCA, these tasks also included a special policy toward the army, since the military dictatorship did not have a fascist character. The conservatism of these opinions is evident, and it may result from the fact that many of the leaders of these parties had risen during the Stalinist period of the 1930s.

A second school of thought—denominated the MDC, the "middle level of capitalism development dependency" group—finds its advocates in other institutes, especially IMEMO. This school believes most Latin American countries have attained a middle level of capitalism with significant industrialization and technological progress, lying somewhere between the most backward countries of Asia and Africa and the industrialized nations of Europe and America. For this school of thought, dependence is still the determinant characteristic of these countries, but it *can be overcome at higher stages of development*.[61] This group attaches considerable importance to internal social contradictions, although it admits that anti-imperialist tasks are still predominant. The crisis in these societies is not structural, but rather a manifestation of neocolonial relations. Its resolution would lead either to revolution or to a stabilization of capitalism through such varied forms as a fascist military dictatorship or a bourgeois democracy. In fact, the fascist solution had already been applied in countries like Argentina, Chile, and Uruguay, and the revolutionary outcome depended on the organizational capabilities of the revolutionary forces and on their "hierarchy of alliances."

One Communist party which identified itself with such views was the PCU (Uruguay). According to its secretary general, Rodney Arismendi, capitalism in Latin America had definitely attained a middle level of development. The situation, he argued, was ready for anti-capitalist transformations, especially since the national bourgeoisie was no longer a "progressive force." For Arismendi, the crisis in Latin America was structural (that is "final" or definitive), although he admitted that fascism could evolve into bourgeois democracy. For him, most military dictatorships in South America were fascist with the exception of the Argentine one.[62] Another Communist party with affinities for this current of thought regarding the general trends in Latin America was the PCES.[63]

For a third school of thought (also representing IMEMO specialists), dependency was not a determinant characteristic of Latin American capitalism. It was one feature, among others, and it could *definitely* be overcome at higher stages of development. The crisis of Latin American capitalism was neither structural nor the product of its dependent situation. Rather, it reflected the general capitalist crisis in the world. Moreover, the major Latin American countries were at the same level of development as some Southern European countries, and they too could evolve toward the stage of state monopoly capitalism (CME).[64]

The PCM (Mexico) and some economists in the PCB (Brazil) shared most of the opinions of this school of thought. In 1978 a group of economists belonging to the PCM's leading organs were invited to Moscow by the journal *Latinskaia Amerika* to participate with Soviet specialists in a debate about the level attained by capitalism in Mexico.[65] For the Mexican guests, their country had attained a middle level of capitalist development and was rapidly advancing toward the stage of state monopoly capitalism. The Mexican state was gradually merging itself to national monopolies, at the same time as the middle and small enterprises were disappearing. For the PCM, the struggle was against big capital, be it national or transnational. Contesting these opinions were some of the ILA's specialists who belonged to the first school of thought.

For R. Freitas from the PCB, Brazil was also already in the stage of state monopoly capitalism, albeit with a fascist variant of military dictatorship. There were already crisis of overproduction, and the military government's state monopoly capitalism strategy was to accumulate capital through the alliance of three forces: foreign monopolies, national capital, and the state. The tactics employed were of a fascist nature and included repression, control of the workers' movement through corporativist measures, and use of nationalistic and chauvinist ideology.[66]

The Soviet authors of *Los Partidos Comunistas en América Latina* share some of the views of this third school. For them, in the last few years, several countries on the continent have arrived at the stage of state monopoly capitalism and foreign capital, which (even though each has pursued its own interests) has promoted the modernization of these economies. These authors also stressed the importance of avoiding any overvaluation of these countries' level of dependence. Therefore, they urged the Communist parties to give more attention to the social struggle against "native bourgeioses" and "follow the Cuban, Chilean, and Nicaraguan experiences" to strive for a "democratic, anti-imperialist, anti-oligarchic, and agrarian revolution."[67]

These schools of thought may be compared with those presented by David Albright in his chapter. Even though there are elements that would need further development in my presentation, clear coincidences exist between his "socialist orientation" category and my "classical dependence" current. All of these specialists stress the underdeveloped and dependent character of these societies and the need to aim for socialist transformations. His "economic interdependence" group also matches the state monopoly capitalism school of thought. The pragmatism of both currents of opinion is evident, although not all those who agree with such views are similarly skeptical about revolutionary perspectives in these countries.

On the whole, this review of the literature demonstrates the diversity of thought and analyses both among Soviet specialists and between the Communist parties. The coincidence between conservative views on both sides, as well as that between innovative analyses, suggests the relation between Latin American Communist parties and the Soviet Union is not as simple as many have supposed.

The Latin American Communist Parties and the International Communist Movement

Traditionally, Latin American Communist parties have been identified as "pro-Soviet." While this has been the case historically, the situation has changed over the years. The Communist parties' attachment to the Soviet Union has provided them with ideological legitimacy, but this dimension has concerned mainly their views on the international situation. As we have seen, their internal line has evolved generally in accordance with their own national circumstances, although certain Soviet foreign policy needs, international discussions, or external events have also had a repercussion in their strategies. Just how much independence any given party has demonstrated vis-à-vis the Soviet Union on international questions has varied. Some examples may serve to illustrate.

The case of the PCM (now PSUM) is perhaps the most exceptional one. Having been one of the most Stalinist parties through the 1960s (it even participated in Stalin's plot to murder Leon Trotsky), the PCM became a "revisionist" party after 1968. Following an internal crisis, the PCM chose to project an image of more independence and internal democracy. This was translated into a strict condemnation of the Soviet invasion of Czechoslovakia in 1968 as "harmful to the rights and sovereignty of each party." During the 1969 Conference of World Communist Parties in Moscow, the PCM dissented with respect to the final document, objecting to the sanctions against China (as a matter of principle, the PCM did not wish to condemn those absent) and to the notion of "democratic centralism" at the international level.[68]

During the 1970s, the PCM reestablished relations with the Chinese Communist party and regarded with benevolence such groups (such as the MAS in Venezuela) which split from other Communist parties. Relations with the Romanian Communist party were also strengthened on account of their common concern for the sovereignty of every Communist state. During this time the PCM even began to identify itself with the "Eurocommunist" analyses.

The early 1980s saw the reinforcement of these trends. The PCM condemned the Soviet invasion of Afghanistan and contacts with the "Eurocommunist" parties in the form of conferences became more regular. Joint communiques published at the conclusion of these meetings always stressed the principles of "party sovereignty," "nonintervention," and the "plurality of paths" to socialism. The PCM also continued to defend China's right to membership in the socialist community, even though the Mexican party did not identify itself with Chinese positions. The struggle of Polish workers to gain an independent trade union movement also received support, since in the PCM's opinion, workers had such a right even under a socialist government.[69]

These positions were not shared by all within the PCM or, after 1981, by all PSUM members. Three organizations in the PSUM were very pro-Soviet, while only one division and a majority of the PCM leadership favored a more independent attitude toward the Soviet Union. The fact that the PCM leadership managed to impose its views in these matters, together with other sources of friction regarding internal politics, led to several desertions after 1982, and by 1985 the PSUM had lost nearly half of its original membership.[70]

Internal dissensions were not the only problems the PSUM had to face because of its independent stance. The CPSU was naturally very disappointed by the PCM's positions and relations between both parties were strained. Discreet, low-level contacts and private criticisms were evident. The disappointment was not only one-sided. The PCM also resented the Soviet government's overtures to the Mexican government (see Brian Latell's chapter), as well as those Soviet analyses which stressed the need to ally with the Mexican bourgeoisie. The latter point ran counter to PCM/PSUM strategy.

By 1983, however, tensions between both parties practically disappeared. Two high-ranking Soviet functionaries (Mikhail Kudachkin and Karen Brutents from the CPSU's International Department) visited Mexico just two months before the creation of the PSUM. Their formal contacts with the party leadership showed some disagreements, but this visit had more to do with Soviet concern for the Central American problems than with relations between both parties. The CPSU gave official approval to the formation of the PSUM, according it the same recognition as the PCM had had.[71] Kudachkin headed the Soviet delegation and was invited to the second PSUM congress in 1983; the PSUM's Secretary General Pablo Gómez headed an official delegation to Moscow in October 1983, a visit prepared far in advance and postponed more than once.[72]

In contrast to the PCM, the PCA in Argentina has shown to be strikingly continuous in its unconditional loyalty to the Soviet Union. Moreover, this party has shown a special zeal in its condemnation of "heresies" from Trotskyism in the 1930s to "Eurocommunism" in the 1970s. For the PCA, there is no place for any theoretical revision. Marxism-Leninism is still valid, in particular its analyses of the state. For the Argentine Communists, the Soviet Union is the most perfect example of "developed socialism" where the state, in the form of proletarian dictatorship, has become the "State of all the People." The PCA approved Soviet positions from Czechoslovakia in 1968 to Afghanistan and Poland in the late 1970s and early 1980s, and has opposed any characterization of equivalent "power blocs" in international relations.[73] The PCA agreed with Soviet policy toward Argentina's military government, and it is even said, although the PCA denies it, that a five percent royalty of all commercial transactions between both governments go to the PCA.[74]

This loyalty has been well corresponded by the CPSU. In the Soviet book about Latin American Communist parties we have already mentioned, the PCA is highly praised, both for its internal strategy ("wisely distinguishing the different factions within the army," its "large influence in the labor movement," and its correct attitude toward the Falklands/Malvinas War) and for its defense of orthodoxy (its "active diffusion of Marxism-Leninism...and other materials against Maoism and other opportunistic currents").[75]

The PCB in Bolivia provides another example of orthodoxy in its links with the Soviet Union and the international Communist movement. The PCB's differences with Ché Guevara during the latter's guerrilla enterprise in Bolivia reflected Soviet disapproval of this enterprise and of Cuban policy at the time. During the Torres regime, the PCB welcomed increased relations with the Soviet Union, especially a $10 million tin sale. Afterwards, notwithstanding the return of the rightist military to power, the Soviet Union maintained normal relations with Bolivia, and the PCB did not seem to mind. Even during their period of full support of the Hernán Siles Suazo government, the PCB openly criticized the government for having condemned the Soviet invasion of Afghanistan.[76]

The PCCh has also followed the tradition of maintaining excellent relations with the CPSU. The party acted as a mediator between President Salvador Allende and the Soviet Union during the UP period, this, despite the minor differences of opinion we have seen regarding the Chilean path to cocialism and, especially, the small amount of aid the USSR and other socialist countries gave to the UP government at a time when it most needed foreign assistance.[77] In any case, the Soviet government seemed to respond to the PCCh's expectations after the coup, in the sense of an energetic condemnation of the military government and of protecting Chilean refugees. Soviet official reactions to the PCCh's new strategy have been, as we have seen, difficult to assess.

In their international views most other Latin American Communist parties have followed a very pro-Soviet position. This is hardly surprising since such views are part of the founding ideology of such parties. By its aid to anti-Communist sectors and regimes, American policy also encourages these views. The surviving members of the old guard have taken care to see the tradition survive. The Communist parties' small size have also made them pragmatically useful (for financial reasons) to adopt pro-Soviet positions. However, there has been a contradiction between this loyalty and their internal politics. This is true not only because of Soviet foreign policy pragmatism and the USSR's goal of establishing relations with all the governments of the region regardless of their political orientation, but also because a rigid ideological attitude has made it difficult for these parties to appeal to a broader national public. Generally, Latin American Communist parties have managed to accommodate themselves to this situation, either praising the governments that establish relations with the socialist countries or understanding the reasons for Soviet relations with reactionary military dictatorships. Whether this loyalty would continue if any of these parties managed to gain power is another question.

Conclusions

The Latin American Communist movement is part of the complex political scenery of the individual countries where it exists, and it has played a significant role in many of them. This has sometimes contradicted, sometimes complemented, Soviet policy toward Latin America. The close relationship between the Communist movement and the Soviet Union has been, nonetheless, maintained over time as part of the theoretical heritage of these parties.

Several general trends are apparent. Latin American Communist parties have carefully maintained a rigid and anachronistic theoretical framework (regarding phases of revolution, vanguards, paths, etc.) which, rather than helping, has prevented them from organizing revolutionary movements. This is not fortuitous. Soviet ideologists have taken care to insure continuation of this theoretical framework: it complements Soviet foreign policy's pragmatic objectives. Not by chance have Communist parties never led revolutions in Latin America; nor will they ever under these conditions. This accounts for the hostility with which the PCES Secretary General Shafik Jorge Handal's analyses have been received by both Soviet and Communist party theoreticians. Nevertheless, the Soviet Union has given evidence of being able to adapt itself to unexpected events like the Nicaraguan revolution. Pragmatism, again, prevails.

Theoretical orthodoxy has not prevented an increase in the strength of some Communist parties and their participation in successful electoral coalitions, as in Chile and in Peru. This proves that orthodoxy does not necessarily mean inefficiency regarding political activity, provided such activity is non-violent. And even here it is necessary to allow for an exception: the PCCh since 1980. The Chilean Communists waited through seven years of clandestinity and repression, however, to change tactics, and Soviet approval of this change is not evident.

Generalizations concerning Latin American Communist parties are impossible to make and at best unfair. Today those Communist parties facing real revolutionary situations are in Central America. Nicaragua has led to a serious questioning of previous strategies, but even here it is far from evident whether the parties in the region have changed tactics or orientation. The weight of bureaucracy and history is perhaps too heavy and, for some parties like the *Partido del Pueblo de Panamá*, the situation is comfortable enough. The Soviet Union, for its part, seems to have lost any hopes of further, immediate revolution in this region. It is not even certain they would presently welcome such a development.

The South American situation seems less revolutionary in the short term, and thus the Communist parties in this region are better equipped to cope through electoral coalitions and support for the consolidation of democracy. The only exception, as we have seen, is in Chile and, perhaps the Andean countries. This also suits Soviet interests, as is argued in the various case study chapters.

Mexico remains an exception, but one which confirms the rule. After all, only in the last few years has the ex-PCM revealed itself as "dissident." On the other hand, the Soviet Union's search for good relations with the Mexican government is too important to pay attention to the PCM's demands. Even here, however, an accommodation has been found.

It is, therefore, simplistic to regard the Latin American Communist parties as totally dependent on the Soviet Union and nothing else. The relation is mutually profitable and mutually consented, the feedback of information is mutual and, although there may be conflicts of interests for *both* sides, these have always been solved. Future perspectives do not announce any change.

Notes

1 *L'Internationale Communiste et les Problèmes Coloniaux (1919–1935): Materiaux pour l'histoire du socialisme international* (Paris: Mouton, 1968).
2 Michael Lowy, *Le Marxisme en Amérique Latine* (Paris: Fr. Maspéro, 1980), pp. 79–92.
3 *Ibid.*, pp. 18–22; Mirochevski, "El populismo en Perú," *Dialéctica,* 1 (June 1942), p. 19.
4 Manuel Caballero, "Tormentosa historia de una fidelidad: el comunismo latinoamericano y la URSS," *Nueva sociedad,* 80 (November–December 1985), pp. 78–85.
5 The report was titled, "On the International Situation: Latin America and the Dangers of War." See *El movimiento revolucionario latinoamericano, versiones de la primera conferencia comunista latinoamericana, Junio de 1929* (Buenos Aires: n.d., Correspondencia Sudamericana), pp. 19–27.
6 The SRI was a subsidiary of the International Worker's Aid, another "front organization" the Comintern had created to aid the Russian peasant victims of the famine. See Rodolfo Cerdas, "Stratégie et Tactique de l'Internationale en Amérique Centrale," these de 3eme cycle, Université de la Sorbonne, 1976, pp. 377–400.
7 According to Miguel Marmol, the number of victims was approximately 30,000. See Roque Dalton, *Miguel Marmol, los sucesos de 1932 en El Salvador* (La Habana: Casa de las Américas, 1983), p. 102; Thomas P. Anderson puts the figure at 10,000. See his *Matanza, El Salvador's Communist Revolt of 1932* (Omaha: University of Nebraska Press, 1971), p. 135.
8 Abguar Bastos, *Prestes et a revolução social* (Rio de Janeiro: Calvino, 1946), p. 323.
9 L. E. Aguilar, *Marxism in Latin America* (New York: Alfred A. Knopf, 1968).
10 See Lowy, *Le Marxisme,* pp. 33–35.
11 See Abelardo Ramos, *Historia del estalinismo en Argentina* (Buenos Aires: Mar Dulce, 1969), p. 176; also E. Guidici, *Imperialismo y liberación nacional* (Buenos Aires: Crónica, 1974), p. 3–4.
12 Comisión política del PGT, *La intervención norteamericana en Guatemala y el derrocamiento del regimen democrático* (Guatemala 1955), pp. 31–32.
13 These ideas were the base of the "Dependence Theory" that would oppose the Communist parties' traditional analyses. See Sergio Bagú, *Economia de la sociedad colonial: ensayo de la historia comparada de América Latina* (Buenos Aires: Editorial Ateneo 1949) and Silvio Frondizi, *La realidad Argentina, ensayo de interpretación sociológica, tomo 11, La revolución socialista* (Buenos Aires: Editorial Praxis, 1956).
14 See Jacques Levesque, *L'URSS et la Révolution Cubaine* (Montreal: Presses de la Fondation Nationale des Sciences Politiques et de l'Université de Montréal, 1976), chapter 2.
15 See Edmé Domínguez, "Etude Comparative des Analyses Socioéconomiques sur l'Amérique Latin des Specialistes Sovietiques et du Mouvement Communiste Latinoamericain, 1970–1979," these de Doctorat de 3eme cycle, JEP, Paris, 1981, pp. 69–77.
16 See Levesque, *L'URSS et la Révolution Cubaine,* pp. 107–24.
17 *Conference des partis communistes de 1969 à Moscou* (Prague: Paix et Socialisme, 1969), pp. 296–336.
18 Michael Lowy, *Le Marxisme Amérique Latine,* pp. 58–59.
19 R. Arismendi, *Lenin y América Latina* (Montevideo: Editorial Pueblos Unidos, 1970).
20 A. Shulgovsky, "Leninist Theory on the National-Democratic transition to Socialist Revolution," *Latinskaia Amerika,* 2 (1970), pp. 55–80.
21 N. Kobo and G. Mirsky, "Some Particularities on the Evolution of the Latin American Armies," *Latinskaia Amerika,* 4 (1971).
22 L. Padilla, "Bolivia: nouvelles perspectives de lutte," *Nouvelle Revue Internationale,* 9 (September 1970), pp. 136–45.

23 These "terror-anarchistic elements" were the *Ejército de Liberación nacional* or ELN (National Liberation Army) that stood for armed struggle.
24 Padilla, "Bolivia," pp. 136–145.
25 "Plenum of the Central Committee of the Peruvian CP," *Unidad*, Lima, July 1, 1969.
26 A. Shulgovsky, *Latin America: Army and Liberation Movements* (Moscow: Znanie, 1972).
27 *La Unidad*, September 15, 1975.
28 "Basic program of the Popular Unity in Chile," *Bulletin d'information*, 12 (1970), pp. 41–49.
29 The Soviet delegation to the PSCh's 23rd congress was headed by S. Rasidov, candidate to the Politburo. He had been the one to head the Soviet delegation to the first Tricontinental Conference in Havana in January 1966. His speech at that time had evinced very enthusiastic support towards the guerilla groups in Latin America. See Edmé Domínguez, these, pp. 158, 230–231.
30 V. Shragin, *Chile: Corvalán's Struggle* (Moscow: izd., Polit. Literat., 1973).
31 A. I. Sobolev, "Revolution and Counterrevolution: the Chilean Experience and the Problem of the Revolutionary Process," *Klass i Sovremennyi Mir*, 2 (1974), pp. 3–22.
32 Central Committee of PCCh, *Mil Días de Revolución* (Santiago: Editorial Paz y Socialismo, 1978).
33 *Ibid.*
34 *Ibid.*
35 Edmé Domínguez, these, p. 372.
36 Robert Vesson, ed., *Yearbook of International Communist Affairs* (YICA), (Stanford: Hoover Institution Press, 1986), pp. 122–23.
37 See: K. Kurin, "Popular Resistance to the Dictatorship," *Mezdunarodnyi Ezhegodnik*," (1979); also O.Ignatiev, "The Victory of the people of Nicaragua," *Kommunist*, 13 (1979), pp. 95–102.
38 According to Maidanik, the PSN's greatest failure had been to mistake the "hierarchy of the unification process" by preferring an alliance with the conservative opposition rather than with others on the left. Similar criticisms were also made by Boris Koval, who said the PSN had been much more preoccupied by its internal struggles than by concern with becoming a real vanguard. Whatever their differences in emphases, all these specialists believed Nicaraguan events had definitely changed the revolutionary perspectives of the continent. See Boris Koval, "La revolución, largo proceso histórico," *América Latina*, 13 (1980), pp. 42–55, 74–70, 101–05.
39 *Ibid.*, pp. 65–73. Also I. Bulichev, "El fortalecimiento de la Unidad Nacional: nuevas victorias," *América Latina*, 7 (1981), pp. 40–56; and Y. Koroliov, "La experiencia del período de transición," *ibid.*, 9 (1984), pp. 43–53.
40 *YICA*, 1974.
41 J. Handal Schafik, "El poder y el carácter y vía de las revolución y la unidad de izquierda," *Fundamentos y Perspectivas*, 4 (1982).
42 *Ibid.*, pp. 39–42.
43 See *Grenada Documents: an Overview and Selection* (Washington D.C.: Departments of State and Department of Defense, 1984), document 26.
44 Such are Jiri Valenta's hypotheses. See J. Valenta, "Leninism in Grenada," *Problems of Communism* (July–August 1984), but a careful reading of the documents contradicts his assumptions.
45 Interviews with Soviet researchers in Moscow, Spring 1984.
46 For a review of the conference see "La unidad, objetivo estratégico revolucionario," *Revista Internacional*, 9 (1982), pp. 49–60.
47 *Los Partidos Communistas de América Latina, en la lucha por la unidad de las fuerzas antimperialistas* (Moscou: Progreso, 1983).
48 *Ibid.*, pp. 70, 99–100.
49 Luis Corvalán, "Discurso del Secretario General del Partido Comunista de Chile-Luis Corvalán," Moscow, September 3, 1980.

50 Carmelo Furci, *The Chilean Communist Party and the Road to Socialism* (London: Zed Books, 1984), pp. 166–67; also Orlando Millas, "Hacia donde va Chile?" *América Latina*, 3 (March 1984), pp. 14–22.
51 Furci, *The Chilean Communist Party*, pp. 167–68.
52 *Los Partidos Comunistas*, pp. 85, 99.
53 Ricardo Falcón and Hugo Quiroga, *Contribución al estudio de la evolución ideológica del Partido Comunista Argentino (1960–1984)* (Buenos Aires: Monografía, 1984), pp. 81–93, 112–16.
54 *Los Partidos*, pp. 91–93; and *YICA*, 1985–1986.
55 *Ibid.*, 1985–1986. Also *Liberación* (Malmö, Sweden), December 1, 1986.
56 *Los Partidos*, pp. 82–85, also *YICA*, 1986.
57 Furci, *The Chilean Communist Party*, pp. 18–19.
58 *Ibid.*, pp. 63–64 and *Los Partidos*, p. 144.
59 *YICA*, 1986.
60 See "Cómo evaluar las particularidades y el nivel de desarrollo capitalista en América Latina?," *América Latina*, 3 (1979) pp. 68–116. This debate has been preceded by several works: Koval, Semionov, and Shulgovsky, *Revoliutsionnye Protsessy v Latinskoi Amerike* (Moscow: Nauka, 1974), for example.
61 "Como evaluar," *ibid.*, and interview with K. Maidanik, Moscow, December 1979.
62 Edmé Domínguez, these, pp. 380–81.
63 "Interview with J. Shafik Handal," *América Latina*, 1 (1980), pp. 23–41.
64 See V. Sheinis, "Strany sredne razvitogo Kapitalizma," *MEMO*, 9 (1977), pp. 105–24.
65 "Acera de la etapa actual del desarrollo Capitalista en México," *América Latina*, 2 (1979), pp. 17–64.
66 Edmé Domínguez, these, pp. 383–85.
67 *Los Partidos*, pp 3–7, 20.
68 Edmé Domínguez, these, pp. 346–47, also, *Conference des partis communistes de 1969 à Moscou.*
69 Arnoldo Martínez Verdugo, *Historia del comunismo en México* (México City: Editorial Grijalbo, 1985), chapter 9 (pp. 365–405).
70 *YICA* 1986. In 1987 a new party, the PMS was created out of the PSUM and other leftist parties. Having abandoned the PCM's old symbols and traditions, it will be interesting to see Soviet reactions to it.
71 Interview with Marco Leonel Posadas, responsible for the Department of International Relations of the PSUM, March 1983.
72 *Latinskaia Amerika*, 3 (1984), pp. 55–66; also interview, *ibid.*
73 Falcón and Quiroga, *Contribución*, pp. 75–80.
74 *YICA* 1984, pp. 83–84.
75 *Los Partidos*, pp. 77–78.
76 *Ibid.*, 1984, 1986.
77 Interview with Orlando Millas, Moscow, December 1979.

5

The Nature and Uses of the Soviet-Cuban Connection

Jorge I. Domínguez

The Soviet Union and Cuba have fashioned relations that have enabled both to play a larger and more effective international role than either could undertake alone. Cuba is objectively far weaker than the USSR and it depends on the Soviets for extensive support. Nonetheless, Cuba has carved out not only a margin of autonomy under Soviet hegemony but even a leadership role: it has induced the Soviets to make commitments that the Soviets alone might not have undertaken to the same extent. This chapter examines the nature of the Soviet-Cuban connection as it can be used to advance their foreign policy objectives toward countries in Latin America and the Caribbean.

A common thread in Cuban and Soviet policies toward Latin America and the Caribbean is their rivalry with the United States. For the Soviets, the foreign policy aims in the region are modest but important: to complicate the U.S. position in the Western Hemisphere and to support the few Soviet friends, especially Cuba and Nicaragua. For Cuba, however, the regime's very survival is at stake in its relations with the United States. Because Western Hemisphere issues are more salient for Cuba, and because its government is better informed about them than the USSR's, Cuban policy toward Latin America and the Caribbean acquires greater significance in the management of Soviet-Cuban relations.

That Cuba has autonomy under Soviet hegemony, and that it often leads the Soviets, may be a source of comfort to Cuba's supporters, but it is the root of deep concern to the U.S. government and its allies. To the extent that Cuba increases the Soviet willingness to take risks in Third World settings, the prospects for international stability consistent with U.S. interests are poorer. It would be a simpler world if Cuba were just a puppet.

Cuba derives extensive economic benefits from, and is thus costly to, the Soviet Union, as Carmelo Mesa-Lago's chapter makes clear. Thus Cuba's "worth" to the Soviet Union depends on military, political, and ideological factors. After all, those tens of thousands of combat troops deployed in Africa are not Hungarians or Poles, but Cubans. The Soviet bloc's ability to bring military power to bear in southern or eastern Africa depends on Cuba. Indeed, Cuba is a small country but with a big power's international reach—so big that it is the USSR's premier ally in the Third World.

The nature of Soviet-Cuban relations combines Soviet hegemony with a degree of Cuban autonomy, a combination which is evident in five major international roles that Cuba has played with regard to the Soviet Union in the 1970s and 1980s: exemplar, vanguard, broker, partner, and supporter. These roles define the uses of the Soviet-Cuban connection. Consistent with this book's focus on Soviet behavior, in this chapter we shall explore these Cuban roles as they are perceived and used by the USSR. Hegemony means, above all, that Cuba accepts Soviet limits on its foreign policy. Three of Cuba's roles are most easily consistent with it. Cuba is supposed to be a good example of what socialism can do for a Third World country's internal development and of the benefits which can be gained from relations with the Soviet Union. Cuban foreign policy, especially toward Third World countries, should also be exemplary in advancing Soviet and Cuban goals. Cuba is also a Soviet partner or supporter on various issues. Though also consistent with Soviet hegemony, more unusual are Cuba's two other roles. Cuba at times serves in a vanguard role, inducing the Soviets to adopt more far-reaching policies. Cuba may also be a broker between the Soviets and Third World governments, helping both sides to collaborate more closely.

That Cuba has played these roles does not mean that all has gone well. Many Cuban policies in the 1960s, and even some in the 1980s, present obstacles to the pursuit of some Soviet objectives or may embarrass the Soviet government. Since Cuba accepted Soviet hegemony in 1968, the island has minimized its political burdens on the Soviet Union and performed its vanguard and broker roles with greater skill and discretion. Careful not to push the Soviets too hard nor to oppose their interests, Cuba never criticizes the Soviets in public. Cuba's views of its roles coincide with Soviet views, with one exception: Cuba does not see its various role performances as a Soviet burden, even in those foreign policy arenas where the Soviets may think so. What the Soviets at times perceive as a burden, the Cubans are likely to see as Soviet unwillingness to follow Cuba's leadership in some areas. Before examining Cuba's behavior in these roles, we will first consider the emergence of Soviet hegemony.

BUILDING SOVIET HEGEMONY

The Soviet and Cuban governments began serious contacts in the Fall 1959, about ten months after Fidel Castro's accession to power. The Soviet Union played no substantive role in Cuba's revolutionary war; the Moscow-allied Communist Party (the *Partido Socialista Popular*, PSP) was barely significant in the struggle against Batista and a latecomer in support of the eventually successful insurgents. Soviet-Cuban relations were cool during the early months of 1959, but as the Cuban government moved toward a break with the United States, it began courting the Soviet Union. Soviet-Cuban links tightened in 1960 when the United States and Cuba came to blows. The Soviet government agreed to purchase all Cuban sugar exports that the United States would no longer buy and Nikita Khrushchev promised, "in a figurative sense," to support Cuba with Soviet missiles if the United States attacked it.[1]

Those figurative missiles became real ones in 1962, leading in October to the missile crisis. The settlement that followed has evolved and modified with time. It led to the withdrawal of Soviet nuclear weapons from Cuba and to a ban on their reintroduction. Restraints were later agreed upon concerning the Soviet troop presence in Cuba. The United States, for its part, refrained from invading Cuba and gradually backed off from supporting those who wished to overthrow the Castro government. Castro was furious at the Soviet decision in 1962 to withdraw the missiles without consulting Cuba in advance; Cuba did not believe U.S. promises not to invade and it now distrusted Soviet defense promises.[2] As time passed, however, Cuban leaders recognized that the 1962 settlement in effect helped to consolidate their regime.

From 1962 through 1968, Cuban-Soviet relations oscillated between collaboration and confrontation, the latter culminating in late 1967 and early 1968, when the Soviet Union coerced Cuba to change key policies. The confrontation was multifaceted. In February 1965, Cuba's Minister of Industries, Ernesto (Ché) Guevara, challenged Soviet economic policies directly, telling the Second Economic Seminar of the Organization of Afro-Asian Solidarity, held in Algiers, that the "development of countries now starting out on the road to liberation should be paid for by the socialist countries." He rejected common Soviet views: "There should not be any more talk about developing mutually beneficial trade based on prices rigged against underdeveloped countries...." With socialist countries trading at world market prices in many products—and, except for the Soviets and the Chinese, purchasing Cuban sugar at those prices—"we must agree that the socialist countries are, in a way, accomplices of imperialist exploitation.... The socialist countries have the moral duty of liquidating their tacit complicity with the exploiting countries of the West."[3]

Serious political disputes ensued as well. In September 1963, Cuba announced it would not adhere to the Nuclear Test Ban Treaty negotiated between the United States and the Soviet Union. In Cuba, factional disputes resulted in repeated defeats (1962, 1964, 1968) for those who had belonged to the Moscow-oriented Communist Party before the revolution. Cuban support for the Soviets in the Sino-Soviet dispute oscillated until early 1966 when Cuba itself became embroiled in a serious confrontation with China.[4]

After mid-1966, Cuban-Soviet relations deteriorated across the board. Cuba took issue with the Soviet Union and its allies on several matters: Soviet willingness to place "state" interests ahead of support for (often small) revolutionary movements; Soviet skepticism as to whether Communist parties should always be committed to armed struggle; the unmilitant Soviet response to the U.S. attack on North Vietnam and to the U.S. intervention in the Dominican Republic; the Soviet acceptance of "capitalist means" in economic relations during the construction of socialism; and, above all, the Soviet demand that the Communist Party of the Soviet Union be respected as the leader of the international Communist movement.

Cuba adopted radical internal policies in the late 1960s somewhat akin to a "cultural revolution." It objected to Communist countries' trade with, and technical assistance to, several Latin American countries at odds with Cuba. As Fidel Castro said: "Lamentably, countries in the socialist camp sometimes make mistakes."[5] Cuba further asserted that only a violent insurrection would bring revolutionaries to power, and it also condemned, publicly and by name, those Moscow-oriented Latin American Communist parties which refused to support or backed away from armed struggle.[6] Cuba even snubbed the USSR symbolically: it was the only Communist country not allied with China whose top leader did not attend the 50th anniversary of the Soviet October Revolution. During this period, Cuba, in effect, claimed the right to be the vanguard of revolutionaries in Latin America, and perhaps elsewhere as well.

At last the Soviet Union had had enough. The Soviets did not end the relationship, but they did insist its nature had to change. Beginning in late 1967, it imposed measured sanctions on Cuba. The Soviets slowed down the rate of petroleum deliveries to Cuba at the same time that they increased oil exports to Cuba's adversaries in Latin America. Because Cuba depended on the USSR for virtually all its petroleum consumption, severe rationing of petroleum products had to be imposed. The Soviets suspended weapons deliveries in 1968 and froze all civilian technical assistance to Cuba, including the training of Cuban university faculty in socialist countries.[7]

Coincidentally, Cuban leaders announced the discovery of a Communist party "microfaction," including some members of the Central Committee. Accused of crimes of opinion and association, microfactionists opposed the leadership's radical internal and foreign policies. They had substantial relations with Soviet, East German, and Czech government and party personnel; the second secretary of the Soviet Embassy in Havana was caught discussing with microfactionists how Soviet oil policy could be used to pressure Cuba. On a more formal level, even Armed Forces Minister Raúl Castro had a serious confrontation with the Chief of Soviet Advisers at the Interior Ministry.[8] Cuban-Soviet relations remained tense for months. Finally, on August 23, Fidel Castro went on national television to discuss the Soviet and Warsaw Pact intervention in Czechoslovakia. He began saying that "some of the things we are about to say are in some cases in conflict with the emotions of many." He went on to state that "we accept the bitter necessity that required the sending of those troops into Czechoslovakia."[9]

The Soviet Union had intended to coerce Cuba, and it succeeded. Power between them was (and is) unequal and it was unequally exercised. At Soviet behest, Cuban internal and foreign policies changed dramatically in the years to come. Nonetheless, many of those changes might have occurred also because Cuban leaders thought them rational. After all, Cuban policies were failing at home and abroad as the 1960s came to an end: Che Guevara himself died trying fruitlessly to provoke an insurrection in Bolivia and Cuba's theory of armed struggle based on a small vanguard (*foco*) was being defeated everywhere. Soviet coercion might not have been needed to reorient Cuban policy. It is not possible to assess the relative weight of external pressure versus leadership rationality as explanations of policy change, though both mattered. Moreover, Soviet preferences were one key fact about which Cuban leaders had to be rational, further confounding the paths of causality. The existence of Cuba's own motivations for policy changes, however, should not obscure what Soviet policy was: the USSR behaved hegemonically and coercively. The events of 1968 proved to be a watershed in Cuban-Soviet relations.

Hegemony is not just the brute exercise of power. It combines structural and ideological components. The first focuses on the asymmetrical distribution of power, but that alone is not enough for a stable hegemony. Most hegemons clothe their power with an ideology that claims to serve the common good, and which enables clients to accept hegemony in the long run as legitimate and beneficial. Benefits often include economic resources transferred from hegemon to client. A stable hegemony depends ultimately on its being wanted by the client as much as on the hegemon's capacity and willingness to exercise power.

These features mark post-1970 Soviet-Cuban relations: the asymmetrical concentration of power in Soviet hands, a shared ideology which legitimizes Cuban subordination to Soviet foreign policy, the institutionalized coordination of policies to benefit hegemon and client, the client's commitment not to oppose the hegemon, and the retention of much client autonomy to formulate and implement foreign policy. This last feature sets Cuba apart from being a mere Soviet puppet; we turn to that later.

CUBA AS AN EXEMPLAR

"Socialism works." Soviet and Cuban foreign policies converge to promote this notion: the more countries that believe it, the more influential Soviet and Cuban policies might be. This is the most general "use" of Soviet-Cuban relations. Cuba advances this goal in two ways: it sets an example of how socialism works in a country's internal and international affairs, and its relations with the USSR are exemplary, too.

The Soviet and Cuban armed forces sponsored a book to describe the evolution of the Cuban armed forces and their "fraternal" cooperation with the Soviet armed forces. These are set in the larger framework of Soviet-Cuban collaboration: "Never before have there been links so just, egalitarian, and fraternal as those established among the states of the socialist community." Quoting Fidel Castro, Soviet-Cuban relations are a "model of truly fraternal relations, truly internationalist, and truly revolutionary." The authors argue that Soviet policy toward Cuba has "always" been to help Cuba to "build socialism" by developing its economic and technical capacities, as well as its defenses. The book details the vast scope of Soviet economic, social, and, with less precision, military aid to Cuba.[10]

The same tone has appeared in other works on Soviet-Cuban relations since the early 1970s. The role of Cuban-Soviet relations as an exemplar for the Third World has been emphasized even more in the 1980s. As an official of the Cuban Communist Party's Central Committee's International Relations Department put it, after comparing Cuban-Soviet relations with the relations of the industrial democracies and the Third World, "[W]e can speak of a favorable prospect for underdeveloped countries in their relations with the socialist countries taking Cuba as an example of that."[11]

The substance and extent of Soviet economic aid to Cuba is discussed in Carmelo Mesa-Lago's chapter, but it is also worth recalling that the Soviets have delivered weapons supplies to Cuba, free of charge, since 1962.[12] The rate of weapons deliveries has increased markedly since the mid-1970s, in part to reward Cuba's successful participation in wars in Angola and in the Horn of Africa, but also to modernize its inventories. The speed of deliveries accelerated in the early 1980s to deter a possible U.S. attack, but its start preceded Ronald Reagan's election.[13]

Raymond Duncan has identified several political dimensions which highlight the Cuban foreign policy example for the Third World: a small country, long dependent on the United States, can break with the United States and reorganize its internal and international affairs. Cuba shows as well that a country can retain its national traditions and style in close alliance with the Soviet Union.[14] Marxism-Leninism is not an exotic European or East Asian flower. It can blossom in the Caribbean, too, and retain its own distinctiveness.

Cuba's internal performance must also be exemplary. Both Cuban and Soviet sources seek to underline Cuba's developmental successes. Cuba must show that development is possible under socialism and that it can be done differently and better than in market-economy countries. As Duncan also puts it, there needs to be a credible "socialist ethic" as a new engine for change. Though there is a scholarly debate both on how much Cuban socialism has accomplished and how much cultural change there has been, Cuba has succeeded in three areas: the armed forces, education, and public health. Although in the latter two areas Cuba built upon a good pre-revolutionary record, it has gained in all three.[15]

Cuba's internationalist programs emphasize those sectors where internal performance has been good, i.e., a supply-side explanation for Cuba's overseas activities. By projecting abroad those area of good internal performance, the larger claim that socialist development "works" becomes more credible—even if, in fact, Cuba's development performance is much poorer in other areas. Thus, for example, by 1983 there were Cuban teachers posted abroad in 20 countries; in 1984 there were 22,000 scholarship students in Cuba from 82 countries; and in 1983, Cuban health workers were posted in 27 countries.[16] Cuba's military impact has, of course, been extraordinary in Angola and in Ethiopia, but there has also been an enduring Cuban military presence in Algeria, Benin, the Congo, Equatorial Guinea, Grenada, Guinea, Guinea-Bissau, Nicaragua, Mozambique, and South Yemen.[17] In addition to services rendered, Cuban military and civilians overseas have been politically reliable and loyal.

From the Soviet view, Cuba's exemplary role has gone further. Fidel Castro has defended Soviet-Cuban relations publicly. One of his best moments was one of his earliest: at the Nonaligned Movement summit in Algiers in 1973, Castro excoriated critics of the Soviet Union within the Movement. He denounced "the theory of two imperialisms" (the United States and the Soviet Union). The Soviet Union, he said, could not be called imperialist: "Where are its monopoly corporations? ... What factories, what mines, what oilfields does it own in the underdeveloped world? What worker is exploited in any country of Asia, Africa, or Latin America by Soviet capital?" With eloquence and feeling, he defended Soviet aid to Cuban security and development, concluding with a phrase that others have interpreted as his advocacy of a natural alliance (a phrase he did not use) between the Third World and the Soviet

Union: "Any estrangement from the socialist camp means weakening and exposing ourselves to the mercy of the still-powerful forces of imperialism."[18]

The Soviets, delighted with the Cuban defense of their relations, have not hesitated to use the phrase "natural alliance" between themselves and the Nonaligned Movement. For example, Leonid Levchenko has written about the "massive" effort at the Algiers summit to "oppose the Movement to its natural ally, the socialist community." He concluded that this effort failed "thanks to a large extent to the Cuban delegation's attitude," and especially to Castro's personal role. In Levchenko's view, Cuba's work helped both the Movement and the socialist countries.[19] In short, Cuba itself, and in its alliance with the Soviet Union, is an example for the Third World, including Latin America. That, the Soviets and the Cubans argue, is the path to the future. If others believe them, everyone would gain.

Cuba as a Negative Example

From the Soviet perspective, however, much about the Cuban government's performance is still not exemplary. Cuba's erratic performance in economic growth is the counterpoint of Cuba's hoped-for "exemplar" role and, therefore, a burden for both Cuban and Soviet policies. Cuba's substantial economic burden on the USSR is examined in Carmelo Mesa-Lago's chapter. Maybe socialism does not generate an efficient economy; and if not, then Cuba is a "negative example."

Again from the Soviet perspective, Cuba was also a negative example in foreign policy prior to 1968. Cuba illustrated how a socialist country could defy the USSR and still get very substantial economic aid from the Soviets. Although there are many fewer instances of such Cuban foreign policy defiance since then, let us illustrate one.

Cuban and Soviet policies toward the Treaty of Tlatelolco—which prohibits the development, deployment, or use of nuclear weapons in Latin America—have differed since 1963. Then, Cuba refused to sign the treaty unless the United States assumed the obligation not to deploy nuclear weapons in the Panama Canal Zone, Puerto Rico and the Virgin Islands, and in Guantanamo and other U.S. bases south of the U.S. mainland. Cuba also demanded a United States guarantee that it would not use nuclear weapons against Tlatelolco treaty signatories. The first set of issues would be covered through the Treaty's Protocol

I, the second set through its Protocol II. However, the United States has never ratified Protocol I, though it did accept Protocol II. The Soviet Union at first supported Cuba in part, abstaining in the United Nations voting which urged the nuclear powers to sign and ratify Protocol II. When the Treaty was signed in 1967, the USSR did not sign Protocol II.

However, in 1978 the USSR signed and ratified Protocol II, doing so in part because it wanted to improve relations with Latin America, and especially with Mexico, which was the prime mover behind the Tlatelolco Treaty. Significantly, the Soviet decision to sign was announced during Mexican President José López Portillo's visit to Moscow. By approving Protocol II, the USSR also wanted to improve the political climate for the SALT II negotiations. Meanwhile, in Washington, the Carter administration also announced its intention to seek ratification of Protocol I. But the United States Senate again failed to ratify Protocol I, and the Cuban position remained unchanged, effectively undercutting Soviet policy. Soviet commentators on these events either ignored the widening divergences between Soviet and Cuban attitudes toward Tlatelolco or simply recorded the Cuban position without comment.[20] Consistent with practice since Cuba accepted Soviet hegemony in 1968, Cuba did not criticize the change in Soviet policy. But the persistence of this difference is an enduring reminder to the Soviets of the limits of Cuba's role as an exemplar of Soviet relations with Third World countries.

CUBA AS A VANGUARD

In the 1960s, Cuba sought to lead revolutionaries in the Americas and beyond, at times scorning the role heretofore played by the Soviet Union and its allies. That policy added to the Soviet-Cuban crisis of 1967–68. Although much changed in subsequent Cuban policies, the view remained in Havana that Cuba should continue to take foreign policy initiatives and lead the Soviet Union and its allies to adopt policies beyond what they would undertake on their own. This is the vanguard role. A close kin is the broker role examined in the next section.

Cuba's continuing vanguard role, however, would have to operate within the confines of Soviet hegemony. Cuba would no longer criticize the Soviet Union or its allies publicly, even if they did not agree to follow Cuba's leadership. Cuba's own decision making would take Soviet interests into account so that in formulating policy, Cuba would not embarrass the Soviet Union or risk a severe crisis. Such consideration, of course, enhanced the chances of ultimate Soviet-Cuban collaboration in new endeavors.

Cuba played this vanguard role most spectacularly and effectively while increasing the Soviet commitment in Angola during 1975–76 (a discussion of which is beyond the scope of this chapter), and subsequently in Central America and the Caribbean (see in this regard the chapter by Raymond Duncan and Peter Clement). Castro has noted Cuba's vanguard role in leading the Soviet Union to become interested in Central America: "One of the great lies that the imperialists use concerning Central America is their attempt to impute the revolutions in this area to the Soviet Union." Instead, the "Soviets did not know even one of the present leaders of Nicaragua ... during the period of revolutionary struggle." As if this were not problematic enough for communism's Mecca, "the same holds true for El Salvador. There, the Communist party is only one of the five left wing organizations joined together in the Farabundo Martí Front. Hewenton: "(w)ith the exception of the Communist party of El Salvador ... militant and independent but," in a dig reminiscent of their disputes in the late 1960s, "small, and not one of the major groups—the Soviet Union did not know the leaders of these revolutionary organizations and had no contact with them. The same goes for Guatemala." Who, then, worked with both Central American insurgents and European Communist powers? "We Cubans ... have relations with the revolutionary movements, we know the revolutionary leaders in the area."[21] Cuba gave weapons, military training, and other support to the *Sandinista* fight against the Somoza government.[22] Moscow discovered Managua through Havana.

In El Salvador, Cuba's activist role has contrasted with the more cautious Soviet role, as evident in the documents captured by Salvadoran and U.S. authorities about the event leading up to the major revolutionary offensive in January 1981. The documents generally confirm Cuba's close support for the Salvadoran insurgency; they also show some Soviet support, albeit quite reluctant. One document reports on the trip of Shafik Jorge Handal, Secretary General of the Salvadoran Communist party to various countries, including the USSR. Although the Soviets expressed solidarity with the Salvadoran revolution and with the Communist party there, they kept referring Handal to other sources of weapons. The Soviets would not commit themselves to help in the transfer of weapons from Vietnam to El Salvador; nor would they supply weapons directly. Handal, upset, complained formally that he was not being received at the level he considered appropriate for his rank, nor getting the decisions he expected. Within a week, the Soviets agreed to train 30 Salvadoran Communists, but they deferred decisions on weapons transfers and for months postponed receiving Handal again. Handal expressed "concern as to the effects that the lack of decision by the Soviets may have, not only regarding the assistance that they themselves can offer but also upon the inclination of the other parties of the European socialist camp to cooperate..."[23]

Though cautious, the Soviets were learning. Revolutions in Latin America, Cuban-Nicaraguan style, were possible, Kiva Maidanik noted triumphantly, over the objections of earlier Soviet writers.[24] The Soviets had to take their prospects seriously. As Sergo Mikoyan summarized discussions among Soviet academics, the Cuban and Nicaraguan revolutions "have shown (and now it can be said that they have demonstrated) that under certain conditions" politico-military movements such as Castroism and *Sandinismo* "can replace the proletariat's political parties in the vanguard role."[25] Other Soviet scholars were more blunt. Tatiana Vorozheikina criticized "armchair analysts" who denounced many revolutionaries "until recently" as "ultra-leftists, Trotskyites, and Maoists." She criticized the Nicaraguan Communist party's "sad experience" which left it "on the margins" of the revolution, and recalled the "right wing opportunist mistakes" of the Salvadoran Communist party in the late 1960s.[26]

The more the Soviets agreed that Cuba was Nicaragua's vanguard, and that jointly they were Latin America's, the more Moscow supported insurgencies. But the defeats suffered by the Salvadoran and the Guatemalan rebels by the mid-1980s counselled caution. For example, some Soviet analysts voiced support for the Contadora Peace process in Central America because it would help consolidate the Sandinista government and reduce U.S. pressures on Cuba. No mention was made about El Salvador, nor was it said that the same Contadora process would require the international abandonment of the Salvadoran guerrillas.[27]

Cuba's vanguard role was also at work in the triangular relations among the Soviet, Cuban, and Nicaraguan governments after 1979. As Theodore Schwab and Harold Sims have shown, "the Communist state with which Nicaragua developed the closest ties was Cuba," especially between 1979 and 1981. The leap in Soviet aid to Nicaragua began in 1981 and became quite evident in 1982, in part in response to changes in Nicaragua and in U.S. policy toward Nicaragua. From the beginning,

Cuba took the lead in assisting the Sandinista government. Whereas the Soviets, at first, emphasized economic and technical collaboration, Cuba was not reluctant to help the Sandinista government in military and security affairs.[28]

For these reasons, Nicaraguan Interior Minister Tomás Borge said in a mid-1984 interview, "I will not deny that the Cuban revolution has exerted a certain very positive influence [in Nicaragua].... The influence of the USSR is rather more remote." He described Nicaragua's relations with Cuba as "excellent"; those with the Soviet Union as "good." He preferred Cuban over Soviet military advisers "for practical reasons." The Cubans, Borge noted, "speak our language and are more keen on our way of life." The Cubans know Soviet equipment and "if we needed technical advice about Soviet weapons, then the Cubans can play that part." Relying on Cuban, rather than Soviet, military advisers, he went on, would "not justify our enemies" in attacking Nicaragua.[29]

Cuban-Soviet relations with regard to Nicaragua also have the features of a "division of labor." Cuba has supplied personnel to Nicaragua, and the Soviet Union has been a source for the supply of weapons, other equipment, and financing. Into the early 1980s, the sequence of events, the tenor of commentary, and the type of involvements continue to point to a Cuban vanguard role, and not just that of a partner in a joint endeavor. By the late 1980s, however, as the Soviet Union increased its support for the Nicaraguan government, Cuba's vanguard role may have begun to fade and the Cuban-Soviet participation in Nicaragua may more nearly approximate a partnership.

In sum, since the early 1960s, Cuba had forged strong and consistent ties to revolutionaries in Central America. The Soviet Union had not. The Soviets gradually reconsidered their views and gave some help to the Salvadoran revolutionaries, though primarily through their allies. In the end, the Soviets may have encouraged—and certainly did not stop—the Cubans from helping the Salvadorans. The Cubans did not push the Soviets too far, but the clear pattern was that of Cuba leading, the Soviet Union following. So too was the case with regard to Nicaragua's government: Cuba led, while the Soviets waited three years to commit themselves directly to the consolidation of the Sandinista regime. Cuba did not act against Soviet interests, but its own commitment served to engage the Soviets, and to convince them that Managua's government could be saved through concerted support.

Cuba as a Reckless Vanguard

From the Soviet perspective, much of Cuba's foreign policy behavior in the 1960s was reckless. Seeking to project its own vanguard role, Cuba condemned Moscow-oriented Communist parties and, instead, supported movements committed to the armed struggle, but which had little chance for success. Since 1970, Cuba has been more prudent in its vanguard behavior. And yet, at times, it has remained a foreign policy burden for the Soviets. One example is the case of relations with Colombia.

Colombian relations with the Soviet Union and other Eastern European countries, begun in the 1950s, had deepened by 1967, when Colombia signed long term bilateral economic agreements with these countries. At that time, Colombia had poor relations with Cuba owing to the latter's support of a guerrilla insurgency. By the late 1970s, however, Cuban-Colombian diplomatic and trade relations improved as well. Colombian trade with the USSR and Eastern Europe had increased significantly from 1978 to 1980, leading one Soviet scholar to cite the trend as an example of how the Soviet Union and Eastern Europe "were willing to promote economic and trade relations with every country, independently of its social and political regime, based on equality, mutual benefit, and noninterference in internal affairs."[30]

Colombia again became a source of conflict between Cuba and the Soviet Union in the early 1980s. In 1980–81, Cuba supported Colombia's insurgent M-19 Movement, fighting against the Colombian government at the very moment that the Soviet Union and Eastern Europe sought to improve their relations with Colombia. Cuba appears to have assisted and trained the M-19 prior to a landing in Colombia, although this fell short of supplying weapons or giving logistical support. This was an unusual step, for Cuba has tended to respect those governments, such as Colombia's, that have reestablished diplomatic and trade relations with Havana. Support of the M-19 provoked Colombia to break relations with Cuba again in 1981. Why Cuba challenged Colombia is difficult to ascertain. Cuba may have acted against Colombia out of peeve: Colombia played a major role in 1979–80 in preventing Cuba's election to the U.N. Security Council, even though Cuba chaired the Nonaligned Movement.[31] Only after Belisario Betancur assumed the Colombian presidency (1982–86) did relations with Cuba again improve, though formal diplomatic links were not restored. Cuba's policies in 1980–81 set back the image of moderation that both it and the Soviet Union had sought to project. They also complicated Soviet and Eastern European relations with Colombia, reminding the Soviet Union of the worst moments in Cuban-Soviet relations during the 1960s. Along with the 1980–81 failure of El Salvador's insurgency, the Colombian events may have cooled Soviet ardor for following Cuba's vanguard leadership in active support for Latin American insurgencies.

CUBA AS BROKER

Cuba has also served as a broker in the ongoing relations between the USSR and other countries. The relations between the People's Revolutionary Government of Grenada (1979–83) and Cuba and the USSR exemplify this role. Four months before the overthrow of the Grenadan government in October 1983, the Grenadan Ambassador to Moscow had written that the Soviets are "very careful, and for us sometimes maddingly slow, in making up their minds about who [sic] to support. They have decided to support us for two main reasons. Cuba has strongly championed our cause," and the Soviets were impressed with Grenada's internal development.[32]

Cuba's brokerage role was necessary because the Soviet interest in Grenada was modest. As the Grenadian embassy reported in late 1982, "the Caribbean—as they [the Soviets] repeatedly state ... is very distant from them. It is, quite frankly, not one of their priority areas." As a result, "we have to work on the Soviets for some considerable time before we reach the state of relationship that, for example, we have with the Cubans."[33] Another reason for Cuba's brokerage role derived in part from Grenada's poor communications with the outside world: Cuba was the transshipment point stipulated in Grenada's agreements with the Soviet Union, Vietnam, and Czechoslovakia.[34]

Cuba even coached the Grenadans on how to bargain with the Soviet Union. In November 1982 the Cuban and Grenadan ministers of communications discussed how to develop Grenada's links to the Intersputnik satellite system: "So it was proposed by the Cuban side that a specialist on this type of station can give some technical assistance and also advise on the discussions with the Soviets. This point was fully agreed by the Grenadian side. Cuba also manifested that it is ready to help in technical aspects, maintenance, and also in the technical conversations with the Soviet Union until Grenada has the prepared personnel."[35] In short, Cuba brokered between Grenada and the Soviet Union, committing the latter beyond its own wishes, and helping Grenada to draw more resources from the USSR.

The vanguard and broker roles emphasize the importance Cuban foreign policy has had in shaping Soviet policy toward Latin America. Cuba has "radicalized" Soviet policy, activating it in Nicaragua and Grenada, and edging the USSR toward support of insurgencies. Cuban officials at times perceive the Soviets as too slow, too cautious, and slightly myopic in their vision of much of the Third World. Some Cuban officials have argued that there are differences in the "temperament" of Cubans and Soviets that are evident in the nature and speed of their respective responses to Third World opportunities and crises: Cubans, they say, are quicker and take the lead. The broker role is also required, these Cuban officials suggest, because the Soviets are not well informed about the Third World and know even less about Latin America and the Caribbean. The governments in these regions, moreover, do not know the Soviet Union or how its foreign policy and aid bureaucracies work. Cuba has experience in both regards and can help to bridge the gap.[36]

From the Soviet perspective, however, the disastrous outcome of the Grenada experience may have called attention to the need for caution in accepting Cuba's brokerage role. In retrospect, the best aspect of Soviet policy toward Grenada was its demonstration of an unwillingness to be drawn even further into supporting a dogmatic regime on an island of little intrinsic interest for Soviet policy.

CUBA AS PARTNER AND SUPPORTER OF THE USSR

Cuba and the Soviet Union have also developed policies where they help each other in partnership to expand their trade, their political influence, and that of local Communist parties. Though there is some coordination, more often their convergences stem from their respective definitions of each government's interests.

At the party level, Moscow-oriented Communist parties at last finally accepted Cuba's leadership of Latin America's Communist movement in 1975, at which time, Cuba in turn agreed that armed struggle was not the only path to power because it might not be feasible everywhere.[37] Although open feuds have not reappeared since, differences remain between the Soviets and the Cubans on the wisdom of the armed struggle as the *only* path to power. Consider two examples from 1980. As Fidel Castro argued, "What do the experiences of Guatemala, El Salvador, Chile, and Bolivia teach us? That there is only one path: revolution. That there is only one way: revolutionary armed struggle."[38] On the other hand, even the Soviet scholar, Kiva Maidanik, who is closest to the Cuban position that armed struggle methods are to be preferred in Central America, has argued such an approach would not work in the continent's more developed countries and has warned against copying it.[39]

At the diplomatic level, a major change occurred around 1970. As Latin American countries sought greater independence from the United States, the Soviet Union and Cuba sought greater influence. All achieved their goals to some degree. In Latin America, a modest step was to promote diplomatic relations with the Soviet Union, and to seek normalization with Cuba. Since 1970, the Soviet Union has had such relations with all South American countries except Chile and Paraguay. Relations have also been developed with a growing number of countries elsewhere in the Americas.[40]

Cuba moved in the same direction, though at a slower pace and along a bumpier road. It dropped its support for many insurgencies in exchange for improved relations with existing governments. As a result, collective interamerican sanctions, imposed on Cuba in 1964, were lifted in 1975. However, Cuba's relations with the English-speaking Caribbean suffered serious setbacks in 1979–80 as a result of several Cuban acts of war (such as the sinking of a Bahamian Coast Guard ship); of adverse reactions in several of the island nations (especially in Jamaica) to the perceived Cuban meddling in their domestic affairs; and of effective Carter administration policies; at the same time, for various reasons, Cuban relations with Spanish America were harmed, too, though less seriously. Cuba resumed the improvement of its relations with South America, though not with the Caribbean, soon thereafter.

The parallel improvement of Cuban and Soviet diplomatic relations with Latin American countries may have been coordinated to some degree, but this was certainly not the case toward all South American countries. For example, Brazil and Uruguay retained diplomatic relations with the USSR throughout the 1960s and beyond, whereas they broke them with Cuba in the mid-1960s, reestablishing them only 20 years later; Argentina maintained diplomatic relations uninterruptedly with the USSR since the mid-1940s, but broke them with Cuba between 1962 and 1973. And whereas the pattern of improved Soviet diplomatic relations with Latin American and Caribbean countries was generally uninterrupted after 1970, Cuba was much more likely to suffer occasional reverses.

A related dimension of the Soviet-Cuban partnership was the manifest increase in Soviet and Cuban trade with Latin American countries since the 1960s (see Elizabeth Valkenier's chapter).[41] However, there has been even less coincidence in the pattern of Soviet and Cuban trade improvement with Latin American countries than was the case in diplomatic relations. For example, Soviet trade with Mexico has been insignificant, though political relations have been important to both countries.[42] Political relations with Mexico have also been important for Cuba since 1959 because Mexico was the only Latin America country never to break relations with Cuba. But unlike commerce with the Soviet Union, Mexican trade with Cuba increased sharply in the 1970s and remained high in the early 1980s. In 1980–82, Cuba even had a large bilateral trade surplus with Mexico.[43]

Divergent, too, has been the Argentine case. There was some Soviet-Argentine trade in the 1960s, even after Cuban-Argentine trade was interrupted. During the Peronist governments (1973–76), Argentine trade with both the Soviet Union and Cuba boomed. However, the real expansion in Soviet-Argentine trade occurred in 1980, when Argentina ignored the U.S. grain embargo which had been called to punish the USSR for its intervention in Afghanistan (see Aldo Vacs' chapter). Cuban-Argentine trade, in contrast, fell sharply in the early 1980s to increase again only in 1983. An enduring similarity in Cuban and Soviet trade with Argentina is that, for the respective size of their economies, they import much from Argentina but export little to it.[44] A sharper divergence is the case of Brazil, which has had important trade relations with the Soviet Union since the early 1970s, but none with Cuba until around 1983.[45]

Soviet and Cuban diplomatic and trade policies shared the intention of improving relations with governments. The moderate tone of these policies (which also involved Cuba's shift from support of revolution in South America) helped each of these governments. Not surprisingly, neither Cuban nor Soviet diplomatic or trade relations improved much with Central America except for Nicaragua, after 1979. From the South American perspective, the less Cuba was feared, the easier it was to deal with it formally (and also with the USSR). In this sense, Cuba and the USSR were partners in their policies toward Latin America, even if overt coordination was probably modest.

The Council for Mutual Economic Assistance has offered another limited means through which Cuba and the Soviet Union coordinated some of their economic policies toward Latin America. CMEA serves as a coordinating mechanism for Soviet bloc economic integration and division of labor. Since Cuba joined CMEA in 1972, it has governed much of Cuban economic relations with Eastern Europe and also aspects of Cuban-Soviet relations. In 1975, Mexico became the first noncommunist country in Latin America to sign a formal agreement with CMEA, though the improvement in Mexican economic relations with European CMEA countries since then has been modest. After 1979 Nicaragua has gradually become integrated into CMEA, and the first session of the Joint CMEA-Nicaragua Collaboration Commission met in September 1984. A month later CMEA heads of government met for the first time outside of Europe—in Havana. The only two Latin American government "observers" were from Mexico and Nicaragua.[46] CMEA provides a means for Nicaragua, Cuba, and the USSR, acting as partners, to enlist further Eastern European support for Sandinista Nicaragua. Outside of Nicaragua, however, CMEA institutions' impact on Soviet and Cuban relations with Latin America has been very modest.

In sum, the Soviet Union and Cuba have identified compatible broad, long-term diplomatic, trade, and party policies whose consequences help each government, even if the processes are distinct, and coordination is limited. It is mainly a partnership of shared consequences.

Cuba has also played a support role for some important Soviet initiatives, primarily outside Latin America and the Caribbean. Cuba supported the new Soviet military alliance with Ethiopia in 1977–78 and sent troops to defeat the Somali invasion. Despite Cuba's chairmanship of the Nonaligned Movement, it sided with the Soviet Union when the latter intervened in Afghanistan. Following the Soviet lead, Cuba also boycotted the Los Angeles Olympics. This support role is the mirror image of the vanguard role. Cuba accepts the Soviet vanguard role in these and other settings, just as it has looked to the Soviet Union to accept Cuba's vanguard role in Latin America and the Caribbean.

Because the USSR has been so cautious and also deferential to Cuba in Latin America and the Caribbean, there are no comparable cases of a Cuban support role for the Soviets in these regions. The closest examples are Cuba's facilitating of Soviet electronic eavesdropping from Cuba and the Soviet use of Cuban airports for long-range reconnaissance aircraft. Although the United States is the main target, these means may also gather intelligence about Mexico, Central America, the Caribbean islands, and northern South America. Therefore, though Cuba plays all five roles in the design of its global policy, the support role does not apply well in the Western Hemisphere.

Jorge I. Domínguez

SUCCESSES AND FAILURES: A BALANCE SHEET

Cuba and the Soviet Union cooperate closely throughout the Third World. Although they do so within a framework of Soviet hegemony, Cuba retains a substantial margin of autonomy. In their relations toward Latin American and Caribbean countries, Cuba's autonomy reaches its zenith. More than in other parts of the world, Cuba leads the Soviet Union into policies and situations in the Western Hemisphere beyond what the Soviets themselves would choose. This explains in part the strong anti-U.S. government edge of combined Soviet and Cuban policies in the Americas.

In the 1960s, Cuba's effort to be a vanguard for revolutionaries failed in part because it directly challenged the Soviet Union. In the 1970s and early 1980s, Cuba succeeded more in playing a vanguard role because it took Soviet interests seriously into account and because it designed policies to engage the Soviet Union, not to repudiate it. Thus Cuba enlisted much more support from the Soviet Union and other Communist countries for insurgencies in Central America in the late 1970s and early 1980s than in the 1960s. Still, Cuba occasionally failed to lead the USSR (as in Colombia), and at times Cuban policy led to fiasco (as in Grenada), in both cases posing burdens for Soviet foreign policy.

Cuba has also served as a vanguard and broker for the Soviet Union in its relations with Nicaragua since 1979 and with Grenada in 1979–83. The Soviet Union welcomed Cuba's intermediary role because it improved Soviet knowledge about Nicaragua and Grenada. Cuba also helped to improve the latter two countries' bargaining capabilities vis-à-vis the Soviet Union. Cuba and Nicaragua were successful in engaging the USSR to support Nicaragua more fully militarily and economically since 1982, but this Soviet policy change did not come in time to rescue Marxism-Leninism in Grenada. On balance, then, Cuba helped to radicalize the Soviet Union in its approach to Central America since the late 1970s.

Cuba has also played its role as an exemplar of successful socialism in the Third World, highlighting its accomplishments while obscuring its failures. It has sought to transform its successes in military and some social sectors into an instrument for influence overseas. Because there have been few takers in the Americas, however, the sustained deployment of Cuban personnel abroad in the Western Hemisphere is concentrated in Nicaragua (and, earlier, in Grenada). Pursuing convergent though distinct policies, Cuba and the Soviet Union have also been partners to promote their diplomatic and trade relations with South American countries and Mexico, even if overt coordination has been modest. They have also worked more closely to coordinate their joint leadership over Communist parties in the Western Hemisphere.

Success, however, should be measured not only by whether Cuba and the Soviet Union work jointly, or whether one leads the other, but by whether they can use their connection to advance their goals. The Americas have witnessed four of Cuba's most spectacular setbacks. Its personnel were expelled from, and relations broken with, Chile in 1973, Jamaica in 1981, and Grenada in 1983. Chile and Grenada were also Soviet setbacks, although in each case Soviet policy has been more cautious than Cuba's. In Chile and in Jamaica, relations with Cuba were a factor, though not decisive, in the removal of Cuba's allies from power in the first through military coup and in the second by election defeat. Cuba's presence in Grenada was a key reason for the U.S. and English-Caribbean intervention. The change in incumbents in these three countries led to the break with Cuba. In 1983, Cuban personnel were also expelled from Suriname as a consequence of the events in Grenada; diplomatic relations have remained in limbo. As in Grenada, Cuba both served as vanguard and broker between Jamaica and (briefly) Suriname and the Soviet Union, although Soviet relations with these countries never developed much.

These failures underscore the high risk the Soviet Union takes in accepting Cuba's vanguard role in the Americas: the only successful insurgency (Grenada's New Jewel Movement came to power in a coup) and the only enduring allied regime in power has been Nicaragua. The Cubans may know more than the Soviets about Latin America and the Caribbean, but the more radical aspects of Cuba's foreign policy toward these countries, be it in support of insurgencies or of governments, have failed to yield much fruit.

Therefore, in the future, the Soviet Union might be more reluctant than it was between 1975 and 1983 to accept Cuba's role as vanguard or broker in the Americas. The insurgency's lack of success in El Salvador, Cuba's reckless policies toward Colombia in 1980–81, and the debacle in Grenada each may have reinforced Soviet predisposition toward more cautious policies in the Americas. The Soviets are likely to continue to minimize the burdens still posed by Cuba and focus instead on political and economic partnership and on the more moderate aspects of Cuba's exemplar role.

For Cuba, however, this would confine its foreign policy to more passive and boring roles—a prospect it will not accept willingly.

Instead, Cuba should be expected to continue to emphasize the vanguard and broker roles toward Nicaragua and revolutionary movements, as well as the more radical aspects of its exemplar role. Cuba had been successful in affirming these roles toward the USSR and other Communist countries, even if, outside of Nicaragua, Cuba could not generate further success in Latin America or the Caribbean. If these indeed become Soviet and Cuban policies, then the comfortable convergence that marked Soviet and Cuban approaches to the nature and uses of their connection in the Americas in recent years may be more difficult to repeat in the 1990s.

Notes

1 Edward González, "Castro's Revolution, Cuban Communist Appeals, and the Soviet Response," *World Politics*, 21:1 (October 1968); George Boughton, "Soviet-Cuban Relations, 1956–1960," *Journal of Inter-American Studies and World Affairs*, 16:4 (November 1974); Andrés Suárez, *Cuba: Castroism and Communism, 1959–1966* (Cambridge: The M.I.T. Press, 1967), chapter 1.

2 Special issue of *International Security*, 8:1 (Summer 1983); summary of "understandings" in Jorge I. Domínguez, "U.S.-Cuban Relations in the mid-1980s," *Journal of Inter-American Studies and World Affairs*, 21:1 (February 1985).

3 *Ché Guevara Speaks*, George Lavan, ed. (New York: Merit Publishers, 1967), pp. 108–09; also published in *Revolución*, February 26, 1965, p. 1.

4 General discussion in Jacques Levesque, *L'URSS et la révolution cubaine* (Montreal: Presses de L'Université de Montréal, 1976), pp. 133–66.

5 *Granma Weekly Review*, July 31, 1966, p. 11.

6 *Granma*, May 15, 1966, pp. 2–3; November 13, 1966, p. 5; *Granma Weekly Review*, March 19, 1967, Supplement, p. 8.

7 *Granma*, January 3, 1968, pp. 2–3, 6; *Current Digest of the Soviet Press*, 19:50 (December 15, 1967), pp. 15–16; Henry Kissinger, *White House Years* (Boston: Little, Brown, 1979), p. 638; Alexis Codina and Joaquín Fernández Núñez, "Apuntes en el XX aniversario del inicio de la formación de economistas," *Economía y desarrollo*, 71 (November-December 1982), p. 23.

8 *Granma*, January 13, 1968, p. 3; January 28, 1968, pp. 1–2; January 29, 1968, pp. 2–3; January 30, 1968, p. 2; February 1, 1968, p. 2.

9 Fidel Castro, *Obras escogidas 1962–1968*, II (Madrid: Editorial Fundamentos, 1976), pp. 182, 224.

10 Ivan Shkadov, Pavel Zhilin, Thelma Bornot Pubillones, and Victor Volsky, *Valentía y fraternidad: el internacionalismo y la amistad combativa entre las Fuerzas Armadas de Cuba y la URSS* (Havana: Editorial de Ciencias Sociales, 1983), pp. 209, 214, and generally chapter 5.

11 Silvia N. Pérez, "La participación de Cuba en la comunidad socialista y su ejemplo para el Tercer Mundo," in *Cuba y los Estados Unidos*, Juan Gabriel Tokatlian, ed. (Buenos Aires: Grupo Editor Latinoamericano, 1984), p. 126.

12 Fidel Castro, "Un pueblo así es un pueblo invencible!" *Cuba socialista*, 2:16 (December 1962), p. 30; *Granma Weekly Review*, August 6, 1972, p. 4.

13 *Granma Weekly Review*, January 4, 1976, p. 7; June 27, 1982, p. 2; *Granma*, December 13, 1982, p. 2; Special Supplement, January 4, 1985, p. 6; *Verde olivo*, 20:1 (January 7, 1979), pp. 12–13; U.S. Department of Defense, *Soviet Military Power* (Washington D.C.: Government Printing Office, 1985), pp. 115, 119–20.

14 Raymond Duncan, *The Soviet Union and Cuba: Interests and Influence* (New York: Praeger, 1985), pp. 138–44.

15 Jorge I. Domínguez, *Cuba: Order and Revolution* (Cambridge: Harvard University Press, 1978), pp. 71–76, 165–73, 184–86, and chapter 9.

16 *Granma Weekly Review*, November 11, 1984, p. 5; *Granma*, November 14, 1984, p. 2; Frank Agüero, "La educación es obra de todos," *Verde Olivo*, 24:52 (December 29, 1983), p. 57.

17 *Granma*, July 2, 1966, p. 12; October 21, 1976, p. 2; August 3, 1983, p. 1; Juana Carrasco, "Encuentro entre hermanos de lucha," *Verde Olivo*, 22:37 (September 13, 1981), p. 55; Carlos Martínez de Salsamendi, "El papel de Cuba en el Tercer Mundo: América Central, el Caribe, y Africa," in *Cuba y Estados Unidos*, pp. 150, 184; Gabriel García Márquez, "Operacion Carlota," *Tricontinental Bimonthly*, 53 (1977), pp. 9–11; Keith Somerville, "The USSR and Southern Africa since 1976," *Journal of Modern African Studies*, 22:1 (1984), p. 86; François Soudan, "Benin: les potions magiques de Kérékou," *Jeune Afrique*, 1242 (October 24, 1984), p. 47; interviews in Havana, March 1985.

18 *Granma Weekly Review*, September 16, 1973, p. 12.

19 Leonid Levchenko, "El papel vanguardista de Cuba," *América Latina*, 3 (1979), pp. 25–26.

20 M. Petrov, "Denuclearised Zone in Latin America," *International Affairs*, 8 (August 1974), pp. 49–50; M. Petrov, "The Soviet Union and the Denuclearised Zone in Latin America," *International Affairs*, 12 (December 1979); Leonid Anisimov and Sajrab Janabadli, "La URSS y el problema de la creación de la zona desnuclearizada en América Latina," *América Latina*, 2 (1979), pp. 7–8; John Redick, "Nuclear Trends in Latin America," in *Governance in the Western Hemisphere*, Viron P. Vaky, ed. (New York: Praeger, 1983), pp. 242–47.

21 *Granma Weekly Review*, December 19, 1982, p. 4.

22 See interview with Interior Minister, Comandante Tomás Borge, in "Revolution in Nicaragua," FRONTLINE, Public Broadcasting System, first aired April 1985.

23 U.S. Department of State, *Communist Interference in El Salvador: Documents Demonstrating Communist Support of the Salvadoran Insurgency* (Washington D.C.: February 23, 1981), Document E. These documents were released along with a U.S. Government "White Paper" on El Salvador. That report's accuracy has been questioned. For example, Document E is in part inconsistent with the White Paper's interpretation of the Soviet role. However, the authenticity of the documents themselves has not been successfully challenged.

24 Kiva Maidanik, "La unidad: un problema clave," *América Latina*, 3 (1980), p. 42 and *passim*.

25 Sergo Mikoyan, "Particularidades y enseñanzas de la revolución en Nicaragua," *Nicaragua: glorioso camino a la victoria* (Moscow: Academia de Ciencias de la URSS, 1981), p. 241.

26 Tatiana Vorozheikina, "Organizaciones revolucionarias de El Salvador: el movimiento popular," *América Latina*, 8 (August 1982), pp. 17–19.

27 Ilia Buliachov, "El Grupo Contadora: intricada ruta hacia la paz," *América Latina*, 1 (1985), pp. 82–85.

28 Theodore Schwab and Harold Sims, "Relations with Communist States," in *Nicaragua: The First Five Years*," Thomas W. Walker, ed. (New York: Praeger, 1985), pp. 447–66.

29 Interview, 1984, "Central America Project," WGBH-TV Educational Foundation, Boston. I was Series Editor for this Project.

30 Anatoli Olshani, "Colaboración económica y comercial con los paises miembros del CAME y Colombia," *América Latina*, 3 (1982), p. 34 and *passim*.
31 *Granma Weekly Review*, March 29, 1981, p. 1; interviews in Havana, March 1985.
32 Document captured by the U.S. armed forces in Grenada in Fall 1983 (hereafter CD), W. Richard Jacobs, "Grenada's Relations with the USSR," Moscow: July 11, 1983, p. 2.
33 CD, Embassy of Grenada in the USSR, "Relations with the CPSU," no date (probably late 1982), p. 2.
34 CD, "Agreement between the Government of Grenada and the Government of the USSR on deliveries from the USSR to Grenada of Special and Other Equipment," July 27, 1982, Article 2, p. 2; CD Embajada de Granada en Cuba, no title, February 18, 1982, p. 1; CD, Czechoslovaka Federal Ministry of Foreign Trade, "Invoice," no date.
35 CD, "Meeting at the Ministry of Communications," November 9, 1982, p. 3.
36 Interviews in Havana, March 1985.
37 "Declaration of the Meeting of Communist Parties of Latin America and the Caribbean," *Tricontinental Bimonthly*, 44 (July–August 1975), pp. 69–108.
38 Speech delivered by Castro, *Tricontinental Bimonthly*, 73 (1980), p. 34.
39 Maidanik, "La unidad," p. 50.
40 Cole Blasier, *The Giant's Rival: The USSR and Latin America* (Pittsburgh: University of Pittsburgh Press, 1983), p. 17.
41 See also *ibid.*, pp. 51–53.
42 Horacio Flores de la Peña, "La colaboración avanza," *América Latina*, 8 (August 1984), p. 28.
43 Comite Estatal de Estadísticas, *Anuario estadístico de Cuba 1983* (Havana), pp. 298–303.
44 Mauricio Lebedinsky, "Segundo simposio soviético-argentino," *América Latina*, 5 (1985), p. 93.
45 Anatoli Glinkin, "URSS-Brasil: 40 años de relaciones diplomáticas," *América Latina*, 5 (1985), pp. 83–84.
46 *Granma Weekly Review*, October 28, 1984, p. 3; November 4, 1984, p. 2; Victor Lukin, "XXXIX reunion del CAME en La Habana," *América Latina* 3 (1985), pp. 93–96.

6

Soviet Economic Relations with Cuba

Carmelo Mesa-Lago
Fernando Gil

SUMMARY OF SOVIET-CUBAN ECONOMIC RELATIONS: 1959–1985

The history of Soviet-Cuban economic relations can be divided into four periods. The first period, 1959–1966, was characterized by the establishment of strong economic linkages between the two nations which were vital to the consolidation and survival of the Revolution: the USSR signed a six-year trade agreement with Cuba, bought the sugar which the island previously sold to the United States, supplied practically all oil and weapons, and granted substantial economic and technical aid. The brief period of conflict between the two nations following the withdrawal of Soviet nuclear missiles in 1962 did not affect the bilateral economic relationship very much. And yet, in the second half of the 1960s, Cuba's unorthodox domestic economic policies as well as its sponsorship of guerrillas in Latin America in confrontations with pro-Soviet Communist parties were a source of mounting tensions. Between 1967 and 1969 (the second period), Cuban-Soviet relations reached a low ebb, the number of agreements signed declined, and the USSR restricted oil supplies, this last move provoking Cuban public criticism. The death of Ernesto (Ché) Guevara in Bolivia in 1967 and the subsequent decline of guerrilla activity in Latin America, combined with Castro's qualified support of the Soviet invasion of Czechoslovakia in 1968—as well as the patent failure of Cuba's unorthodox domestic economic policies in 1970—played a crucial role in restoring strong Soviet economic support to Cuba in the third period (1970–1975). An intergovernmental economic commission was established between the two countries, and Cuba entered CMEA and began receiving preferential treatment.

TABLE 6.1
Historical Highlights of Cuban-Soviet Economic Relations 1959–1985

Date	*Event*
February 1960	A bilateral 5 year (1960–1964) trade agreement signed in Havana by Premier Mikoyan grants Cuba MFN status, commits the USSR to buy 1 million tons of sugar annually, and to supply oil, machinery and chemicals. The USSR also provides credit for U.S. $100 million to purchase and construct new factories and for geological exploration in 1961–1965.
June–July 1960	U.S. refineries refuse to refine Soviet crude hence are nationalized and start to process Soviet oil. The U.S. reduces Cuba's sugar quota and the USSR promises to buy (at market prices) all sugar turned away by the U.S. and to increase oil supplies.
1961–1963	Soviet technical assistance plus additional development loans ($54 million) are granted for a fishing port and fleet, irrigation facilities, nickel industry, housing and fertilizer factory; more than 1,000 Soviet technicians start working in Cuba.
January 1964	The USSR signs a long-term agreement to purchase 24 million tons of Cuban sugar in 1965–1970.
September 1965	The USSR provides economic and technical aid ($133 million) to mechanize Cuba's sugar harvest and modernize sugar industry in 1965–1970.
1965–1966	Soviet development loans ($46 million) are provided for sugar industry and geological prospecting.
1967–1968	Cuban-Soviet relations reach a trough due to conflicts over Cuba's unorthodox domestic economic model and foreign policy. The number of agreements signed is the lowest since 1960. The USSR restricts oil supplies in 1967 and Castro denounces this action at the beginning of 1968.
1970	After Cuba's support of the Soviet invasion of Czechoslovakia in August 1968—and the beginning of Cuba's return to Soviet orthodoxy—Cuba introduces shifts in domestic and foreign policies:

TABLE 6.1 (cont.)

Date	*Event*
	both countries establish an Intergovernmental Commission for Economic and Scientific-Technical Cooperation (IC) and the USSR promises aid on oil refining, electricity, sugar and nickel industries, manufacturing of agricultural machinery, etc. In April of the same year Castro acknowledges that the USSR has supplied military equipment free in 1961–69 for $1.5 billion.
July 1972	Cuba becomes a full member of CMEA, receiving special developing member status including preferential trade treatment by more developed members.
December 1972	The IC signs four agreements in Moscow: (1) postpones payment of Cuban debt from trade deficits and development loans incurred in 1960–1972 until 1986 (to be repaid in 25 years) interest-free until repayment begins. (2) grants credit to cover Cuban trade deficits with USSR in 1973–1975 whose payment is also postponed until 1986, interest-free; (3) sets subsidized prices for Cuban sugar and nickel exports in 1973–1975; and (4) grants a credit ($362 million) to be paid over 25 years starting in 1976, for development of nickel, textile, energy, transportation, mechanization of sugar harvest, geological exploration, irrigation, etc.
1973–1975	Numerous Soviet-Cuban agreements are signed on metallurgy, electricity, new nickel plants, television, reconstruction of sugar mills, atomic energy, and construction of a sugarcane harvester factory. These projects are partly financed with the 1972 credit as well as with new Soviet credits ($387 million).
February 1976	First Cuban-Soviet five year economic and trade agreement (1976–1980) establishes mechanisms to be exchanged, a two-fold increase of trade value, and determines prices of goods (with new subsidies on sugar, nickel, and oil). Later agreements in 1976 commit Soviet aid on the construction of a nuclear power plant, a steel mill, and other industrial and agricultural projects for 1976–1980 for an estimated total of 1.5 billion. Also a long-term economic and technical cooperation agreement (1976–80) adjusts the value of Cuban imports from the USSR to the value of Cuban exports.
December 1979	In a speech to the National Assembly, President Castro unveils deficiencies in Soviet and CMEA supplies and their negative effects on the Cuban economy.
June 1980	CMEA and Cuba sign a ten year plan for economic and scientific-technological development with emphasis on sugar industry machinery, a nickel plant ($870 million for this alone), citrus, nuclear and electric energy, hydro-economic resources, and geological

TABLE 6.1 (cont.)

Date	*Event*
	prospecting; low interest loans (for an undisclosed amount) are provided to buy equipment, inputs, etc.
July 1981	Three agreements are signed with CMEA for 1981–1990: (1) $1 billion in credits ($600 million in 1981–1985 and $420 million in 1986–1990) to build 11 new sugar mills and modernize another 23 in order to increase sugar exports to USSR, GDR, and Bulgaria at prices above world market prices; (2) $762 million (half in 1981–1985) to expand citrus output to 2.5 million tons and increase exports (to USSR, GDR, Czechoslovakia, Hungary, and Bulgaria) to 1.5 million tons in 1990; and (3) on agriculture (no date available). Loans (part in hard currency) to be repaid in 17 years—4 of grace—at 2 percent interest.
August 1981	Second Soviet-Cuban five year economic and trade agreement (1981–1985) is signed, but no specifics are revealed.
July 1984	Annual Cuban-Soviet protocol on economic and scientific-technical cooperation provides for continuation of nuclear and thermo-electric plants, continuation of nickel plant funding in Punta Gorda (and remodeling of two existing plants), oil exploration and exploitation, improvement of cane harvester, new unit of steel complex, oil refinery, and textile plants.
October 1984	Cuban-Soviet long-term cooperation agreement, 1985–2000 signed at CMEA meeting held in Havana emphasizes increased efficiency in Cuban existing resources, saving in fuel and inputs, improvement in quality, increase in traditional and new exports, self-sufficiency in foodstuffs, strengthening Cuba's integration in CMEA and independence from capitalist countries, creation of Soviet-Cuban joint enterprises and joint exports to third countries, and processing Soviet raw materials in Cuba. The USSR commits aid in agriculture, energy, metallurgy, electronics, machinery, chemistry, construction, and transportation.
December 1984	Castro declares that absolute priority will be given to investments to increase exports to the USSR and other socialist countries, that commitments to them must be honored, and that the practice of diverting exports, earmarked for socialist countries, to hard-currency countries will be terminated. He reports that the USSR has guaranteed fuel deliveries for 1986–1990 and that any saving Cuba makes can be sold for hard currency.
June 1985	Cuban-Soviet annual protocol on trade and payments is the highest ever: $9.9 million; Cuba is expected to increase exports of sugar, citrus, and nickel, and the USSR to augment deliveries of oil and oil products, foodstuffs, fertilizer, steel, machinery, and equipment. In

TABLE 6.1 (cont.)

Date	*Event*
	a new form of cooperation, Cuban garment factories receive Soviet inputs and produce goods for the USSR in exchange for additional inputs for domestic production.
April 1986	At the annual session of the Cuban-Soviet Intergovernmental Commission for Economic, Scientific, and Technical Cooperation, four agreements for 1986–1990 are signed. One increases Soviet investment credit by 50% over the previous quinquenium (reported as $3 billion); another document deals with the trade exchange agreement for 1986–1990; other agreements cover planning coordination and technical aid.

Sources: Cole Blasier, "COMECON in Cuban Development," Blasier and Mesa-Lago, eds. in *Cuba in the World,* (Pittsburgh: University of Pittsburgh Press, 1979), pp. 229–40; Lawrence Theriot and Je Nelle Matheson, "Soviet Economic Relations with non-European CMEA: Cuba, Vietnam, and Mongolia," in Joint Economic Committee, *Soviet Economy in Time of Change* (Washington D.C.: Government Printing Office, 1979), II, pp. 551–57; Oscar Pino Santos & Osvaldo Martínez, "Relaciones economicas de Cuba con los países miembros del CAME," Santiago, Economic Commission for Latin America, November 1979; Jorge Pérez-López and René Pérez López, *A Calender of Cuban Bilateral Agreements 1959–1976* (Pittsburgh: University of Pittsburgh, 1980); Sergio G. Roca, "Cuba's International Economic Relations in the 1980s," Columbia University, December 6, 1985; and *Granma* and *Granma Weekly Review*, 1980–1986.

Several agreements were then signed which postponed the payment of Cuba's debt to the USSR, granted new Soviet credits to the island, introduced significant subsidies to Cuban industries making exports to the USSR, and provided substantial Soviet technical aid. In the fourth and current period (from 1976 on), Soviet-Cuban relations were strengthened even more with the introduction of the Soviet model of economic organization. There was—and is—close cooperation between the two nations in the African wars in Angola and Ethiopia. During this period, the Soviet-Cuban economic relationship has become routinized and strengthened, and Soviet support has significantly increased. Thus since 1976, the two nations have signed three five-year trade and economic agreements (1976–1980, 1981–1985, and 1986–1990) plus a long-term economic cooperation treaty (1986–2000). Soviet subsidies to Cuban exports have increased significantly as have Soviet trade credits and other development aid.

As Table 6.2 shows, the expansion of Soviet economic aid to Cuba since 1976 has resulted in greater Cuban economic reliance upon the

TABLE 6.2
Cuba's Economic Reliance on the USSR
1961–1975 and 1976–1984

Indicators	*1961–1975*	*1976–1984*
Cuba's percent of total trade with USSR[a]	48%	64%
Percent of Cuba's sugar exports (value) to USSR[a]	45%	72%
Percent of Cuban imports supplied by the USSR[a]	52%	62%
Percent of Cuba's oil imports supplied by the USSR[a]	98%	99%
Cuba's terms of trade with USSR[b]	187	86
Soviet economic aid to Cuba[c]	$7.0 billion	$33.8 billion
Average per year	$ .5 billion	$3.7 billion
% of Cuba's GSP at end of period	4%	18%
Cuban debt to USSR[d]	$4.8 billion	$3.7 billion
Average per year	$320 million	$869 million

a. Annual average.
b. In 1974 and 1984; 1968 = 100.
c. Cumulative in each period.
d. Cumulative in each period; does not take repayment into account.
Sources: Tables 6.4, 6.5, 6.7, 6.10, 6.11, 6.13.

USSR: Cuban foreign trade with the USSR increased from an average of 48 percent of trade value in 1961–1975 to 64 percent in 1976–1984; sugar exports to the USSR jumped from 45 percent to 72 percent of the Cuban total; Soviet economic aid (including both subsidies and loans) rose 700 percent from an annual average of $470 million to $3.7 billion (or an increment from 4 percent to 18 percent of Cuba's Global Social Product—GSP[1]): Cuba's debt with the USSR significantly expanded, although under very generous terms: but Cuba's terms of trade with the Soviets deteriorated. The decade since 1976 has seen increased Cuban dependence on Soviet imports (and thus less flexibility to trade with market economies) regardless of fluctuation of world sugar prices, and continued dependency on Soviet fuels despite Cuba's increase in domestic output as well as Cuba's reexport of Soviet oil for hard currency. Similarly, Cuban trade deficits with the USSR have grown dramatically (after a notable elimination of such deficits in 1975–1978)[2] and there has been a significant expansion of Soviet military supplies to the island.

THE NATURE AND ROOTS OF CUBAN DEPENDENCY

Historically Cuba has been a monoculture economy, concentrating its efforts on producing a few raw materials for export and foreign exchange (fundamentally sugar) while producing very few of the goods it consumes.[3] Naturally, foreign trade has been pivotal to Cuba's economy, and export concentration has made the economy more vulnerable to world price fluctuations than if it had a more diversified base. Under the Revolution, output for domestic consumption has been expanded somewhat (which combined with rationing has induced a decline in manufacture imports), but the country has become more dependent on imports of capital goods and fuels. Furthermore, export concentration has continued and the nation's dependence on foreign trade has worsened.

Table 6.3 demonstrates Cuba's increasing dependency. From 1959–1974, the average percentage of exports and total transactions over GSP were respectively 9.7 percent and 24 percent, but such averages doubled to 20.7 percent and 45.2 percent from 1975–1986. The table also shows that export concentration (sugar exports as a percentage of total exports) has fluctuated from 74 percent to 90 percent in the entire period, without a significant steady reduction on sugar dependency.[4] The value of Cuban exports and trade dependency indicators are positively correlated to sugar prices (in the world and Soviet markets); paradoxically, when prices and the value of exports are low (with a negative effect on the economy), trade dependency seems to decline and vice-versa. There is also a significant relationship between international sugar prices and Cuban GSP.

Throughout the Revolution, the value of merchandise exports have been lower than the value of merchandise imports. Until 1972, the value of exports was basically stagnant owing to low Cuban sugar harvests (except for the record crop of 1970) combined with low world sugar prices, except for 1963–1964 when Soviet prices for Cuban sugar imports were slightly above the world market price. World sugar prices oscillated in the 1970s, but the average price in 1973–1985 was 3.3 times

TABLE 6.3
Cuba's Foreign Commerce and Trade Dependency, 1959–1986

	Total Merchandise Trade[a]					*Trade Dependency*		
						(% of GSP)		
Years	Export *(f.o.b.)*	Imports *(c.i.f.)*	*Total Transactions*	*Trade Balance*	*Trade Balance (millions US$)*[b]	*Total Transactions*	*Exports*	*Export Concentration: Sugar Exports as % Total Exports*
1959	636.0	674.8	1,310.8	−38.8	−38.8	n.a.	n.a.	75
1960	608.3	579.9	1,188.2	28.4	28.4	n.a.	n.a.	78
1961	626.4	638.7	1,265.1	−12.3	−12.3	n.a.	n.a.	85
1962	522.3	759.3	1,281.6	−237.0	−237.0	24.8	10.1	83
1963	545.1	867.3	1,412.4	−322.2	−322.2	25.1	9.7	87
1964	714.3	1,018.8	1,733.1	−304.5	−304.5	26.4	10.9	88
1965	690.6	866.2	1,556.8	−175.6	−175.6	23.0	10.2	86
1966	597.8	925.5	1,523.3	−327.7	−327.7	22.3	8.8	85
1967	705.0	999.1	1,704.1	−294.1	−294.1	23.6	9.8	86
1968	651.4	1,102.3	1,753.7	−450.9	−450.9	23.7	8.9	77
1969	666.7	1,221.7	1,888.4	−555.0	−555.0	26.1	9.2	76
1970	1,049.5	1,311.0	2,360.5	−261.5	−261.5	27.6	12.3	77
1971	861.2	1,386.6	2,248.7	−526.3	−571.4	25.2	9.6	76
1972	770.9	1,189.8	1,960.7	−418.9	−454.8	18.9	7.4	74

1973	1,153.0	1,462.6	2,615.6	−309.6	−379.9	22.0	9.7	75
1974	2,236.5	2,225.9	4,462.4	10.6	12.8	33.2	16.7	87
1975	2,952.2	3,113.1	6,065.3	−160.9	−194.1	38.3–43.6	18.7–21.2	90
1976	2,692.3	3,179.7	5,872.0	−487.4	−594.4	37.0–41.7	17.0–19.1	87
1977	2,918.4	3,461.6	6,380.0	−543.2	−684.1	43.5	19.9	83
1978	3,440.1	3,573.8	7,013.9	−133.7	−177.8	43.0	21.1	87
1979	3,499.2	3,687.5	7,186.7	−188.3	−259.7	42.3	20.6	86
1980	3,966.7	4,627.0	8,593.7	−660.3	−931.3	48.8	22.5	84
1981	4,233.8	5,114.0	9,337.8	−890.2	−1,139.8	42.1	19.0	79
1982	4,933.2	5,530.6	10,463.8	−597.4	−717.2	45.3	21.3	77
1982	5,534.9	6,222.1	11,757.0	−687.2	−797.2	48.3	22.7	74
1983	5,462.1	7,207.2	12,669.3	−1,745,1	−1,949.8	48.5	20.9	76
1984	5,983.0	7,983.2	13,966.3	−2,000.3	−2,180.3	51.9	22.2	74
1985	5,325.0	7,569.0	12,894.0	−2,244.0	−2,715.2	48.3	20.0	n.a.
1986								
Cumulative Trade Deficit (1959–1986):				−14,533.	−16,958.5			

a. Figures are in millions of Cuban Pesos.

b. Based on Cuba's official exchange rate unilaterally set since 1971.

Sources: Comité Estatal de Estadísticas (CEE), *Anuario Estadístico de Cuba (AEC) 1984* (La Habana, 1985) except for 1985 which is from Banco Nacional de Cuba, CEE, *Cuba Quarterly Economic Report*, December 1985. Conversion pesos/U.S. dollars using Cuba's exchange rates. Percent of GSP estimated by the authors based on Cuba's official series; for 1975–1976 there are two series, hence the two percentages. Export concentration from Mesa-Lago and Jorge Pérez-López, "Imbroglios on the Cuban Economy," *Comparative Economic Studies*. 27:1 (Spring, 1985), p. 78 and *AEC 1984*.

the average price of 1959–1972. Furthermore, Soviet prices in 1973–1985 were 5.7 times higher than in 1959–1972. This basically explains the expansion in the value of Cuban exports since 1973. On the other hand, imports increased since 1963 due to a step-up in importing capital and intermediate goods and fuels against a backdrop of rising prices of imported goods.

In the 27 years of the Revolution, Cuba has generated a merchandise trade surplus only twice (1960 and 1974, for a total of 39 million pesos); in the remaining years the trade balance has been in the red, resulting in a cumulative deficit of 14.5 billion pesos ($17 billion) in 1959–1986. The trade deficit worsened in the 1980s. During the last five-year plan (1981–1985) the deficit increased 190 percent over the previous quinquenium; and the combined deficit in 1980–1985 was 14 percent higher than the cumulative deficit of the previous 21 years. The current five-year plan (1986–1990) has as its major goals, the vigorous expansion of exports and the tight control of imports, but the reduction of the 1986 deficit will be difficult due to the severe damage on the sugar crop inflicted by Hurricane Kate.

In almost 28 years, and despite the radical changes in Cuba's economic and social structure and the enormous concentration of state power, the Revolution has been unable to solve the problems of export concentration, trade dependency, and trade deficits. In fact, some of these problems have worsened in the last decade. Herein lies the root of Cuba's continued economic reliance on the USSR.

TRADE-PARTNER CONCENTRATION AND INTERNATIONAL DIVISION OF LABOR

Historically, Cuba's economy has been highly integrated with that of a single developed country; heavy reliance on one major trade partner has made the island more vulnerable to economic and political influence. Prior to the Revolution, about two-thirds of Cuba's trade was with the United States, and it normally resulted in a deficit against Cuba. The mounting conflict between the two nations resulted in a rapid decline of trade by 1962; the USSR and CMEA, however, gradually substituted for U.S. trade and today they greatly surpass the previous U.S. trade share.

The history of Soviet-Cuban trade under the Revolution is presented in Table 6.4. Figures, however, should be taken with caution for two reasons: (1) the peso-dollar exchange rates are set unilaterally by Cuba since the peso is not freely exchanged in the international market; and (2) Soviet-Cuban trade is essentially a barter exchange and prices derived from Soviet or Cuban data are not indicative of hard currency flows, i.e., they do not necessarily reflect real economic value.[5]

In 1961–1975, the USSR's share of Cuba's trade transactions averaged 48 percent, but in 1976–1986 it increased to 65 percent; the total CMEA average share (including the USSR) rose from 68 percent to 77 percent in the same periods and reached 86 percent in 1983–1986.[6] Currently Cuba is the seventh largest USSR trade partner, accounting for 5 percent of total Soviet trade. Also, within CMEA, Cuba is the country with the smallest percentage of imports from market countries. Amazingly, despite the relative distances involved, Cuba imports less from the West than Eastern Europe.

Between 1962 and 1974, Cuban trade with the USSR always ended in a deficit. In this period, the Soviet share of Cuba's total trade deficit averaged 80 percent, and in 1972–1974 the deficit with the USSR alone was higher than Cuba's total deficit. This situation changed dramatically in 1975–1978, when Cuban trade with the USSR resulted in a substantial surplus owing to the concessionary prices granted by the USSR to Cuban sugar and nickel and Soviet oil (more on this below). And yet the trade deficit reappeared after 1979, reaching a record of around $1 billion in 1980–1981 and 1984–1985 ($1.4 billion in 1986). The Cuban-Soviet cumulative merchandise trade balance in 1959–1886 resulted in a deficit of $9.3 billion, but without Soviet subsidies (concessionary prices) such a deficit would have been more than five time higher. Cuban trade with other CMEA members has resulted in a small deficit amounting to a minor share of Cuba's total deficit.

The above figures indicate an increase in Cuba's trade dependence with the USSR and CMEA countries. Such trade is largely deficitary in spite of enormous Soviet subsidies. Based on the latter, Cuban leaders and scholars have often argued that their relationship with the USSR (and socialist international economic relations in general) are completely different than the exploitative relations Cuba had in the past with the United States (and capitalist international relations with developing countries in general).[7] In 1962, CMEA adopted a policy of "international socialist division of labor" through which member nations specialized on products in which they have a comparative advantage, thus reducing costs, avoiding duplication of production, facilitating coordination and integration, with alleged gains for all.

TABLE 6.4
Cuba's Merchandise Trade with the USSR and CMEA, 1959–1986
(in million Cuban pesos)

Years	Exports (f.o.b.)	Imports (c.i.f.)	Soviet-Cuban Transactions	% of Total Cuban transactions with USSR	% of Total Cuban transactions with CMEA	Trade Balance: Million Pesos	Trade Balance: Million U.S. Dollars	Trade Balance: Without Soviet Trade Subsidies	% of Soviet Deficit over Cuba's Total Trade Deficit
1959	12.9	.01	12.9	1.0	1.0	12.9	12.9	12.9[c]	0[a]
1960	103.5	80.2	183.7	15.5	17.1	23.3	23.3	23.3[c]	0[b]
1961	303.7	262.6	566.3	44.8	57.0	41.1	41.1	37.3[c]	0[a]
1962	221.9	411.6	633.3	49.4	67.0	−189.5	−189.5	−191.9[c]	80.0
1963	163.9	460.9	624.8	44.2	63.3	−297.0	−297.0	−294.8[c]	92.2
1964	275.0	410.0	685.0	39.5	51.8	−135.0	−135.0	−135.3[c]	44.3
1965	322.5	428.4	750.9	48.2	61.5	−105.9	−105.9	−115.2[c]	60.3
1966	274.0	521.2	795.2	52.2	67.3	−247.2	−247.2	−255.0[c]	75.4
1967	366.1	582.0	948.1	55.6	68.4	−215.9	−215.9	−432.9	73.4
1968	289.6	671.8	961.4	54.8	68.3	−383.2	−383.2	−538.2	84.8
1969	233.0	657.9	890.9	47.2	62.0	−424.9	−424.9	−491.9	76.6

1970	529.0	690.6	1,219.6	51.7	64.0	−161.6	−161.6	−371.6	61.8
1971	303.7	730.8	1,034.5	46.0	59.5	−427.1	−439.9	−538.9	81.2
1972	224.1	714.4	938.5	47.9	60.2	−479.3	−523.4	−536.4	117.0
1973	476.7	811.0	1,287.7	49.2	61.7	−334.3	−410.2	−605.2	108.0
1974	811.2	1,024.9	1,836.1	41.1	52.9	−213.7	−275.8	−341.8	213.7[b]
1975	1,661.9	1,250.2	2,912.1	48.0	56.0	411.7	496.6	−273.4	0[a]
1976	1,638.3	1,490.2	3,128.5	53.3	63.5	148.1	180.6	−1,246.4	0[a]
1977	2,965.8	1,858.3	3,924.1	61.5	71.6	207.5	261.3	−1,719.7	0[a]
1978	2,495.5	2,327.7	4,823.2	68.8	79.2	167.8	223.1	−2,457.9	0[a]
1979	2,370.0	2,513.4	4,883.4	68.0	79.1	−143.4	−197.8	−2,898.8	76.2
1980	2,253.5	2,903.7	5,157.2	60.0	71.7	−650.2	−916.8	−3,354.6	98.5
1981	2,357.5	3,234.0	5,591.5	59.9	74.0	−876.5	−1,121.9	−3,839.9	98.5
1982	3,289.6	3,744.4	7,034.0	67.2	81.5	−454.8	−545.8	−4,327.8	76.1
1983	3,881.8	4,245.3	8,127.1	69.1	83.1	−363.5	−421.7	−4,412.7	52.9
1984	3,952.2	4,782.4	8,734.6	68.8	82.6	−830.2	−935.1	−5,156.1	48.0
1985	4,478.7	5,373.0	9,851.7	70.5	83.0	−894.3	−1,073.0	n.a.	53.6
1986	3,933.6	5,313.9	9,247.5	71.2	86.2	−1,380.3	−1,670.2	n.a.	61.5

a. There was a deficit in the total trade balance.
b. There was a surplus in the total trade balance.
c. Only sugar subsidies.
Source: Junta Central de Planificación, *Boletin Estadistico (BE) 1970, AEC 1972–1985, Cuba Quarterly Economic Report*, December 1986, and Table 6.3. The estimate of Cuban deficit without Soviet trade subsidies (to sugar, nickel, oil) is based on Table 6.12.

Theoretically, the socialist policy avoids the advantage which developed capitalist nations enjoy over less developed partners. Nevertheless, as Elizabeth Valkenier reports in her chapter, in the early 1970s, Soviet experts abandoned the fiction of two separate competing world markets and acknowledged the existence of a single world market with socialist and capitalist segments. By the end of the decade, under pressure from increasing economic interdependence, the Soviet Union went further, recognizing a world-wide international division of labor (not a separate one for each segment of the world market) based on comparative advantage. Having done this, as Valkenier argues, Soviet experts stopped advocating import substituting industrialization for the LDCs and insisted instead that production of raw materials in LDCs best contributes to the international division of labor.

Within CMEA, Cuba has been assigned the role of supplier of raw materials in exchange for capital and intermediate and manufactured goods from the USSR and other developed member nations. Interestingly, CMEA relations with the rest of Latin America follow a similar pattern: member countries export machinery, equipment, chemicals, and manufactures, while importing raw materials. Such behavior has prompted the Economic Commission for Latin America (ECLA) to observe asymmetry in these relations similar to those existing between capitalist developed countries and Latin America.[8]

Although the issue of whether or not Cuba benefits from the international socialist division of labor will be analyzed in the following sections, here we should suggest some problems resulting from Cuba's integration into CMEA: (1) since Cuba needs vital Soviet and CMEA supplies for its own development, such needs must be incorporated into Soviet/CMEA production plans, hence making Cuban plans dependent on foreign decision; (2) due to the rigidity and length of the plans, Cuba must foresee its needs with five years of anticipation, reducing flexibility in its decision making and restricting its ability to obtain unplanned goods; (3) collective participation in CMEA's Cuban projects requires complex coordination among various countries, thus increasing the Soviet role and often resulting in significant building delays; (4) better trade based on nonconvertible currency ties up the island's trade, hence reducing its capacity to select partners; (5) significantly longer distances between Cuba and the USSR and other CMEA members (compared to the United States and Canada) substantially increase freight costs and the delivery time; and, (6) the solution of problems is delayed by the complex CMEA bureaucracy.[9] Despite Cuba's enormous effort to expand its merchant marine in 1980, its ships carried only 20 percent of the nation's foreign trade, the rest being handled by rented or foreign ships (mostly from CMEA). If trade were shifted to the West, Cuba's current merchant marine could handle practically all of its overseas commerce.[10]

PRINCIPAL CUBAN EXPORTS TO THE USSR AND PRICE SUBSIDIES

The USSR, and to a lesser extent the remaining CMEA members, are the principal buyers of most Cuban exports: sugar, nickel, citrus, alcoholic beverages, and cigarettes. They only buy a small fraction of Cuba's cigar exports and practically no fish exports. The USSR gives concessionary prices to Cuban sugar and nickel, but no information is available on other products. Table 6.5 contrasts, in quantity and value, the proportion of various Cuban exports bought by the USSR. The Soviet share of Cuba's sugar exports (in quantum) increased from 38 percent in 1965–1975 to 52 percent in 1976–1984 (about the same proportion the United States bought from Cuba prior to the revolution), but in value terms—because of Soviet subsidized prices—the shares increased respectively to 45 percent and 72 percent. In the same periods, the quantum share of sugar bought by the rest of CMEA and other socialist countries declined from 18 percent to 13 percent, but the total share going to all socialist countries increased from 56 percent to 65 percent.

Table 6.6 shows that in only three years (1963, 1972, and 1974) was the Soviet price paid for Cuban sugar below the world price. In all cases a decline in Cuba's sugar output—combined in the 1970s with a decline of U.S. output, an increase in world demand, and inflation—induced an increase in world price,[11] and the fixed Soviet price lagged behind. In the 1960s, a decline in the world price automatically restored the concessionary fixed Soviet price, but in 1972–1975 the USSR had to increase its price to catch up with booming prices in the world market. To cope with this problem, in 1975 the USSR agreed to fix a minimum price of 30 cents (in peso—then $0.29) per pound of sugar in 1976–1980, but it indexed this price with the prices of a Soviet import basket containing oil, steel, machinery, food, and other "basic goods."[12] In the meantime, world demand for sugar slowed down, world output and stocks increased significantly (with the incentive of record prices), and the production of sugar substitutes expanded once its production

TABLE 6.5

Cuban Exports[a] of Major Products to the USSR, 1965–1984 (Quantum Percentages and Value Percentages of Total Exports)

	Sugar		Nickel[c]		Citrus		Alcoholic Beverages		Tobacco				
									Cigarettes		Cigars		Total
Years[b]	*Quantum*	*Value*	*Quantum*	*Value*	*Quantum*	*Value*	*Quantum*	*Value*	*Quantum*	*Value*	*Quantum*	*Value*	*Value*
1965	46.2	56.6	67.0	67.2	0.0	0.0	9.6	19.9	10.2	9.6	4.7	3.4	2.2
1967	43.5	56.0	n.a.	n.a.	0.0	0.0	33.1	45.9	83.5	83.5	4.2	3.4	30.5
1968	39.7	50.8	50.8	43.6	4.9	4.8	36.9	50.4	88.3	88.2	8.4	8.4	29.4
1969	28.2	36.3	56.4	45.8	19.2	20.1	33.1	38.8	88.5	89.0	7.9	7.8	35.6
1970	45.0	51.8	53.5	65.7	24.9	25.4	13.7	18.2	80.4	81.2	5.2	5.0	20.1
1971	28.7	32.4	68.1	68.8	33.2	35.1	0.0	0.0	66.8	66.8	8.0	8.8	9.3
1972	26.5	26.2	57.0	63.0	28.8	29.3	34.9	63.7	63.2	63.3	14.7	15.5	13.2
1973	34.6	42.4	50.8	62.8	32.8	31.5	46.6	59.0	92.5	92.4	16.8	17.6	24.3
1974	36.0	36.6	52.9	65.1	36.6	34.1	65.9	72.0	93.3	93.2	11.9	12.7	22.8
1975	55.5	58.4	58.3	66.3	32.3	32.0	77.8	86.2	98.1	98.0	16.4	15.0	28.6
1976	52.7	65.3	53.9	58.9	39.3	39.4	77.9	84.5	90.1	89.6	7.8	5.8	12.6
1977	60.8	77.0	72.2	75.1	35.7	36.3	75.6	80.5	83.0	82.0	8.9	7.0	14.4
1978	54.7	79.0	47.0	56.0	36.1	36.8	69.7	75.2	94.9	94.8	0.0	0.0	13.0
1979	53.4	76.4	38.8	44.6	37.1	37.0	71.2	73.9	82.9	81.8	0.5	0.3	9.0
1980	44.2	61.8	48.0	49.2	39.2	39.5	72.3	74.4	97.5	96.9	3.1	1.6	5.8
1981	45.4	58.7	49.0	64.3	33.2	35.7	73.5	72.1	27.3	28.0	4.0	1.7	1.6
1982	57.3	73.4	47.6	66.4	30.2	31.9	80.0	80.1	82.0	80.7	3.0	1.0	4.9
1983	50.5	75.8	48.1	68.9	39.5	40.9	80.0	80.0	78.6	77.8	5.1	1.7	9.1
1984	52.1	77.4	49.7	67.0	41.0	41.6	80.1	79.5	78.1	74.3	6.4	2.7	3.8

a. Cuba does not export any fish or seafood to the USSR.
b. The years 1959–1964 and 1966 are not available from Cuban statistical yearbooks.
c. Cuba exports practically all its nickel sulfide to the USSR, but only small quantities of sinter and oxide.
Source: *AEC 1972* to *1984*.

TABLE 6.6
Prices of Sugar and Nickel in the Soviet-Cuban Market and the World Market 1960–1984[a]
(in U.S. cents per pound)

	Raw Sugar			Nickel Sulfide		
Years	*USSR*	*World*	*Ratio*	*USSR*	*World*	*Ratio*
1960	3.2	3.1	1.03	n.a.	74.0	n.a.
1961	4.1	2.9	1.41	n.a.	77.6	n.a.
1962	4.1	2.9	1.41	n.a.	79.9	n.a.
1963	6.1	8.5	0.72	n.a.	79.0	n.a.
1964	6.1	5.9	1.03	n.a.	79.0	n.a.
1965	6.1	2.1	2.90	n.a.	78.6	n.a.
1966	6.1	1.9	3.21	n.a.	78.7	n.a.
1967	6.1	2.0	3.05	n.a.	86.5	n.a.
1968	6.1	2.0	3.05	72.1	94.1	0.77
1969	6.1	3.4	1.79	81.8	107.2	0.76
1970	6.1	3.8	1.60	283.8	129.1	2.20
1971	6.1	4.5	1.36	201.7	133.0	1.52
1972	6.4	7.4	0.86	194.5	139.7	1.39
1973	12.1	9.6	1.26	273.6	153.0	1.79
1974	19.2	29.7	0.66	273.2	173.5	1.57
1975	26.4	20.4	1.29	273.2	205.8	1.33
1976	27.6	11.5	2.40	276.2	225.6	1.22
1977	27.9	8.1	3.44	285.2	236.0	1.21
1978	36.1	7.8	4.63	298.1	209.1	1.42
1979	36.8	9.7	3.79	316.9	271.5	1.16
1980	47.5	28.2	1.68	319.3	295.7	1.08
1981	35.1	16.9	2.08	489.2	270.0	1.81
1982	34.2	8.4	4.07	489.2	219.4	2.23
1983	45.9	8.5	5.40	489.2	212.0	2.30
1984	43.9	5.2	8.44	491.7	215.6	2.28

a. Cuba is the largest single world exporter of sugar and past fluctuations in that country's production have affected its exports to the world sugar market (approximately 15 million metric tons) by about 1 million tons. Hence, there is a negative correlation between Cuban sugar output and world market prices. A 1% increase in Cuba's share of the world market can induce a −0.7% decline in the world price and vice-versa. See C. Suan Tan, *Cuba–USSR Sugar Trade*, The World Bank, Division Working Paper, 1986–2, June 1986.

Sources: Jorge Pérez-López, "Sugar and Petroleum in Cuban–Soviet Terms of Trade," in Cole Blasier and Mesa-Lago, eds., *Cuba in the World* (Pittsburgh: University of Pittsburgh Press, 1979), pp. 282–83; Mesa–Lago, *The Economy of Socialist Cuba* (Albuquerque: University of New Mexico Press, 1981), pp. 88–91; José A. González, "Comercio Exterior entre Cuba y la Unión Soviética: Resultado económico e implicaciones políticas," University of Pittsburgh, December 1984; and authors' updating based on *AEC 1983* and *1984*, and IMF, *International Financial Statistics 1980 to 1985*.

costs became competitive. Accordingly, in 1976, the world sugar price began to decline, while the Soviet price increased, reaching a ratio of 4.6 in 1978 (See Table 6.6). The epidemic of sugar cane rust badly afflicted plantations in Cuba and the Caribbean in 1979–1981, inducing a decline in sugar exports and a second boom in prices. This should not have affected the Soviet-Cuban index, and yet the Soviet prices rose notably in 1980. The restoration of Cuban (and other sugar exporters') production in 1982–1985 coincided with the conversion of the European Economic Community from net importer to significant exporter (now with a 17 percent share of world exports) and the reduction of Japanese imports. The continuous expansion of high-fructose corn syrup (now costing one-third less than sugar from cane) and sluggish world demand further induced a sharp decline in world sugar prices. Throughout this period, the world price steadily declined, hence new record ratios of Soviet/world price of 5.4 and 8.4 were set in 1983 and 1984, to Cuba's advantage. Significantly, the average ratio of Soviet/world price increased from 1.7 in 1960–1975 to 4.0 in the 1976–1984 period.

The USSR is the largest sugar producer in the world, but with the exception of the second half of the 1960s, it has had to import sugar to satisfy domestic needs. In 1960–1964 when the USSR began buying Cuban sugar in large quantities, it had a deficit of 1.4 million metric tons, Cuba filling most of it. However, in 1965–1969, despite a Soviet sugar surplus and declining world prices, the USSR continued to buy Cuban sugar at highly concessionary prices. Since 1970, the USSR has suffered an increasing shortfall in its domestic sugar needs. Cuba has increased its sugar sales to the USSR in the last fifteen years, but the question is by how much and for how long the Soviets will continue to pay concessionary prices.[13] Furthermore, when Cuban sugar output has been low and world prices high (e.g., 1963, 1974, 1980–1981), the USSR has allowed Cuba to sell part of its export in the world market to obtain badly needed hard currency. Some scholars have argued that if Cuba had sold its sugar to the United States, at preferential U.S. prices, it would have earned more than by selling it to the USSR. One study using Cuba's total sugar exports calculated that in 1962–1972, Cuba lost a cumulative $780 million for that concept.[14] Another study based on Cuban sugar exports to the USSR and the U.S. import price, estimated the cumulative loss at $415 million in 1960–1972, but showed Cuban gains since 1973 which gradually reduced the deficit and generated a $1 billion cumulative surplus by 1976.[15] In the present study we have extended the analysis to 1984 and applied the methodology of each of the two studies estimating cumulative surpluses for Cuba. $32 billion for

1962–1984 in the first case and $13 billion for 1960–1984 in the second. Furthermore, the U.S. sugar market has shrunk since the mid-1970s due to the domestic production of sugar substitutes (particularly corn syrup now used in the soft drink industry), as well as dietary and health considerations. U.S. sugar import quotas further declined by 30 percent in 1984–1986 with an estimated loss of $300 million in export earnings for Caribbean sugar producers.[16]

Until 1971, the USSR bought one-fourth of Cuba's exports of nickel-cobalt sinter, and about two-fifths of its oxide. Beginning in 1982, the Soviet Union stopped purchases of both products, (except in 1983–1984, it bought about one-fifth of Cuban oxide). On the other hand, Cuba increased its sales of nickel sulfide to the USSR from an 85 percent share in 1968 to 100 percent since 1973 (see Table 6.5). Since 1981, Cuba has sold less nickel to the USSR than in the 1960s and 1970s, but what was sold was at a higher price. Only in 1968–1969 (see Table 6.6) has the Soviet price for nickel been below the world price. Since the 1970s, the Soviet price has been set for the five-year plan periods, but when world prices have greatly increased (as in 1976–1977), the Soviet price has been raised. In 1981–1984, as the nickel world price declined, Cuba greatly benefitted from the Soviet concessionary price which was more than double the world price.[17]

Cuba has difficulties in exporting its citrus to market economies (owing to marketing and quality problems), while these products are in high demand in CMEA. Hence, the USSR has been buying an increasing amount of Cuban citrus exports with no essential difference between the Soviet price and the price offered by other buyers (see table 6.5). However, the Soviet-Cuban 1985–2000 agreement apparently guarantees preferential prices for citrus exports, higher than world market prices, as well as a stable CMEA market. Cuba is expected to increase citrus exports to CMEA countries by 300 percent between 1985 and 1990, although they have fallen short of their commitments in the past.[18]

Cuba also exports most of its rum and other alcoholic beverages to the USSR. Soviet prices were higher than those of other CMEA buyers until 1973 when they became equal or slightly lower. In 1982–1984, Cuba sold 80 percent of these products to the USSR and the rest to other CMEA countries. The Soviet share of Cuba's total tobacco exports has declined, but the Russians keep buying 85 percent of exports of cigarettes, while the rest go to other CMEA members. On the other hand, Cuban cigars are in high demand and command good prices in the West, hence the Soviet share of these exports has declined from 9 percent to 4 percent.

TABLE 6.7

Percentage Distribution of Cuban Imports supplied by USSR, all Socialist, and Market Economies, 1967–1984

Imports[a]	*1967*	*1968*	*1969*	*1970*	*1971*	*1972*	*1973*	*1974*	*1975*	*1976*	*1977*	*1978*	*1979*	*1980*	*1981*	*1982*	*1983*	*1984*
Foodstuffs																		
USSR	67.8	66.6	64.2	60.2	58.0	63.8	60.6	52.6	54.4	65.4	73.6	76.3	75.7	59.2	64.7	67.9	62.0	63.3
Socialist	82.5	86.8	85.4	75.2	71.1	77.4	75.2	71.6	66.4	77.1	80.8	87.4	87.7	74.6	75.6	86.6	78.0	74.9
Market	17.5	13.2	14.6	24.8	28.9	22.6	24.8	28.4	33.6	22.9	19.2	12.7	12.3	25.4	24.4	13.4	22.0	25.1
Raw Materials																		
USSR	82.0	85.8	78.2	75.3	77.6	85.5	89.6	74.5	77.7	81.9	86.5	86.9	87.2	74.9	82.6	86.2	80.7	79.0
Socialist	86.4	90.4	83.2	80.4	84.6	90.6	92.0	77.5	80.6	86.5	89.2	91.4	90.5	76.7	84.5	89.3	83.6	80.8
Market	13.6	16.7	16.8	19.6	15.4	9.4	8.0	22.5	19.4	13.5	10.8	8.6	9.5	23.3	15.5	10.7	16.4	19.2
Fuel																		
USSR	99.3	98.6	97.9	97.6	98.0	97.5	99.3	97.6	98.3	99.4	99.6	99.5	99.7	97.9	99.4	99.1	99.0	n.a.
Socialist	99.3	98.6	97.9	97.6	98.0	97.5	99.3	97.6	98.3	99.4	99.6	99.5	99.7	97.9	99.4	99.1	99.0	n.a.
Market	0.7	1.4	2.1	2.4	2.0	2.6	0.7	2.4	1.7	0.6	0.4	0.5	0.3	2.1	0.6	0.9	1.0	n.a.
Chemicals																		
USSR	41.4	28.8	20.7	23.4	34.6	41.0	31.0	31.0	23.9	41.8	57.7	56.5	46.6	43.9	38.9	38.5	43.5	43.4
Socialist	46.1	37.2	28.4	33.0	51.5	53.5	37.1	39.2	36.2	57.6	71.1	71.0	59.0	54.7	56.9	58.9	61.9	62.2
Market	53.9	62.8	71.6	67.0	48.5	46.5	62.9	60.8	63.8	42.7	28.9	29.0	41.1	45.3	43.1	41.1	38.1	37.8

Manufactures																		
USSR	51.0	56.8	43.9	48.3	50.8	52.8	39.2	33.5	27.1	39.9	42.1	47.1	47.4	46.8	46.3	49.4	53.9	46.7
Socialist	81.2	89.0	71.7	53.9	54.8	76.7	63.1	49.1	47.4	57.5	60.9	72.9	67.8	69.3	68.8	72.6	71.6	66.9
Market	18.8	11.0	28.3	46.1	45.2	23.3	36.9	50.9	52.6	42.5	39.1	27.3	32.2	30.7	31.2	27.4	28.5	33.1
Machinery																		
USSR	36.7	42.3	49.0	47.4	36.3	54.6	53.6	46.1	34.8	38.7	30.4	62.5	71.4	67.9	66.0	67.7	71.5	64.2
Socialist	75.1	69.9	72.3	64.3	52.0	63.7	64.1	56.2	41.1	42.8	33.8	66.7	76.9	74.6	72.8	76.4	77.8	71.3
Market	24.9	30.1	27.7	35.7	48.0	36.3	35.9	43.8	59.0	57.2	66.2	33.3	23.1	25.4	27.2	23.6	22.3	28.7
								a										
Transport																		
USSR	54.0	48.8	32.0	34.4	29.9	51.0	38.5	22.9	18.3	16.9	29.0	34.5	52.9	53.3	43.4	44.1	46.0	43.7
Socialist	68.4	56.9	42.9	46.0	45.8	62.3	46.3	27.0	21.1	19.1	31.3	36.2	59.0	58.2	56.6	62.9	70.3	63.6
Market	31.6	43.1	57.1	54.0	54.2	37.7	53.7	73.0	78.9	80.9	68.7	63.8	41.0	41.8	43.4	37.1	29.7	36.4
Total																		
USSR	58.3	60.9	53.9	52.7	52.8	60.0	55.4	46.0	40.2	46.9	53.7	65.1	68.2	62.8	63.2	67.7	68.2	66.3
Socialist	77.1	75.2	71.7	66.4	65.3	76.9	70.8	60.8	51.5	58.6	67.6	79.7	82.8	78.1	78.5	88.7	87.0	84.0
Market	22.9	24.8	28.3	33.6	34.7	23.1	29.2	39.2	48.5	41.4	32.4	20.3	17.2	21.9	21.5	11.3	13.0	16.0

a. Selected imports representing an average of two-thirds of all imports in the period. Market economies includes "others," presumably non-socialist countries. Starting with the year 1972 (as reported in the *AEC 1977*) the row "others" appears more disaggregated, showing imports from both socialist and market partners. Changes, however, are small, and hence it was guessed that the previous distribution was not distorted.

Source: Estimates based on *AEC 1970* to *1984*.

Carmelo Mesa-Lago and Fernando Gil

SOVIET IMPORTS: BLESSING OR CURSE?

A quick glance at the section on foreign trade in Cuba's 1985 statistical yearbook indicates how dependent that nation is on imports: while the list of exports occupies 10 pages, that of imports extends for 24 pages. An analysis of the 1958–1985 percentage composition of imports detects the following trends: declining foodstuffs (from 21 percent to 12 percent), manufactures and chemicals (30 percent to 21 percent), and raw materials (7 percent to 4 percent); stagnant machinery and transportation (around 31 percent); and increasing fuels and minerals (11 percent to 33 percent).[19]

The USSR is the major provider of Cuba's imports, increasing from 54 percent to 66 percent in 1962–1985, while imports from all socialist countries (including CMEA members and others) rose from 77 percent to 84 percent in 1967–1984 (see Tables 6.3, 6.4 and 6.7). Cuba's imports from the USSR represent, as an average in 1967–1984, in relation to the island's total imports in each category, 99 percent of fuels, 82 percent of raw materials, 64 percent of foodstuffs, 52 percent of machinery, 48 percent of manufactures, 39 percent of transportation equipment, and 38 percent of chemicals. Although there are fluctuations in these percentages throughout the entire period, the Soviet supply of capital and intermediate goods steadily increases, while shares of other imports are more steady, except for manufactures which show a slight decline (see Table 6.7).

The composition of Soviet exports to Cuba in 1965–1984 is presented in Table 6.8. Fuels take an increasing share of Soviet exports (16 percent to 35 percent), followed by machinery and transportation (steady at about 28 percent), and other unidentified exports (increasing from 9 percent to 15 percent). The rest—foodstuffs, manufacturers chemicals, and raw materials—show a declining trend. A serious obstacle to the analysis of Cuban imports' value is the lack of information on the complexity and quality of machinery, transportation equipment, manufactures, and chemicals. Data are available, however, on 3 homogenous imports: crude oil (which in 1983–1984 represented 17 percent of the total value of Cuban imports and 20 percent of Soviet exports to Cuba), wheat, and corn (which combined equaled 4 percent of both Cuban imports and Soviet exports). Table 6.9 contrasts Soviet world market prices for these three goods for the period 1960–1984.

Cuba obviously has benefitted from Soviet concessionary oil prices. Until the 1973 energy crisis, the island paid a price equal to or slightly

TABLE 6.8
Percentage Distribution of Soviet Exports to Cuba, 1965–1984

Items	*1965*	*1970*	*1975*	*1980*	*1984*
Foodstuffs	24.1	17.2	19.0	11.2	8.4
of which grains	7.4	4.5	5.1	3.9	4.0
Raw Materials	5.1	5.5	4.1	3.3	3.4
Fuels[a]	16.5	11.9	21.8	26.7	35.3
Chemicals	5.5	3.3	3.5	3.1	2.4
Manufactures[b]	11.8	12.6	10.9	8.9	8.3
Machinery and Transportation	28.3	34.9	24.4	32.4	27.4
Others	87.7	14.6	16.3	14.4	14.8
Totals	100.0	100.0	100.0	100.0	100.0

a. Oil and oil products.
b. Ferrous and nonferrous metals and consumer goods; other manufactures may be included in "others."
Sources: Authors' estimates based on *Vneshnaiia torgovlia, USSR 1966, 1970, 1976, 1980*, and *1984*.

below the world oil price. Beginning in 1975, a formula for pricing Soviet oil exports to CMEA members was established based on a five-year moving average of world market prices (except for 1975 when a three-year average was used). Since then, despite this formula, the average Soviet price (until 1984) has been about half the world price. With declining world oil prices in 1983–1984, however, the gap between the Soviet and the world price has closed (from 0.42 in 1980 to 0.60 in 1984) and, with continued application of the formula, the Soviet price may surpass the world price (more on this below).

Contrary to oil, Cuba has lost in its imports of Soviet grains. Table 6.9 shows that only during the inflationary years of 1973–1974 was the Soviet price of wheat highly beneficial to Cuba. Between 1960 and 1984, Cuba paid an annual average of eight cents per bushel over the world price. The same is true of Soviet corn imports for which Cuba paid an annual average of six cents per bushel above the world price. The USSR imports these grains from the West and, hence, has to arrange with major producers (e.g., Canada, Argentina) to supply Cuba directly and then be reimbursed in hard currency by Moscow. On a visit to Cuba in 1977, U.S. grain producers made the point that the U.S. could supply such grains as much as 30 percent more cheaply than the USSR.[20]

Because grains only represent about 4 percent of Soviet exports to Cuba (in contrast to 20 percent of oil exports), on balance Cuba gains. But what is the situation of other exports such as machinery and transportation equipment, manufactures, chemicals, etc., which all together account for 60 percent of Soviet exports to Cuba? Scholars of divergent ideological inclinations have asserted that Soviet goods (particularly capital goods) offered in intra-CMEA trade are characterized by poor quality and/or high prices, but none have provided evidence that this is the case with Cuba.[21]

In a previous work, Mesa-Lago has indirectly approached this question by looking at shifts of Cuban trade away from the USSR towards market economies whenever the world price of sugar has been very high, thus providing the island with hard currency to choose better—or lower priced—goods. A simple glance at Table 6.7 indicates that in 1969, 1974, and 1980, when the world prices of sugar increased significantly, the total Soviet share in all imports in all categories except fuels declined sharply, while the market economies' share increased. Conversely, when world sugar prices declined notably, as in 1976–1978, Cuba cut back on Western imports and shifted its trade back to the USSR. The pursuit of this line of argument with a selected group of machinery, transportation, and manufacturing goods (e.g. bulldozers, tractors, loaders, trucks, steel sheets and tubes, and fertilizers) produces even more remarkable results. For instance, in 1972 when world sugar prices were low, Cuba imported 100 percent of all bulldozers from the USSR, but in 1975 when prices were high only 2 percent were imported; a reverse to 100 percent Soviet imports occurred in 1978 when the price was again low, but a decrease in imports to 34 percent took place in 1980 when the price was high. This seems to confirm the hypothesis that when Cuba has the purchasing power to select trade partners for its imports, the island chooses market economies via-à-vis the USSR. If Soviet goods were advantageous in quality and/or price (as fuels are), Cuba certainly would not shift her trade away from the USSR.[22]

To test this hypothesis further, in a more comprehensive and systematic manner, a correlation exercise was conducted relating annual percentage changes of imports from Soviet and market economies (see Table 6.9). A first test using the period 1968–1980 resulted in high correlation coefficients, e.g., for total imports: -0.7354 for the USSR (as the world price of sugar increases, Soviet imports decrease) and 0.4865

TABLE 6.9
Prices of Crude Oil, Wheat and Corn in the Soviet Market and the World Market, 1960–1984

Years	Crude Oil[a]			Wheat[b]			Corn[b]		
	USSR	World	Ratio	USSR	World	Ratio	USSR	World	Ratio
1960	1.74	1.92	0.91	1.61	1.58	1.02	n.a.	1.26	n.a.
1961	1.66	1.86	0.89	1.69	1.60	1.06	1.33	1.21	1.10
1962	1.60	1.80	0.89	1.72	1.75	0.98	1.32	1.24	1.06
1963	1.81	1.80	1.01	1.68	1.76	0.95	1.22	1.37	0.89
1964	1.78	1.80	0.99	1.87	1.84	1.02	1.35	1.39	0.97
1965	1.79	1.80	0.99	2.06	1.62	1.27	1.47	1.41	1.04
1966	1.78	1.80	0.99	1.87	1.72	1.09	1.46	1.47	0.99
1967	1.76	1.80	0.98	1.83	1.79	1.02	1.42	1.38	1.03
1968	1.78	1.80	0.99	1.91	1.71	1.12	1.23	1.21	1.02
1969	1.75	1.80	0.97	1.71	1.59	1.08	1.27	1.32	0.96
1970	1.75	1.80	0.97	1.63	1.50	1.09	1.40	1.48	0.95
1971	1.74	2.19	0.79	1.67	1.68	0.99	1.67	1.48	1.13
1972	2.16	2.46	0.87	1.88	1.90	0.99	1.56	1.42	1.10
1973	2.85	3.29	0.87	1.96	3.81	0.51	1.98	2.48	0.80
1974	3.19	11.58	0.28	3.29	4.90	0.67	3.76	3.36	1.12
1975	5.81	11.53	0.50	4.57	4.06	1.12	3.70	3.03	1.22
1976	5.90	12.38	0.48	4.28	3.62	1.18	3.40	2.85	1.19
1977	7.50	12.40	0.60	4.00	2.81	1.42	3.46	2.42	1.43
1978	10.15	12.70	0.80	2.94	3.48	0.84	2.49	2.56	0.97
1979	12.15	17.26	0.70	3.73	4.36	0.86	3.27	2.94	1.11
1980	12.14	28.67	0.42	4.58	4.70	0.97	2.54	3.19	0.80
1981	16.07	32.50	0.49	6.41	4.76	1.35	4.57	3.32	1.38
1982	19.52	33.47	0.58	5.05	4.36	1.16	3.52	2.75	1.28
1983	18.12	29.31	0.62	7.02	4.28	1.64	2.94	3.45	0.85
1984	17.25[c]	28.47	0.60	6.32	4.15	1.52	4.11	3.45	1.19

a. U.S. dollars per barrel, world price based on Saudi Arabian light crude. There is no precise information on the quality of Soviet crude, but it has been usually considered medium grade, not as good as Saudi crude but better, for instance, than Venezuelan crude. Therefore, the index may overestimate somewhat the amount of the subsidy.

b. U.S. dollars per bushel.

c. Estimate.

Source: see sources, Table 6.6.

TABLE 6.10
Soviet Supply of Oil and Oil Products to Cuba, 1963–1984
(in thousands of metric tons)

	Crude Oil						
				Percentage Distribution of Supply			Soviet supply of crude oil and oil products
Years	Domestic Production	Total Imports[a]	Total Supply	Domestically Produced	Imported from the USSR	Imported from other countries[b]	
1963	31	3,709	3,740	0.8	n.a.	n.a.	4,078[c]
1964	37	3,469	3,506	1.0	n.a.	n.a.	4,562[c]
1965	57	3,483	3,540	1.6	n.a.	n.a.	4,588[c]
1966	69	3,826	3,895	1.8	n.a.	n.a.	5,048[c]
1967	116	3,713	3,829	3.0	96.3	0.7	5,097[c]
1968	197	3,851	4,048	4.9	93.8	1.3	5,225
1969	206	4,156	4,362	4.7	92.3	3.0	5,681
1970	159	4,261	4,420	3.6	94.1	2.3	6,016
1971	120	4,757	4,877	2.5	95.6	1.9	6,817
1972	112	4,749	4,861	2.1	95.5	2.4	6,671
1973	138	5,243	5,381	2.6	96.7	0.7	7,154
1974	168	5,875	6,043	2.8	94.9	2.3	7,766
1975	226	5,797	6,023	3.7	94.7	1.6	7,748
1976	235	5,797	6,032	3.9	95.5	0.6	8,231
1977	256	6,201	6,457	4.0	95.6	0.4	9,236
1978	288	6,359	6,647	4.3	95.2	0.5	9,623
1979	288	6,131	6,419	4.5	95.2	0.3	9,875
1980	274	6,025	6,298	4.3	93.7	2.0	10,564
1981	259	6,355	6,608	3.8	95.6	0.6	11,089
1982	541	6,247	6,788	8.0	91.2	0.8	11,668
1983	742	6,861	7,603	9.8	89.3	0.9	12,410
1984	770	7,235	8,005	9.6	n.a.	n.a.	12,485

a. Part of Soviet oil imports was reexported by Cuba in the 1980s.
b. Unspecified countries.
c. Estimates.

Sources: 1963–1972 partly based on Pérex-López, "Sugar and Petroleum in Cuban-Soviet Terms of Trade," p. 276. Rest from Mesá-Lago, *The Economy of Socialist Cuba* (Albuquerque: University of New Mexico Press, 1981), p. 100; and *AEC 1080* to *1985*.

for market economies (as the price of sugar increases, market economy imports also increase). In all disaggregated import categories, the sign was negative for the USSR and positive for market economies, but surprisingly the highest resulting correlation coefficients were registered in raw materials (-0.8182 and 0.87393) and foodstuffs, (-0.7068 and 0.4651). In the second test using selected years when world sugar prices reached record increases (1969, 1974, and 1980) or record declines (1976), the resulting correlation coefficients were even higher and became significant in all categories except for transportation. A third test, using the entire period 1968–1984, resulted in lower correlation coefficients, suggesting that the relationship has weakened in recent years. The apparent reason for this is that in the 1980s, Cuba's flexibility to shift trade toward market economies has been greatly reduced and the island is more economically locked than ever with the USSR, as the significant increase in Cuban trade with the USSR indicates. Cuba's expanding trade deficits and scarcity of hard currency (aggravated by hard currency debt service), combined with increased Soviet subsidies, have strengthened the Cuban-Soviet linkage and provided the USSR greater economic leverage over Cuba.

Although a sensitive topic, current Cuban leaders and former technicians, as well as foreign scholars, have referred to a number of disadvantages with Soviet/CMEA imports. Supplies are submitted to either Soviet/CMEA surpluses (or are goods of obsolete technology) or higher demand priorities (e.g., domestic or Eastern European needs), rather than Cuban needs. The USSR and CMEA countries have failed to deliver, or have substantially delayed, the supply of certain technologies and services because they do not produce them and refuse to buy them in hard currency from developed market economies. Examples of this are the Soviet failure to deliver a fuel-efficient nickel smelter plant for Punta Gorda, a plant to process nickel by-products from the René Ramos Latour plant into pig iron (and then steel), a factory to produce cars and trucks, and know-how to develop Cuba's tourist industry. Production failures in CMEA countries often result in nondelivery or delays in supplies, provoking both bottlenecks or stoppages in Cuban production and grave scarcities. In 1979, the Soviet Union failed to deliver 40 percent of an agreed 500,000 metric tons of wood, badly affecting the Cuban construction industry. On another occasion, a CMEA member's cancellation of a chicken cargo forced Cuba to slaughter underweight cattle in order to fulfill domestic food needs. Traditional supplies are often discontinued or substituted by other products without previous notification or on very short notice (e.g., recent cases have been fertilizers and motorized equipment), and supplies agreed upon to maintain an installed plant at full capacity are often insufficient, provoking slowdowns or forcing Cuba to import needed goods from market economies. (The José Martí iron and steel plant worked at only 70 percent capacity for a long time due to such problems.) Often agreed upon technical services and spare parts for an already installed plant are not delivered (this happened in 1979 with the cane-harvester—KTP 1—factory), and in other cases services are provided at high costs (e.g., to deliver a significant share of output of the serviced plant). Further, the cost of Soviet technicians in Cuba is high, as 80 percent of their salary must be paid in hard currency. They must also have housing, transportation, health care and other services, and special stores. Because of the USSR incentive system, Soviet managers try to increase the price of goods to be delivered (in order to increase bonuses), resulting in overpricing. This occurred in the José Martí steel plant. It took Cubans several months to prove the overpricing, and four years for the Russians to return the corresponding credit. A final disadvantage to reliance on Soviet/CMEA trade is that Soviet ships transporting goods to Cuba usually have a smaller loading capacity than that which is required to transport the purchased supplies; hence extra warehouse and dock costs have to be paid by Cuba.[23]

SOVIET SUPPLY OF FUELS

Cuba is not well endowed with energy resources, and in the 1970s, ranked among the least able of 88 developing countries to meet current and projected energy needs from domestic sources. It does not have significant coal resources, its hydro potential is very low, and the known oil and gas deposits are quite limited. CMEA lacks the technology both for off shore oil exploration and solar energy development on a relatively cheap, large-scale basis. Unlike Brazil, Cuba has not shown interest in the production of gasohol out of sugar. A nuclear power plant with two units is being installed by the USSR in Cuba, and operation of the first reactor has been officially promised by the end of the current decade. This plant, however, will reduce oil imports by 20 percent (2.4 million tons of fuels), and Cuba will still depend on importation of enriched uranium from the USSR. Sugar cane bagasse (crushed waste material) has been traditionally used as a fuel for the sugar harvest, but its share as a source of energy has sharply declined since the 1960s at the same time that oil use has increased.[24] Table 6.10 shows that Cuba's production of crude oil has steadily increased, but in 1983 Cuba still imported more than 90 percent of her crude oil supply. In 1967–1983, the USSR supplied an average of 94 percent of Cuban crude oil imports and 99 percent of oil and oil-derivative imports.[25]

Soviet oil comes from Black Sea ports, 6,400 miles away and, in 1972 (when consumption was 40 percent lower than today), required an expensive flotilla of 150 medium-sized Soviet tankers—practically one tanker every other day—to keep Cuba supplied at an average trip of 42 days per tanker. (A recent statement by the dean of Soviet Latin Americanists suggests that the burden to the USSR was even heavier—two oil tankers daily for 20 years.) Transportation costs are very high: in the 1970s and 1980s they were equivalent to around seven percent of the total cost of Soviet oil imports. Since 1976, the USSR and Venezuela have swapped oil destined to Cuba and Spain respectively, although this only affected five percent of Cuban oil imports in 1979. A similar Soviet agreement with Mexico apparently has not materialized. Such arrangements reduce transportation costs, but not Soviet losses in hard currency; furthermore, oil imports are attributed to the USSR.

A cut in Soviet oil supply would paralyze the country in a very short time span. This nearly occurred in 1967 when the USSR delivered only 80 percent of the agreed supply of oil to the island (in retaliation for Cuba's unorthodox policies at the time) while publicly announcing an increase of oil exports to Brazil, then one of Cuba's archenemies. This move rapidly reduced Cuba's oil reserves, including those of the military, forced gasoline rationing and—according to some observers—prompted Castro's subsequent, albeit qualified, endorsement of the Soviet invasion of Czechoslovakia.

Available evidence suggests USSR oil reserves are decreasing. In 1984–1985 alone, oil output fell by more than three percent. As a result, the Soviet Union should find it increasingly difficult to satisfy its own energy needs, not to mention to export to the West in order to generate hard currency and to supply CMEA members. In 1985, Soviet oil exports to the West declined by 40 percent and export reductions to CMEA clients have also been reported (e.g., a 30 percent cut to Bulgaria).[26] According to Castro, Soviet supply of oil derivative in 1981–1985 has been guaranteed at 61 million metric tons for a 28 percent increase over the previous quinquenium. In 1981–1984, 47.6 million metric tons were actually delivered, thus 13.4 million remained to be delivered in 1984–1985. Whether such levels of deliveries indeed materialized, at a time when the Soviet Union was cutting oil supplies elsewhere, cannot be determined because Cuba's 1985 statistical yearbook and statistical compendia did not provide such data.[27]

At the end of 1984, Castro announced that the USSR had guaranteed oil supplies for the current quinquenium, but did not disclose the amount. Western sources, drawing on indirect information, have estimated these supplies at 50 to 55 million metric tons.[28] If both these estimates (and Castro's supply figures for 1981–1985) are correct, the Soviet oil supply to Cuba in 1986–1990 would be 10 to 12 percent less than in the previous quinquenium. Such a cut—combined with a decline in world oil prices plus comparatively higher Soviet oil prices to CMEA—could drastically curtail Cuba's reexport of oil and the corresponding hard currency revenue.

Since the mid-1970s, Cuba has been reexporting gasoline to the West, but in 1980 it apparently also began reexporting Soviet crude oil. In 1983–1984, reexported oil and oil products accounted for more than 10 percent of the island's total exports, and 40 percent of its hard currency exports. In 1982, world oil prices peaked, but thereafter declined by more than 50 percent; conversely, intra-CMEA oil prices—calculated on the basis of a moving five-year average of previous world prices—rose through 1985 and early 1986, practically eliminating the gap with world prices. Unless the Soviet price formula is changed, or Cuba is granted preferential treatment, Soviet oil prices, at least in 1986, should be higher than world prices.[29] U.S. estimates of Cuba's available oil and oil products for reexport in 1986–1990 indicate more than a one-third decline in relation to 1983–1984 reexports. Possibilities for a cut in domestic fuel consumption are very small since most conservation measures have already been taken, and because nuclear energy will not be able to reduce dependence on oil until the end of the 1980s at best. If world oil prices continue at current depressed levels, Cuba's already reduced reexports would be paid at half the 1982–1983 prices, generating only a net one-third of what they once did.

IMPROVEMENT AND DETERIORATION IN THE TERMS OF TRADE

The barter or commodity terms of trade measure imports a country can obtain with a unit of its exports. A deterioration in the terms of trade means that a country can buy fewer units of imports with a given quantity of exports, while an improvement in the terms of trade implies the opposite.

For more than two decades, Western specialists on international trade have discussed whether the USSR has taken advantage of its socialist trade partners by exporting to them at higher prices and importing from them at lower prices than it does with trade partners from market economies. Mendershausen opened the debate arguing that, in 1955–1958, the USSR extracted a trade surplus from Eastern Europe. Conversely, Marrese and Vanous found that, in 1960–1980, the USSR paid a trade subsidy to the six European CMEA members. Reviewing the Marrese-Vanous estimates, Marer concluded that the USSR extracted a surplus from Rumania and that Soviet subsidies to the other CMEA members had been overestimated. Holzman analyzed the period 1960–1978, finding Rumania and Bulgaria had suffered a loss in their trade with the USSR, but that the opposite was true for the rest of CMEA. He explained the different direction of the trade transfer based on the nature of products traded: raw material exporters (including fuel exporters) suffer a loss, while capital and manufactured goods exporters benefited from a subsidy.[30]

Several studies have tried to answer that question in the Cuban case. One study compared Cuba's terms of trade with socialist and market economies between 1968 and 1975, reaching the conclusion that Cuba's terms with market economies were 95 percentage points better than with socialist economies. A second study compared Cuba's terms of trade both globally and with the USSR from 1968 to 1974, concluding that the former were 22 percentage points better than the latter. These two studies were faulty in that they introduced a bias in favor of market economies, at least concerning exports. In both, the year base and the year end were abnormal: while in 1968 the USSR paid Cuba three times the world sugar price, in 1975 the USSR paid basically the world sugar price; hence the two studies introduced a bias in favor of market economies at least concerning exports. A third study estimated Cuba's sugar-oil terms of trade with the USSR in 1960–1976. It showed an improvement in 1960–1963, no significant changes in 1963–1972, improvement in 1973–1974, and deterioration in 1975–1976. Unfortunately, the latter study is based only on one Cuban export and one import (albeit the most important), and does not provide information on the recent period 1977–1985.

One way to improve our knowledge of this subject is to expand the goods included and the period of the analysis. Table 6.11 compares

TABLE 6.11

Terms of Trade[a] of Cuba with the USSR, 1968–1984

	Value of Exports (in U.S. cents per pound)					Value of Imports (in U.S. cents per pound)								Index 1968=100	
	Sugar		Nickel		Total	Oil		Wheat		Corn		Total	Px	Soviet	World
1968	6.0	99.2	72.1	0.8	6.6	0.6	92.4	3.2	4.9	2.2	2.7	0.8	8.6	100.0	100.0
1969	5.9	98.8	81.8	1.2	6.8	0.6	92.2	2.8	6.0	2.3	1.8	0.8	9.1	105.8	169.4
1970	5.9	99.5	283.8	0.5	7.3	0.6	92.3	2.7	4.9	2.5	2.8	0.7	10.4	120.9	161.1
1971	6.1	99.0	201.7	1.0	8.0	0.6	92.5	2.8	5.8	3.0	1.7	0.8	10.7	124.4	183.3
1972	6.4	98.4	194.5	1.6	9.4	0.7	93.4	3.1	5.8	2.8	0.8	0.9	10.7	124.4	272.2
1973	12.1	98.8	273.6	1.2	15.2	0.9	93.6	3.3	5.3	3.5	1.1	1.1	13.8	160.4	225.0
1974	19.2	99.1	273.2	0.9	21.5	1.1	94.0	5.5	4.9	6.7	1.1	1.3	16.1	187.2	213.8
1975	26.4	99.4	273.2	0.6	27.8	1.9	94.3	7.6	4.7	6.6	1.0	2.2	12.4	144.2	150.0
1976	27.6	99.4	276.2	0.6	29.1	2.0	94.8	7.1	4.2	6.1	1.0	2.2	13.1	152.3	91.7
1977	27.9	99.5	285.2	0.5	29.2	2.5	92.0	6.6	5.9	6.2	2.1	2.8	10.4	120.9	61.1
1978	36.1	99.6	298.1	0.6	37.7	3.4	92.1	4.9	5.3	4.4	2.6	3.5	10.8	125.6	58.3
1979	36.8	99.6	316.9	0.4	37.9	4.0	91.6	6.2	6.3	5.8	2.1	4.2	9.0	104.6	52.8
1980	47.5	99.4	319.3	0.6	49.1	4.0	92.1	7.6	5.8	4.5	2.1	4.3	11.5	133.7	88.9
1981	35.1	99.5	626.2	0.5	38.0	5.4	91.2	10.6	6.9	8.1	1.9	5.8	6.6	76.7	63.9
1982	34.0	99.6	587.1	0.4	36.2	6.5	90.6	8.4	7.2	6.3	2.2	6.6	5.5	63.9	25.0
1983	45.9	99.8	567.5	0.2	46.9	6.0	91.3	11.7	7.2	5.2	1.5	6.4	7.3	84.9	25.0
1984	43.9	99.8	549.3	0.2	44.9	5.7	90.5	10.5	7.5	7.3	1.9	6.1	7.4	86.0	16.7

P = price W = weight

a. Includes only two exports (sugar and nickel) and three imports (oil, wheat, and corn).

b. Estimated using world prices rather than Soviet prices.

Sources: Based on González, "Comercio Exterior entre Cuba y la Unión Soviética," updated with *AEC 1984* and *Vneshniaia torgovlia SSSRv 1984*.

Cuban-Soviet terms of trade for the period 1968–1984 based on sugar and nickel—exports which together represent an average of 90 percent of total Cuban exports to the USSR—and 3 Cuban imports (oil, wheat, and corn) which represent 26 percent of Cuban imports from the USSR for the period, but whose share has increased significantly over time, rising from 16 percent in 1970 to 39 percent in 1984.[31] These products were selected since they are of homogenous quality and because data exist on Soviet and world market prices for all of them. The exercise, however, leaves out most Soviet imports to Cuba (e.g., capital and intermediate and manufactured goods) for which no information is available on quality and price, hence its results must be taken with caution. Table 6.11 provides estimates of an index of Cuba's terms of trade with the USSR, based on Soviet prices; in addition, there is a second index, for comparative purposes, as if trade between the two countries had been conducted in world prices.

The first index (Soviet prices) indicates a steady improvement in Cuba's terms of trade, particularly between 1970 and 1974, then a decline, although with oscillations. The best 4 years for Cuba were 1973–1976 and the worst 4 years 1981–1984; terms of trade in 1984 were 14 percentage points below the 1968 level, and 101 percentage points below the 1974 level. The second index shows that if Cuban-Soviet trade had been conducted in world prices, Cuba would have benefited in 1969–1972, but it would have lost badly thereafter. Terms of trade on this index would have been, in 1984, 83 percentage points below the 1968 level. This comparison indicates that although Cuba's terms of trade with the USSR have deteriorated since 1977, the deterioration would have been much worse if Cuba had traded with market economies (not taking preferential prices into account).[32]

An example given by Castro at the end of 1984 illustrates the comparative advantage in terms of trade Cuba still apparently enjoys with the USSR (despite the deterioration in these terms): if Cuba had sold 7 million metric tons of sugar (practically the entire harvest) at the prevailing world market prices in 1984, with that income it could only have bought 20 percent (actually 23 percent) of its oil needs at world market prices.[33] Earlier we raised the issue that when Cuba has had hard currency to buy from developed market economies, it has shifted its trade from the USSR to the West, an indication that the latter may offer better technology quality and/or lower prices than the USSR. Unfortunately, this important question cannot be settled in this paper.

TABLE 6.12
Soviet Trade Subsidies to Cuba, 1960–1984
(in millions of U.S. dollars)

	Estimates Based on World Prices						
Years	*Sugar*	*Nickel*	*Oil*	*Wheat*	*Corn*	*Total*	*Total at U.S. Import Prices*
1960	2	n.a.	3	0	0	5	−78
1961	85	n.a.	6	−1	0	90	−115
1962	57	n.a.	6	0	0	63	−76
1963	−50	n.a.	0	1	0	−49	−27
1964	7	n.a.	1	0	0	8	−10
1965	194	n.a.	0	−4	0	190	−18
1966	174	n.a.	1	−1	0	174	−8
1967	217	0	1	0	0	218	−36
1968	164	−7	1	−2	0	156	−45
1969	76	−9	2	−2	0	67	−45
1970	150	58	2	−1	1	210	−45
1971	54	25	21	0	−1	99	−19
1972	−24	22	15	3	0	13	−11
1973	89	52	24	28	2	195	174
1974	−467	40	471	23	−1	66	76
1975	413	27	339	−7	−2	770	637
1976	998	21	419	−9	−2	1,427	1,394
1977	1,661	21	333	−26	−8	1,981	1,748
1978	2,455	34	180	11	1	2,681	2,156
1979	2,303	14	371	16	−3	2,701	2,206
1980	1,137	9	1,283	3	6	2,438	2,347
1981	1,288	153	1,339	−50	−12	2,718	2,510
1982	2,499	136	1,196	−43	−9	3,782	2,648
1983	2,926	137	1,021	−97	4	3,991	2,927
1984	3,120	121	1,053	−79	6	4,221	2,997
Total	19,528	854	8,088	−237	−18	28,215	21,284

Source: Same as table 6.11 plus *International Financial Statistics 1985*, *Commodity Trade and Price Trends 1985*, and CIA *The Cuban Economy: A Statistical Review* (Washington D.C., June 1984).

THE COLOSSAL SOVIET AID: AMOUNT AND TERMS

The task of estimating Soviet aid to Cuba is as colossal as its presumed magnitude. The only data Cuban and Soviet statistical yearbooks report are on merchandise trade, hence allowing us to calculate the trade deficit, but not the balance of payments. There are no statistics on the cost of total Soviet economic aid and technical assistance, either yearly or cumulative; scattered data on this was not published until the mid-1970s, thereafter only percentage changes over previous quinquenium are reported although, occasionally, the cost of a single project is released. Cuba has never disclosed the amount of its debt with the USSR (not even when part of such debt was postponed in 1972 and 1986), and Western estimates only roughly calculate the amount of Soviet loans. Even so, since we do not know how much has been repaid, it is not possible to accurately estimate the outstanding debt.[34]

Soviet aid to Cuba assumes several forms. The first—annual credits to finance the Soviet-Cuban trade deficit and direct aid for economic development—are loans that must be repaid. The others are non-repayable grants in the form of subsidies to support the price of Cuban exports (e.g., sugar, nickel), imports from the USSR (e.g., oil), and military aid. Table 6.13 presents rough estimates of all except the latter.

The calculation of the trade subsidy is based only on five products (sugar, nickel, oil, wheat, and corn) at world prices as explained earlier (see Table 6.12). The total subsidy is approximately $28.2 billion. It could be smaller if Cuban imports from the USSR are priced higher than world market prices, but it is probably not larger since other Soviet imports are unlikely to be subsidized. Furthermore, if U.S. import prices (the highest possible) instead of world prices had been used to estimate the Soviet subsidy, it would have been substantially smaller. Thus the total subsidy for 5 products in 1960–1984 would have been $21.3 billion, or $7 billion less. Hence the total cumulative trade subsidy for the entire period lies between $21.3 and $28.2 billion.

The estimate of the trade-deficit aid is easier to substantiate since the USSR covers Cuba's annual trade deficits with credits. We have assumed that no Soviet credit was extended in 1975–1978, when the merchandise trade between the two countries ended in a surplus for Cuba. In that period, the price of Cuban exports (basically sugar and nickel) was tied to the price of a basket of Soviet imports (including oil and other unspecified "basic goods") which greatly benefited

Cuba because Soviet aid shifted from repayable trade-deficit loans to nonrepayable trade subsidies. The latter increased 24 fold in 1975–1978 compared with 1971–1974. On the other hand, trade subsidies in 1979–1982 only increased 1.3 times over 1975–1978. The situation reverted after 1979 to the previous status. Neither Cuban nor Soviet leaders have publicly explained the reason for this shift, which resulted in a loss for Cuba, but apparently the USSR considered that the adjustment mechanism was too detrimental.[35] The cumulative trade deficit in 1960–1984 amounted to $7.9 billion, but half of it was provided in the last five years of the period. The shift from grants to loans could only reduce the Soviet burden, if indeed Cuba repays such loans. The important economic reforms introduced on the island in late 1984 and thereafter (explained in the next section) must be interpreted in light of mounting Cuban trade deficits with loans from the USSR.

The component of economic aid most difficult to estimate is development credits, in terms of both their amount and impact. One Soviet source has estimated that in 1984 industrial plants built in Cuba with Soviet aid produced 100 percent of rolled ferrous metals, sugar cane harvesters, and TV and radio sets; 95 percent of steel; 80 percent of nitrogen fertilizers; 60 percent of construction metal works; 50 percent of electricity, etc.[36] Table 6.13 data for 1959–1975 came from Cuban reports of individual loans in specific years (see Table 6.1). The global figure for 1976–1980 is based both on scattered data on loans for the five-year period, table 6.1, and a statement by Cuban Vice-President Carlos Rafael Rodríguez in the sense that economic aid in that period was planned to increase 2.5 times over the previous quinquenium.[37] Economic aid for 1986–1990, according to Rodríguez, totalled 2.5 billion rubles ($3.4 billion), an increment of 50 percent over 1981–1985 ($2.3 billion).[38] Total development aid for 1960–1985 is roughly estimated at $5 billion.

Data of Soviet military aid to Cuba is even harder to obtain. Castro reported the amount as $1.5 billion provided free, presumably for 1961–1969.[39] No other official figure has ever been released. Two recent Western estimates set military aid at $1.7 billion for 1981–1983 and $3 billion for 1981–1984. Taking the lowest of the two estimates, and assuming that aid in the interim period of 1969–1980 was given at an average of the two cited figures, Soviet military aid can be grossly estimated at $4 billion, for a total of $7.2 billion for 1961–1983. According to Cuban Vice-President Raúl Castro, Cuba received free about $13.4 billion from 1960 to 1985.[40] This is a huge sum for a small country like Cuba, and is all the more notable since the USSR has supplied

TABLE 6.13
Soviet Economic Assistance to Cuba, 1960–1984
(million U.S. dollars)

	Our Estimates					CIA Estimates			
Years	*Trade Subsidy*[a]	*Trade Deficit Credit*	*Develop-ment Aid*	*Total without Dev. Aid*	*% of GSP*	*Trade Subsidy*	*Trade Deficit Credit plus Dev. Aid*	*Total*	*% of GSP*
1960–1970	1,131	2,083	344	3,214	—	1,020	2,250	3,270	—
1971	199	440		539	5.8	120	450	570	6.2
1972	13	523		536	4.8	49	565	614	5.5
1973	195	410	749 (1971–1975)	605	4.1	181	430	611	4.2
1974	66	276		342	2.1	43	295	338	2.1
1975	770	0		770	4.0–4.6	914	150	1,064	5.6–6.3
1976	1,427	0		1,427	7.4–8.3	1,384	185	1,569	8.1–9.1
1977	1,981	0		1,981	10.7	2,040	230	2,270	12.3
1978	2,681	0	1,872 (1976–1980)	2,681	12.4	2,626	320	2,946	13.6
1979	2,701	198		2,899	12.4	2,718	460	3,178	13.6
1980	2,438	917		3,355	13.5	2,633	830	3,463	14.0
1981	2,718	1,122		3,840	13.5	3,145	1,415	4,560	16.0
1982	3,782	546	2,266[b] (1981–1984)	4,328	15.6	3,690	975	4,665	16.8
1983	3,991	422		4,413	15.6	3,190	1,070	4,260	15.1
1984	4,221	935		5,156	17.7	3,620	1,000	4,620	15.9
Totals	28,214	7,872	5,231[c]	36,086		27,373	10,625	37,998	

a. Based on world prices; excludes nickel subsidies for 1960–1966.
b. 1981–1985.
c. Includes 1985.
Sources: Our estimates for Tables 6.1, 6.4, and 6.12 and explanations in the text; CIA estimates from *The Cuban Economy* and *Handbook of Economic Statistics 1986*. Percent of GSP are authors' estimates based on Cuba's GSP series converted to U.S. dollars using official exchange rates; in 1975–1976 there were two GSP series, hence the two percentages.

practically all of the island's advanced military equipment apparently at no cost.

The probable maximum total economic aid received by Cuba in 1959–1984 (including trade subsidies, trade deficit credits, and development aid) totals $41.3 billion, a figure which rises to $48.5 billion if military aid is added. Once again, this figure would be $7 million lower if U.S. import prices were used, and would diminish further if Cuban losses in relation to the bulk of Soviet imports and our estimates of both development and military aid are too high. Our estimates of total economic aid for 1960–1984 are about $2.9 billion higher than those of the CIA (see Table 6.13). The combined value of trade subsidies and credit alone in relation to GSP increases—according to our estimates—from 5.8 percent of GSP in 1971 to 17.7 percent in 1984. If the corresponding annual average of the five-year estimated value of development aid is added for 1984, the proportion rises to 19.4 percent of GSP, and if the estimated military aid is also included, the figure reaches 21.3 percent of GSP. Thus total Soviet aid in 1984 may have been as high as $5.6 billion or $15.4 million daily. Because information on aid to Cuba from other CMEA countries is even more scarce and fragmentary than figures for Soviet aid, it is practically impossible to calculate. Since 1974, however, Cuba has been a member of the CMEA's International Investment Bank and the International Bank for Economic Cooperation, and as such has received hard- and soft-currency loans and credits, but their amounts are unknown.

Terms of Soviet loans to Cuba are generous by world standards, particularly in view of the latter's increasing cost since the late 1970s. According to official information, typical Soviet trade loans have an amortization period of 12 years and a rate of interest not higher than 4 percent. For equipment purchases, payment begins the year after delivery, while in projects and plants, payment starts two years after the last delivery needed to put the project in operation. For development loans, the amortization period is 25 years and the rate of interest is 2 percent.[41] Many of these loans are repaid with Cuban goods. The Soviet Union has also been extraordinarily flexible in rescheduling Cuba's debt payments. It postponed payment of both the debt and interest accumulated from 1963 to 1972 until 1986, with payment to be stretched out for 25 years. A loan to cover Cuba's trade deficits with the USSR in 1973–1975 was also postponed with similar conditions.[42] According to a Western source, in October 1984, the USSR agreed to reschedule *all* Cuban debt repayments falling due before 1990.[43] Cuban sources told a U.S. specialist in mid-1985 that the debt due in 1986 had been postponed for another five years; payment should begin in 1990 for a 25-year period.[44] President Castro has referred to the postponement of the debt in a general manner without giving specifics:

> The debts [with the USSR] resulting from [trade] imbalances and [development] credits do not harm us in the least. Every time we have proposed a five-, ten-, or fifteen-year postponement and without interest, this has been conceded without any difficulty.... Our debt with the socialist countries is rescheduled practically automatically on a long-term, no-interest basis.[45]

Such postponements, without interest, are another important form of Soviet economic aid to Cuba. Not only do they defer payment of the principal (making these funds available for domestic needs), but Cuba saves a significant sum in interest payments.

What is the current total foreign debt of Cuba? Data on the hard-currency debt has been up-to-date and precise since 1982 when Cuba had to renegotiate such debt. It stood at $2,989 million at the end of 1984 and increased to $3,259 million at the end of 1985.[46] But the exact debt to the USSR is difficult to calculate, and that to other CMEA countries is practically impossible to assess. According to Table 6.13 total Soviet loans granted to Cuba in 1960–1984 amount to $13 billion (this includes development credits in 1985, but not trade deficit credits for that year), and the trade deficit in the USSR in 1985 was about $1 billion. Our estimate of total loans granted to Cuba in 1960–1985, therefore, is about $14 billion. Assuming this estimate is correct, we still do not know how much of this debt has been repaid. A Cuban economist has criticized a previous estimate by Mesa-Lago, arguing he did not take into account what Cuba had paid to the USSR since 1961; this economist, however, does not provide a figure on such amortization.[47] And yet if Castro's statement reproduced above is to be taken seriously, Cuba's debt with socialist countries is automatically rescheduled. Furthermore, the National Bank has reported that "...the average cost of the foreign debt incurred [with market economies] during the 1970–1981 period was about 15 times higher than the cost of the outstanding debt with the *socialist countries* in the same period."[48] We lack data on the amount of the debt service for hard-currency loans. However, the National Bank has provided the annual total percentage of the debt service (including amortization and interests of both hard-currency and socialist-country loans) in relation to the total foreign revenue Cuba received in 1975–1982 (we extrapolated the percentages for 1970–1974).[49]

In order to roughly estimate the "cost" of the Soviet debt we first estimated Cuba's total foreign revenue for each year in 1970–1981 (value of exports, plus other revenue, plus Soviet loans, plus hard-currency loans), and applied to each year the percentage released by the National

TABLE 6.14
Comparisons of Cuba's Foreign Dept with other Latin American Countries, 1985

Country	Total Debt[a] (millions of U.S.$)	GDP (millions U.S.$)	Population (thousands of persons)	Exports (FOB) (millions of U.S.$)	Debt GDP % (1)	Debt p/c (U.S.$) (2)	Debt/ Exports % (3)	Ranking Worst to Best 1	2	3	Average
Argentina	50,000	60,251	30,564	8,398	83	1,636	595	5	6	2	2
Bolivia	3,1909[b]	5,403	6,429	620	59	496	515	10	16	6	9
Brazil	101,930	249,137	134,500	25,639	41	758	398	15	11	10	13
Chile	19,580[c]	21,947	12,081	3,646	89	1,621	537	4	7	5	5
Columbia	13,350	32,961	26,526	3,671	41	503	364	16	14	12	16
Costa Rica	4,240	4,309	2,523	903	98	1,681	470	3	3	7	2
Cuba	16,700	29,300[d]	10,153	5,943	57[d]	1,645	281	12	5	15	9
Dominican Republic	2,760	7,665	6,257	738	36	441	374	18	17	11	17
Ecuador	7,300	12,462	9,378	2,851	59	778	256	11	10	18	15
El Salvador	2,100	3,746	4,857	752	56	432	279	13	18	16	18
Guatemala	2,450	9,686	7,963	1,062	25	308	231	20	19	19	20
Haiti	650[b]	1,757	5,498	223	37	118	291	17	20	14	19
Honduras	2,440	3,142	4,369	835	78	558	292	6	13	13	9
Mexico	97,700	178,289	79,327	21,866	55	1,232	447	14	9	9	9
Nicaragua	4,370[b]	2,764	3,272	297	158	1,336	1,471	1	8	1	1
Panama	5,140	4,841	2,183	1,949	106	2,355	264	2	1	17	6
Paraguay	1,850	6,559	3,691	323	28	501	573	19	15	4	14
Peru	13,750	20,772	19,696	2,966	66	698	464	9	12	8	7
Uruguay	4,900	6,473	2,931	853	76	1,672	574	7	4	3	4
Venezuela	30,300	42,528	17,355	14,1797	71	1,746	213	8	2	20	8

a. Public and private disbursed.
b. Public debt only.
c. Excludes debt with IMF and short-term credits for foreign trade operations.
d. GSP.

Sources: Latin America (except Cuba) GDP, population and exports from IDB, *Economic and Social Progress in Latin America 1986* (Washington, D.C., 1986); and total debt from ECLA, "Preliminary Overview of the Latin American Economy 1985," *Notas sobre la Economía y el Desarrollo*, 424–425 (December 1985). Cuba's GSP and population from Comité Estatal de Estadísticas, *Cuba en Cifras 1985*; exports from Table 6.3, and foreign debt from calculations in the text.

Bank as a total debt service.[50] We disaggregated the resulting figure according to the 1:15 ratio given by the National Bank, obtaining an estimate of only $360 million as Cuba's debt service to the USSR in 1970–1981. This figure would be somewhat higher if we had included loans from other socialist countries, but the data are not available. It is difficult to conceive that in neither 1961–1969 nor 1982–1984 Cuba's debt service to the USSR did not surpass the $360 million mark. Therefore we may grossly estimate the debt service to the USSR between 1961 and 1985 as totalling approximately $1 billion, a very low figure indeed since it includes both amortization and payment of interests. Assuming one half of this figure was repayment of principal, the outstanding debt with the USSR alone should be around $13.5 billion. When the $3.2 billion of the hard-currency debt is added, Cuba's total debt reaches $16.7 billion, and even this excludes the debt with other socialist countries.

In 1985 Cuba's total foreign debt was the fifth largest among 20 Latin American countries, surpassed by Brazil, Mexico, Argentina, Venezuela, and Chile (see Table 6.14). Cuba's debt per capita was $1,645, while the total debt was equal to 57 percent of GSP and 281 percent of exports. From worst to best, Cuba was ranked as follows: fifth in terms of the debt per capita; twelfth in debt/GDP—GSP for Cuba; and fifteenth in debt/exports. Using a nonweighted average of the three indicators, Cuba ranked ninth in Latin America, meaning that eight countries were better off than Cuba, and eight worse off. The 1985 comparison shows a significant improvement over Cuba's situation ten years earlier when the island's debt status was the very worst of Latin America.[51] In the last decade, Latin American indebtedness has rapidly accelerated in comparison with Cuba's. The latter's hard-currency debt represents only 19 percent of the total debt; the rest is with the USSR and thus is on much better terms than those endured by Latin America in general. Soviet largesse (both in the amount and terms of the aid) has partly protected Cuba from the 1980s crisis that has so badly affected Latin America. By providing subsidies to Cuban exports and postponing debt repayment free of interest, the USSR has significantly contributed to the relatively good economic growth rates Cuba enjoyed in 1981–1985 in the midst of the worst Latin American economic performance since the Great Depression.

One important question that remains unanswered is why does not the USSR cancel the Cuban debt? After all, if the Russians automatically reschedule the Cuban debt on a long-term, no-interest basis, and are reasonably convinced Cuba cannot pay it back, they could at least gain favorable international publicity by cancelling the debt. This action would not only be the ultimate proof of Soviet generosity and fraternal socialist economic relations, but would present a challenge to developed capitalist nations, particularly the U.S. government and U.S. bank creditors in Latin America. This probably was the shrewd game that Castro played in 1985 (on the eve of negotiations to repay the 1972 postponed Cuban debt), when he held a meeting of Latin American personalities in Havana and asked the Latin Americans to cancel their debts unilaterally.[52] As Elizabeth Valkenier argues in her chapter, Castro's radical position clashed with the cautious Gorbachev's stand in favor of a "fair for all" (presumably negotiated) debt solution, to avoid "grave socioeconomic and political consequences for international relations." Understandably, the Soviet media almost ignored the Havana meeting and the Cuban debt was postponed once again. Postponing rather than canceling the debt is a clear sign that the Soviet Union is willing to relinquish a crucial bargaining chip with which to press Cuba to improve its use of Soviet aid and to honor its economic commitments.

THE FUTURE OF THE SOVIET-CUBAN ECONOMIC PARTNERSHIP

Soviet economic aid to Cuba is unparalleled by both Soviet aid standards with client states and U.S. aid to Latin America. Obviously, the Cuban Revolution would not have survived without the colossal Soviet assistance; but a more important issue is that the Cuban economy—with its current organization—cannot function in the future without such vital support. Despite the latter, Cuba has not been able to significantly reduce, much less eliminate, some of its traditional structural economic problems such as dependence on sugar and external economic aid. Arguably, Soviet aid has contributed to maintaining these distortions of the Cuban economy. Soviet subsidies appear to be beneficial in the short run, but they have been disruptive in the long run, allowing Cuba to maintain its costly dependence on sugar. How likely is it that the USSR will increase or even maintain the level of aid to Cuba in the long run?

It has been estimated that in 1966–1974 Cuba took four percent of total Soviet assistance, that in 1979 Soviet economic aid to Cuba exceeded total aid to all noncommunist Third World countries, and that by the end of the 1970s, Cuba had received more Soviet aid than any other developing country outside the USSR Eurasian orbit.[53] These estimates were made before Soviet aid to Cuba increased enormously. In 1984 alone, Cuba received 39 percent of total Soviet economic aid (extended to both Communist countries and less developed countries), 50 percent of all Soviet aid extended to all communist countries, and 2.3 times the Soviet economic aid extended to less developed countries. Even so, we estimate that in 1985 total Soviet aid to Cuba (including military aid) took less than 0.3 percent of Soviet GNP.[54]

The Soviet Union does not obtain great economic returns from its partnership with Cuba, nor does it have direct investment or own means of production in the island (although it is increasingly sharing in the output of those plants it built pursuant to compensation agreements). Cuban exports are not strategically important to the USSR, and some imports (like oil) are extremely costly in the sense that they could generate hard currency for the Soviets. Whatever disadvantages Cuba endures in this relationship (tied credits, possible higher prices/poorer technology in some Soviet imports, and dependency), these are more than compensated by the advantages. The Cubans argue that socialist solidarity is the only reason behind Soviet cooperation, but this reasoning does not apply to other Soviet client states and socialist or bloc-aligned countries (Soviet aid to Nicaragua has been a tiny fraction of aid to Cuba). The major gains obtained by the USSR appear to be of a political and military nature: Cuba's strategic location in the Western Hemisphere close to U.S. shores, her crucial role in the expansion of socialism in Africa, her support of the USSR within the Nonaligned Movement and in the Soviet controversy with China, her endorsement and support of guerrilla movements and revolutionary governments in Latin America, and her status as a showcase of Soviet generosity. (For a comprehensive discussion on these and other political issues see Jorge Domínguez's chapter in this book.)

In deciding what level of economic aid to extend to Cuba in the future, the USSR has to balance these political gains with an increasingly heavier economic burden. The year 1984 seems to have been a turning point in the Soviet-Cuban relationship. Cuba's overall foreign trade deficit reached a record $1.9 billion (about half of it with the USSR), Soviet subsidies and loans surpassed for the first time the $5 billion mark (19 percent of Cuba's GSP), the world price of sugar declined to the lowest level in 14 years without immediate prospects of a significant recuperation, and Soviet supplies of oil and oil products approximated the 13 billion-ton mark. All of this happened as the Soviet leadership elite was changing, and Castro could no longer rely on old and predictable friends.

A Western analyst has recently argued that 1984–1985 was a period of chilly relations between the two countries highlighted by Castro's conspicuous absence at both Chernenko's funeral and the CMEA meeting in Moscow.[55] According to the evidence presented in Valkenier's chapter, the situation should not improve under Gorbachev's tenure. Several issues raised in his report to the 27th CPSU Congress in February 1986 (as well as in the current Soviet five-year plan) obviously conflict with Castro's interests. Earlier we noted Soviet acknowledgment of a single world market, interdependence, the LDCs' natural role as raw material producers, and the call for a fair, presumably negotiated, solution of the debt crisis. Gorbachev also placed priority on building up the Soviet economy over the needs of "national liberation movements" in the Third World countries. Moreover, to argue that Soviet foreign trade must be built on "principles of mutual benefit," implies the avoidance of generous support of LDCs. The call for a removal of trade barriers (rather than the preferential agreements favoring LDCs advocated by the Group of 77), the tough stand of Soviet trade negotiators with Latin American trade partners, and the resistance to the request of the Third World that the USSR give 0.7 percent of its budget to LDCs are all additional signs of a toughened Soviet position.

In October 1984, CMEA held its 39th meeting in Havana, the first time such a gathering had been held outside of Eastern Europe. This could be taken as a Soviet concession to Havana, but from another perspective it might be seen instead as a Soviet way to put additional pressure on Cuba to improve its economic performance and become more self-sufficient. In his speech to the CMEA meeting, Castro acknowledged delays in Cuban exports to CMEA and blamed these on domestic deficiencies. He then announced production increments in Cuban sugar and other raw materials exported to CMEA, and promised to increase economic efficiency.[56]

Later in the year a series of significant changes in Cuba's economic policies and bureaucracy took place. Castro appointed a small team of loyalists to drastically modify the investment plan (emphasizing export promotion and import substitution), taking this function away from the Central Planning Board (JUCEPLAN). In the long-range plan (1985–2000) signed with the USSR, 11 out of 14 policy directives were designed to transfer more of the cost of development to Cuba in an attempt to make the island more self-financing, among which were increasing sugar and nickel exports to the USSR, reducing Soviet imports, partially substituting Soviet oil imports by increases in Cuban domestic output and savings, and generally improving economic efficiency. Similar in thrust were the objectives outlined in the 1986–1990 Cuban plan, namely to fulfill export commitments with socialist countries, increase hard-currency foreign earnings, and use foreign aid more effectively.

The above measures—and the tenor of Castro's main report to the 3rd Congress of Cuba's Communist Party was highly critical of Cuba's economic deficiencies, emphasizing the need to improve efficiency, end corruption, and strengthen discipline—coincide with Gorbachev's campaign of economic self-discipline as to domestic and foreign commitments.[57] On the other hand, since mid-1985, Castro has also taken actions of a different nature which seem to put him on a collision course with the Soviet leadership. After criticizing many of its features as "neo-capitalist," Castro dismissed the head of JUCEPLAN, Humberto Pérez, a Moscow-trained economist and the architect of the Soviet-style System of Economic Management and Planning (SDPE) which began to be introduced in Cuba in the mid-1970s. Moreover, in a drive against "capitalist-type enterprises" which were mainly motivated by profits instead of the common good, Castro announced the elimination of the free peasant markets, suspended productivity bonuses, criticized the private sale of houses and apartments, condemned such things as authors' royalties and other economic incentives, and launched a "rectification campaign" which stressed the importance of nonmaterial incentives.

These measures were reminiscent of the moral economy of the second half of the 1960s which climaxed with the "Revolutionary Offensive" and open confrontation with the USSR in 1968, and which ended in chaos and economic disruption in 1970. These measures should have caused both concern in Moscow and confusion in Cuba since it is difficult to believe that the problems of the Cuban economy can be corrected through another shift to the left. More economically rational and palatable to the USSR would have been for the Cuban leadership to push the economic reform towards a more liberal stand à la Hungary. But a shift toward the market would have required significant economic and political decentralization, something the Cuban leaders are reluctant to consider.

If Castro continues to move leftward while his measures to expand exports, reduce imports, cut down on deficits, and improve efficiency are not successful, a confrontation with the USSR is highly probably.[58] Certainly low world prices for sugar and oil are not going to help in increasing exports. Restrictions on certain imports could well create bottlenecks and induce output declines. It appears that the Cuban leadership has forgotten the lessons of recent history: moral incentives have negative effects on output, discipline, and efficiency. Another interpretation of Cuba's apparent deviation from Soviet orthodoxy might suggest that Castro has lost his bargaining chips with the USSR (e.g., his role in Africa is no longer paying dividends, but instead has become a costly burden) and this may be a trick to recuperate his leverage in order to maintain the generous Soviet aid. Or perhaps Castro, after unsuccessfully trying various socialist models in the past, is now uncertain of the way to go and (as in 1964–1966) he is gaining time until he comes up with a new, inventive path. The difference with past experiments is, however, that the Soviet leadership is probably less patient, while the Cuban people should be weary of waiting for the materialization of the promised dream after almost three decades of revolution.

Notes

1 The authors gratefully acknowledge the detailed and valuable review of a first draft of this chapter by Jorge Pérez-López, as well as other comments from (or materials supplied by) Cole Blasier, Jorge Domínguez, José Alonso, Janet Chapman, Kevin Sontheimer and Jose Mencinger. In the Soviet Material Product System, GSP is the annual value from all the material production sphere, both material goods (i.e., agriculture, fishing, mining, industry, and construction) and material services (i.e., transportation, communication, and trade). Hence GSP excludes nonmaterial services such as administration, finance, defense, health care, education, housing, etc. For details see C. Mesa-Lago and Jorge Pérez-López, *A Study of Cuba's Material Product System, its Conversion to the System of National Accounts, and Estimation of Gross Domestic Product per Capita and Growth Rates* (Washington D.C.: World Bank Staff Working Papers, 1985), p. 770.

2 These findings contradict previous research conducted by William LeoGrande, "Cuban Dependency: A Comparison of Pre- and Post-Revolutionary International Economic Relations," *Cuban Studies*, 9:2 (July 1979), pp. 1–28. LeoGrande covers in his study the period 1959–1976, prior to the increase in Cuban dependency.

3 For recent comprehensive analyses of Cuba's economy, see Mesa-Lago, *The Economy of Socialist Cuba: A Two-Decade Appraisal* (Albuquerque: University of New Mexico Press, 1981) and Claes Brundenius, *Revolutionary Cuba: The Challenge of Economic Growth with Equity* (Boulder: Westview Press, 1984). For a debate on several economic issues between Brundenius/Zimbalist and Mesa-Lago/Pérez López, see *Comparative Economic Studies*, 27:1 (Spring), pp. 21–83; 27:3 (Fall), pp. 115–131; and 27:4 (Winter), pp. 67–84.

4 Brundenius has criticized Mesa-Lago's previous analysis of trade dependency based on two points: (a) the use of CMP which is smaller than both GSP and GDP, hence leading to higher percentages of trade dependency; and (b) the comparison of exports (and imports) in current prices with GMP allegedly in constant prices, thus also resulting in higher percentages. Concerning the first point, Table 6.3 reports trade dependency over GSP showing indeed smaller percentages than with GMP, but a similar increasing trend. Furthermore, a Cuban GDP series for the 1970s proves that GDP is systematically *smaller* than GSP, hence percentages of trade dependency calculated over GDP are higher than corresponding percentages over GSP. Concerning the second argument, GSP includes trade which is affected by inflation; Brundenius has later alleged that GSP is constant in prices, a point contradicted by the Cuban data. He also argues that both trade-partner concentration and sugar export concentration indicators are biased (inflated) because of Soviet subsidies to Cuban sugar exports. This argument is absurd since by the same token it could lead to exclude revenue from Soviet trade subsidies in the calculation of Cuban GSP. Furthermore, it would also lead to similar adjustments in relation to U.S. preferential prices paid to Cuban sugar exports prior to the revolution.

5 See Lawrence Theriot and Je Nelle Matheson, "Soviet Economic Relations with Non-European CMEA: Cuba, the Soviet Union, and Mongolia," in Joint Economic Committee, *Soviet Economy in Time of Change* (Washington D.C.: Government Printing Office, 1979), II, p. 560.

6 Fidel Castro, "Main Report to the 3rd Congress," *Granma Weekly Review*, February 16, 1986, p. 4.

7 See, as examples, Castro, "Speech on the 19th Anniversary of the Attack on the Moncada Garrison," *Granma Weekly Review*, August 6, 1972, pp. 3–6; and José Luis Rodríguez, "Un enfoque burgués del sector externo de la economía cubana," *Cuba Socialista*, 14 (March–April 1985), pp. 83–84.

8 CEPAL "Comercio y cooperación entre países de América Latina y países miembros del CAME," Santiago, Estudios e Informes de la CEPAL, 1985, pp. 71–72.

9 Some of these problems are reported by a former Cuban trade official, Luis Negrete, "Commercial Relations Between Cuba, the Soviet Union, and the Other MEAC [CMEA] countries," n./p., 1986, pp. 6–7. Even Carlos R. Rodríguez acknowledges the flaws of CMEA in "Press Conference on the 39th Session of CMEA," *Granma Weekly Review*, October 28, 1984, p. 4.

10 Mesa-Lago, *The Economy...*, pp. 101–02; and "The Cuban Merchant Marine," *Granma Weekly Review*, Special Supplement, September 20, 1981, pp. 5–6.

11 Cuba is the largest single world exporter of sugar. Past fluctuations in that country's production have affected its exports to the world sugar market (approximately 15 million metric tons) by about 1 million tons. Hence, there is a negative correlation between Cuban sugar output and world market prices: a 1 percent increase in Cuba's share of the world market can induce a -0.7 percent decline in the world price and vice-versa. See C. Suan Tan, *Cuba-USSR Sugar Trade*, The World Bank, Division Working Paper, 1986–2, June 1986.

12 For more details, see Mesa–Lago, "The Economy: Caution, Frugality, and Resilient Ideology," in Jorge Domínguez, ed., *Cuba: Internal and International Affairs* (Beverly Hills: Sage Publications, 1982), p. 122.

13 The Soviet shortfall amounted to 1.5 million tons in 1970–1974, 3.1 million in 1975–1979, and 5.3 million in 1980–1984; Cuba has supplied, in these respective periods, 85, 90, and 59 percent of Soviet needs. International Sugar Organization, *Annual Reports* and *Statistical Bulletins*.

14 John T. Smith, "Sugar Dependency in Cuba: Capitalism vs. Socialism," in Mitchell A. Seligson, ed., *The Gap Between Rich and Poor* (Boulder: Westview Press, 1985), pp. 369–74.

15 William W. Redell, "Cuban-Soviet Sugar Trade, 1960–1976: How Great was the Subsidy?," *The Journal of Developing Areas*, 17:3 (1983), pp. 365–82.

16 Clifford Krauss, "U.S. Sugar Quotas Impede U.S. Policies Toward Latin America," *The Wall Street Journal*, September 26, 1986, pp. 1, 16.

17 According to a Cuban-CMEA agreement, when the nickel plant (which had been started at the end of 1984 in Camarioca-Holguin with CMEA credit and technical aid) is in full production, half of its output (15,000 tons) will be exported to CMEA members as repayment for their loans.

18 C. R. Rodríguez, "Press Conference," p. 3.

19 Mesa-Lago, *The Economy*, p. 92; also see below, note 27.

20 See, as examples, Theriot and Matheson, "Soviet Economic Relations," p. 561; and Andrew Zimbalist, "Soviet Aid, U.S. Blockade and the Cuban Economy," *The ACES Bulletin*, 24:4 (Winter 1984), p. 142.

21 Mesa-Lago, *The Economy*, pp. 97–99.

22 See E. Guevara, *Revolución*, February 26, 1965, p. 1 (quoted in Domínguez' chapter); Castro, "Speech Analyzing Events in Czechoslovakia," *Granma Weekly Review*, August 25, 1968, p. 2 and "Discurso en la clausura del II periodo de sesiones de 1979 de la Asamblea Nacional del Poder Popular," Palacio de las Convenciones, December 27, 1979; Negrete, "Commercial Relations," pp. 3–35; C. R. Rodríguez, "Press Conference," pp. 3–4 and quoted by *Le Monde*, January 1975, pp. 1–4; and Lawrence Theriot, *Cuba Faces the Economic Realities of the 1980s* (Washington D.C., Joint Economic Committee, 1982), p. 36.

23 Mesa-Lago, *The Economy*, pp. 99–101. On nuclear power see *Granma Weekly Review*, October 28, 1984, p. 2.

24 Jorge Pérez-López, "Cuba as an Oil Trader: Petroleum Deals in a Falling Market," *Caribbean Review*, 15:2 (Spring 1986), pp. 26–29, 43–44.

25 *Ibid.*

26 *Anuario Estadístico de Cuba 1984*, *Cuba en Cifras 1985*, and *Guía Estadística 1985*.

27 Castro, "Speech at the First National Forum on Energy," *Granma Weekly Review*, December 16, 1984, pp. 13–14; and Pérez-López, "Cuba as an Oil Trader."

28 Pérez-López, "Cuban Oil Re-exports: Significance and Prospects," forthcoming in *The Energy Journal*.

29 Horst Mendershausen, "Terms of Trade Between the Soviet Union and Smaller Communist Countries, 1955–1957," *Review of Economics and Statistics*, 61:2 (May 1959), pp. 106–18, and "The Terms of Soviet-Satellite Trade: A Broadened Analysis," *ibid.* 62:2 (May 1960), pp. 152–63; Michael Marrese and Jan Vanous, *Soviet Subsidization of Trade with Eastern Europe* (Berkeley: University of California Institute of International Studies, 1983); Paul Marer, "The Political Economy of Soviet Relations with Eastern Europe," in *Soviet Policy in Eastern Europe*, Sarah M. Terry, ed. (New Haven: Yale University Press, 1984), pp. 155–88; and Franklyn Holzman, "The Significance of Soviet Subsidies to Eastern Europe," in *Comparative Economic Studies*, 28:1 (Spring 1986), pp. 54–65.

30 The three studies are the following: CIA, *The Cuban Economy: A Statistical Review 1968–1976* (Washington D.C.: Government Printing Office, 1976), p. 13, table 23; Jorge Domínguez, *Cuba: Order and Revolution* (Cambridge: Harvard University Press, 1978), pp. 155–56; and Jorge Pérez-López, "Sugar and Petroleum in Cuban-Soviet Terms of Trade," in Cole Blasier and C. Mesa-Lago, eds. *Cuba in the World* (Pittsburgh: University of Pittsburgh Press, 1979), pp. 273–96.

31 A note of caution with Table 6.11 is that the base year is 1968 when Soviet-Cuban relations were rather tense, in the midst of the Maoist-Guevarist period, before relations improved in the 1970s. For that reason, Cuban terms of trade were not very favorable in that year, and indeed the total trade subsidy declined by 28 percent in 1968 and by 57 percent in 1969. This may induce an upward bias in the index, but the trend still should be proper.

32 Quoted by Sergio Roca, "Cuba's International Economic Relations in the 1980s," Symposium on the Future of Cuba, Columbia University, December 6, 1985, p. 9.
33 See Cole Blasier, "COMECON in Cuban Development," in *Cuba in the World*, pp. 227–28.
34 This information was given by José Luis Rodríguez to Jorge Domínguez in a visit of the latter to Cuba in the summer of 1986. Personal conversation with Domínguez in Pittsburgh, August 16, 1986.
35 N. Leonov, "USSR-Cuba: Fraternal Cooperation in Action," *International Affairs*, 11 (1984), p. 25.
36 *Granma Weekly Review*, April 25, 1976, p. 9.
37 Rodríguez reported this as "new Soviet credits" in an interview with Prensa Latina partly reproduced in BBC, *Weekly Economic Report*, Part IV, April 2, 1986, pp. 3–5. The *Washington Post* (April 12, 1986, p. A 20) reported the figure as $3 million as based on *Granma*. However, *Granma* (April 11, 1986) did not provide the amount of the credits, although it did report the 50 percent increase over the previous quinquenium.
38 Castro, "Discurso en conmemoración del Centenario del Natalicio de Vladimir Ilich Lenin," *Granma*, April 23, 1970, p. 3. For a full description and references on this subject, see Jorge Domínguez' chapter and U.S. Department of Defense, *Soviet Military Power* (Washington D.C.: Government Printing Office, 1985), pp. 115–20.
39 Pamela Falk, *Cuba Foreign Policy: Caribbean Tempest* (Lexington: Lexington Books, 1985), p. 136.
40 J. L. Rodríguez, "Un enfoque burgués," p. 95. On Raúl Castro's claims, see AlfonsoChardy,"ArmswasteadmittedbyCubanRaúlCastro,"*MiamiHerald*,September 12, 1987, p. 1A.
41 Oscar Pino Santos y Osvaldo Martínez, "Relaciones económicas de Cuba con los países miembros del CAME" (Santiago de Chile: CEPAL, November 1979), pp. 52–72.
42 *Latin American Weekly Report*, December 21, 1984, p. 7.
43 Cole Blasier, conversations with high Cuban officials in Havana, June 1, 1985. José Luis Rodríguez confirmed this to Jorge Domínguez in Havana, June 1986, but said that the terms had not yet been settled. This is interpreted by Domínguez as a Soviet way to increase its leverage in negotiations with the Cubans.
44 Castro, "Speech," p. 14, and "Speech at the Close of the Meeting on the Situation of Latin America," *Granma Weekly Review*, June 16, 1985, pp. 15–17.
45 Banco Nacional de Cuba (BNC), *Economic Report*, February 1985 and March 1986; and BNC-Comité Estatal de Estadística, *Quarterly Economic Report*, September 1985.
46 J. L. Rodríguez, "Un eforque," p. 97.
47 BNC, *Informe Económico*, August 1982, p. 46.
48 *Ibid.*, p. 47.
49 Calculations were based on Table 6.3, United Nations Conference on Trade and Development (UNTAD), *Cuba: Recent Economic Development and Future Prospects*, November 1982; BNC, *Economic Reports 1982* to *1986*.
50 Mesa-Lago's, *The Economy*, p. 106. For other comparisons, see J. L. Rodríguez, "Un enfoque burgués," pp. 102–03; Susan Eckstein, "The Cuban Revolution in Comparative Perspective," LASA Meeting, Mexico City, September 1983, table 6.5; and Donald Putnam Henry et al., *An Analysis of Cuban Debt* (Santa Monica: Rand Corporation, May 1984), p. 13; Brundenius (*Revolutionary Cuba*, p. 66) does the Cuban comparison with the rest of Latin America restricting the Cuban foreign debt to the hard-currency part, hence excluding the debt with the USSR (81 percent of the total debt), and obviously reaching rosier conclusions.
51 Castro, *Interview Granted to the Mexican Daily Excelsior* (La Habana: Editora Política, 1985), pp. 23–24, 26.
52 Blasier, *The Giant's Rival*, pp. 225 and 231.

53 Author calculations based on data from the CIA, *Handbook of Economic Statistics 1986* (Washington D.C.: Government Printing Office 1986), pp. 25, 111–15.

54 W. Raymond Duncan, "Castro and Gorbachev: Politics of Accommodation," *Problems of Communism*, 35:2 (March–April 1986), pp. 49–50. Duncan is incorrect, however, in asserting that an indication of the Soviet stick was the limited economic aid to Cuba of $4 billion in 1984; actual aid was around $5.6 billion, 15 percent more than in 1983 (see table 6.13).

55 Castro, "Address...to the 39th Session of the Council for Mutual Economic Assistance," *Granma Weekly Review*, November 11, 1984, p. 5.

56 Castro, "Main Report," Jorge Pérez-López, "Cuban Economy in the 1980s," *Problems of Communism*, 35:5 (September 1986), pp. 16–34; Roca, "Cuba's International Economic Relations," pp. 14–17; Jorge Pérez-López, "Cuban Economic Performance during 1981–1985 and Prospects for 1986–1990," 1986; and Edward González and David Ronfeldt, *Castro, Cuba, and the World* (Santa Monica: The Rand Corporation, June 1986), p. 81.

57 For analysis of various scenarios of the Cuban future, see Duncan, "Castro and Gorbachev," pp. 55–56, and González and Ronfeldt, *Castro, Cuba, and the World*, pp. 87ff.

58 For a review of the "Rectification Process" and my own analysis of viable alternatives for Cuba, see "The Cuban Economy in the 1980s: The Return of Ideology," in *Socialist Cuba: Past Interpretations and Future Challenges*, Sergio Roca, ed. (Boulder: Westview Press, 1988).

7

Soviet Trade Relations with Latin America

Robert K. Evanson

This chapter is an attempt to summarize Soviet economic and military trade in Latin America and assess its political and economic importance. What is the current level of Soviet trade with Latin America? What purposes are apparent, and how do the Soviets attempt to utilize trade and aid to accomplish these purposes? What have been the Soviet successes and failures in this regard and the reasons for them? What factors are most likely to influence future trends in Soviet economic relations with the region? The primary emphasis in this chapter is on economic (nonmilitary) trade, because the USSR ships arms to very few countries in Latin America. Economic aid is treated largely as an aspect of trade, since most Soviet nonmilitary assistance is extended in the form of trade credits.

OUTLINE OF SOVIET-LATIN AMERICAN COMMERCE

Prior to the 1960s, Soviet trade with Latin America was miniscule, although Soviet initiatives had resulted in formal trade agreements and modest increases in trade with Argentina after 1953 and with Brazil after 1959. The big breakthrough came in the wake of the Cuban Revolution, when the USSR began to fill the trade vacuum created by the loss of U.S. markets for Cuban sugar and other products. Since then the number of Soviet trading partners in Latin America has grown steadily. The USSR has been buying and selling regularly for 15 or more years with 8 of the 12 South American states. Trade with Paraguay and with post-Allende Chile has been negligible. The Soviets sell small amounts to Venezuela on a fairly regular basis, but buy almost nothing; trade with Surinme has been intermittent.

There has been a dramatic long-term rise in the ruble value of Soviet nonmilitary trade with Latin America. If one excludes Cuba, whose trade with the Soviet Union exceeds that of all the other Latin American states combined, the value rose from 60 million rubles in 1960 to 1.6 billion in 1980 and to over 3 billion in the early 1980s.[1] Recent figures reveal, however, that the upward trend has stopped at least for the moment. Cuban sources reported a 1.2 billion ruble increase in all Soviet-Latin American trade for 1985,[2] but figures from the International Monetary Fund (IMF) indicate a net decline in trade for the same year if one excludes Cuba.[3] Soviet statistics for trade with selected Latin American states published in 1987 suggest that the non-Cuban figure for 1985 rested somewhere below 2.5 billion rubles; the same source also reveals a further, more precipitous decline in

TABLE 7.1
Soviet Trade with Nine Latin American States, 1979, 1985, 1986

Country	Imports from USSR (in millions of rubles)			Exports to USSR (in millions of rubles)		
	1979	*1985*	*1986*	*1979*	*1985*	*1986*
Argentina	24.8	63.0	53.3	288.7	1229.9	192.4
Brazil	19.9	70.2	30.3	160.0	380.0	236.5
Columbia	9.0	5.2	4.9	3.0	21.2	0.0
Cuba	2113.2	3877.4	3802.3	2136.0	4140.1	3800.2
Mexico	0.7	4.2	4.3	4.1	16.1	7.6
Nicaragua	*	212.9	276.4	*	0.2	7.7
Panama	10.3	7.1	10.5	0.2	**	**
Peru	2.8	11.3	9.2	9.9	108.5	75.2
Uruguay	1.6	33.5	4.3	11.7	32.4	20.6

* No data available.
** No measurable trade.
Source: *Vneshniaia torgovlia*, 3 (1979 supplement), and 3 (1987 supplement).

1986 (see Table 7.1). Responsible for both the upsurge of trade in the early 1980s and the recent drop were Soviet purchases of foodstuffs, especially Argentine grain. These purchases varied in volume from year to year, and grain prices declined in the mid-1980s. It is too early to tell to what extent Soviet purchases of grain were temporarily inflated by the imposition of the U.S. embargo in 1979 and now are seeking a more realistic level, but this clearly has been a factor. Until that picture is clarified, it would be premature to draw any firm long-term conclusions from the decline in Soviet-Latin American trade in 1985–86. A more detailed discussion of Argentine-Soviet trade appears below.

Table 7.1 presents in millions of rubles the value of Soviet nonmilitary trade in 1979, 1985, and 1986 with the nine Latin American countries included in Soviet-published trade data. These are not necessarily the nine largest Soviet trading partners in the region. Table 7.2 presents a different set of figures, in dollars, for Soviet trade with the 13 largest partners in 1985. Bolivia, Costa Rica, the Dominican Republic, and Jamaica appear in this list, but not in Table 7.1, which includes one

TABLE 7.2
The USSR's Largest Trading Partners in Latin America, 1985

Country	*Imports from USSR (in millions of U.S. dollars)*	*Exports to USSR (in millions of U.S. dollars)*
Argentina	35	1,330
Bolivia	4	10
Brazil	91	495
Columbia	4	21
Costa Rica	0	7
Cuba	6,448*	5,374*
Dominican Republic	0	8
Ecuador	1	8
Jamaica	3	31
Mexico	7	7
Nicaragua	39	10
Peru	2	8
Uruguay	25	64

* Figures were given in Cuban pesos and converted to U.S. dollars at the official conversion rate as of September 1985.

Sources: International Monetary Fund, *Direction of Trade Statistics Yearbook 1985* (New York: IMF, 1985); U.S. Department of State, private communication with various officials, 1987.

country, Panama, that does not appear in Table 7.2. The uncertain nature of foreign trade statistics can be seen by comparing the figures for 1985 in the two tables. The enormous discrepancies between the Soviet and IMF figures for several of these trade relationships, which result from the IMF's exclusion of countertrade, cannot be removed by converting rubles to dollars; in some cases—Peru, Nicaragua, and Mexico—conversion would make the gap more obvious.

Although the figures in Tables 7.1 and 7.2 must be taken with caution, they do allow comparisons of the relative sizes of various Soviet trade relationships as well as of trends over time. Both tables illustrate the enormity of Soviet-Cuban trade and the large volumes of Soviet purchases between 1979 and 1985, and the growth of Soviet shipments to Nicaragua, which were too small in 1979 to be included in the annual Soviet trade chart. Table 7.2 greatly understates the value of Soviet economic deliveries to Nicaragua, perhaps owing to the exclusion of certain types of aid. The U.S. Department of Defense, for example, estimates $300 million in Soviet economic assistance to Nicaragua in 1986 alone.[4] Table 7.1 also highlights the sharp decline in Soviet-Latin American trade from 1985 to 1986, particularly in Latin American exports. Finally, both tables illustrate the trade deficits the Soviets run with most of the countries of Latin America. These deficits work an economic hardship on the USSR that sometimes discourage Soviet purchases as well.

Perhaps more telling than the dollar or ruble values are Soviet and allied percentage shares of Latin American trade, since they provide one measure of the importance of Soviet and Soviet bloc trade to the economies of the region. While the Soviet share of total Latin American trade has grown, it remains rather small—extremely so when Cuba is excluded—and did not reach four percent until the 1980s. Table 7.3 presents Soviet and combined Soviet-East European average annual percentage shares of the nonmilitary imports and exports from the 13 states in Table 7.2 during 1974–82, the most recent period for which such data are available (the dates for Bolivia are 1974–79). Only in the case of Cuba have Soviet and East European shares been large on both sides of the ledger; the shares of Argentine exports have also been very impressive. In several other cases—Bolivia, Brazil, Peru, and Uruguay—the export shares during 1974–82 were by no means negligible. Soviet and East European trade with Nicaragua grew in the 1980s and is not reflected in Table 7.3.

According to Nicaraguan government sources, the Council for Mutual Economic Assistance share of Nicaraguan imports and exports grew form 0 percent and 3 percent, respectively, in 1980 to 26 percent and 6 percent in 1984.[5] The ruble value of Soviet-Nicaraguan trade grew from 51.9 million rubles in 1983 to 138.1 million rubles in 1984.[6] That amount in turn doubled by 1986 (Table 7.1), while Nicaragua's overall trade declined.[7] The USSR has become the major oil supplier of Nicaragua (between 80 and 90 percent since 1985) and a source of food, machinery and equipment, transportation vehicles, and oil-based products. In contrast, Nicaragua ships little of value to the Soviet Union, fostering this trade relationship entirely for political reasons. (For a discussion, see the chapter by Peter Clement and Raymond Duncan.) At this point, Nicaragua maintains trade with a large number of states, but as its economy and its ability to pay its creditors has deteriorated, it has become increasingly dependent on and more fully integrated into the Soviet bloc's economic subsystem.[8]

As reported in Aldo Vacs' chapter, the USSR became Argentina's biggest customer in the early 1980s, buying $3.4 billion in goods in 1981 (that is, one-third of all Argentine exports for that year and including 80 percent of grain exports).[9] The value of Soviet purchases during 1982–85 ranged between $1.3 billion and $1.6 billion. In 1986, however, Argentine exports to the Soviet Union plummeted to less than one-sixth the value of Soviet purchases in 1985 (Table 7.1). The record of 1982–85 suggests that both 1981 and 1986 were aberrations; Argentine exports to the USSR in the future will no doubt fall somewhere between these two extremes. In January 1986, the two countries signed a new five-year trade agreement in which the Soviet Union promised to buy at least 4.5 million tons of grain annually,[10] which is more than 5 times the volume bought in 1986, and less than one-third of the 15 million tons purchased in 1981.[11] Soviet representatives were quick to reassure their Argentine counterparts that their country would make up for the 1986 shortfall in subsequent years.[12]

The future pattern of Soviet-Argentine trade relations is as yet unclear. The USSR has been hit by a severe shortage of hard currency as a result of declining prices for its oil exports and has begun to seek cheaper, subsidized grain from other sources. In 1986, the Soviet Union may have been waiting for Argentine prices to drop to the level of the competition, and they may also have been pressuring Argentina to honor its commitment to increase its imports of Soviet manufactures to alleviate what has been one of the worst imbalances in all of Soviet trade (Tables 7.1 and 7.2).[13] Future levels of Soviet purchases may depend in part on Argentina's ability to sell at competitive prices, but the USSR has been willing

TABLE 7.3
Soviet and Soviet/East European Shares of Trade with Latin America, 1974–1982

Country	*Average Trade with USSR* Exports (%)	Imports (%)	*Average Trade with USSR and Eastern Europe* Exports (%)	Imports (%)
Argentina	12.4	0.4	14.1	1.7
Bolivia (1974–79)	4.1	0.8	6.3	2.0
Brazil	2.5	0.3	6.8	1.7
Columbia	0.4	0.2	3.4	1.6
Costa Rica	0.2	0.1	1.7	0.5
Cuba	70.3	56.9	78.8	68.1
Dominican Republic	1.6	0.0[a]	1.8	0.0[a]
Ecuador	0.5	0.1	2.5	1.2
Jamaica	1.8	0.0[a]	2.1	0.2
Mexico	0.0[a]	0.0[a]	0.4	0.4
Nicaragua	0.7	0.6	1.9	1.5
Peru	1.8	0.2	6.2	1.5
Uruguay	4.1	0.2	7.0	1.4

a. 0.0% = less than 0.1%.

Source: United Nations, *Yearbook of International Trade Statistics* (New York: United Nations, 1983).

in the past to endure large deficits with Argentina and has a deep economic and political investment in close trade relations. Argentina has provided a reliable market for grain when other sources have proved inadequate, and it has a large domestic market the Soviets have labored hard to cultivate. Trade may also be a foundation on which the Soviets can build greater political cooperation, a matter that is treated below.

The Soviet Union buys a great deal of foodstuffs from Brazil and is purchasing increasing amounts of iron ore and pig iron. (See Aldo Vacs' chapter.) In the past, Brazil has bought almost nothing but oil, but the Soviets are involved in the development of Brazil's energy industries and are pushing hard to sell more manufactured products. Soviet purchases rose from $226 million in 1979 to $864 million in 1983.[14] Tables 7.1 and 7.2 reveal a decline in 1985 and 1986, principally reflecting a fall in Soviet food orders. A $1.5 billion trade agreement signed in November 1985, if fully implemented—such protocols often are not—would triple the 1985 level of trade between the two countries.[15] In Brazil, as in Argentina, the Soviets are attracted by potentially huge domestic markets which they have had only modest success in penetrating.

At one time in the 1970s, as Ruben Berríos notes in his chapter, Peru was the Soviet Union's fourth largest trading partner in Latin America behind Cuba, Argentina, and Brazil. Soviet-bloc states granted extensive credit and established cooperative relationships in many of Peru's economic sectors, including mining, agriculture, chemicals, fishing, oil, hydroelectricity, and transportation.[16] Most of the credit and the lion's share of the trade have involved the East European allies (Table 7.3). Peru's principal shipments to the USSR have been minerals, wool, fish, and other foodstuffs; in return, it has received machinery and heavy equipment, military weaponry, and technical assistance for its oil, mining, and fishing industries, and for the development of irrigation and hydroelectric power.

The Soviet share of Peruvian trade, which was tiny during the late 1970s, grew even smaller in the early 1980s, and the common Soviet and East European percentage of Peru's exports dropped from 6.7 percent in 1976–80 to 1.7 percent in 1981–82.[17] Soviet arms sales declined as well. This trade decline may have been due in part to a lack of commitment by the civilian government of Fernando Belaunde, who returned to power in 1980 after 12 years of military rule. During the 1980s, Peru's debt problems further complicated Soviet bloc-Peruvian trade. However, in November 1983 Peru and the USSR reached a countertrade agreement under which repayment of nearly half of Peru's Soviet debt was postponed, and of what was left, Peru began to pay in kind (up to 75 percent of it in the form of nontraditional products) rather than in hard currency.[18] Peru has made similar arrangements with several other CMEA states. These agreements have provided an enormous stimulus to some of Peru's domestic industries and have at least temporarily made the Soviet Union a major market for Peruvian exports (Table 7.1). The latter now include large amounts of textiles, lumber, footwear, finished metal products, and computers.[19] In addition, the two states have extended their cooperative fishing arrangement through 1990, despite disagreements over financial details and division of the catch. Soviet vessels are allowed to make a catch reportedly worth up to $1.8 billion a year, and to dock in Peruvian ports for food, fuel, and repairs.[20] These privileges have drawn domestic criticism in Peru, since they allow many thousands of Soviet personnel into Peruvian ports and could easily provide cover for intelligence activities.

The Soviet Union looks to Bolivia largely for tin, and delivers machinery, equipment, and technology for Bolivia's mining and fuel industries in return. In the 1970s, tin sales pushed Bolivia past Peru as the USSR's fourth largest trading partner in Latin America. Trade declined in the 1980s as labor unrest, an antiquated mining infrastructure, and the collapse of metal prices on the world market brought Bolivian tin, atimony, copper, and lead output to their lowest levels since the 1930s.[21] Heavy Soviet involvement in revitalizing Bolivia's mining sector suggests a strong mutual commitment to future trade.

Since 1984, the Soviets have resumed purchases of bauxite from Guyana, which in turn is buying Soviet aircraft, agricultural machinery, electronic equipment, and pharmaceuticals. They also have discussed possible cooperation in gold and diamonds.[22] The Soviet Union signed a similar accord with Jamaica in 1984 under which it is to purchase 1 million tons of bauxite a year for 7 years. Jamaica buys Soviet autos and tractors, but 80 percent of the Soviet purchases are to be paid for in hard currency.[23] The Jamaican export figure in table 7.2 reflects this agreement, but the Soviets reportedly fell short of their commitments under the deal in 1986–87.[24] The USSR also has recently emerged as a major buyer of sugar from the Dominican Republic, purchasing large amounts in 1982–83 and signing a three-year agreement in February 1987 under which it will buy 50,000 tons a year at a very low price, thereby taking advantage of the Dominican Republic's desperate need for customers in the wake of a cut in the United States' sugar quota.[25]

The USSR has paid considerable attention to Mexico, whose political influence, strategic location, frequently strained relations with the U.S., and large domestic market have made it an attractive target.[26] Soviet political and cultural relations with Mexico have long been cordial, and the USSR has made repeated diplomatic overtures in the 1980s focusing on such issues as the war in Central America and President Reagan's Strategic Defense Initiative. Despite repeated efforts by both governments, however, Soviet-Mexican trade has never really taken off. In the past, Mexico exchanged fruits and other consumer items for small amounts of oil, machinery, and technical assistance. The sum total of Mexican-Soviet trade during the 1970s barely exceeded 83 million rubles,[27] and the trade totals in Tables 7.1 and 7.2 for 1985–1986 suggest only modest improvement.

In recent years a flurry of promotional activity has resulted in promises of greater economic cooperation between Mexico and the Soviet Union in a number of areas. In 1984, the two states signed an agreement under which the USSR was to construct and enlarge foundries and other enterprises in the Mexican iron and steel industry. The Soviet Union also would provide technical advice and equipment, and accept payment in kind.[28] That same year it was announced that the USSR would build two textile factories in Chihuahua.[29] More recently, Mexico and the Soviet Union agreed to the joint construction of a copper-smelting plant, and the Soviets expressed an interest in investing 40 percent of the total capital in Mexican petrochemicals and steel.[30] Mexico has shown an interest in the joint manufacture of tractors, agreeing to send industrial employees to the Soviet Union for training.[31] Mexico is now selling pipes and drilling equipment for the Soviet oil industry, and the two states have also agreed to consult on petroleum pricing policies.[32] Thus they are increasing the variety of their trade products and modes of cooperation. A lack of product diversity was identified by Mexico's Secretary of Commerce and Commercial Development as a major barrier to past trade.[33] For his part, a Soviet trade representative spoke about low productivity in some Mexican industries,[34] a problem that might be alleviated by technical assistance in areas such as steel and oil, where the Soviets have extensive experience. On the other hand, previous promotional efforts by both countries have led to few results, and Mexico's economy remains closely tied to that of the United States.

An important aspect of Soviet trade with Latin America, to which we have only alluded, is arms shipments. The latter grew from $.06 billion in 1973–76 to $2.1 billion in 1977–80 and $3.6 billion in 1981–84.[35] Unlike economic trade, however, Soviet military trade with Latin America is basically confined to only a few countries: Cuba, Nicaragua and Peru. For a time the USSR shipped arms to Grenada, and in 1985 it sold three military helicopters to Guyana.[36] Soviet military aid to Cuba and Nicaragua has increased sharply in recent years. The U.S. Department of Defense estimates that of the $9 billion in military equipment delivered to Cuba free of charge from 1960 to 1986, nearly 60 percent arrived in the 1980s; in addition, the Soviets station about 2,800 military advisers in Cuba.[37] U.S. government sources also trace a rise in the value of Soviet arms aid to Nicaragua from $6 million in 1980 to $250 million in 1984, followed by a dip to $115 million in 1985 and a jump to $580 million in 1986. In metric tonnage, Soviet and East European shipments increased from 6,300 in 1981 to 17,960 in 1984, followed by a decline to 13,900 in 1985 and a leap to over 23,000 in 1986. The number of Soviet advisers in Nicaragua was estimated at 50–70 in 1986.[38] For a complete picture of military aid, one should also include the ultimately Soviet-subsidized Cuban and other bloc military and security advisers in Nicaragua, estimated by U.S. sources at 2,000 to 2,500; Nicaragua alone acknowledged 786 in 1985.[39]

According to U.S. Department of Defense estimates, the Soviet Union sold approximately $1.5 billion in arms to Peru during 1973–1986.[40] Peruvian purchases of Soviet tanks, missiles, helicopters, Sukhoi-22 supersonic fighter bombers, radar, and artillery during 1974–78 comprised, in another U.S. government estimate, some 65 percent of the country's total arms purchases for that period; [41] a different, reputable source puts the figure at 41 percent for the same period.[42] Sales began in 1973, increasing in value after 1975 as Peru became engaged in an arms race with Ecuador and Chile. Unable to procure advanced weaponry from the United States, Peru did some comparative shopping and found Soviet prices and terms of credit were the most attractive.[43] Arms sales served to reduce the USSR's trade imbalance with Peru, although a good part of the gain was lost when it became necessary to reschedule Peru's debt. The sales also gave the Soviets access to influential Peruvian military elites at a time of strained relations with the U.S., setting an example of military cooperation in a region that has been deeply suspicious of Soviet intentions.

Subsequently, the Peruvian air force, under the strongly pro-American civilian administration of Fernando Belaunde, leaned more heavily towards French Mirage fighters, reducing the Soviet share of Peruvian weapons purchases to 36 percent in 1979–83.[44] On the other hand, the Soviets have continued to sell weapons to Peru's army, provide spare parts, exchange military missions, train Peruvian military personnel in the USSR, and station about 115 military advisers in Peru for unit training and equipment maintenance.[45] The current government of President Alan García has cut back on military spending in the face of the debt crisis, so it is unlikely that Soviet arms sales will rise in the immediate future. Nevertheless, because Soviet-Peruvian military cooperation has survived several military and civilian regimes in Lima, the relationship should remain a fixture in both countries' foreign policies for the foreseeable future.

The level of overall Soviet trade with Latin America in the short run, therefore, has been in flux, some partnerships waxing, others waning. The long-term trend in Soviet purchases, however, has been strongly upward, and the USSR has been pressing hard for increased sales to Latin American markets. Based on the evidence of the 1980s, it has been much more successful at buying than at selling.

SOVIET POLITICAL USES OF TRADE

The USSR has important economic and political interests in Latin America. Economically, the Soviets seek access to valuable commodities, especially metals and foodstuffs, and strive to expand the sales of their own products, particularly manufactures, in local markets. Politically, the region is an arena for competition with the United States; Soviet involvement there is essential to its status as a global superpower. Because Latin America is so far away from the Soviet Union and U.S. influence so formidable, Soviet involvement there has increased more slowly than elsewhere in the Third World. However, as its logistical capabilities have grown and events in Latin America have presented new challenges to U.S. interests, the Soviet Union has found the temptation to exploit these events irresistible. Obviously, Latin America does not hold as much importance to the USSR as Third World areas close to the Soviet periphery, such as the Middle East and Southern Asia. Nonetheless, precisely because Latin America is such a vital concern to the United States, it takes on greater importance to the Soviets than its lack of geographical proximity would otherwise justify.

The Soviets seek to establish a permanent political and economic presence in Latin America, and a capacity to influence events there to the detriment of the United States. The disparity in power between the U.S. and the Soviet Union in Latin America has enhanced the importance of economic tactics as a Soviet political weapon. Few states in the region have thus far been willing to buy Soviet arms, which comprise the largest portion of Soviet shipments to other parts of the Third World. Certainly the USSR cannot intervene directly with military power, or even indirectly through thousands of Cuban proxy troops, the way it did in Africa in the 1970s. Sheer distance, U.S. influence, and ideological suspicions limit Latin American openness to Soviet diplomatic influence. As a result, the Soviet Union has at times fallen back on economic trade and aid as the most politically feasible alternative; at the same time, it has sought to supplement economic trade with arms shipments wherever possible.

One must be careful, of course, not to assume that every Soviet economic decision is guided exclusively, or even primarily by political motives. Political and economic goals are intertwined in every state's foreign policies, and Soviet behavior toward Latin America is no different. There are, however, a number of cases in which trade has served Soviet political interests in Latin America. Trade has often provided an entry for the USSR in opening or strengthening relations with countries in the region, and it has not been unusual for the Soviet Union to begin trading with a country before it establishes diplomatic relations: it was mutual economic interest, Brazil's desire to reduce its economic dependence on the United States, and a Soviet wish to exploit that desire that led to a Soviet trade agreement with the civilian government of Juscelino Kubitschek in 1959. The Soviets used the allure of expanded trade in an attempt to win Brazilian assent to the establishment of diplomatic relations, and to encourage Janio Quadros' "independent foreign policy" in 1961–63.[46]

Similarly, as Aldo Vacs notes in his chapter, trade provided a breakthrough in Soviet relations with Argentina, beginning with the Alejandro Lanusse regime in 1971 and accelerating under the conservative governments of the late 1970s and early 1980s. Soviet policymakers were attracted both to Argentina's abundance of foodstuffs and large domestic market, and to its flirtation with political nonalignment under Lanusse and then the Peronistas. The Soviet Union also used such political ploys as defending the human rights record of the military junta in the face of U.S. criticism, and giving diplomatic support to Argentina in the Falklands/Malvinas War, but trade has been the USSR's principal mechanism for cultivating contacts with local elites and establishing an accepted presence in Argentine society.

Still another example of politically motivated trade was the trade agreement signed with Omar Torrijos of Panama. The accord was extremely modest from an economic perspective, and of little use to Torrijos' effort to gain Panamanian control of the U.S. controlled Canal, but it appears that the USSR wanted a trade agreement partly to symbolize an improvement in relations at a time when overt political or military cooperation would have been unacceptable and risky to Panama. Such trade, the Soviet Union may have thought, could be a building block for closer future relations with the country destined to control the Panama Canal.

In addition to aiding Soviet efforts to establish a longterm presence in Latin America, trade has been used to lend political, economic, and military support to governments at odds with the United States. The Cuban and Nicaraguan cases are the most obvious. They are discussed elsewhere in this book. The Soviet Union also responded economically when the three Andean states of Ecuador, Peru, and Bolivia entered into conflict with the United States in the late 1960s. Ecuador resumed its "Tuna War" with the U.S. in 1968, expelled the U.S. ambassador, squabbled with U.S. oil companies over concessions, and provoked cuts in U.S. military and economic aid. The USSR and several of its allies signed trade agreements with Ecuador in 1969, but most of the trade gains were made by Eastern Europe, not the USSR.[47] In Peru in October 1968, and in Bolivia the following September, military groups seized power and soon nationalized U.S. oil company holdings and denounced the United States. These actions induced the Soviets to reevaluate the political roles of certain "progressive" military elites in Latin America,[48] and opened the door to trade agreements in which the Soviet Union granted credits for various development projects and agreed to purchase nonferrous metals and foodstuffs from Peru and tin from Bolivia. A subsequent Bolivian coup in October 1970 under General Juan José Torres, who shifted his country further to the left, was rewarded by larger Soviet credits and increased trade. In the Peruvian case, representatives for both sides praised the trade pact as aiding Peru's economic independence of the United States,[49] while in Bolivia the Soviet Union helped build a tin smelter to reduce that country's reliance on smelters in the West.[50]

The Soviet Union also employed trade in support of the Marxist government of Salvador Allende in Chile (1970–73). Allende's nationalization of U.S. companies' holdings brought his regime into bitter conflict with the United States, and his radical domestic policies and alliance with the Communist party made him ideologically attractive to the USSR. Actually, Soviet trade credits had already been extended to his predecessor, Eduardo Frei, who had asserted a much more cautious independence from the U.S. Under Allende, these credits were refinanced at lower interest and supplemented by new ones, and the USSR provided technical advisers for Chile's copper and fishing industries. Later the Soviet Union and its allies granted loans and agreed to purchase larger amounts of copper. Some writers have argued that the Soviets were not generous to a Marxist regime in dire financial need,[51] and the $260 million in credits and loans extended by the USSR[52] certainly was modest in comparison to its aid to Cuba. But aid was on the rise at the time of the coup. Chile was too large a country for the Soviet Union to keep afloat; and Allende, unlike Castro, had alternative sources of trade and aid and was slow in seeking assistance, and by the time he did so the Soviets may have considered him a lost cause.

Quarrels with the U.S. also preceded Soviet trade agreements with Guyana and Jamaica. In the 1970s their socialist governments joined the Nonaligned Movement, denounced U.S. "imperialism," gave diplomatic support to Cuba, and led the formation of the International Bauxite Association. The first Soviet purchase of bauxite came shortly after Guyana nationalized U.S. and Canadian bauxite firms in 1973. Soviet purchases of Jamaican bauxite followed the Michael Manley government's declaration of a pro-Cuban policy after its election in 1972. Both governments were seeking new markets and external support in the wake of their challenges to U.S. interests, winning Soviet praise for their changes in policy.[53]

There are several current situations where the Soviets pursue business-like trade relations that are economically beneficial to both parties, but where they view trade as having potential or actual political value as well. The USSR has major economic interests in Argentina and Brazil, but the two states are also leaning increasingly towards nonalignment and are politically too important to be viewed solely as trading partners. In Soviet relations with Argentina, for example, economic trade may ease the way to military trade during a political crisis, and port privileges for Soviet fishing vessels could be a precedent for extending similar privileges for Soviet warships. In the case of Mexico, the USSR clearly would like to sell more of its products in the domestic market. However, some Soviet analysts also admire Mexico's increasingly assertive foreign policy and see a potential for breaking the ties binding it to the United States.[54] Undoubtedly, the Soviet Union hopes that improved trade and cooperation in such important sectors as oil will help to strengthen Mexico's economic independence vis-à-vis the U.S. and put the USSR in a better position to influence future events there.

SOVIET ECONOMIC TACTICS

The Soviet Union has been very pragmatic in its pursuit of commodities and markets in Latin America. It was noted above that trade breakthroughs often have followed political shifts in Latin American states' foreign and domestic policies. In many cases, the USSR has launched a trade initiative at least partly for political reasons, but the relationship has persisted despite adverse changes in political circumstances. Once a mutually beneficial trade relationship has been established, neither side wants to give it up. Soviet trade with Brazil was not harmed by the onset of anti-Communist military rule in

1964, for example, nor did trade with Peru suffer from the fall of Juan Velasco Alvarado in 1975. Soviet-Bolivian trade positively flourished under the conservative military regime of Colonel Hugo Banzer after 1971, as did trade with Argentina under the right wing generals who ruled after 1976. The recent resurgence of Soviet-Jamaican trade began in the more conservative post-Michael Manley period.

Today the Soviet Union seldom has trouble finding sellers because Latin Americans need to export as much as possible. A number of factors are increasing this urgency. The debt crisis has worsened and no one expects it to diminish in the near future. At the same time, certain Latin American exports have run into barriers in traditional markets. A major cause of the recent rise in Soviet purchases of sugar from the Dominican Republic, Jamaica, Guyana, and other Caribbean countries, for example, has been the reduction in the quota by the United States.[55] Jamaica and Guyana have also been hurt by a glut in the international bauxite market and would like to sell the Soviets more than the USSR is willing to accept.[56]

Protectionist measures in the United States have spurred Latin American countries to seek markets in the Soviet bloc. The government of Brazil frequently complains about U.S. quotas affecting its products (such as shoes and carbon steel), and Argentina has bitterly criticized U.S. and West European sales of subsidized grains. Argentina's President Raúl Alfonsín also has said that unless the West opens its doors to greater Argentine exports, his country will have no choice but to trade more heavily with the socialist states.[57] The Soviets buy bananas and other products from Nicaragua no longer saleable in the U.S., and Honduras began to expand trade with the Soviet Union in 1987 because of a loss of Western markets.[58]

The Soviet Union also takes action to assure the availability of desired goods. One common approach has been to provide technical assistance to Latin American industries that mine and process valuable metals. This effort is most noteworthy in Bolivia, where the Soviets have made available enormous amounts of money—$500 million dollars in 1984–85 alone—for the tin and other mineral industries, which are in a severe state of disrepair. As noted earlier, the USSR has also helped Bolivia build its own smelters to reduce its reliance on the West. It has also extended credit and accepted payment in kind, attractive policies to Bolivia and other states in the region that are struggling under a debt burden.[59] In Bolivia, Argentina, Mexico, Brazil, and elsewhere, Soviet representatives also foster relations with people in the public and private sectors in the capital and other locales, in the process of building good will and providing steady access to tin, grain, and other materials.

The Soviet Union has become deeply concerned about its huge trade deficits in the region, but thus far has been willing to endure them. Its willingness to do so stems from the need for certain products, the hope of eventually breaking through the barriers Soviet so as to expand exports, and probably also a realization of the political importance of trade in a region where Soviet military and diplomatic options are rather limited. There are a number of reasons for the deficits; the availability of alternative sources for any product the Soviets can offer, lingering anti-Communism, a lack of complementarity with many local economies, and, perhaps most of all, a Latin American conviction that Soviet manufactured products are of inferior quality. Indeed, many Latin Americans would rather pay more for a Western or Japanese alternative.[60] This problem becomes acute in Soviet dealing with the more advanced economies in the region.

The Soviet Union has sought to overcome the deficit problem in a number of ways, sending trade delegations and pursuing the same kinds of contacts it employs in promoting itself as buyer. The Soviets push for joint development projects to guarantee the infusion of their machinery and equipment, and accept payment in kind to make the deal more attractive. They extend credits, often at long-term, low interest, and require the recipient to use the credits to buy Soviet goods. The Soviets also have insisted on incorporating clauses into some trade treaties that require the Latin American partner to purchase a specified amount of manufactured goods, as in their most recent agreement with Argentina.[61] They train Latin Americans in the Soviet Union to establish a working relationship and familiarity with Soviet products, and they also threaten to reduce their imports, and have at times done so; they try to sell arms, as they have done in Peru.

Recent Soviet approaches to Mexico provide excellent illustrations of many of these techniques. The USSR has flooded Mexico with trade delegations to the public and private sectors at the federal and state levels. In 1983, the two countries formed a Joint Commission for Economic Trade and Cooperation, and in 1986 they agreed to form a coordinating group to promote joint developments in Mexico. Soviet officials have used formal meetings and the Mexican media to offer technological assistance in oil and natural gas, copper smelting, steel, heavy industry, transportation, hydroelectric power, and other areas where close cooperation would lead to Soviet sales of machinery and equipment. The Soviets have also pressed for closer merchant marine cooperation, an area with implications for intelligence, as well as trade.[62]

THE SOVIET ECONOMIC CHALLENGE IN LATIN AMERICA

Trade has helped the Soviet Union establish a permanent presence, both economic and political, in Latin America, and has given it access to strategically important raw materials. Soviet economic and military assistance has been crucial to the financial and political survival of Marxist-Leninist regimes in Cuba and Nicaragua. Soviet economic intervention may also have strengthened the resolve of other governments in confrontations with the United States; if so, the effects must have been mainly psychological, because the levels of Soviet aid—tendered chiefly in the form of trade credits and technical advisers—have seldom been as impressive as in the Cuban and Nicaraguan cases.

What trade and aid have not done, again excepting the cases of Cuba and Nicaragua, is give the USSR significant political influence in Latin America. One reason may be that Soviet and bloc trade shares are not great enough to give the Soviets significant economic leverage. It is not clear, however, that trade at any level can produce measurable political influence unless other important factors are at work. The Soviet economic role could not be what it is today if Cuba and Nicaragua were not engaged in political warfare with the United States, and thereby in a state of extreme dependence on the Soviet bloc. In contrast, the USSR has gained little visible political influence from its large share of Argentine exports, or from its military sales to Peru.

The record suggests, therefore, that Soviet economic influence would be greater if more Marxist revolutions occurred in the region. Soviet economic constraints may be too great, however, to allow the USSR to assist future Latin American revolutions unless they occur in countries as small as Cuba or Nicaragua. Chile may have provided an object lesson in that regard. On the other hand, the recent Soviet record of resolute military and economic support for Nicaragua and of increasing aid for Cuba suggests that the USSR will endure significant costs to maintain its alliance system in the region. The Soviet Union's policy of aid without a formal military commitment leaves it in what is essentially a no lose situation, since it can sustain both regimes without risking an irrevocable military confrontation with the United States.

A worsening of the debt crisis, in which Latin American states default and are cut off from further Western assistance, could open the door to a greater Soviet economic role. Once again, however, the USSR faces severe economic constraints that limit its capacity to fill whatever gaps would be left by the West. The Soviet Union, which in the past has not been inclined to provide large-scale economic support to non-Communist regimes in Latin America, would have to accept the possibility of nonpayment of its credits and loans. Instead of a general effort, therefore, the Soviet Union might instead target one or two countries with which it has had significant past economic cooperation for an intensive aid effort.

An analyst considering scenarios of future Soviet breakthroughs would have to consider Argentina, because it has important strategic and ideological interests that sometimes conflict with those of the West. The Soviets have courted Argentina principally to protect their access to foodstuffs, but they also would like to see it move at least to permanent nonalignment, and perhaps to eventual military cooperation. A renewal of the Falklands/Malvinas War and another Western arms embargo could induce Argentina to buy Soviet weapons, a move it has not taken thus far despite probable Soviet approaches. Arms sales would serve to improve Soviet relations with Argentina's conservative military elites, who were willing to trade with the Soviets in nonmilitary goods when they were in power. Arms sales of sufficient value would also further consolidate economic relations by reducing the Soviet balance of payments deficit. A collapse of debt arrangements would further set the stage for greater collaboration between the two states.

The level of Soviet economic activities in Latin America will have to increase considerably and do so in the context of a growing political crisis in the region to present a serious threat to U.S. interests in the near future. Barring further Marxist-Leninist revolutions, the growth of Soviet influence is not likely to come in quick and dramatic fashion. The Soviets are thinking in terms of the long-run with slow, patient efforts at establishing a presence in the economic infrastructure of Latin America through the various tactics described above. Full exploitation of its economic contacts in the years ahead will require drastic improvement in the Soviet Union's economic productivity and the quality of its exports. Future losses of influence by the U.S. are likely to be principally the result of developments indigenous to

Latin America, but the Soviet Union may be able to encourage these developments by providing alternative markets and sources of supply.

Notes

1 Cole Blasier, *The Giant's Rival: The USSR and Latin America* (Pittsburgh: University of Pittsburgh Press, 1983), p. 54.
2 Radio Havana, January 3, 1986, in Federal Broadcast Information Service—Latin America (hereafter FBIS-LAM), January 3, 1986, p. Q1.
3 International Monetary Fund (hereafter IMF), *Direction of Trade Statistics Yearbook 1985* (Washington D.C.: IMF, 1986), p. 395.
4 U.S. Department of Defense, *Soviet Military Power 1987* (Washington D.C.: U.S. Department of Defense, 1987), p. 143.
5 M. Edelman, "Lifelines: Nicaragua and the Socialist Countries," *NACLA Reports on the Americas*, 19:3 (1985), p. 49.
6 Managua Radio Sandino, May 14, 1985, in FBIS-LAM, May 16, 1985, p. P14.
7 According to IMF statistics, total Nicaraguan imports declined by 12.3 percent in 1985 and exports by 24.8 percent, IMF, *Direction of Trade*, p. 299.
8 Nicaragua continues to lose non-Communist sources of aid and trade. The most recent is France, which announced that it was ending all aid due to anti-democratic practices by the Sandinista regime. *The Times of the Americas*, March 11, 1987, p.3.
9 Aldo César Vacs, *Discreet Partners: Argentina and the USSR Since 1971* (Pittsburgh: University of Pittsburgh Press, 1984), p. 62; *Noticias Argentinas*, February 21, 1984, in FBIS-LAM, February 27, 1984, p. B9; and *Folha de São Paulo*, February 7, 1985, in FBIS-LAM, February 11, 1985, p. D3.
10 *Clarin* (Buenos Aires), July 22, 1986, in FBIS-LAM, July 24, 1986, p. B1.
11 *Washington Post*, August 12, 1986, p. A11.
12 See, for example, *Washington Post*, November 4, 1986, p. A12.
13 See *Noticias Argentinas*, September 25, 1986, in FBIS-LAM, September 30, 1986, p. B2, for one of many Soviet warnings to Argentina tying future trade levels to a reduction of the deficit.
14 United Nations, *Yearbook of International Trade Statistics 1983* (New York: United Nations, 1983), p. 101.
15 *O Globo* (Rio de Janiero), November 10, 1985, in FBIS-LAM, November 12, 1985, p. D1.
16 For valuable descriptions of Peru's economic relations with the Soviet Union and its allies in the 1969–74 period, see Leon Goure and Morris Rothenberg, *Soviet Penetration of Latin America* (Miami: University of Miami, 1975), pp. 146–49; and A. I. Ol'shanyi, "Peru i Strany SEV," *Latinskaia Amerika* 2 (1974), pp. 79–92.
17 UN, *Yearbook of International Trade*, various years.
18 *Times of the Americas*, December 21, 1983, p. 18.
19 *Ibid.*, December 21, 1983, p. 18, and June 6, 1984, p. 3; and Lima Radio del Pacifico, September 16, 1986, in FBIS-LAM, September 17, 1986, p. J1.
20 Lima TV, September 13, 1986, in FBIS-LAM, September 4, 1986, p. J1; and Madrid EFE, September 4, 1986, in *ibid.*, September 5, 1986, p. J2.
21 *Times of the Americas*, April 24, 1985, p. 11.
22 Bridgetown CANA, October 19, 1985, in FBIS-LAM, October 22, 1985, p. T1; January 25, 1986 in *Times of the Americas*, January 28, 1986, p. T1; and February 3, 1986, in *ibid.*, February 6, 1986, p. T1.

23 *Times of the Americas*, January 16, 1985, p. 10.
24 U.S. Embassy, Kingston, Jamaica, private communication, March 28, 1987.
25 *Times of the Americas*, January 16, 1985, p. 10.
26 See the article by Brian Latell in this volume for an analysis of Mexico's political attractiveness to the Soviet Union.
27 Blasier, *Giant's Rival*, tables 4 and 5.
28 Notimex, February 24, 1984, in FBIS-LAM, February 28, 1984, p. M4.
29 Mexico City International Service, June 28, 1984, in FBIS-LAM, June 29, 1984, p. M2.
30 *Excelsior* Mexico City, October 21, 1986, in FBIS-LAM, October 26, 1986, p. M3.
31 Notimex, February 25, 1984, in FBIS-LAM, February 29, 1984, p. M2; and June 27, 1984, in *ibid.*, July 3, 1984, p. M1.
32 Mexico City *Excelsior*, November 15, 1983, in FBIS-LAM, December 6, 1984, p. M1; and October 21, 1986, in *ibid.*, October 27, 1986, p. M3.
33 Mexico City *Excelsior*, October 21, 1986, in FBIS-LAM, October 27, 1986, p. M3.
34 *Times of the Americas*, July 17, 1986, p. 2.
35 U.S. Arms Control and Disarmament Agency (hereafter ACDA), *World Military Expenditures and Arms Transfers 1985* (Washington D.C.: ACDA, 1985), p. 44.
36 On the sale of Soviet helicopters to Guyana, see Bridgetown CANA, October 19, 1985, in FBIS-LAM, October 22, 1985, p. T1.
37 U.S. Department of Defense (hereafter DOD), *Soviet Military Power 1986*, (Washington D.C.: DOD, 1986), p. 129; and DOD, *Soviet Military Power 1987*, p. 141.
38 U.S. Department of State, unpublished manuscript, 1987; DOD, *Soviet Military Power 1985* (Washington D.C.: DOD, 1985), p. 121; and DOD, *Soviet Military Power 1987*, p. 143. See the Clement and Duncan chapter for more references.
39 DOD, *Soviet Military Power 1987*, p. 141; and *New York Times*, March 20, 1985, p. 5.
40 DOD, *Soviet Military Power 1987*, p. 143.
41 ACDA, *World Military Expenditures and Arms Transfers 1971–1980* (Washington D.C.: ACDA, 1980), p. 162.
42 Stockholm International Peace Research Institute (hereafter SIPRI), *World Armaments and Disarmament: SIPRI Yearbook 1980* (London: SIPRI, 1980), p. 115.
43 Stephen M. Gorman and Ronald Bruce St. John, "Challenge to Peruvian Foreign Policy," in Gorman, ed., *Post Revolutionary Peru: The Politics of Transformation* (Boulder: Westview Press, 1982), pp. 182, 186–90; *Christian Science Monitor*, December 17, 1973, p. 1; *New York Times*, October 13, 1976, p. 63.
44 DOD, *Soviet Military Power 1986*, p. 133.
45 *Ibid.*, p. 131; *ibid.*, (1987), p. 143.
46 *New York Times*, October 21, 1958, p. 9; and May 4, 1961, p. 4.
47 Gouré and Rothenberg, *Soviet Penetration*, pp. 134–35, 154; R. J. Bromley, *Development Planning in Ecuador* (Sussex: Latin American Publications Fund, 1977), p. 11, 13–14; and the *New York Times*, various issues, 1967–71.
48 See, for example, the authoritative comments of Soviet General Secretary Leonid Brezhnev and alternate Politburo member Boris Ponomarev in, retrospectively, *Pravda*, March 3, 1971, p. 3 and *Kommunist*, 15 (October 1971), p. 62.
49 *New York Times*, February 18, 1969, p. 1, and April 18, 1969, p. 7; and L. Becerra and J. Dickman, "U.S. Imperialist Policy in Latin America," *World Marxist Review*, 13 (July 1970), p. 84.
50 Herbert S. Klein, *Bolivia: Evolution of a Multi-Ethnic Society* (New York: Oxford University Press, 1982), p. 251.
51 Blasier, *Giant's Rival*, pp. 38–39; Joseph S. Nogee and J. W. Sloan, "Allende's Chile and the Soviet Union: A Policy Lesson for Latin American Nations Seeking Autonomy," *The Journal of Interamerican Studies and World Affairs*, 21:3 (1979), pp. 339–368; and Paul Sigmund, *The Overthrow of Allende and the Politics of Chile 1964–1976* (Pittsburgh: University of Pittsburgh Press, 1981), pp. 284–85.
52 Nogee and Sloan, "Allende's Chile and the Soviet Union," p. 353.

53 W. Raymond Duncan, "Soviet and Cuban Interests in the Caribbean," in R. Millett and W. M. Will, eds., *The Restless Caribbean: Changing Patterns of International Relations* (New York: Praeger Publishers, 1979), p. 140.
54 See, for example, I. K. Sheremet'ev, "Vneshnye i vnutrennye faktori v kapitalisticheskom razvitii," *Latinskaia Amerika*, 8 (1980), p. 38.
55 The United States reduced the quota of sugar from the Caricom countries by 44 percent in 1986; the Dominican Republic was hit by a 47 percent cut. See *Times of the Americas*, January 14, 1987, pp. 5, 14.
56 Bridgetown CANA, January 29, 1986, in FBIS-LAM, January 30, 1986, p. S2.
57 *Washington Post*, August 11, 1986, p. A15; and Hamburg DPA Radio, December 17, 1983, in FBIS-LAM, December 19, 1983, p. B10.
58 *Times of the Americas*, February 25, 1987, p. 2, and May 20, 1987, p. 5.
59 *Ibid.*, December 4, 1985, p. 4.
60 *Folha de São Paulo*, February 7, 1985, in FBIS-LAM, February 11, 1985, p. D3.
61 *Noticias Argentinas* (Buenos Aires), October 19, 1985, in FBIS-LAM, October 22, 1985, p. B1.
62 *Unomasuno* (Mexico City), December 12, 1985, in FBIS-LAM, December 31, 1985, p. M1.

8

Eastern Europe and Latin America

Michael Radu

The role of the East European allies of the Soviet Union in Latin America has undergone dramatic changes since the late 1970s. Until a decade ago, Moscow's six East European allies within the Warsaw Pact were motivated by a combination with national interests (economic and political) and Soviet geopolitical requirements. Since the Nicaraguan Revolution, and in conjunction to its own economic difficulties, Eastern Europe's role has shifted decisively toward that of a simple surrogate of the USSR. In geographic terms this shift translated into lower priority being given to South America and a disproportionate increase in activities in Central America and the Caribbean. Economically the trend is toward fewer investments and less trade throughout the Americas, and increased levels of concessionary aid and soft credits to radical regimes and groups, such as Nicaragua, Grenada, El Salvador, and Guyana.

PRELIMINARY CONSIDERATIONS

The role of the Soviet Union's Warsaw Pact partners (Poland, Czechoslovakia, Romania, East Germany, and Hungary) in Latin America has seldom been examined in all its aspects. Traditionally, the involvement of Eastern Europe has been treated as part of the Soviet Union's geostrategic interests in the Western Hemisphere. Two important issues require further investigation: the goals of the East European states, individually and collectively, and the relationship between their goals and those of the USSR. The investigation must clarify the degree and type of coordination between the Soviets and their allies in Latin America, at different political, military, and economic levels.

The obstacles to the research of Latin American-East European relations are considerable, particularly concerning data collection. Regarding trade, for instance, Latin American sources are not always complete, while the East European ones, when they do exist at all, are seldom reliable. Even in those few instances when East European data are regularly available (mostly in the cases of Hungary and Poland), they further confuse the issues with their peculiar conceptual definitions. For instance, such terms as "aid," "assistance," and "trade volume" are plagued by definitional minefields. "Aid" to Third World countries generally consist of tied loans, normally (and vaguely) defined as low or noninterest, which in reality are nothing more than subsidies to otherwise uncompetitive domestic industries. Capital or equity participation in Third World ventures by East European state-owned companies are sometimes also presented as "aid," as are commercial credits in nonconvertible currencies. Furthermore, a significant amount of East European trade with the Third World, including Latin America, is based on barter of triangular trade arrangements, all of which are impossible to quantify in dollars with any precision.

Political support, particularly when provided as "services" in the form of security police and other regime-consolidation expertise and personnel, is practically impossible to define in monetary terms. Nevertheless, it is invaluable and often paid for by the recipient Third World regime. Such services are provided by the East Europeans to countries like Nicaragua, Guyana, and (between 1979–1983) Grenada.

Military sales and aid to Latin American countries are equally difficult to quantify, because they are often based on either "credit" or "aid." Their real value is distorted by the Soviet bloc's peculiar calculations of military hardware costs and its low labor costs. Totally impossible to assess is the distinction between actual Soviet costs, however calculated, and those hidden into licenses sold to the East Europeans. "Real" Czech, Romanian, Polish, East German, or Hungarian costs are further lost in the maze of intra-CMEA or intra-Warsaw Pact economic, political, and military exchanges.

Such problems notwithstanding, the East European role in Latin America should simultaneously be viewed in terms of "national," bloc, and Soviet interests, and interpreted in light of the overall East European impact on the superpowers' imbalance of power and influence in the Western Hemisphere. Outside such an integrated framework, the East European role cannot be understood. It should not be assessed as *primarily* a function of their own "national interests," unless one assumes that the Warsaw Treaty Organization (WTO) member governments have the wherewithal, interest, and latitude to operate as free actors—a totally unwarranted assumption.

The first and basic issue to consider is whether Eastern Europe actually "needs" ties to Latin America. Individual Warsaw Pact countries can legitimately claim that their activities in Latin America are in pursuit of national interests only if such "needs" can be established. The second deals with the degree of involvement, as well as the type of activities characterizing East European presence in the Western Hemisphere. Both provide important insights for understanding both the Soviet goals in Latin America and the nature of Soviet-East European relations. Third, the impact of the East European presence in Latin America must be properly evaluated either as serving its own national interests in a small way, or as part of the U.S.-Soviet struggle for regional hegemony. For all these reasons, a historical and cultural background of East European ties to Latin America is necessary.

THE ORIGINS OF EAST EUROPEAN TIES TO LATIN AMERICA

Any relations Eastern Europe had with Latin America before the satellization of the East European states are largely irrelevant to this chapter. At any rate, Eastern Europe has been neither culturally close to Latin America, nor did they ever have any historical claim to ties with the continent. Finally, even the influence of any East European immigrants remains negligible in Latin America, except the Croatians in the Southern Cone countries, a subject outside the scope of this study.

For the American public and policy makers, East European ties to Latin America first gained prominence, or at least attention, during the Arbenz regime (1951–1954) in Guatemala. At the time, Czechoslovakia, a known manufacturer of weapons, was the only East European country with any significant presence in the Western Hemisphere. Its curious reputation as a democratic, rather than a Communist country, despite the 1948 coup d'état, helped conceal the political motives of the presence. These skewed perceptions and the nature of the Arbenz regime, thoroughly infiltrated by the *Partido Guatemalteco de Trabajo* (PGT), the local Communist party, explains the flurry of negotiations between Guatemala City and Prague. Furthermore, the Mexican government's peculiar notion of democracy and independence in Czechoslovakia accounted for the presence of a Czech Consul-General in Mexico City. From Mexico City, the center of Soviet activities in the Western Hemisphere, the Czechs conducted their operations in Guatemala and beyond.

The episode that first drew Washington's attention to both Central America and the Eastern European role there was the Czechoslovakian sale of weapons to Guatemala. In January 1954, a Czech ambassador came to Guatemala City, becoming the first and only East European diplomat of that rank in the country. That month also witnessed the presence of an official, albeit discrete, Guatemalan negotiator in Switzerland, who met with Czech arms manufacturers.[1] Subsequently, the negotiator, Major Alfonso Martínez Estevez, went to Prague for the final arrangements. In a pre-run of the first USSR-Egypt arms deals, a consignment of Czech weapons was transferred through the Polish port of Stettin and carried by a Swedish flag carrier to Guatemala.[2] The deal sparked Washington's planned bonfire, which eventually led to Arbenz's ouster.

As a convenient alternative location for Soviet-dominated or controlled organizations, Prague played a disproportionate role in the advancement of Soviet interests in Latin America until the late 1960s.[3] It hosted some of the USSR's most effective global operations, such as the *The World Marxist Review* and trade union fronts. A far more cosmopolitan city than Moscow, this Mecca of Leninism also attracted some of the most important Latin American revolutionaries during the 1960s. Among them were Roque Dalton of El Salvador, Heriberto Padilla of Cuba, Manuel Pellecer of Guatemala, and even the exiled Arbenz. They established essential networks with Soviet and fellow Latin militants committed to continental revolution, especially through the *World Marxist Review,* which remains important even today.

In the late 1960s, East Berlin replaced Prague as the center of leftist revolutionary activities. Among the reasons for this shift were East Germany's increasingly high profile in the Third World, the convenient proximity of West Berlin, and its higher standard of living. Many Allende supporters, who had been freed from Chilean prisons, went into Romanian custody after the 1973 debacle, later took refuge in East Berlin, where they felt free to plot their return to power.[4] At least two of the most prominent leaders of the Nicaraguan FSLN, *comandante de la revolución,* Jaime Wheelock Román and the late Enrique Schmitt Cuadra, were close to the East Germans and lived in East Berlin during the early 1970s. As clarified later, key Nicaraguan personalities established close links with the German Democratic Republic that would later be instrumental in the creation of the *Sandinista* secret police and security apparatus.

Romania had so few ties with Latin America before the mid-1960s as to be largely irrelevant. Trade with the continent, for instance, was always minimal. Even Latin American literature and art were hardly known in Romania before that time, and it was only during the 1970s that a rush of translations and travel journals paralleled Romania's move toward closer relations. In an attempt to compensate for the absence of serious relations in the past, Nicolae Ceausescu tried to make arcane historical claims to ties with Latin America based on a common linguistic heritage.

Latin American relations with Eastern Europe for the most part mirrored their attitude toward the Soviet Union and communism in general, at least until the 1970s. Latin America's alliance with the Soviets in World War II resulted in the establishment of diplomatic relations between them, followed by the opening of similar ties with East European states during the pre-Cold War period 1945–1948. The effect of the Cold War was so devastating that by the end of the 1950s the Soviets and their East European satellites had diplomatic representation in only a handful of Latin American capitals: Montevideo, Mexico City, Buenos Aires, and Rio de Janeiro.[5] During the 1960s, the Soviet bloc was perceived, however incorrectly, as closely associated with Cuba's adventurism and export of revolution. Only by the late 1960s, when Castro's revolutionary offensive was widely considered a dismal failure, were the East Europeans and Soviets again accepted as legitimate trade and diplomatic partners. By 1974, Poland and Romania had formal relations (embassies, trade missions) with 15 Latin American countries, followed by East Germany with 12, Czechoslovakia and Hungary with 11, and Bulgaria with 9.[6]

Today, all Latin American countries, save Paraguay, have diplomatic or trade ties with at least one Warsaw Pact member, although Guatemala, El Salvador, and Honduras limit their ties to commercial exchanges. The heaviest concentrations of Warsaw Pact presence (diplomatic, commercial, and sometimes open military and security) in Latin America today are in Managua, Georgetown, Lima, Buenos Aires, and Mexico City. Managua and Buenos Aires, followed closely by Mexico City, have the most extensive diplomatic ties to the Communist countries, while Santiago is the most restrictive of Latin capitals with embassies from Romania and China only.

POLITICS AND ECONOMIC TRENDS

The *Sandinista* Revolution of 1979 clearly induced the East Europeans to drastically expand their economic aid to Central America. Perhaps the most salient aspect of that expansion is the growing imbalance between aid to Central America and that to South America. The gap between actual economic benefit from trading with Central America and the commercial primacy accorded it suggests a growing politicization and coordination with Soviet strategic interests in the region. For example, the combined GDP of the five largest Central American countries (Guatemala, Costa Rica, Nicaragua, El Salvador, and Honduras) was smaller than that of Colombia alone, in 1965 as well as in 1984.[7] Yet, the total East European economic aid and credits to the two regions between 1971 and 1984 was $1.095 billion for Central America and only $1.689 billion for *all of* South America.[8] Before 1971 (or more precisely, before 1979), East European aid to Central America was nonexistent, while South America received $270 million.[9]

The hypothesis that the East Europeans play the role of Soviet surrogates in Central America is further strengthened by the differences between direct Soviet and East European levels of assistance to the region. Between 1971 and 1984, the East European countries supplied $1.095 billion as compared to the Soviets' $640 million.[10] In South America, Eastern Europeans supplied $1.689 billion while the Soviets nearly matched them with $1.25 billion over the same period.[11]

Where the economic rewards of granting credits do exist, as in South America, the East Europeans are more interested than the Soviets. The need for markets and raw materials, which interest the Soviets less, motivated East European countries' trade policy with South America. In Central America, however, where neither raw materials nor sizable markets exist, and where credits and aid are clearly a losing proposition, the East Europeans are assuming the economic costs of Soviet extra-economic (i.e., strategic and ideological) interests.

The importance of Nicaragua, for example, is underscored by the fact that before 1980 (beginning essentially in 1979, the first year of *Sandinista* rule), the East Europeans provided that country with $20 million in aid and grants. From 1980–84 the level of aid rose to $470 million.[12]

The highly ideological purposes of East European aid and economic credits to the Caribbean and Central America are visible in the blatant preference for radical or revolutionary regimes. For example, the Cooperative Republic of Guyana received $155 million in 1984, and Grenada under New Jewel collected $45 million. Jamaica under Michael Manley was blessed with $285 million, whereas the government of Edward Seaga was denied the honor.[13] In other words, over 90 percent of East European aid and grants to these regions went to precisely four Marxist-Leninist or leftist radical regimes: Nicaragua, Guyana, Grenada, and Jamaica. Since the only significant economic attraction in those countries is the bauxite found in Jamaica and Guyana, it becomes obvious that political rather than economic considerations dominate the relations between Eastern Europe and these countries.

The Eastern European economic policy in the Caribbean Basin contrasts sharply with their trade practices in South America. In the case of the latter, the amounts of credits and aid are generally proportionate to the value and availability of markets. Brazil loomed largest in Eastern European trade policy, for it received $780 million in credits and aid between 1954 and 1985. During the same period, Argentina garnered $300 million, followed by Peru with $255 million, and Colombia with $110 million.[14] These countries were also the scene of maximum activity for Eastern European multinational state corporations. Poland's *Rybex* was active in Peru (fisheries), Czechoslovakia's *Fincom* (later renamed *Transkata*) in Argentina (mining). By providing credits to major markets for facilitating the sale of their own products, the Eastern Europeans behaved like any other state in South America. Fully aware of those countries' inability to repay credits or to pay for imports, the Eastern Europeans provided largely concessionary aid and long-term, easy credits to radical regimes in Central America and the Caribbean, while they pursued their own specific economic interests in South America.

Of the total instances of state-owned multinational investments in the Third World by 1983, East Germany was proportionally most active; both instances of East Berlin's overseas operations occurred in Latin America. It was followed by Czechoslovakia with 24 out of a total of 38 such investments in the Third World, and Hungary, with

11 out of a total of 44. By comparison, Poland had 6 investments in Latin America out of a total of 37 in the entire Third World; Romania 8 out of 54 (the highest total within Comecon); Bulgaria 1 out of 34; the USSR 1 out of 27; and the Comecon as a whole, 52 out of 236.[15]

The same disparity between economic interest and political motivations that highlights trade relations also characterizes personnel exchanges between the Soviet bloc and Latin America. Of a total of 1,410 economic and technical advisers present in Latin America in 1984, Nicaragua had received 475, leftist-dominated Peru 245, and Guyana 20.[16] There were also 11,130 Latin American students trained in Eastern Europe and the USSR in 1984, of which most were from Colombia (2,140), Nicaragua (1,885), Costa Rica (1,569), Peru (1,185), and the Dominican Republic (1,045).[17] Once again, there is no clear relationship between the size of a country and the number of trainees it has in the Soviet bloc, but there is a clear bias in favor of leftist and/or Central American and Caribbean countries. The presence of some 275 Soviet and East European military personnel in Latin America in 1984—100 in Peru (presumably Soviet, since the Peruvians have bought Soviet-made weapons) and 150 in Nicaragua—reveals a similar pattern.[18] Among the 1,320 Latin Americans receiving military training in the Soviet bloc between 1955 and 1984, 910 were Peruvians, 405 Nicaraguans, and 5 Grenadians.[19] Once again, the Caribbean Basin area commanded a disproportionate share of Soviet bloc attention.

THE CASES OF NICARAGUA, EL SALVADOR AND GRENADA

The East Germans have been the pivotal element in the development of the Nicaraguan military and security apparatus. They provided most of the military trucks used by the *Sandinista* Popular Army (EPS)—the IfAs which have become the Nicaraguan synonym for heavy army trucks; hospitals and medical care for the EPS; and internal security advisors. In addition, the East Germans also train and equip the *Sandinista* Special Operations Forces. A very publicized shipment from the GDR included 24 trucks, which arrived in Corinto on July 24, 1986.[20] According to the U.S. government, there are also some 60 East Germans acting as security advisers in Nicaragua—more than Soviets, but well within the range of a well-known Third World pattern.[21] The total cost of GDR aid to Nicaragua, mostly in military and paramilitary advice and services, vehicles, and technical support, is at least $200 million and will drastically increase in light of the new burden of providing oil to Managua.

According to the Managua regime, Czechoslovakia has provided $100 million in credits to Nicaragua as of July 1986,[22] including some 500 trucks and tractors, footwear manufacturing facilities, textile plants, and services. By July 1987, Czechoslovakia's aid to Nicaragua reached $143 million, of which $60 million was committed in 1988 mostly for textile and cement plants.[23] According to Nicaraguan Economy and Planning Minister Henry Ruiz, the Czechs are also to provide about 20 technicians in those fields.

The Bulgarians are known to have trained Nicaraguan MIG fighter pilots as well as pilots for Soviet-built helicopters. Open involvement in such activities, along with Sofia's intelligence support for the *Sandinistas*, is less than surprising at present because of that country's increasingly active role as a Soviet surrogate in the Third World and Western Europe. This surrogacy coincides with Sofia's growing commercial interest in the developing countries. Its trade turnover with the Third World grew by 597 percent (admittedly from a smaller initial base) during the 1970–1980 period, second in the European CMEA only to Hungary's 782 percent increase.[24] What is still unusual is the open and significant Bulgarian role in such a remote and historically alien region as Central America.

The Eastern European role in Nicaragua was best described by former Nicaraguan counterintelligence officer Miguel Bolaños Hunter:

> The East German advisors were mainly involved in electronic bugging and the tapping of microphones in section F6. We had one East German advisor in my section, F2. He would come specifically to talk to the person in charge of the West German embassy....The Bulgarians had a center for the analysis of information....We used to gather information for the Center of Information and Analysis and they would process it. They gave us advice through our chief. The chief was the only one who dealt directly with the Bulgarians.[25]

Eastern European assistance to the Salvadoran Marxist-Leninist insurgents best attests to their surrogate role. The captured National Liberation Front-Farabundo Martí (FMLN) documents from El Salvador fully substantiate the Eastern European involvement. The travel notes of Shafik Handal, the general secretary of the staunchly pro-Soviet Salvadoran Communist Party, on Eastern Europe document the various offers of material aid he received from the leaders there.[26] In Bulgaria, where he met Dimitur Stanichev, the Central Committee secretary for international relations of the BCP, Handal was offered 300 German rebuilt submachine guns which were to be sent "by their own means or in coordination with the [East] Germans or the Czechs."[27] In Czechoslovakia, Handal was received by no less prominent a figure than Vasil Bilak, the second most important party leader and secretary of the CC for international relations, who also promised Czech weapons (to be transported by East German ships). The Hungarians offered uniforms and radios. Arrangements were also made for Western weapons in Angola and Ethiopia to be shipped to El Salvador, while Hungary would replace them for the Angolans and Ethiopians. As in Hungary, Bulgaria, and Czechoslovakia, Handal was received in East Germany by the Central Committee secretary for international relations, Hermann Axen, who mentioned that 1.9 tons of medicines, megaphones, batteries, and cameras had already been sent to Managua for the Salvadorans. At the same time, East Berlin told Moscow that the GDR had decided to send an additional 2.3 million Marks worth of aid to the Salvadorans. In addition, Handal obtained tentative support from the East Germans for training of FMLN cadres in military and covert operations.[28]

Eastern European activities in Grenada also indicated subservience to Soviet objectives. After Bernard Coard's visit to Prague, the Czechs provided free of charge 3,000 7.62mm automatic rifles and bazooka projectiles.[29] The Grenadan *quid pro quo* was merely a trade agreement with Czechoslovakia stipulating the export of 80 tons of nutmeg every year, starting in 1984.[30] East Germans advised the New Jewel Movement on Leninist party building and offered support for party press training, while Bulgarians provided military aid according to a treaty with Bishop's government. The Czechs trained radio anchormen for Radio Free Grenada—a station used to stir up domestic unrest throughout the English-speaking Caribbean during the New Jewel regime. Grenadan cadres were to be trained at the Bulgarian Party's Academy of Social Sciences and Management.[31] The explicit statement of East German goals—to concentrate attention on Grenada, Nicaragua, and Cuba in the Caribbean region,—reflects the general attitude among East European governments, perfectly consistent with expressed Soviet goals and actions in the region.[32]

The pattern of Soviet military involvement in Nicaragua is consistent with historic experience in such previous cases as Guatemala under Arbenz and Egypt under Nasser. In Nicaragua, the role of "scout" previously played by Czechoslovakia in Guatemala and Egypt—an introduction of Soviet bloc weapons where the Soviets themselves were unsure of American reaction—was played by Libya and Poland. Thus the politically sensitive build-up of Nicaraguan air power was achieved despite Washington's declared objections to allowing Nicaraguan air supremacy to supplement Managua's clear regional superiority in ground forces. Initially the Soviets did not send advanced aircraft to Managua, but encouraged Libya to do so. Qaddafi promptly sent Italian-made SF-260 trainer-tactical support planes in 1982, followed by Soviet-made transport planes of the AN-26 type ("nonlethal instruments"). Next came Polish-made Mi-2 helicopter cargoes, also in 1982. It was only in late 1984 that the first Soviet first-line Mi-8 and the lethal Mi-24 "Hind" attack helicopter appeared over the Nicaraguan skies.[33]

Finally, the past East European surrogacy in Nicaragua involved significant economic losses, motivated by political gains in supporting world-wide "progressive" regimes and in ingratiating themselves with Moscow. East Germany "invested" over $200 million in aid,[34] followed by Czechoslovakia with $100 million. Bulgaria injected a significant but not precisely known figure, whereas Poland and Hungary contributed very little, and Romania practically nothing. Only in the case of Czechoslovakia are there any data regarding the relationship between the different forms of economic assistance given to Nicaragua. Thus, in April 1986 the Czech ambassador to Nicaragua, Gustav Stopka, stated that Prague had provided $250 million "through credits and donations" to Nicaragua; repayment on the credits will start only after 1990.[35] Three months later, the embassy's chargé d'affaires, Vlastimil Kalecki, was more specific: credits to Nicaragua amounted "to more than $100 million."[36] The implication is that about 40 percent of Czech assistance to Nicaragua was in the form of soft credits and the rest in outright grants or "donations." Interestingly, services, such as various types of advisers, were included as credit rather than grant.

The Eastern European "economic exchanges" with Nicaragua are suspect at best, although both sides claim mutual benefits. Nicaragua, once the proud exporter of meat, now imports it from Bulgaria. Soviet wheat (!) and oil supplies keep the fledgling Nicaraguan economy afloat. The same commitment applies to military support. Soviet bloc arms supplies to Managua reached over $500 million in 1985,[37] and are now approaching $1 billion, despite Nicaragua's patent inability to pay for anything. Thus when Nicaraguan soldiers are sent to East Germany for treatment of injuries—a pattern borrowed from the Cubans in Angola—those services are free of charge, like training and intelligence support from the Eastern Europeans.[38] In effect, Eastern Europe subsidizes a welfare state, which would otherwise collapse of its own inefficacy. Ironically, the sustenance of the Nicaraguan state weighs adversely on the Eastern European countries themselves.

At least in the cases of Nicaragua and El Salvador, the minor Warsaw Pact members are simply surrogates prepared to do or pay more than the Soviets would or could, in terms of financial or political costs to themselves. The fact that Western media pays so little attention to the East Europeans' activities in Nicaragua seems to go a long way in explaining the existence and likely persistence of this pattern.

Unless one takes their faith in "proletarian internationalism" far too seriously, Prague, East Berlin, Budapest, Sofia, and Warsaw are vulnerable to Soviet pressures to subsidize Moscow's activities in areas of marginal or nonexistent economic interest to themselves. The most glaring recent example of this exploitation is the case of Soviet oil supplies to Nicaragua. After the Soviets announced a drastic reduction in their oil supplies to Managua, the *Sandinistas* were compelled to find alternative sources, despite their bankrupt economy. Once again "internationalism" came into place, and the East Europeans picked up the tab. Until this year, the Soviet union provided all of Nicaragua's annual petroleum needs, or about 750,000 tons. Since July 1987 the Soviet contribution has dropped to 300,000 tons annually; instead, Czechoslovakia and the GDR will provide 90,000 tons each, Cuba and Hungary 60,000 tons each, and Bulgaria 40,000, with the difference to be obtained following credit negotiations with Mexico and Venezuela.[39] All East European countries involved, together now providing Nicaragua with more oil than the USSR, are nonproducers; on the contrary, they buy their own oil primarily from the USSR, at prices rapidly moving to world market levels. By supplying Nicaragua, they have to either buy more oil from the USSR and non-Communist suppliers, or curtail their own domestic consumption. Thus they directly and purposefully (if not necessarily willingly) reduce Soviet costs in sustaining Managua at direct cost to themselves.

By using the East Europeans, the Soviets minimize the cost of imperial expansion, while still challenging the United States in a very sensitive area. Thus, the inevitable conclusion is that in Central America and the Caribbean, the East Europeans' involvement is an exclusive function of Soviet goals. Their activities are coordinated with, and even in, Moscow (according to Shafik Handal's testimony), and they are willing to bear economic losses.

Michael Radu

THE CASE OF SOUTH AMERICA: ECONOMIC CONTRACTION AT HOME AND ABROAD

Unlike Central America and the Caribbean, South America raises a number of different, but equally important economic and financial issues for the East Europeans. There is ample evidence of downward trends in bilateral exchanges on both fronts. East European economic aid and credits to Latin America, exclusive of Nicaragua, have gone down consistently since 1980. Thus, in 1980 the Nicaraguans received only $15 million, the same as Bolivia, but far less than Brazil's $150 million (out of a total of $225 million for the continent as a whole).[40] However, by 1981 Nicaragua received $90 million out of a total for Latin America of $100 million, and in 1983 it boasted $255 million out of a total of $265 million for the entire continent. It was only in 1984, when Guyana received what amounted to emergency aid from its East European friends, that Nicaragua's share represented only $25 million out of the total $270 million, with Guyana getting $155 million.[41]

The downward trend in East European economic ties with Latin America is linked to the global problem of foreign debt. As Latin American nations (Brazil, Argentina, Mexico, Peru, and Chile) started having insuperable foreign debt problems, their interest in exporting or importing goods to and from an Eastern Europe starved for hard currency waned, and the importance of obtaining it themselves became dominant. Brazil became a major weapons exporter, thus competing with Czechoslovakia, Romania, and East Germany. Argentina has always demanded hard cash payments for its agricultural products, as did Brazil, Chile, and Peru for their minerals, and Colombia for its coffee. At the same time, the East Europeans, also plagued by foreign debt, decided that providing *credits* to countries rapidly becoming successful competitors with their own industrial exports was increasingly unrealistic. Thus, except for obtaining important minerals, like Guyanese alumina and bauxite, or iron ore (in the case of Romania), East European investments in Latin America have been curbed.

Similarly, the general pattern of East European *investments* in Latin America followed that of its investments in the Third World in general, which in turn were a delayed copy of such investments in the West. Hence, Comecon investments in the West, 16.1 percent of total foreign investment in 1965–69, reached a peak of 29.3 percent in 1970–1974, a plateau of 29.1 percent in 1975–1979, then dropped sharply to 11.2 percent in 1980–1983 and probably—given the absence of reliable data—have continued that downward trend since.[42] Similarly, Third World investments started at a modest 12.1 percent in 1965–1969, peaked at 32.9 percent in 1970–1974, dropped slightly to 30.3 percent in 1975–1979, and dramatically to 20.3 percent in 1980–1983.[43] The differential between the drop in investments in the West and in the Third World, including Latin America, was due to the differences in the need of operating in hard-currency areas, in the ability of obtaining hard currency, and in the capability of paying off hard-currency debts.

The East European countries reacted differently to each of these issues. East Germany, the least exposed of the six European CMEA members to the Third World—and the informal beneficiary of support from the European Economic Community—was the least involved. Romania, the most exposed, contracted the most (although mostly in its favorite area of investment, which was Sub-Saharan Africa). The others were somewhere between those extremes.

Finally, the commercial role of Eastern Europe in Latin America, as in the Third World in general, depends heavily on their particular interests: manufacturing (Czechoslovakia), fishing (Poland), raw materials (Romania), medical and electrical supplies (Hungary), and services (the others and the USSR). In these circumstances, such ideological considerations as the survivability of leftist regimes and the fate of Michael Manley of Jamaica certainly did not improve East European credit risk assessments of Latin American states. On the contrary, they produced a strategy which involves lower exposure throughout the continent and the tolerance of increased economic costs on purely political and ideological grounds.

ASSESSMENT

In essence, the emphasis of the East European commercial interests in Latin America has shifted significantly during the past decade. General trends indicate a declining overall involvement, and an even more dramatic decline in the relative autonomy of those states vis-à-vis the Soviet Union. They also point to a growing concentration of activities in a few ideologically friendly and economically insignificant states, mostly in Central America and the Caribbean.

The overall East European contribution to Soviet strategic goals in Latin America, and particularly in Central America, is the establishment of a cumulative economic base aimed at long-term Soviet geopolitical interests which are not their own. Thus, Bulgaria signed a three-year, $170 million aid agreement with Nicaragua in March 1983, when the Soviets themselves only offered $220 million in aid to Managua the year before.[44] East Germany and Czechoslovakia each gave aid to Nicaragua in amounts close to that of the Soviet themselves. The record indicates that in Nicaragua, Grenada, El Salvador, Guyana, and in Manley's Jamaica, the *economic* risks for Soviet power projection are largely assumed by Moscow's Warsaw Pact allies. Since they are in the forefront of military training, the latter also shoulder some of the political risks of escalating Soviet bloc involvement in Central America, such as U.S. retaliation. That the East Europeans can scarcely take such risks and can ill-afford such economically wasteful endeavors only underline their overall submissiveness to Moscow's Latin American policies.

Their increased economic and political vulnerability help explain their strong, albeit discreet, resistance to Nicaraguan demands to join Comecon, and thus institutionalize Managua's right to receive aid. The Eastern Europeans manifested similar attitudes toward Angola and Mozambique. A Nicaraguan entrance into CMEA would entail severe economic consequences and unwieldy formal obligations, complications that Eastern Europe would rather avoid. Whether this fear causes the East Europeans to assume the relatively less costly burden of aid is unclear and, possibly, irrelevant.

The East European role in Central America is clearly supportive, having little if anything to do with national interests. In this context, claims by some observers that Soviet bloc aid to Nicaragua is "strikingly low" seem uninformed, precisely because East European aid commitments alone neared $1 billion by 1984. This huge sum for a country of 3 million inhabitants,[45] compares only to such exceptionally high per capita aid recipient countries as Cuba and Vietnam for the Soviet bloc, or Israel and Greece for the United States. Furthermore, that Eastern Europe (and some Western states) and not the Soviets subsidize Nicaragua's survival as a Marxist-Leninist regime only exposes the fallacy of the claim that the Soviets are unwilling or unable to "afford" another expensive client like Cuba.[46] Not only do the Soviets not have to "afford" such costs, they have actually succeeded in having their satellite states underwrite the *Sandinistas'* economic and political actions and errors. The Eastern European role in El Salvador, where the very nature of the situation obviates any relevance of the "national" or economic interest of East Berlin or Prague, is simply a part of the Soviets' novel resolution to the financial strain of revolution. There, once again, the East Europeans provided the bulk of the FMLN outside support at their own cost, with Moscow taking a relatively detached and "neutral" attitude while directing East Germany, Hungary, Bulgaria, or Czechoslovakia as secondary players in its own orchestra. Specific East European economic or political interests in Africa, the Middle East, or the Far East may parallel Soviet global aims and, thus, possibly benefit both sides. That, however, is not the case in Latin America.

The latest trends and the recent concentration on Central America indicate a drastic shift toward almost total East European subservience to Soviet interests at a growing cost to their own economies, prestige, political credibility, and autonomy. Their behavior raises important question regarding U.S. attitudes toward Eastern European countries, especially the assumption that they should be seen as different, perhaps autonomous, parts of the Soviet sphere of influence. In Latin America, East European states clearly appear to be an integral parcel of Soviet strategic planning.

Notes

1 Probably not coincidentally, Major Alfonso Martínez Estevez, generally considered to have been the Guatemalan Communists' tool in the assassination of Arbenz's main and only serious political rival, Col. Francisco Xavier Arana, was also in charge of the delicate negotiations with Prague regarding Guatemalan imports of Czech weapons. See Ronald M. Schneider, *Communism in Guatemala* (New York: Frederick A. Praeger Publishers, 1958), pp. 30, 294.

2 *Ibid.*, pp. 308–309.

3 For an interesting first hand testimony of the atmosphere in Prague during the late 1960s, at least from the standpoint of the Latin American representative to the *World Marxist Review*, including the spicy episode of Salvadoran CP representative Roque Dalton being almost killed for daring to date Andrei Gromyko's daughter, see Heriberto Padilla, "El otro mundo de Roque Dalton," *Linden Lane Magazine*, 4:4 (October–December 1985), p. 14.

4 Michael Radu, ed., *Eastern Europe and the Third World* (New York: Praeger, 1982), p. 251.

5 See Leon Gouré and Morris Rothenberg, *Soviet Penetration of Latin America* (Miami: Center for Advanced International Studies, University of Miami, 1975), pp. 129–30.

6 *Ibid.*, p. 131.

7 The World Bank, *World Development Report*, 1986, pp. 184–85.

8 U.S. Department of State, *Warsaw Pact Economic Aid to Non-Communist LDCs, 1984*, (Washington D.C.: May 1986), p. 10.

9 *Ibid.*
10 *Ibid.*
11 *Ibid.*
12 *Ibid.*, p. 15.
13 *Ibid.*
14 *Ibid.*, pp. 14–15.
15 *Comecon Foreign Investment Data Bank*, East-West Project (Ottowa: Carleton University); Carl H. McMillan, *Partners in East–West Economic Relations* (New York: Pergammon Press, 1980), pp. 36–37.
16 U.S. Department of State, *Warsaw Pact Economic Aid.*
17 *Ibid.*, p. 17.
18 *Ibid.*, p. 20.
19 *Ibid.*, p. 21.
20 Federal Broadcast Service–Latin America (FBIS-LAM), July 28, 1986, p. 13.
21 *Ibid.*, p. 14.
22 U.S. Department of State and the Department of Defense, *The Sandinista Military Build-up* (Washington D.C.: Government Printing Office, 1985), p. 29.
23 Henry Kissinger, (Chair), *The Report of the National Bipartisan Commission on Central America*, July 3, 1987, p. 200.
24 McMillan, p. 17.
25 Testimony of Miguel Bolaños Hunter in Uri Ra'anan, Robert L. Pfaltzgraff, Jr., Richard H. Schultz, Ernst Halperin, Igor Lukés, eds., *Hydra of Carnage* (Lexington, MA: Lexington Books, 1986), pp. 313–14.
26 Reproduced in *Hydra of Carnage*, pp. 335–39.
27 *Ibid.*, p. 336.
28 *Ibid.*, p. 337.
29 *Ibid.*, p. 379.
30 Charles Gati, "Fraternal Assistance: Eastern Europe in Grenada," in Jiri Valenta and Herbert J. Ellison, eds., *Grenada and Soviet/Cuban Policy* (Boulder: Westview Press, 1986), p. 90.
31 *Ibid.*, p. 90.
32 *Ibid.*, p. 91.
33 U.S. Department of State, *The Sandinista Military Build-Up* (Washington D.C.: 1985 Government Printing Office), p. 17.
34 JPRS-LAM, September 5, 1985, p. 49.
35 *FBIS-LAM*, April 24, 1986, p. P11.
36 *Ibid.*, July 28, 1986, p. P14. Most of those credits went for over 500 trucks and tractors, textile machinery and services.
37 *The Wall Street Journal*, April 3, 1985.
38 See *FBIS-LAM*, August 13, 1985, p. P11.
39 *Central America Report*, July 3, 1987, p. 200.
40 U.S. Department of State, *Warsaw Pact Economic Aid*, 1986, pp. 14–15.
41 *Ibid.*
42 McMillan, p. 162.
43 *Ibid.*, p. 162.
44 Pedro Ramet and Fernando López-Alves, "Moscow and the Revolutionary Left in Latin America" (Summer 1984), p. 354.
45 *Ibid.*
46 See, for instance, the typical claim by Stephen Kinzer, "Soviet Help to Sandinistas: No Blank Check," *The New York Times*, March 28, 1984.

III

Soviet Policy Toward Latin America

9

The Soviet Union and Central America

Peter Clement
W. Raymond Duncan

INTRODUCTION

A number of factors have converged to increase the importance of examining Soviet policy in Central America during the 1980s. For one, Central America has emerged as one of those Third World regions—along with the Middle East and southern Africa—which have so starkly contributed to East-West tensions. The consequences of these strains significantly affect the international system in terms of superpower relations—relations vividly dramatized by undermined detente, absent Soviet-U.S. arms agreements, and spiraling arms spending. Because the Soviet Union and the United States have not developed a "code of conduct" regarding the relationship between regional actions and broader East-West interests, Soviet diplomacy in Central America very likely will continue to contribute to serious conflict with the United States,[1] and East-West relations will suffer as a consequence.

Central America, moreover, is a Third World locale whose geographic proximity to the United States quickly arouses American security sensitivities. Cuba's growing role in the area, the 1979 *Sandinista* revolution in Nicaragua, the growth of various leftist insurgencies in El Salvador, Guatemala, and Honduras, and the onset of potentially destabilizing economic and political problems in Mexico have prompted Washington to focus attention on the geostrategic significance of Central America.[2]

Any assessment of Soviet policy in Central America must include an analysis of the Soviet-Cuban nexus. Unlike Soviet-Cuban cooperation in other Third World arenas, however, the links between Soviet and Cuban foreign policies are somewhat different in Central America.[3] This is especially true when analyzing Nicaragua—the only Latin American country where Havana directly participated in the armed overthrow of an incumbent regime. Elsewhere in Latin America, Castro's support for armed struggle movements has failed to produce similar results, not to mention the severe Soviet-Cuban clashes provoked on issues of revolutionary strategy and tactics. The Cuban-backed *Sandinista* regime—located in a geographically proximate region, with ethnic and linguistic similarities, and shared experiences regarding antipathy toward their common neighbor to the North—makes Central America of special geostrategic signifiance to Cuba.[4] Cuba's special interest in and knowledge about Central America has led Havana to assume the lead role in Cuban-Soviet initiatives in this part of the world; assessing Havana's position relative to the Soviet policies in the region helps clarify how Cuba serves Soviet interests while pursuing its own objectives.

Quite apart from these broader geostrategic concerns, a review of Soviet policy is instructive as a case study of Soviet influence-building efforts and tactics in the Third World. It is all the more intriguing in that Central America offers attractive opportunities for an expanding Soviet presence, yet its location in the U.S. strategic backyard requires Moscow to steer a careful course while trying to maximize benefits and minimize costs in foreign policy. The attraction of the region is clear; it is a virtual laboratory of contrasting political systems: Nicaragua's revolutionary regime; El Salvador's centrist civilian government with its restless military and persistent leftist insurgents; Guatemala and Honduras with their precarious democratically elected governments, leftist guerrilla movements and strong military heritage; and Panama with its cycles of political instability. Evaluating Soviet adaptation to these differing political systems should indicate the sophistication of Moscow's Latin American policies, while also allowing us to consider the effects of Central American events on Soviet decision-making toward Latin America more generally.

Finally, analyzing Soviet policy in Central America should provide us with an opportunity to study evolving Soviet Third World perceptions under Mikhail Gorbachev.[5] Gorbachev's policies in Central America may reflect on his commitment to an active Third World policy, and allow us to gauge the extent to which Third World clients are an "imperial burden" or a "political asset" for the Soviet Union.[6]

EVOLUTION OF MOSCOW'S CENTRAL AMERICAN POLICY

The Soviet approach to Central America shares much in common with its general policy toward Latin America. Historically, neither Central nor South America attracted significant Soviet attention, largely because Moscow, subscribing to an assumption of "geographic fatalism," considered that national liberation movements had little hope of success, if only because of the historically dominant U.S. role in the Western Hemisphere.[7]

The *Sandinista* victory over Anastasio Somoza in July 1979 brought Central America into a distinct regional focus for Soviet policy-makers and analysts. Soviet leaders moved rapidly to establish formal relations with Nicaragua—more swiftly than they had with Cuba— due largely to Havana's role in training and unifying the *Sandinista* leadership and in lending material assistance to their efforts to bring about Somoza's overthrow.

Although Moscow appears neither to have anticipated the *Sandinista* victory nor given Central America high priority, the Marxist victory galvanized Soviet attention and greatly altered Moscow's views of other revolutionary opportunities in Central America—especially El Salvador. Following the *Sandinista* victory, Soviet observers concluded that the Cuban model for political change (exploiting armed struggle and guerrilla warfare) could be translated into a formula for "political-military fronts," offering a viable alternative to Moscow's traditional tack of peaceful change through nonviolent united leftist fronts.[8]

By 1982–83, however, Soviet optimism about revolutionary opportunities through armed struggle had distinctly waned. With the failure of El Salvador's touted January 1981 "final offensive," followed by declining guerrilla fortunes in Grenada, Moscow downscaled its talk of "new Nicaraguas," avoided conspicuous backing of armed struggle movements outside Nicaragua, and began to reemphasize broad united fronts of various leftist groups in the region.[9] As opposed to its first blush of enthusiasm about possibilities for armed struggle, Moscow turned toward support of regional Contadora negotiations to resolve the Central American conflicts, a tactic which offered the Soviet Union an additional opportunity to assert itself as a political equal with the United States, while reinforcing its moderate image. Toward this end, Moscow initiated links with the Guatemalan government through that country's newly democratically elected President, Vinicio Cerezo Arevalo. A key factor in this shift was the realization that growing U.S. pressures on Nicaragua posed a potential threat to Cuba, Moscow's most important asset in Central America.

MOSCOW'S OBJECTIVES AND POLICY TECHNIQUES IN CENTRAL AMERICA

Central America has attracted increasing Soviet attention since the late 1970s, owing in no small part to the region's geostrategic location. Like Moscow's principal Latin American and Third World client, Cuba, Central American states are positioned off the U.S. southern flank. Next to them are sea routes carrying nearly 50 percent of all crude oil and other foreign cargo shipped to the United States. The region is also the point of origin for critical raw materials: Mexico supplies approximately 33 percent of crude oil to the United States, followed by 8 percent from Venezuela and Trinidad and Tobago, and 56 percent of refined petroleum products coming from other area refineries.[10] In the event of a Soviet armed attack in Europe, as much as 70 percent of U.S. seaborne reenforcements to NATO would need to transit the sea lanes of the Gulf coast or the Panama Canal.[11] Even if future "Nicaraguas" and "Cubas" are not spawned, Soviet activities in Central America produce significant benefits from Moscow's perspective: diversion of U.S. attention and resources away from regions of genuine Soviet security concerns in Europe and Asia, and political turmoil in the United States over the appropriate policies to pursue in Central America.

Soviet motivations in Central America are a mix of superpower ambitions, pursuit of traditional national interests through power politics, and the Marxist-Leninist imperative of promoting socialist models of economic and political change at as low a cost as possible.[12] Low costs are measured both in financial terms—by not having to commit extraordinarily high levels of economic support—and in political terms—by a diplomacy aimed at preserving revolutionary regimes (e.g., Nicaragua) and discreetly bolstering leftist movements without provoking a direct confrontation with the United States.

Caution is central to Soviet policy calculations vis-à-vis Central America. Foremost is a pragmatic appreciation of the U.S. political, economic, and military sway over the region, as well as the great geographical divide between the USSR and Central America. U.S. willingness to counter the *Sandinistas* by supporting the anti-*Sandinista* insurgents has reinforced this appreciation, as did the United States' October 1983 intervention in Grenada.

Beyond geography, a national/cultural divide separates Soviet leaders from Central American revolutionaries, further adding to Soviet wariness. One way of phrasing the difference is in terms of the Latin affinity for "caudillismo" and personalistic politics. But more to the point, perhaps, is the Soviet preference for organizational predictability, for political parties guided by rational principles of control and structure, and whose leaders' charisma has been routinized. The rift between Maurice Bishop and Bernard Coard which led to the demise of the pro-Soviet regime in Grenada reinforced Soviet concerns on this score, as have the devastating factionalist feuding and personalist rivalries within the Salvadoran left. In many ways, such internecine feuding and clash of egos has made various Latin leftist groups somewhat more resistant to outside influence and control, thereby impeding Soviet efforts to build a stable and predictable degree of influence.[13]

Of course, these examples could hardly have surprised the Soviets, who had endured a difficult and at times tumultuous relationship with Cuba during the first decade of Castro's rule. During that period, the Soviets had to contend with a strong-willed and temperamental Fidel Castro. His public airing of suspicions and differences on ideology and tactics in the mid-1960s could only have been anathema to the disciplined and more secretive Soviets. As the Soviets have discovered elsewhere in Latin America, the latent anti-Americanism found in much of the region does not automatically translate into support for the Soviet Union or affinity with its style.

Further complicating Soviet efforts are the political and economic costs inherent in trying to build and consolidate a socialist state so close to U.S. shores. As Cuba demonstrates, the economic costs alone can be quite high. Then, there is the question of "defending" fellow socialist states—a commitment the Soviets have sought to avoid, even in the case of Cuba.

The consolidation of the regime in Nicaragua has become another major element of Moscow's Central America strategy. Soviet willingness to provide a growing, albeit still managable, portion of Managua's economic needs attests to the USSR's interest in cultivating a major client on the Central American mainland and positioning itself to exploit potential opportunities yet to emerge there.[14] In pursuing this objective, however, the Soviets have followed a rather consistent low-profile approach, themselves providing essentially material goods and a limited number of military advisers, Cuba contributing a substantially larger contingent of personnel.[15]

While the Soviets are not as optimistic about the near-term prospects for revolutionary change through armed struggle (as they were, for example, at the time of the Salvadoran guerrillas' January 1981 "final offensive"), they nevertheless continue to support a number of "political-military fronts" throughout the region (in El Salvador, Guatemala, and Honduras). These umbrella organizations include the Communist parties. Typically, they engage in two-track policies, pursuing armed struggle actions, but also seeking negotiations to end fighting and to allow for leftist participation and power-sharing in government.[16] These political-military fronts have also conducted more traditional Communist activities, such as penetrating labor and student groups.[17] This multifaceted approach is interesting not only because it has involved the orthodox Communist parties in the armed struggle, but because it has also had the effect of pulling in guerrilla groups.

Since 1981, the Soviet Union has backed a wide range of military and political activities in Central America, employing diplomacy, party-to-party ties, and other standard Soviet operating techniques, such as radio broadcasts, disinformation, active measures, and building a network for support of Central American leftists in Mexico and South America.[18] Soviet support of insurgency is not always a constant in Soviet foreign policy, but rather one of several variables in a group of policy tools.

Moscow seeks to exploit anti-U.S. nationalism in its various forms. In Panama, for example, the Soviet-line Communist party gears its efforts toward fomenting anti-U.S. sentiment over control of the Canal; and like Moscow, it has been quick to side with General Manuel A. Noriega—commander of the national Guard and power behind presidential politics—as he has battled U.S. charges that he is linked to drug trafficking by claiming these are an attempt to forestall the

Canal's turnover to Panama, set for the year 2000.[19] Conscious of simmering anti-U.S. resentment in Panama, and of that country's utility as an espionage and trade center, Cuba has also backed Noriega; indeed, Fidel Castro singled out the Panamanian military for praise at the February 1986 Cuban Communist Party Congress.[20]

The Contadora process provides an interesting example of Moscow's tactical flexibility in regard to U.S. policy in Central America. Moscow, for example, was initially ambivalent about the Contadora process—presumably out of concern that U.S. influence over the Contadora group (Mexico, Colombia, Venezuela, and Panama) would be exploited so as to transform this regional initiative into a multilateral instrument aimed at imposing U.S. demands upon the *Sandinistas*. Once it became evident that Contadora had a life of its own, and, more importantly, as the U.S. became somewhat disenchanted with the prospects for and viability of a Contadora-sponsored solution, Moscow became an outspoken advocate of the process. Soviet Foreign Minister Shevardnadze, for example, underscored Moscow's positive view of the Contadora process during an October 1986 visit to Mexico City.[21]

Cuba plays a pivotal role in Soviet calculations with respect to Central America, insofar as Havana has taken the lead in supporting Nicaragua and the leftist movements of Central America. Moscow benefits greatly from Havana's experience in assisting revolutionary groups—this growing out of Castro's guerrilla struggle against Fulgencio Batista during the late 1950s and Cuba's support for insurgent movements in Latin America and Africa beginning in the early 1960s.[22] Since then, Cuba has provided financial support, military training, and organizational advice for leftist insurgents from practically every country in Latin America.[23] In addition, from the mid-1970s to the early 1980s, over 20,000 students from preschool through university levels studied at Cuba's Isle of Youth educational complex. Other Cuban activities in the Caribbean and Central America have included: (1) working to unite various leftist groups; (2) providing ideological and organizational training for urban and guerrilla warfare; (3) using military aid and advisers to gain influence over guerrilla fronts and; (4) using Cuba's extensive cultural exchange and propaganda activities to support covert operations and armed struggle.[24]

Cuba, rather than the USSR, played the leading role in supporting the *Sandinistas* fortunes prior to the overthrow of Anastasio Somoza in July 1979. Indeed, Fidel Castro's 1959 revolution served as the inspiration for Carlos Fonseca Amador, Tomás Borge, and Silvio Mayorga, former Nicaraguan student activists who founded the FSLN in July 1961 and led it on the path of armed struggle.[25] And it was Fidel Castro who unified the three factions of the FSLN in 1978, making possible the toppling of the Somoza dynasty one year later. Once in power, the FSLN leadership drew again upon Cuba's assistance in creating mass organizations, the *Sandinista* military and security organizations, as well as a unified National Directorate as the instruments through which to control and direct Nicaragua's revolutionary process.[26] Cuba, in addition, has provided badly needed educational, medical, and technical assistance—complementing and paralleling Soviet economic and military support.[27]

The Soviet Union, in short, can thank the Cubans for helping to bring Somoza down and guaranteeing the *Sandinista's* hold on power. Without the Cubans, the Soviets probably would not have paid much attention to the FSLN, given the *Sandinista*'s opposition to the pro-Soviet Nicaraguan Socialist Party (PSN), which small and politically weak, subscribed to the classic Soviet line emphasizing peaceful change through conversion of the urban workers rather than armed struggle.[28] The Cubans, with their natural revolutionary, ethnic, and linguistic affinity with the *Sandinistas*, helped the FSLN maintain its unity and political leadership after the civil war with Somoza had been won.

THE CUBA PARADIGM: THE LESSONS OF THE CUBAN EXPERIENCE FOR SOVIET POLICY IN NICARAGUA

Although Cuba played a greater role in abetting the *Sandinista* revolution, the Soviets have carefully developed their own bilateral relationship with the *Sandinistas* since 1979. Soviet policy toward Nicaragua in the 1980s suggests Moscow is applying "lessons learned" during the development of the Soviet-Cuban relationship.

The extent to which the Cuban experience has influenced Soviet thinking about Nicaragua was clearly reflected during a spring 1983 interview with the London *Guardian*. In the midst of a discussion of Soviet policy toward Nicaragua, Viktor Vol'skiy, director of the Moscow-based Latin America Institute, stated that the USSR had "to send oil to Cuba—two tankers a day for twenty years"—and that "we would like not to have to repeat that on a larger scale."[29] Given the costly and sometimes turbulent nature of the Soviet-Cuban relationship over the past 27 years, not to mention its impact on U.S.-Soviet relations, it is not surprising that Soviet leaders would shape policy toward Nicaragua with an eye toward the "lessons" learned in their dealings with Cuba.

In reviewing Soviet policy and activities in Nicaragua since the July 1979 *Sandinista* takeover, a number of parallels and contrasts strongly suggest that the Cuban experience has indeed influenced Moscow's relationship with the Managua regime. Perhaps the most obvious contrast is the extent to which the Soviets have maintained a surprisingly low profile in their dealings with Managua, be it in the political/diplomatic, economic, or military realm. Some seven years after the *Sandinista* revolution, not a single Soviet Politburo member has visited Managua. In contrast, just 13 months after Castro's 1959 seizure of power, a large Soviet delegation (headed by high-ranking Presidium member Anastas Mikoyan) spent 10 days in Havana and concluded a number of major long-term trade agreements. That move had been all the more remarkable since formal diplomatic relations had not yet been established.

Further Soviet boldness was exemplified by the delivery of ICBMs in the late summer of 1962. That move had the ancillary effect of satisfying Castro's call for a defense commitment, although it clearly was not the motivating factor in Moscow's decision.[30] While the Cuban missile crisis was the most serious consequence to grow out of Moscow's military relationship with Cuba, it was not the last time U.S. concerns about that relationship exacerbated U.S.-Soviet relations. Controversy over the Soviet combat brigade in Cuba during the fall of 1979, for example, proved to be a key factor in the U.S. Congress' decision not to ratify the SALT II arms control agreement, which in turn contributed to the demise of detente.[31]

Moscow has eschewed a high profile in providing military assistance to Nicaragua during the 1980s. Thus, while the USSR itself has provided nearly one-third of the estimated $580 million in Communist military assistance to Managua between 1980 and 1985, most of the military hardware has actually been delivered by the East Europeans or third parties, such as Algeria.[32] Indeed, the controversial delivery of Mi-24 helicopter gunships by the Soviet ship *Bakuriani* during the November 1984 U.S. presidential campaign, represented the first direct Soviet delivery of a major military system to Nicaragua. Moscow's conscious effort to maintain its public distance from Managua to obscure its military assistance role presumably also reflected the Soviets' concern lest their actions prompt a strong reaction from the

Reagan administration, a concern reinforced by events in Grenada in October 1983.

The military assistance component of Soviet-Nicaraguan relations nonetheless offers some interesting parallels with that of the Soviet-Cuban relationship. For example, although there has not been a "crisis" such as the 1962 missile crisis, in both cases an unwritten but tacitly understood U.S.-Soviet "threshold level" seems to have evolved over time. Soviet-American "understanding" which ended the Cuban missile crisis established the general "threshold mark" in Soviet-Cuban military relations to which Moscow has thus far adhered, i.e., the introduction of nuclear weapons in Cuba.[33]

In Nicaragua, Moscow seems to be abiding by U.S. injunctions not to introduce advanced fighter aircraft. Soviet silence on this matter, however, can not yet be taken to mean consent, as it did in the Cuban missile crisis. The USSR may choose to ignore the U.S. injunctions at a later date, especially since the U.S. threshold level is much lower than it was in Cuba. In any case, to date the Soviets have interpreted the U.S. warnings to mean that systems short of the advanced fighter aircraft threshold are permissible. Thus, in support of a growing *Sandinista* military—which now numbers some 75,000 active duty armed forces and security forces, as well as 44,000 in the reserves and unmobilized militia—Moscow and its bloc allies have provided Mi-24 helicopter gunships, T-54/55 tanks, Mi-8 transport helicopters, armored personnel carriers, anti-aircraft missiles, transport trucks, and associated small arms and ammunition.[34]

Despite the growing Communist military aid program, the Soviets have sought to maintain a very low profile, allowing the Cubans and East Europeans to provide the bulk of military and economic technicians working in Nicaragua. An estimated 50 to 70 Soviet military/security advisers work alongside some 2500–3500 Cuban military advisers; in addition, Cuba provides some 3000–4000 economic and technical advisers.[35] Moscow's sensitivity on the question of its *military* role in Nicaragua was reflected in an official refutation of U.S. assertions that "hundreds" of Russian military advisers are working in Nicaragua. A Soviet television broadcast reported in mid-June 1986 that "the number of Soviet military specialists in Nicaragua at the invitation of the country's government does not exceed the number of fingers on the President's hand—if, of course, this number equals five, as is the case with other people."[36] Again, the reluctance to maintain a larger presence probably stems from Moscow's Cuban experience, particularly the controversy with the United States provoked by the presence of the Soviet combat brigade in Cuba in 1979. Of course, Moscow's policy and tactical flexibility have been enhanced by instruments not available to it in the Cuban case, i.e., allies who share common interests and are prepared to perform a surrogate function.

The question of advanced fighter aircraft has apparently prompted some frictions between Moscow and Managua, perhaps not unlike those between Moscow and Havana when Castro sought security guarantees from the Soviets in the early 1960s. Reports that the Nicaraguans had received training on MiG-21 fighter aircraft in the Soviet bloc in the early 1980s, as well as the ongoing construction of a major new airfield runway at Punta Huete, suggests that Moscow may well have agreed to deliver such aircraft, presumably before the U.S. demarches on this issue.[37] President Daniel Ortega's public assertions of Nicaragua's right to acquire advanced fighter aircraft in March and September 1983, and on the eve of a June 1984 trip to Moscow—as well as Moscow's studied silence on these statements—strongly suggest that Managua was seeking (with little success) to pressure Moscow into delivering such aircraft.[38]

Ortega's tactic of going public to pressure or embarrass Moscow into meeting Nicaraguan requests for jet fighters is strongly reminiscent of Castro's public statements between 1960 and 1962, in which he sought to elicit Soviet acknowledgment that Cuba was part of the "socialist community." Castro hoped such a statement would, in turn, imply a Soviet defense commitment. As Jacques Levesque has aptly stated, "it is not by chance that the Cuban leader chose the Bay of Pigs invasion as the moment to declare the Socialist character of the Cuban Revolution."[39]

In this context of thresholds and "commitments," Gorbachev's prospective visit to Latin America will pose some dilemmas for the Soviet leadership. Apart from Brezhnev's 1974 visit to the Second Cuban Party Congress in Havana, no Soviet general secretary has every been to Latin America proper. Inasmuch as media accounts suggest Gorbachev's itinerary includes Argentina, Brazil, and Mexico, the Soviet leader could be expected to stop over in Nicaragua. However, a stop in Managua might be detrimental to Nicaragua—the U.S. Congress reversed an earlier decision to cut off aid to the Nicaraguan insurgents when Daniel Ortega went to Moscow in April 1984. Because of President Reagan's strong personal views on Nicaragua, Gorbachev presumably would have to weigh the implications of a symbolic visit in Managua with ongoing equities in U.S.-Soviet relations, particularly if an arms agreement was at hand. On the other hand, to totally shun the *Sandinistas* might be construed by Soviet Third World clients elsewhere—and potential critics within the Soviet leadership—as a sign of Gorbachev's weakness.

On a broader strategic level, Moscow has not yet moved to fully translate its growing investment in Nicaragua into a net strategic gain vis-à-vis the United States. Brezhnev, and now Gorbachev, have no need for an "easy fix" to attain a symbolic nuclear parity as Khrushchev attempted to do by introducing nuclear missiles into Cuba in 1962. Still, U.S. willingness to go to the brink of war to underscore its sensitivities on that occasion probably remains an important factor in Soviet strategic calculations concerning Nicaragua.

In comparing the evolution of Soviet-Cuban and Soviet-Nicaraguan relations, some interesting contrasts are immediately apparent. During the stormy decade of the 1960s, the Soviet Union and Castro openly clashed over revolutionary tactics in Latin America, leading to major strains in bilateral relations. At one point, Castro even accused Moscow of conspiring with party oppositionists—the so-called "microfaction"—and meddling in Cuban internal affairs. There is little evidence of such Soviet meddling in the case of Nicaragua, despite apparent differences over Managua's efforts to push revolution beyond its borders in the early 1980s. While there are reputed "hardliners" within the *Sandinista* leadership (such as Tomás Borge and Bayardo Arce), there is little evidence to indicate that Moscow has sought to cultivate them more than others in the ruling group.[40]

The 1960s experience in Cuba may have prompted a more circumspect Soviet approach to dealing with Nicaragua's new leaders. Indeed, the Soviets have eschewed public polemics and recriminations with Managua, despite *Sandinista* policies that have frequently run counter to Soviet advice. In the early 1980s, statements of Soviet leaders clearly suggested limits to economic largesse, admonishing the FSLN to proceed slowly in the construction of a socialist economy.[41] Indeed, the Soviets, mindful of the effect radical measures had on the Cuban economy in the 1960s, have actively encouraged Managua to maintain its economic and trade links with various Western powers.[42] Nonetheless, because *Sandinista* foreign and economic policies have stifled the private sector, scared off foreign investment, and prompted the U.S. to impose economic sanctions, Nicaragua, as Cuba before it, has had to seek increased economic assistance from the Soviet Union. In the early 1980s, however, the Soviet Union was not forthcoming in the area of economic assistance. Between 1981 and 1984, for example, total Soviet bloc aid was estimated at between $200–250 million, of which $75–150 million came from the USSR.[43] Most Soviet aid in that period came in the form of long-term development credits for hydroelectricity and agriculture-related projects. There were, on the other hand, few infusions of hard currency support.[44]

Nonetheless, since 1985 Moscow has given signs of increasing economic aid to Nicaragua, despite its own economic difficulties.[45] The most important development since late 1984 has been Managua's increased dependence upon the USSR for its oil needs. According to recent public statements from Nicaraguan officials, the USSR provided at least 80 to 90 percent of Managua's oil needs in 1985, and almost all oil in 1986 (up to 3.5 million barrels). The Nicaraguan trade minister acknowledged, moreover, that the oil costs are being covered by Soviet credits which Managua has been unable to repay.[46] Given Nicaragua's current economic straits, it seems unlikely Managua will be able to pay these, or any new oil debts, any time soon. In addition to oil, the export of other Soviet items, such as machinery and motor vehicles, have tripled between 1983 and 1984. Managua, meanwhile, has exported virtually nothing to the USSR.[47] Increased Soviet largesse may reflect in part Moscow's determination to offset a perceived U.S. challenge. Moreover, increasing economic aid levels is a relatively low-cost and low-risk policy.

In any event, Nicaragua is not likely to become a Cuba-style economic drain, at least in the near to mid-term. Nicaragua differs from Cuba in several important respects. For example, it has a population of some 3 million, whereas Cuba numbers some 10 million, and as a much less industrialized country, it requires less to sustain its economy.

Moscow presumably hopes the current Nicaraguan economic crisis will not persist as in the case of Cuba. Still, the Soviet experience in Cuba has demonstrated how the growth of economic dependence, while admittedly costly, does provide a reliable and, in some ways, almost irreversible form of leverage and influence. Indeed, during the polemics over revolutionary tactics in the 1960s, Moscow successfully brought the economic weapon to bear on Castro: by reducing the rates of increase in oil deliveries at a moment of growing Cuban need in 1967–1968, Moscow sent a message that Castro could not ignore.

Seen in this context, Moscow's growing economic largess to the *Sandinistas* is a shrewd policy move. It sustains Nicaragua against a U.S.-backed insurgency, thereby burnishing Moscow's credentials as a key backer of revolutionary regimes besieged by the "forces of imperialism." By supporting the young *Sandinista* leadership at a critical moment in its genesis, Moscow is making an investment in the future, ingratiating itself with those who will remember "who their friends were." Thus, Moscow is sowing the seeds of influence and possible leverage by creating a dependency that will insure the "Soviet factor" cannot be ignored in future *Sandinista* policy calculations.

Against this backdrop, Castro reportedly cautioned the *Sandinistas* not to repeat his economic experience, one which has made Cuba almost totally dependent upon the Soviet Union.[48] If so, Managua seems to have ignored his advice, progressively isolating itself from the West, and even seeking membership in CMEA.[49] However, Managua certainly does not appear to be close to the kind of economic integration achieved by Cuba since its entry into CMEA in 1972. Still, recent developments in Nicaragua offer some possible parallels to the Cuban experience. As noted above, the beginning of Soviet oil deliveries in late 1983 and early 1984 marked an important benchmark, symbolizing Moscow's growing willingness to shoulder part of Managua's economic burdens as well as Nicaragua's increased dependence upon the Soviet Union for its energy supplies. In October 1985, a Soviet economic delegation headed by a deputy chairman of the Soviet State Planning Commission (GOSPLAN) spent ten days in Managua, presumably advising the *Sandinistas* on how to centralize and "rationalize" the national economy.[50] Virtually unnoticed in the Western press, this visit—which was openly discussed in the Soviet media—may have served a function similar to that which restructured the Cuban planning mechanisms in 1970–1971.

In this context, a recent *Pravda* account entitled "Nicaragua: A Difficult Formation Process," published on the seventh anniversary of the *Sandinista* revolution, offers some telling indicators of possible Soviet "advice on questions of central planning and direction." After noting the effects of the insurgency war on the national economy, the article states:

> Of course, there are internal difficulties as well. Recently, for example, substantial shortcomings were revealed in the organization of the labor process in the country as a whole. People are violating production discipline, not working as long as they should, and failing to meet production targets. The situation is bad in agriculture as well. Many peasants who have obtained land and have no obligation to the state are farming in such a way as to satisfy only their families' needs. To a large extent, this is why Nicaragua has recently been short of food supplies.[51]

The critical policy-suggestive tone of this piece stands in marked contrast to the article issued a year earlier on the occasion of the sixth anniversary. That article made no mention of the growing economic problems. Quite the contrary, it asserted that "the country is implementing a democratic agrarian reform and has created hundreds of peasant cooperatives and state farms which are operating successfully on land appropriated from local landowners and foreign companies."[52]

Moscow's willingness to offer a more critical and candid assessment than in the 1986 article suggests that the Soviets are now more directly concerned, and by implication, more prepared to offer advice in order to remedy those problems. Implicit in the article was Moscow's preference for a more systematic and centralized organization of labor resources, as well as a greater State role in monitoring agricultural activity. The importance of this economic issue was underscored again in December 1986, when Nicaraguan Planning Minister Henry Ruiz, accompanied by President Daniel Ortega and the Nicaraguan Defense and Foreign Ministers, travelled to Moscow. Upon their return to Managua, Ruiz declared that the new Soviet aid promises would be "of great importance."[53]

BEYOND NICARAGUA: SOVIET ACTIVITY ELSEWHERE IN CENTRAL AMERICA

The Soviet Union has followed a two-track policy of helping leftist insurgents while seeking to improve state-to-state relations in Central America. In this effort, its principal instruments have been Cuba and the region's Communist parties. Cuba remains a revolutionary model for many Central American guerrillas—especially in El Salvador, but also among the less powerful movements of Honduras and Guatemala.[54] As a Honduran leftist who fought with the *Sandinistas* explained in 1985, "for the first time young Communists could see a revolution triumph, a revolution that spoke Spanish."[55] Rebels interviewed in 1985 reported that Cuban embassies served as refuges and bankers for Central American leftists traveling abroad, and that senior rebel officials in El Salvador and Guatemala have received advanced guerrilla training in Cuba.[56] The education of guerrillas in Cuba is overseen by the Department of Special Operations of the Cuban Army and the Department of the Americas, headed by Manuel Piñeiro.[57] Piñeiro, a close friend of Fidel Castro, draws on two decades of guerrilla experience in the region and knows many of the area's leftist insurgent commanders personally.[58] Among other topics taught in Cuba's courses are how to recruit spies, maintain security, forge secret communications, and interrogate prisoners.[59]

Through the mid-1980s, the guerrilla movements in Central America continued to receive Cuban backing, but more in the form of training in Havana, support for travel abroad, diplomatic attention, and propaganda, rather than direct weapons supplies. The latter appear to have peaked in early 1981 when the El Salvadoran leftists failed to replicate the victory of their comrades in neighboring Nicaragua.[60] Cuba's diminished profile in backing El Salvador's guerrillas stemmed in part from the October 1983 U.S. intervention in Grenada, which rang alarm bells in Havana and Moscow about possible further U.S. actions in Central America, especially in Nicaragua. As a result, Cuba seemed to shift toward rebuilding its image as a responsible regional actor less bent upon destabilizing Central America. Democratic elections in Costa Rica, El Salvador, Guatemala, and Honduras during the mid-1980s, moreover, may have figured in Havana's shift from blatant and direct material support of guerrilla movements in the area to a more conciliatory tack of improving state-to-state relations. Cuba's endorsement of the Contadora process complemented its effort to upgrade bilateral ties with the Central American states.[61] This two-track approach—helping leftist insurgents while seeking to improve state-to-state relations—parallels Soviet policy in Central and South America.[62]

A second important adjunct to Soviet policy in Central America has been its support for indigenous pro-Soviet Communist parties. Their status differs from country to country: in El Salvador, Guatemala, and Honduras, they are illegal; while Costa Rica's Communist party is tolerated by a government that would rather see Communist deputies debating in the National Assembly than Communist guerrillas fighting in the streets.[63] Panama's Communist party lost its recognized status after the May 1984 elections because it received less than three percent of the votes cast. Central America's three illegal parties in El Salvador, Guatemala, and Honduras—following Soviet advice after Moscow's euphoric reception of the *Sandinista* armed struggle victory—have joined forces with leftist, Marxist guerrilla groups in political-military umbrella organizations dedicated to a combination of armed struggle and political organization.[64]

In countries where the pro-Soviet Communist parties are not outlawed (Costa Rica, Nicaragua, and, until 1984, Panama), Marxist groups work within the legal structure, following traditional Communist tactics. These endeavors include working to build their electoral strength through broad united fronts, infiltrating worker and student organizations, and utilizing front organizations, like the World Peace Council, to maximize power and build a respectable image of responsibility.[65] The People's Party of Panama (PPP—with an estimated 750 members) and Costa Rica's Popular Vanguard Party (PVP—membership estimated at 3,500) fall into this category.[66]

Nicaragua is a case apart, where two small Communist parties—the Nicaraguan Socialist Party (PSN) and the Communist Party of Nicaragua (PCN)—pose an interesting, albeit minor, dilemma for the USSR. The PCN, for example, has moved away from the "patriotic front" of parties that had backed or coalesced with the *Sandinistas*.[67] In part, this move stems from the USSR's establishment of various party-to-party accords with the *Sandinistas*, agreements which implicitly challenge the legitimacy of the PCN. Moreover, the PCN rejects the *Sandinistas'* claim to be true Marxists and accuses them of illegally restricting PCN activities among worker and trade union groups.[68] The Moscow-orientated Nicaraguan Socialist Party (PSN), meanwhile, has been relegated to obscurity by the Soviets, despite its stature as "Moscow's party" for so many years during Somoza's rule. Neither the PCN, the PSN, the leftist Popular Christian Social Party (PPSC), or the Popular Action Movement–Marxist-Leninist (MAP-ML) fared well during the November 1984 election sweep by the *Sandinistas*.[69] Still, the existence of these small parties serves as a minor nuisance to the *Sandinistas* who obviously see themselves as carrying the mantle of "revolution" in Nicaragua.[70]

Among the illegal Communist parties working in political-military fronts are El Salvador's Communist Party (PCES), the oldest Marxist-Leninist movement in the country, and the Guatemalan Party of Labor (PGT). Led by Shafik Jorge Handal, with an estimated membership of 1,000, the pro-Soviet PCES joined the armed struggle movement in 1980 as part of the Farabundo Martí National Liberation Front (FMLN), and since then has actively participated in FMLN politics.[71] In Guatemala, the estimated 500 member Soviet-backed Guatemalan Party of Labor (PGT) adheres to the position that the revolution can triumph only through the use of force, and since 1981 has committed itself to armed struggle.[72] Still, in keeping with its pro-Soviet orientation, the PGT continues to favor the formation of a "unified revolutionary front"—led by itself, of course—whose goal is to combine military action with political organization among the masses.[73]

Toward this end, the military arm of the PGT, the Rebel Armed Forces (FAR), joined with Guatemala's three other guerrilla groups in February

1982 to form the Guatemalan National Revolutionary Alliance (URNG), an organization dedicated to combining political and military work.[74] The URNG has called for a "revolutionary people's war" through a "great front of patriotic unity."[75] Both the PGT and PCES adhere closely to the Soviet positions on international affairs: strengthening solidarity with the USSR, defending the *Sandinista* revolution against U.S. pressure, and condemning the U.S. use of Honduran territory for actions against Nicaragua.[76]

The Honduran Communist Party (PCH), with about 650 members, has followed the example of its counterparts in El Salvador and Guatemala by joining the country's major Marxist-Leninist organization, the Honduran Revolutionary Movement (MHR) which was founded in 1982 as an umbrella group to unite Honduras' proliferating small leftist guerrilla groups.[77] The MHR's advocacy of armed struggle and other subversive activities has not found much support in Honduran society. Nevertheless, because the large U.S. presence has kindled nationalist resentment in Honduras, there has been an upsurge of MHR activities in unions, church organizations, and among peace groups. The result has been a downturn in armed insurgency during the mid-1980s.[78] As in El Salvador and Guatemala, pursuit of a two-track policy involving both armed struggle and political action under specific country conditions has been clear.

Central America's small Communist parties, and the armed struggle coalitions they have joined, have both hindered and promoted Soviet interests in the region. On the negative side, most of them have a history of factionalism and personalist rivalries which have led to a proliferation of leftist groups and revolutionary rifts, all undermining the unity advocated by both Moscow and Havana.[79]

In El Salvador, the FMLN's ill-fated January 1981 offensive produced serious rifts over how closely to rely on advice from the Cubans and Soviets as opposed to carrying on a fiercely independent struggle.[80] These intensified during the mid-1980s as the Cubans and Soviets increasingly advocated a peaceful political negotiation of the conflict.[81] Personalistic rivalries pitted Salvador Cayetano Carpio, the intensely independent leader of the Popular Liberation Forces (FPL), and Fabio Castillo, founder of the Central American Revolutionary Workers' Party faction, against much of the rest of the FMLN (including Shafik Handal, almost irrationally disliked by Carpio).[82] In 1983, Carpio became implicated in the murder of his second-in-command, Melinda Montes, who had come to support a more integrated command structure within the FMLN and political negotiations with the El

Salvador government. When ordered to divulge information about his rebel group and to go to Cuba for an "extended rest," Mr. Carpio went to his home and shot himself.[83] Since then, the FMLN groups have moved toward closer military coordination on the battlefield, and peace negotiations within the government.[84] Throughout this feuding, the Soviets continued to support the PCES and accorded PCES leaders public prominence, presumably to enhance influence of the PCES within the broader coalition of leftist parties.

Internecine feuding within the various Marxist groups elsewhere in Central America has undermined unified political action. The Honduran Revolutionary Movement's unity exists essentially on paper only, as was evident when the PCH split following the ouster of the party's General Secretary, Rigoberto Padillo Rush, in 1985.[85] Moreover, other groups, such as the Morazanista Front of National Liberation (FMLH), are gaining stature, while the PCH is preoccupied with its internal problems. The FMLH gained some publicity, for example, after seizing a Tegucigalpa radio station in 1985.[86]

In Guatemala there is intraparty conflict between the Guatemalan Party of Labor (PGT), which supports a military wing called the Rebel Armed Forces (FAR), and a PGT offshoot called the PGT-Leadership Nucleus, which argues that the party itself must entirely assume the task of armed struggle.[87] And, as in the case of Honduras, other groups are gaining stature and credibility as the PGT handles its internal dissension. Thus, the Guerrilla Army of the Poor (EGP) and the Armed People's Organization (ORPA) have expanded their military activities.[88]

Costa Rica's Popular Vanguard Party has been marked by falling outs and bitter rivalries over a variety of issues.[89] Leftist parties have proliferated in Panama, complicating the chances for a viable unified front there. They include the Tendencia, or *Fracción*, which broke away from the People's Party of Panama in 1974; the Maoist Communist Party/Marxist-Leninist, which violently opposed the PPP in the early 1980s; and the Socialist Workers' Party (PST), officially recognized in 1983. Panama also accorded legal status in 1983 to the Workers' Revolutionary Party (PRT), a Trotskyist organization.[90]

Despite becoming weakened by widespread factional feuding, Central America's pro-Soviet Communist parties and leftist movements clearly advance Soviet interests by echoing Moscow's foreign policy positions and working to unify leftist groups in their countries. The Soviets, Cubans, and Nicaraguans keep abreast of these various issues through frequent and high-level contact with each other. Nicaraguan President Daniel Ortega, for example, attended the Cuban Communist

Party's 3rd Congress in early February 1986 with expressions of praise for the Cubans, while Bayardo Arce, one of the nine *comandantes* within the ruling FSLN National Directorate, attended Moscow's 27th Congress of the CPSU in February–March 1986.[91] Arce expressed his profound gratitude to the USSR and was allowed to hold a news conference during which he strongly defended the *Sandinista* revolution and warned against possible U.S. direct intervention in Nicaragua.[92]

Similarly, El Salvador's FMLN sent Communist Party leader Shafik Handal to the PCC Congress, where he defended the FMLN's two-track policy of military and political action and called for a negotiated political solution to El Salvador's conflict.[93] Handal also attended Moscow's 27th Party Congress, carrying a parallel message of warm greetings from the FMLN and expressing support for Gorbachev's main address.[94] The visit of a high-level CPSU delegation headed by M.A. Ponomarev to the 8th Congress of the People's Party of Panama in January 1986 underscored Moscow's growing interest in other potential hotspots in Central America beyond El Salvador and Nicaragua.[95]

Notes

1 On Soviet-U.S. discussions of a "code of conduct" to manage U.S.-Soviet rivalry in the Third World areas (which was set in motion by the Richard Nixon-Leonid Brezhnev detente process of 1972), see Alexander L. George, ed., *Managing U.S.-Soviet Rivalry* (Boulder, CO: Westview Press, 1983), Introduction and chapter 5.

2 Much has been written about Mexico's mounting economic difficulties and potential political instability. See, for example, Brian Latell, *Mexico at the Crossroads: The Many Crises of the Political System* (Palo Alto: Stanford University, Hoover Institution, 1986).

3 See W. Raymond Duncan, *The Soviet Union and Cuba, Interests and Influence* (New York: Praeger, 1985), chapter 6; U.S. Department of State and Department of Defense, *The Soviet-Cuban Connection; in Central America and the Caribbean* (Washington D.C.: Government Printing Office, 1985).

4 *The Soviet-Cuban Connection*, H. Michael Erisman, *Cuba's International Relations; The Anatomy of a Nationalistic Foreign Policy* (Boulder, CO: Westview Press, 1985), pp. 137–48; Joseph Whelan, *The Soviet Union in the Third World, 1980–85: An Imperial Burden or Political Asset?* Report prepared for the Committee on Foreign Affairs, U.S. House of Representatives, (Washington D.C.: Government Printing Office, 1985), pp. 319–39.

5 See Francis Fukayama, "Gorbachev and the Third World," *Foreign Affairs*, 64: 4 (Spring 1986), pp. 715–31.

6 Whelan, *The Soviet Union in the Third World*.

7 On Soviet policy in Latin America before the Cuban Revolution, see Stephan Clissold, ed., *Soviet Relations with Latin America* (London: Oxford University Press, 1970); and Gregory J. Oswald and Anthony J. Strover, *The Soviet Union and Latin*

America (New York: Praeger, 1970). United States policy in Latin America prior to Cuba's revolution is acutely assessed by Gordon Connel-Smith, *The Inter-American System* (London: Oxford University Press, 1966).

8 See Robert S. Leiken, ed. *Central America: Anatomy of a Conflict* (New York: Pergamon Press, 1984); and his *Soviet Strategy in Latin America* (New York: Praeger, 1982), one of the Washington Papers (10: 93). (Published with the Center for Strategic and International Studies, Georgetown University, Washington D.C.)

9 See Whelan, *The Soviet Union in the Third World*, pp. 335–40.

10 *The Latin American Times*, 63, January 1985, p. 6.

11 *Ibid.*

12 See Seweryn Bialer, "Soviet Foreign Policy: Sources, Perceptions, Trends," in Bialer, ed., *The Domestic Context of Soviet Foreign Policy* (Boulder, CO: Westview Press, 1981), chapter 15.

13 For an excellent discussion of the domestic political struggle within Grenada's New Jewel Movement, see Jiri Valenta, "Leninism in Grenada," in *Problems of Communism*, (July–August 1984), pp.1–23. This author believes the evidence of a Soviet-Cuban rift over whom to support—Coard vs. Bishop—is less than fully persuasive. However, there can be no doubt of Soviet-Cuban tensions over the subsequent explanation of what transpired in October 1983. While Fidel Castro explicitly laid the blame on Bernard Coard, the official Soviet position was that U.S. "special services" had penetrated the upper echelons of the party, and then created a provocation to justify the U.S. intervention. In this regard, see Fidel Castro's speech in November 1983 on the occasion of the return of Cuban dead from Granada, and *Pravda's* version of that speech.

14 See Fukuyama, "Gorbachev and the Third World."

15 *The Soviet-Cuban Connection in Central America and the Caribbean*, also Department of State and Department of Defense, *The Challenge to Democracy in Central America* (Government Printing Office, Washington D.C.: 1986), pp. 17–37.

16 See annual *Yearbook on International Communist Affairs* (Palo Alto: Stanford University, Hoover Institution), by year from 1982–86.

17 *Ibid.*, 1986, pp. 108–109, 87–94, 98–103.

18 *Ibid.*, pp. 113–118.

19 *Washington Post*, August 13, 1986.

20 Havana International Service in Spanish, 6 July 1986, FBIS-LAM, July 8, 1986, p. Q1.

21 See, for example, Shevardnadze's dinner speech in Mexico City, published in *Pravda*, October 5, 1986, p.6.

22 See D. Bruce Jackson, *Castro, The Kremlin, and Communism in Latin America* (Baltimore: The Johns Hopkins University Press, 1969).

23 See *The Challenge to Democracy in Central America* and *The Soviet-Cuban Connection in Central America and the Caribbean*, pp.8–10.

24 U.S. Department of State, Special Report No. 90, December 14, 1981, pp.1, 4.

25 Shirley Christian, *Nicaragua: Revolution in the Family* (New York: Vintage Books, 1986), chapter 2.

26 *Ibid.*, Epilogue.

27 *Ibid.*

28 See Leiken, "Fantasies and Facts: The Soviet Union and Nicaragua," *Current History*, 83 (October 1984), p.316.

29 *The Guardian* (London) April 28, 1983, p.1.

30 Historians differ somewhat on Khrushchev's motivations in sending missiles to Cuba. On balance, it would seem that meeting Havana's request for a commitment was secondary to the broader strategic implications of the move for the U.S.-Soviet balance. Herbert Dinerstein, in *The Making of a Missile Crisis* (Baltimore: The Johns Hopkins University Press, 1976), p. 156, argues that the successful emplacement of the missiles would have advanced by a decade Soviet attainment of nuclear

parity. Jacques Levesque has stated that the issue of defending Cuba is what initially prompted consideration of the move. See Jacques Levesque, *The USSR and the Cuban Revolution: Soviet Ideological and Strategical Perspectives, 1959–1977* (New York: Praeger, 1978), p. 39.

31 For a thorough examination of the Soviet combat brigade controversy and its repercussions on U.S. domestic politics and the SALT II debates, see Gloria Duffy, "Crisis Mangling and the Cuban Brigade," in *International Security* (Summer 1983) pp. 68–87.

32 See *Soviet Military Power 1986* (Washington D.C.: Government Printing Office, 1986), p. 131 for data on deliveries to Nicaragua.

33 See Henry Kissinger, *White House Years* (Boston: Little, Brown, and Company, 1979), pp.636–51 for an exact chronology of events related to the Cienfuegos episode in 1970; see also Ray Garthoff, "Handling the Cienfuegos Crisis," in *International Security* (Summer 1983), pp. 46–66. For details on the MiG-23 issue, see Ray Garthoff, *Detente and Confrontation*, pp. 617–18. Of course, at various points, the Soviets have probed the parameters of the 1962 understanding, as with nuclear ship visits to Cienfuegos in 1970; similarly, when MiG-23s were initially delivered to Cuba in 1978, U.S. officials sought—and received—Soviet assurances that the aircraft could not carry nuclear payloads.

34 *The Challenge to Democracy in Central America*, pp. 19–23.

35 *Soviet Military Power 1986*, pp. 130–31.

36 Moscow Television Service, June 16, 1986, cited in *Foreign Broadcast Information Service-Soviet Union Daily Report* (hereafter as FBIS-SOV), June 19, 1986, p. A2.

37 For details on these reports, see the *Washington Post*, June 19, 1983, p. 1, and the *New York Times*, August 2, 1983, p. 3, and August 10, 1983, p. 1.

38 See for example, Ortega's comments as reported in the *Washington Post*, October 2, 1983, p. 1.

39 Levesque, p. 32.

40 See Jiri and Virginia Valenta, "Sandinistas in Power," in *Problems of Communism* (September-October 1985), pp. 1–27, for a more detailed discussion of the views and differences among members of the *Sandinista* leadership, especially pp. 8–11.

41 See, for example, Brezhnev's dinner speech of May 3, 1982 in TASS, May 4, 1982, in which he frequently alluded to the great geographic expanses between Managua and Moscow, and praised efforts to develop a nonaligned posture, i.e., to keep doors open to the West and the U.S. A year later, Andropov continued this distancing tack, asserting that Nicaragua had all the necessary resources to defend its motherland. See TASS, March 25, 1983.

42 For a review of Soviet-Nicaraguan relations and Soviet circumspection in cultivating the new revolutionary government, see Peter Clement, "Moscow and Nicaragua: Two Sides of Soviet Policy," in *Comparative Strategy*, 5:1 (1985), pp. 75–91; also see Robert S. Leiken, "Fantasies and Facts: The Soviet Union and Nicaragua," in *Current History* 83 (October 1984), pp. 314–37, 344–45.

43 Soviet economic aid figures are provided in Joseph Whelan and Michael Dixon, *The Soviet Union in the Third World, 1980–65: An Imperial Burden or Political Asset?* Congressional Research Service Report for the House Committee on Foreign Affairs, September 23, 1985, pp. 334–35. This study is an excellent, exhaustive review of Soviet policies in the Third World, and offers a comprehensive bibliography of books and articles related to this subject.

44 *Ibid*.

45 Moscow's economic problems at home, and its shifting views on the realities of aid and development efforts in the Third World are thoroughly examined in Elizabeth Valkenier, *The Soviet Union and the Third World: An Economic Bind* (New York: Praeger, 1983).

46 See Peter Ford, "Nicaragua Struggles for its Economic Survival," in *The Christian Science Monitor*, April 3, 1986, p. 9; and Stephen Kinzer, "Sandinista Says Soviets Will Meet Almost All Nicaragua's Oil Needs," in *The New York Times*, May 21, 1986, p. 1.
47 Theodore Shabad, "Nicaragua Said to Triple Imports from Soviets," in *The New York Times*, May 12, 1985, p.1. The author cited statistics from the Soviet journal *Foreign Trade*, to demonstrate the point.
48 Garthoff, *Detente and Confrontation*, p. 1055.
49 Stephen Kinzer, "Nicaragua Reports Soviet Bloc is Stepping Up Aid," in *The New York Times*, October 27, 1985, p. 1.
50 For Soviet accounts of this visit, see *Pravda*, October 23, 1985, p. 5.
51 *Pravda*, July 19, 1986, p. 4.
52 *Pravda*, July 19, 1985, p. 4.
53 See *The New York Times*, December 28, 1986, p. 12.
54 James LeMoyne, "A Region in Conflict," *New York Times Magazine*, April 1986, p. 19.
55 *Ibid.*
56 *Ibid.*
57 *Ibid.*; also *The Challenge to Democracy in Central America*, pp. 55–56.
58 LeMoyne, "A Region in Conflict," p. 19.
59 *Ibid.*
60 *Ibid.*, *The Soviet-Cuban Connection in Central America and the Caribbean*, pp. 31–36; *Latin America Weekly Report*, July 3, 1986, p. 5.
61 See *The New York Times*, August 5, 1983.
62 Duncan, *The Soviet Union and Cuba*, chapter 6; Whelan, *The Soviet Union in the Third World, 1980–85*, part V.
63 See Richard F. Staar, ed., *1985 Yearbook on International Communist Affairs* (Palo Alto: Hoover Institution Press, 1985).
64 *Ibid.*
65 *Ibid.*
66 *Ibid.*
67 See the *New York Times*, January 15, 1987 for a recent account of the feuding between the Nicaraguan Communists and the *Sandinistas*.
68 See Pedro Ramet and Fernando López-Alves, "Moscow and the Revolutionary Left in Latin America," *Orbis* (Summer 1984), pp. 341–62.
69 Staar, ed., *Yearbook on International Communist Affairs, 1985*.
70 *Ibid.*
71 See U.S. State Department, Special Report Number 90.
72 Staar, ed., *Yearbook on International Communist Affairs, 1985*.
73 *Ibid.*
74 *Ibid.*, pp. 89–95.
75 *Ibid.*
76 *Ibid.*
77 *Ibid.*, pp. 100–01.
78 *Ibid.*
79 LeMoyne, "A Region in Conflict," pp. 16 ff.
80 *Ibid.*
81 *Ibid.*, p. 71 ff.
82 *Ibid.*
83 *Ibid.*
84 *Ibid.*
85 Staar, ed., *Yearbook on International Communist Affairs 1985*.
86 *Ibid.*
87 Staar, ed., *Yearbook on International Communist Affairs 1985*, p. 93.
88 *Ibid.*, pp. 93–95.

89 *Ibid.*
90 *Ibid.*, 1984.
91 Moscow Television Service, March 6, 1986, FBIS-SOV, *International Affairs*, March 7, 1986, p. K1.
92 *Ibid.*
93 Prensa Latina (Havana), February 6, 1986, FBIS-LAM, February 11, 1986, p. 2.
94 *Pravda*, March 5, 1986, FBIS-SOV, *International Affairs*, March 24, 1986, p.01.
95 Moscow Television Service, January 24, 1986, FBIS-SOV, *International Affairs*, January 27, 1986, p. K1.

10

The USSR and Mexico

Brian Latell

For more than six decades, Mexico has been one of the most important Soviet interests in Latin America, and today only the costly relationships with Cuba and Nicaragua provide Moscow with greater dividends and advantages. Since the mid-1970s, moreover, Mexico has risen steadily in the hierarchy of Soviet global interests, a trend that has gained added force since Mikhail Gorbachev's accession to power. This rising Soviet interest has been reflected in the statements of Gorbachev and other high level officials in the Soviet media, and in the published works of the growing number of Soviet scholars concerned with Mexico. It has also been evident in the numerous accords that have been implemented by the two countries, in the wider array and higher level of official contacts, and new areas of agreement in their foreign policies.

In other important respects, however, Moscow's relationship with Mexico is of less value and significance than its ties with other leading Latin American countries. In particular, Mexican political and military leaders continue to look exclusively to Western countries for military supplies and other defense requirements. Mexico sends more military personnel to the United States for training than to any other country, and none is known to have trained in the USSR, Cuba, or Eastern

Europe. Mexican leaders clearly have been sensitive to U.S. security concerns—and to the mostly conservative and traditional attitudes of their own top officers—and have eschewed any institutionalized military relationship with the USSR.

Furthermore, although Soviet and Mexican leaders have endeavored since the mid-1970s to expand and diversify their trade, the results have been marginal. Mexican exports to the USSR in 1986 were valued at only about $4.9 million, down from $5.7 the year before. And, as a percentage of Mexico's total exports, in 1986 they amounted to only 0.05 percent.[1] In the same year, almost 68 percent of Mexican exports were sold in the United States, and even El Salvador, Honduras, Costa Rica, Guatemala, and Puerto Rico each bought more Mexican goods than did the USSR. Thus, despite continuing cooperation with the Council for Mutual Economic Assistance (CMEA), and the hosting of a CMEA trade fair in November 1984, Mexico's trade with the USSR remains negligible. Unless one or both partners is willing to make significant concessions for strictly political reasons, moreover, the prospects for any significant increase will remain bleak for the foreseeable future.

Thus, although recent Mexican administrations have often taken the lead in broadening and intensifying ties with the USSR, they have also adroitly managed the relationship and exploited it for their own purposes. Above all, Mexican officials have sought to demonstrate their independence of the United States and to assert Mexican nationalism through closer relations with the Kremlin. The Soviet connection also advances important internal Mexican goals. It has provided a succession of administrations, and the political system generally, with greater legitimacy and flexibility in dealing with Communist and other leftist opposition forces. By presiding over a steady expansion of bilateral relations with the USSR, Cuba, and other Communist countries, Mexican leaders have been better able to coopt and assuage their left wing critics, as well as to bolster official claims that they and the PRI continue to embody the revolutionary aspirations of earlier years.

This approach has been especially effective in limiting the strength and credibility of the PRI's Marxist opposition. Through a number of reorganizations and name changes in recent decades, the Communist party has remained small and ineffective, seemingly more easily manipulated by the PRI than by Moscow. Over the last two decades, Mexico's Communists have generally been the most critical of the USSR among the major Latin American parties, and in recent years have been close in orientation to leading Euro-Communist parties.[2] The Mexican Communist Party merged with several smaller left wing groups in 1981 to form the Unified Mexican Socialist Party (PSUM), and though this was accomplished with strong Soviet encouragement, the new party proved no more malleable or reliable than the old. In another reorganization in early 1987, the PSUM joined forces with several smaller leftists groups to form the Mexican Socialist Party (PMS). Through all of these realignments, however, the Communists have remained a peripheral political force in Mexico and strongly at odds with Moscow.

MUTUAL FASCINATION AND AFFINITIES

Since the 1920s, Mexico has often taken the lead among the Latin American nations in seeking to broaden ties and areas of cooperation with the Soviet Union, becoming in 1924 the first country in the Western Hemisphere to establish diplomatic relations with the USSR. Those early ties reflected the sense of mutual fascination and strong affinities that grew out of the Mexican and Russian revolutions. They were the first great twentieth century social upheavals, and although ideology was not an important factor in Mexico, the two revolutions had a number of similar causes and characteristics and have also had some comparable results. Most notably, both countries have been dominated by hegomonic political parties that assert that they alone embody the aspirations of workers, peasants, and other previously neglected groups, and claim to be the sole guardians of their country's revolutionary and nationalistic ideas. A sense of shared experience and purpose came to characterize their views of each other. President Plutarco Calles referred to those unique bonds when he said in 1926 that the "social struggles of the two peoples are in many respects analogous."[3]

Popular, academic, and official views of Mexico in the Soviet Union have also been shaped since the 1920s by a sense of shared history. The colorful Madame Alexandra Kollontai, Moscow's first ambassador in Mexico City, spoke in 1926 of a "spiritual union," and effused that "in the entire world there aren't two countries that have such an affinity."[4] Russian revolutionary artists and intellectuals—in particular the poet Vladimir Mayakovsky and the filmmaker Sergei Eisenstein—were enthralled by Mexico's blend of peoples and cultures, produced works with heroic Mexican themes, and collaborated with Mexican artists. No other Latin American country had ever attracted such a fervid Russian interest, and, with the exception of Cuba since Fidel Castro's rise to power, none has done so since.[5]

These high levels of mutual attraction have provided a solid foundation for a bilateral relationship. Even during the break in diplomatic ties from 1930 to 1942, and the period from the mid-1940s through the late 1950s when Mexican governments were distinctly cool to the USSR and wary of Soviet interference in their domestic affairs, pro-Soviet and Marxist sentiment remained strong. Marxist intellectuals and opposition leaders, left wing elements of the PRI, and nationalists of diverse persuasions pressed for closer ties with Moscow. Some were motivated by the belief—advocated most effectively by the Marxist labor leader Vicente Lombardo Toledano—that the original objectives of the Revolution could only be fulfilled through the adoption of Marxist models and doctrines. Although that view has failed to attract widespread popular support, the belief that closer ties with Moscow help reduce Mexico's dependence on the United States and provide greater international maneuverability and prestige has steadily gained ground in recent decades.

It was on such bases, therefore, that Soviet-Mexican relations began rapidly to deepen and diversify in the mid-1970s. Luis Echeverría took the initiative by traveling to the Soviet Union in April 1973 and by subsequently institutionalizing an extensive network of new bilateral arrangements. His successor, José López Portillo, was equally ardent in expanding relations, and he too traveled to the USSR and developed a large number of new accords. Indeed, during just a few years in the mid and late 1970s, more agreements were negotiated between Mexico and the USSR than during the preceding 50 years.[6]

THE EXPANSION OF STATE-TO-STATE RELATIONS

Unlike any other president in Mexican history, Echeverría devoted himself to expanding Mexico's international prestige and leverage. While in office, he visited 35 countries, most of them developing nations, but with the exception of an 8 day trip to 5 U.S. cities in June 1972, none of his sojourns abroad were as long as the 8-day one in the Soviet Union in April 1973. Echeverría was only the third Latin American head of state to visit the USSR—Fidel Castro and Salvador Allende had preceded him—but the reception he received in

Moscow must have been disappointing. Met on his arrival by President Podgorny, who also hosted the state banquet for him that night in the Kremlin, Echeverría had only two, apparently brief and formal meetings with General Secretary Leonid Brezhnev.

Echeverría's efforts to win Soviet support for the Tlatelolco Treaty banning nuclear weapons in Latin America—a major Mexican interest since the 1960s—were spurned. His failure to win Soviet backing for Protocol II of the treaty was in sharp contrast, moreover, with the accessions of the other four countries with nuclear weapons. The United States and the United Kingdom had already signed Protocol II, and during the same six-nation trip that included the stop in the USSR, Echeverría won French and Chinese approval as well. The opposition of Soviet leaders to Protocol II was so strong, however, that Echeverría could not even get them to include an indirect reference to Tlatelolco in the joint communique issued at the end of his visit.[7]

Echeverría's other principal foreign policy priority—the Charter of Economic Rights and Duties of States—which unlike the Tlatelolco Treaty, he had engineered personally and for which he campaigned indefatigably throughout his administration, received only tepid support from Soviet leaders. The charter was treated gingerly in the joint communique, and was ignored entirely by President Podgorny in his speech at the Kremlin banquet welcoming the Mexican delegation.[8] Although the USSR voted at the United Nations in December 1974 with 120 other countries in favor of the charter[9] (the United States and 5 other countries voted against), Soviet objections to several of its provisions remained strong. Specifically the reference to "hegemony and spheres of influence" in its first chapter clearly signaled the Mexican authors' view that both great powers were guilty of abusing the rights of their neighbors.[10]

Soviet leaders had other, even stronger reasons to be wary of the Mexican president. In early 1973, Echeverría was still widely viewed both in Mexico and internationally as an authoritarian and mercurial guardian of traditional interests. In 1968, when he was Secretary of Government in the administration of Gustavo Díaz Ordaz, he had ordered troops to fire on civilian demonstrators in Mexico City, and hundreds of deaths and injuries resulted in what has been known since then as the Tlatelolco Massacre. In March, 1971, furthermore, several months after his inauguration, relations with the USSR reached a new low when he expelled five Soviet diplomats from Mexico amid charges that the USSR had connived with North Korea in providing guerrilla training to a group of Mexican terrorists.

Nonetheless, Echeverría's visit to the Soviet Union gave impetus to a steady and significant expansion in state-to-state relations during the remainder of his term. Numerous bilateral accords were approved, including, in August 1975, the first agreement concluded between a non-Communist Latin American country and CMEA. The first high-level exchanges of parliamentary delegations also took place during the latter years of the Echeverría administration.

During the second half of Echeverría's administration, and largely because of the initiatives he took with Soviet leaders, Mexico began to rise in the hierarchy of their international interests. Moscow was also attracted to Mexico because of favorable developments there and adverse ones elsewhere in the region. The Allende government in Chile had been overthrown in a military coup in September 1973; in Peru, the reformist zeal of the populist regime of General Juan Velasco Alvarado by then had abated; and in August 1975 he too was overthrown in a coup that resulted in a more conservative government. In addition, it was in 1974 that Mexico virtually overnight became considerably more important in world affairs following the first credible reports that it had discovered enormous new deposits of petroleum. It was also important, from Moscow's perspective, that the highly nationalistic positions Echeverría adopted both in domestic and foreign policy had created significant new areas in which Soviet and Mexican interests and objectives seemed to converge.

MEXICO BECOMES A MAJOR SOVIET INTEREST

Relations continued to broaden and intensify during the ensuing administration of José López Portillo. He also visited the USSR, spending over a week there in May 1978, but unlike Echeverría was met at Moscow airport by Brezhnev and other Soviet leaders and was given a warm reception in the media.

López Portillo's main accomplishment was winning Soviet accession to the Tlatelolco Treaty.[11] Foreign Minister Andrei Gromyko signed Protocol II on May 18, 1978 during the Mexican president's visit, although Soviet statements continued for a period to note that some differences remained.[12] Nonetheless, as Jorge Domínguez indicates in his chapter in this volume, the Brezhnev leadership by then had come to place a high priority on broadening relations with Mexico and other major Latin American countries, and also wanted to improve the political climate for the SALT II negotiations with the United States. The joint communique issued at the end of López Portillo's visit contained numerous statements of agreement in those areas. It advocated a "reduction of armed forces and of both conventional and nuclear armaments, and universal and complete disarmament under effective international control."[13] The two governments also agreed on the need for a "complete and universal ban on nuclear weapons tests," the termination of "the production of such weapons," and the "reduction of stockpiles, right up to their complete elimination." They "stressed the need for the UN General Assembly special session on disarmament" that began the same month, and called for a "world disarmament conference."

The shift in Soviet policy with regard to the Tlatelolco accord was an important watershed that marked the beginning of a gradually widening of cooperation between Mexico and the Soviet Union in support of international peace and disarmament. Mexico's "extremely active and constructive role" in these respects, especially in comparison to other Latin American countries, was described in glowing terms in a March 1980 article in *Latinskaia Amerika* which praised

> Mexico's attempts to promote a positive resolution of the complex problems in the relations between the USSR and the United States, its initiative on the creation of a non-nuclear zone in Latin America, its active participation in the preparations for the World Conference on Disarmament, and its call for a special session of the UN General Assembly on disarmament, reflect a position which is in the interests of peace and genuine disarmament.[14]

Since the Soviet accession to Protocol II of the Tlatelolco Treaty, high level bilateral consultations and pronouncements have reiterated areas of Mexican-Soviet agreement on issues related to international peace and disarmament, while often indirectly criticizing U.S. defense policies. Following Mexican Foreign Secretary Jorge Castañeda's consultations with senior Soviet officials in Moscow in May 1981, for example, the joint communique printed in *Pravda* voiced "profound concern in connection with the growth of the arms race, particularly in the sphere of the production of mass-destruction weapons."[15] The two sides stated their intention to work together at the United Nations on behalf of disarmament and to strengthen the nuclear-free zone in Latin America, and "the Soviet side noted Mexico's high prestige and growing role in the international arena and its active and constructive contribution to the efforts of peace-loving states to normalize the international situation and curb the arms race."

Although these and other positions that Castañeda endorsed while in Moscow were carefully crafted and might appear to apply equally to both great powers, the context and timing of his visit strongly suggested that Mexico and the USSR were in agreement that the Reagan administration was adopting an aggressive international stance. Castañeda's visit occurred just five months after Reagan's inauguration, and only two months after the U.S. Congress was presented with a defense budget intended substantially to increase military expenditures.

MEXICO, CUBA, AND CENTRAL AMERICA

Mexico's importance as a regional power willing to confront the United States and to act as an ally of Marxist and revolutionary forces in the Caribbean Basin reached its zenith during the last few years of López Portillo's administration. Soviet interests in the region were significantly bolstered between 1979 and 1982 by Mexico's concerted efforts to help the *Sandinistas* win and then consolidate power in Nicaragua, to support Marxist and revolutionary forces in El Salvador, and to expand relations and cooperation with Cuba. No other Mexican president before or since López Portillo has collaborated so closely with Fidel Castro, and between May 1979 and August 1981 the two leaders held annual summits at which, among other things, they apparently coordinated their countries' Central American policies.

In May 1979—just days after Castro and López Portillo conferred on the Mexican island of Cozumel—Mexico severed diplomatic relations with the Somoza dictatorship in Nicaragua and urged other Latin American governments to do the same. The ensuing damage to Somoza's legitimacy was profound, and the *Sandinista* National Directorate promptly issued a statement expressing "revolutionary joy" at the Mexican action.[16] During its first few years in power, moreover, the *Sandinista* government was the recipient of substantial Mexican economic support, mainly through deliveries of petroleum at reduced prices and on credit. López Portillo publicly told visiting Nicaraguan leader Daniel Ortega in May 1981 that "Mexico will defend the Nicaraguan cause as if it were its very own,"[17] and traveled to Managua the following February where he announced a three part plan calling for talks between the United States and Cuba, negotiations in El Salvador, and a nonaggression pact among Nicaragua and its neighbors.

Mexican policy toward El Salvador also directly and powerfully confronted U.S. interests during the last few years of López Portillo's administration. In 1980 his government withdrew its ambassador and downgraded its embassy in San Salvador to a consulate, while becoming increasingly critical of the military and other conservative elements there. In addition, Mexico invited the Salvadoran Democratic Revolutionary Front (FDR) to join a Mexican-sponsored coalition of progressive Latin American political parties, and most importantly, joined with the Mitterrand government in France in August 1981 in recognizing the coalition of the FDR and the Marxist Farabundo Martí National Liberation Front (FMLN) as a "representative political force." Although no other European or Latin American government emulated that initiative, the international legitimacy and backing of the Salvadoran revolutionary movement was greatly enhanced in the aftermath of the Franco-Mexican declaration.

The close Cuba-Mexican collaboration that developed toward the end of López Portillo's term also buoyed Soviet interest in Mexico's more aggressive regional power aspirations, and at least temporarily bolstered Soviet interests in the Caribbean Basin. In a press conference in Cozumel during the 1979 visit, Castro strongly criticized the United States and, in a probable reference to the agenda of his discussions with López Portillo, asserted that "the development of solidarity as a force for checking foreign meddling in Central America, particularly that of the United States, must not be delayed."[18]

The second Castro-López Portillo summit took place in Cuba in August 1980. The Mexican president was accorded the unusual honor of a mass rally in Havana's Revolutionary Plaza where Castro spoke of Mexico's support for the "heroic struggle of the Nicaraguan people" and its long time role as a haven for Latin American revolutionaries.[19] The two leaders met a third time, again on Cozumel, in August 1981, about two weeks before the Franco-Mexican declaration recognizing the Salvadoran insurgents was issued. Following the second Cozumel exchange, *Pravda* noted the "coincidence of the Mexican and Cuban positions in regard to the need to halt U.S. interference in the internal affairs of El Salvador."[20]

Cuban–Mexican ties and cooperation expanded in a variety of other ways as well. Trade, which in earlier years had remained at negligible levels, grew rapidly beginning in 1979, mainly as a result of large Mexican purchases of Cuban sugar. In 1980, for instance, Cuban sales to Mexico constituted about five percent of total exports, even surpassing those to such countries as Bulgaria and East Germany.[21] In 1981 Mexico purchased $190 million of Cuban products, while selling $25 million.[22] Radical and enduring changes in Mexico's trading and domestic spending patterns followed the economic and financial crisis that occurred in August 1982, however, and the large trade deficits with Cuba of the preceding few years were reversed. In 1985, Mexico purchased only about $7 million of Cuban goods, while exporting more than $85 million of Mexican products.[23]

SOVIET ACADEMIC VIEWS OF MEXICO

As Mexico broadened its ties with the USSR and Cuba, and challenged U.S. interests between 1973 and 1982, the Soviet view of Mexico's international importance evolved from relative indifference to unprecedented interest. The change has been particularly evident in the substantial body of Soviet academic literature that has appeared since the late 1970s. A growing number of Soviet scholars are doing research on Mexico, and judging from the frequency of articles and books they have published, interest is greater than in any other Latin American country except Cuba.

Since 1980, more than 20 Soviet scholars have published major articles either wholly or largely concerned with contemporary Mexican issues in leading Soviet academic journals. Some of the authors, like Igor Sheremet'ev, who has been described as the "top specialist on Mexico"[24] at the Latin America Institute in Moscow, have been long time, well-informed observers.[25] Others, like Irina Zorina of the Institute of World Economy and International Relations (IMEMO) have developed a primary interest in Mexico more recently, in her case after having concentrated on Chile in the early 1970s. Unlike most of her academic colleagues, Zorina has recent first hand knowledge of Mexico; she worked for several months in 1985 at the Center for Research and Economic Education (CIDE) in Mexico City. Still others are doctoral candidates and emerging young specialists who have seemingly been attracted to Mexican studies in recent years.

The majority of the published work by Soviet scholars has been concerned with Mexican foreign policy, and particularly with relations with the United States. A principal purpose of that literature is to provide Soviet officials with policy-relevant propositions and conclusions about Mexico's changing regional and global relationships. It is especially significant in that regard that by the early 1980s, a consensus was beginning to emerge among Soviet scholars that viewed Mexico as an increasingly strong and independent world actor. In August 1980, V. P. Lukin wrote in *Latinskaia Amerika* that Mexico had emerged as a major "regional center of power" in the Western Hemisphere with "large, independent economic and political potentials."[26] In another article in the same issue, Sheremet'ev saw Mexico as the "most probable candidate" in Latin America assuming "a relatively independent position...within the world capitalist system."[27]

Not all specialists have agreed with this view. At a 1982 debate sponsored by *Latinskaia Amerika*, A. F. Shulgovsky was quoted, for instance, as stating that "when a particular Latin American country shows interest in broader ties with the socialist countries, this fact alone does not attest to anti-imperialist foreign policy aims.[28] Another participant—V.N. Dmitriyev—claimed in contrast that even during the economic crisis that occurred in the last year of López Portillo's term, "the efforts of U.S. imperialism" to force changes in Mexican foreign policy "were unsuccessful." On balance, there is reason to believe that Dmitriyev's conclusion—that earlier "generalizations about dependence are obviously inadequate today"—reflected the thinking of a majority of the participants in the debate, as well as of the remaining scholars and officials interested in it.

A key argument that has been used effectively by those specialists who believe that Mexico has become increasingly "anti-imperialist" is that since the mid or late 1970s, it has acquired substantial new leverage in dealing with the United States. Instead of viewing Mexico as being helplessly manipulable by its powerful northern neighbor, Soviet analysis has increasingly focused on its strengths. In the late 1970s and early 1980s, for example, Soviet scholars wrote extensively about the enhanced international power that Mexico's oil wealth had provided the Echeverría and López Portillo governments. M. L. Chumakova, in an article published in early 1983, wrote that "although Mexican oil has not been a panacea for the chronic illnesses of a dependent capitalist economy, its significance for increasing the negotiating potential, ensuring greater freedom of maneuver in negotiations with the imperialist centers, and pursuing an independent foreign policy line is difficult to overestimate."[29] In the aftermath of Mexico's economic crisis that began in mid-1982, and the subsequent sharp drop in oil prices, however, it became clear that Chumakova had indeed overestimated the oil "weapon," and since then this theme has been largely absent from Soviet analyses.

Soviet scholars continue to focus on Mexico's independent policies in Central America and the Caribbean, and on the significant leverage in its dealings with the United States that those positions have provided, and one specialist, V. P. Sudarev of the Latin America Institute, argued in 1982 that the "emergence of hot spots" in Central America had reduced Mexico's dependence on the United States. Other Soviet officials and scholars have concluded in recent years that Mexico is in a good position to influence the internal political and policy processes in the United States to its advantage. Writing in *Latinskaia Amerika* in August 1980, V. P. Lukin commented on Mexico's "serious levers for affecting the North American domestic political process."[30] Although he did not clarify exactly what leverage he had in mind, it appears from the context that he was referring to the large Mexican-American population in the United States.

GORBACHEV'S INTEREST IN MEXICO

The analysis of leading scholars apparently has helped to shape a more assertive Soviet policy toward Mexico in the 1980s. One leading analyst, who is also a high level party official, has evidently been particularly influential in persuading General Secretary Gorbachev that Mexico should be placed higher in the Soviet hierarchy of global interests than it was under Brezhnev. Karen Brutents, a deputy chief of the Communist Party's International Department[31] and a Latin America specialist known to have traveled twice to Mexico in recent years,[32] may be in the forefront of those who have concluded that Mexico is of prime international strategic importance. Writing in early 1984 in *Kommunist*, Brutents argued that Mexico, India, and Brazil, "add a multipolar character to the capitalist world and create within it an additional counterweight to U.S. policy."[33] An earlier comparison of Mexico and India (as well as of Nigeria and Venezuela) as countries "already clearly recognized as states taking an anti-imperialist position in international affairs" was made by Irina Zorina in August 1982.[34]

Since July 1986, Gorbachev has been publicly associated with the view of Mexico advocated most forcefully by Brutents and Zorina.

In a major foreign policy address in Vladivostok on July 28, 1986, the general secretary spoke of the Pacific Basin and of the need for "urgent, radical" new approaches to security in that region. He described three categories of Pacific and Asian countries, and it was significant that he included Mexico among the eight "major" states of the region along with the U.S., USSR, China, India, Japan, Vietnam, and Indonesia. Gorbachev cited Canada, the Philippines, Australia, and New Zealand among the "medium sized" Pacific states, and then mentioned that there are also "dozens" of smaller countries in that region.[35] His emphasis on Mexico was neither casual nor accidental. In a speech in Mexico City in October 1986, Foreign Minister Shevardnadze referred to the importance of Gorbachev's Vladivostok address and called for cooperation with Mexico in "strengthening security in the Pacific."[36]

The Shevardnadze visit—his first to a Latin American country other than Cuba—also provided opportunities for criticism by both the USSR and Mexico of the United States. The joint communique issued at the end of his visit set new precedents in the continuing development of Mexican-Soviet cooperation on issues relating to international peace and disarmament. It also indirectly criticized the U.S. Strategic Defense Initiative and expressed "reciprocal interest" in an exchange of official visits by Gorbachev and Miguel de la Madrid. In addition, both governments declared their intent to further expand trade and other forms of cooperation, and to begin regular consultations at the foreign ministry level.[37] The latter agreement was advanced in May 1987, when Bernardo Sepúlveda became the third consecutive Mexican foreign secretary to visit the USSR.

Sepulveda's visit provided strong additional evidence of the high priority Moscow has placed on expanding relations with Mexico since Gorbachev's rise to power. The foreign secretary was received warmly by the Soviet media and by a number of ranking Soviet officials, including President Gromyko, Foreign Minister Schevardnadze, and Deputy Premier Kamentsev. And, although Gorbachev had earlier passed up opportunities to meet with the Brazilian, Argentine, and Uruguayan foreign ministers during their visits to Moscow, he had a wide-ranging exchange with Sepulveda, indicating the Soviet Union's desire "to improve [relations] further."[38] The treatment Sepulveda received—even warmer than that the Brezhnev regime afforded former Foreign Secretary Castañeda in 1981—demonstrated above all Moscow's keen interest in Mexico's nationalistic foreign policy. Gorbachev was quoted by TASS as commenting on "the independence and vigor of Mexico's foreign policy," and praised its leadership in the Contadora and Delhi Six groups of countries.[39]

Rising Soviet interest in Mexico has also been evident in recent years in greater propaganda and media coverage. In particular, the numerous stresses and misunderstandings that have undermined U.S.-Mexican relations have become recurring themes in Mexico City since the early 1980s, has had frequent press conferences, published interviews, and made numerous public appearances. Soviet access to public opinion in Mexico has been greatly enhanced since October 1980, furthermore, by a convention which provides for exchanges and cooperation in radio, television, and film.[40] This was augmented by an information exchange agreement between the Soviet news agency TASS and NOTIMEX, the Mexican government information agency.[41]

THE SOVIET VIEW OF MEXICO'S DOMESTIC AFFAIRS

Despite their heightened general interest in Mexico, Soviet scholars seem to have only a superficial understanding of its byzantine and fascinating political dynamics or of the implications of its unfolding economic crisis. Although the academic literature on Mexican foreign policy is substantial, few articles have been published on internal political and economic issues in recent years, and, with the notable exceptions of Sheremetyev and Zorina, the scope of those discussions is narrow and unsophisticated by the standards of U.S. scholarship.

The central dilemma for Soviet analysts and observers revolves around how to treat the PRI. In power without interruption since the late 1920s, that party has provided all of Mexico's presidents, governors, other top officials and the overwhelming majority not only in both houses of the national legislature, but in all 31 of the state assemblies as well. The legitimacy of the PRI is based in large measure, moreover, on its pretensions to be the guardian and repository of the ideals of the Mexican Revolution, and thus also to be the progressive representative of workers, peasants, and other once neglected groups. By preserving its monopoly of political power in this manner for five and a half decades, the PRI has been the sole source and arbiter of all national policy.

Thus, of necessity, Soviet policy has concentrated on broadening and intensifying relations with the PRI, and both Soviet spokesmen and scholars with only one notable exception, have avoided sharply criticizing the party as a whole. High level Soviet visitors to Mexico City have made it a point to call at PRI headquarters, while paying little attention to the opposition parties, the Communists included. Moreover, Soviet policy in the 1980s has clearly emphasized the need to develop close personal ties between top PRI and Mexican government officials and Soviet leaders.[42]

During his visit to Mexico in October 1986, Shevardnadze hinted broadly that de la Madrid and Gorbachev had already developed a close personal relationship. According to TASS, he said that "amicable, confidential relations" had developed between the two leaders, and that they maintained "a private correspondence on key issues of world politics."[43]

But, despite, the desire to develop closer ties with leading PRI and government officials, Soviet scholars and spokesmen are also constrained by the requirement that they maintain a correct ideological distance from the party. The PRI, after all, is dominated by Mexico's "national bourgeoisie" according to Soviet analysis, and is a long way from acting as the vanguard of the Mexican proletariat. In fact, the party's labor branch—one of its largest and most influential—and its venerable labor chieftains have been criticized in the Soviet academic literature for being bureaucratic, corrupt, and elitist.[44] A few small Marxist-oriented or dominated unions are endorsed and encouraged by Soviet scholars, and some independent Marxist intellectuals—notably Alonso Aguilar and a group associated with him and the journal *Estrategia*—have received considerable and favorable attention.[45]

In contrast, Mexico's Communist party gets only qualified and limited Soviet support. One reliable measure of Moscow's attitude toward the PSUM (and, more recently, the PMS) was the treatment it received in the *World Marxist Review*. Between 1983 and 1986 the *World Marxist Review* carried major articles by the top Communist party leaders of 14 Latin American and Caribbean countries, but no ranking Mexican communist official was given space.[46]

The absence of an effective pro-Soviet Communist party in Mexico helps to justify Moscow's preferred policy of encouraging left wing elements and affiliates of the PRI. Thus, the belief expressed in varying degrees by Mexican Marxists and radicals that the PRI can only fulfill its original revolutionary commitments by adopting Marxist-Leninist doctrines and strategies is subtly echoed in some of the Soviet literature. M. L. Chumakova wrote in *Latinskaia Amerika* in February 1983, for example, that "Mexico's support for the revolutionary-democratic forces in Central America and the Caribbean countries was brought about by...the adherence of party-government circles to the idea of permanent Mexican revolution."[47] Soviet interest in cultivating the left wing of the PRI has also been evident in the frequent and favorable treatment afforded to former president Echeverría. In his capacity as the director of a radical Center for Third World Studies in Mexico City, he made at least two publicized trips to Moscow in recent years.[48]

At least one prominent Soviet scholar has begun, however, to write critically and candidly about the PRI and the political system it dominates. Irina Zorina, who also seems the most knowledgeable and astute observer of Mexican internal dynamics, described a catalogue of the party's problems in *MEMO* in October 1985, concluding that the PRI had been "faring poorly."[49] "Its leadership," she wrote, "has not updated the party rhetoric for a long time and has not changed the methods of liaison with the masses [and] has in recent years found itself increasingly less effective, particularly under the conditions of economic crisis." In contrast, Zorina conceded implicitly that the center-right National Action Party (PAN)—the largest and most rapidly growing opposition force in Mexico—had stolen the initiative from the ruling party. The PAN, she claimed "has increasingly made use of the struggle methods of the forces of the left: taken to the streets and organized demonstrations, striving for a mobilization of the population in the provincial centers."[50] By contrast, she said, left wing forces "are disconnected and do not have a serious chance of changing the political situation." Zorina even took the unprecedented step of asserting that the PRI candidate in the gubernatorial elections in the key northern state of Sonora in 1985 was "unpopular" and "manifestly lost to the united right," though "local authorities rigged the vote to prevent the loss of the governorship." The PRI, she observed dryly, "is not very well adapted to operating as a customary bourgeois party."

Zorina seems to have concluded, perhaps in part as a result of her stay in Mexico City in 1985, that the PRI has lost vitality and popularity. "It is becoming increasingly apparent...that the party today lacks social dynamism...and that populism...is drying up also."[51] Although similar analyses by U.S. and Mexican scholars and journalists have been widely circulated since 1985,[52] Zorina's views have thus far not been reiterated in the Soviet media or by any of her academic colleagues. Because of her seniority as a Latin America specialist and her position at the prestigious Institute of World Economy and International Relations, Zorina's published views may well reflect those of important colleagues—such as Brutents—and could, therefore, signal the beginning of an important change in Soviet attitudes toward the PRI. On the other hand, her earlier record of iconoclasm in analysis of the failures of the Allende regime in Chile,[53] may signify that Zorina is above all, an unusually independent and unpredictable analyst more respected for her area expertise than for whatever policy recommendations her work might imply.

DE LA MADRID AND THE USSR

When he took office in December 1982, Miguel de la Madrid inherited relationships with both the USSR and Cuba that were more complex, dynamic, and stable than they had ever been before. Although ties with Havana have cooled since then, Mexican-Soviet relations have continued to broaden and intensify. The frequency and level of parliamentary, government, and other exchanges with Moscow have increased, the binational commissions have agreed to a number of new protocols and exchanges (at least one major new treaty has been negotiated) and Mexico's leadership in the Contadora and Delhi Six groups of countries has won enthusiastic Soviet support. Although as of mid-1987 de la Madrid had not traveled to the USSR, three of his top aides—the secretaries of government, foreign relations, and commerce and industrial development—had met with senior Soviet officials during separate visits to Moscow.

Unlike his two immediate predecessors, de la Madrid has been preoccupied throughout his administration with Mexico's grave economic and financial problems, and his limited foreign traveling has been mainly for the purpose of promoting exports and attracting investment. He has been no less committed to the highly nationalistic principles and goals of Mexican foreign policy, especially in regard to relations with the United States,[54] but has pursued Mexican foreign policy objectives more pragmatically than either Echeverría or López Portillo.

Mexico's ties with revolutionary governments and groups in the Western Hemisphere have been more formal and reserved since de la Madrid took office than at any time since the early 1970s. He has not traveled to Cuba, received Castro in Mexico, or provided significant rhetorical or diplomatic support for Havana. In addition, de la Madrid has reduced Mexico's economic support for the Managua regime, and his administration normalized relations with El Salvador after José Napoleón Duarte won the presidential elections there in 1984.

Despite these and other policy shifts, de la Madrid has continued forcefully to assert Mexico's regional power aspirations, as well as its roles as a leading broker between East and West and advocate for great power disarmament. In particular, the de la Madrid administration's leadership in the Contadora negotiating process has enhanced Mexico's legitimacy as an independent broker, while also generating tensions with the Reagan administration and winning strong Soviet and Cuban support.

Soviet leaders and scholars have enthusiastically supported Mexico's role in Contadora. Frequent references and discussions of its significance have appeared in the academic and official literature, typically with an emphasis on how Contadora illustrates Mexico's independence of the United States, its legitimacy as a regional power, and its "principled" foreign policy. *Pravda*'s coverage of the joint communique issued at the end of Shevardnadze's visit to Mexico stated, for example, "that the solution to the Central American crisis depends mainly on the states of the region themselves, and that the conflict must not be looked at from the narrow perspective of East-West confrontation."[55]

Soviet leaders and spokesmen have generally been even more enthusiastic about Mexico's active role with the Delhi Six countries. De la Madrid met in January 1985 in New Delhi with the leaders of India, Greece, Sweden, Argentina, and Tanzania, and together they called for a halt to testing of nuclear weapons and a ban on the development of space weapons. In August 1986, Mexico hosted a second meeting of the DS leaders at the Pacific resort of Ixtapa. They urged the United States and the USSR to cease nuclear testing under a verification plan that they devised, and, in a criticism aimed primarily at the Reagan administration, called for an end to the development of space weapons. Through its activism in this forum, the de la Madrid government has given new impetus to Mexican efforts on behalf of international peace and disarmament that date to the 1960s.

CONCLUSIONS

The expanding Soviet-Mexican relationship has served important international objectives of both countries, and unless de la Madrid is succeeded by a distinctly more conservative president, it seems likely that ties will continue to broaden and solidify, and that economic and other types of cooperation will also gradually increase. A loose, highly flexible, and selective partnership has developed in which both countries support certain key interests of the other. At the United Nations, Mexico and the Soviet Union in recent years have been in agreement in a large percentage of votes, and the convergence of certain of their key interests has also been increasingly evident in other international fora. By 1987, these trends appeared so firmly established and to enjoy such broad support among Mexican elites, that they seem likely to become more solidly entrenched in the years ahead.

The institutionalization of the bilateral relationship has been of substantial value to the USSR. Mexico City is one of the principal intellectual, media, and publishing centers in the Spanish-speaking world, and in recent years—in part as a result of treaties and other agreements—a substantial volume of information about the USSR, the people, cultures, and international positions has flowed through Mexico. Since the 1920s, moreover, the Soviet embassy in Mexico has been one of the largest and most important in the region, and today may only be exceeded in those respects by Moscow's large official presence in Havana. In 1965, Karl Schmitt wrote that "only the staff of the United States embassy in Mexico is larger than that of the Soviet Union,"[56] and both Mexican and U.S. press reports in subsequent years have frequently reiterated the same conclusion. At least one major incident of espionage involving U.S. citizens and Soviet intelligence officers assigned to the Mexico City embassy is known to have occurred in recent years.[57]

On balance, however, Mexican leaders have been sensitive to concerns in the United States about Soviet activities and missions across the border. Despite apparent Soviet interest, for instance, in opening one or more additional consulates in Mexico (the USSR has a consulate in Vera Cruz, Mexico's principal Gulf port), the de la Madrid administration has been reluctant to permit any further expansion outside of the capital of Moscow's large official representation.

As already indicated, furthermore, another potentially key area in which warming trends in bilateral relations have failed to yield significant new benefits is the military sphere. The first tentative contacts between the militaries of the two countries occurred in 1973 during Echeverría's administration,[58] but they led to no further exchanges until López Portillo cautiously explored the possibilities of expanding military ties. In September 1987, Soviet Marshal Peredelsky visited Mexico to take part in the independence day celebrations.[59] He appears to have been the highest level Soviet military officer officially ever to have traveled to Mexico. Two years later, Mexican Defense Minister Felix Galván López visited Moscow and Leningrad. He met with the late Soviet Defense Minister Dmitri Ustinov and other top military officers, visited the Frunze Military Academy, and, according to *Krasnaya Zvezda*, "familiarized himself with examples of military equipment and the Soviet serviceman's life and routine."[60] If in fact he had been authorized to shop for Soviet military hardware, nothing came of it. There were no other indications in the Soviet media, furthermore, to suggest what objectives—other than symbolic ones—either side may have had in mind. During the first four and a half years of the de la Madrid administration, there were no important contacts between the militaries of the two countries.

Mexican leaders realize that any major increase in the numbers of Soviet personnel or change in the types of activities they engage in in Mexico (particularly if any were to occur along the border with the United States) would be viewed widely as a serious challenge to U.S. security interests and would likely result in major new tensions in bilateral relations. It has been much more difficult for them, however, to assuage fears in the United States that sudden, destabilizing political change could occur in Mexico and bring in its wake dramatic gains in Soviet presence and influence.

Concerns about such a watershed involving the three nations will inevitably increase through the remainder of the 1980s and beyond if, as seems likely, Mexican-Soviet relations become more complex and extended. Mexico will continue to seek a larger and more prestigious international role while endeavoring to assert greater independence of the United States. The Soviet Union will remain a useful partner in Mexico's pursuit of those goals, and continue to seek new allies among Mexican elites with the hope of eventually achieving more permanent and tangible gains. And, given the extraordinary array of other daunting bilateral issues in the Mexican-U.S. relationship, the potential for serious misunderstandings arising from Mexican foreign policy positions and initiatives—particularly any involving the Soviet Union and its allies—will continue to be high.

Notes

1 *Estadísticas del Comercio Exterior de México* (Mexico City: Instituto Nacional de Estadística Geografiá e Informática, 1986).

2 Barry Carr, *Mexican Communism, 1968—1983; Eurocommunism in the Americas?* (San Diego: Center for U.S.–Mexican Studies, University of California, San Diego, 1985).
3 *Relaciones Mexicano-Sovieticas, 1917—1980* (Mexico City: Archivo Histórico Diplomático Mexicano, 1981), p.44.
4 *Ibid.* p.61.
5 *Foreign Broadcast Information Service-Soviet Union Daily Report* (hereafter FBIS-SOV), October 8, 1986, p. K2. Soviet Foreign Minister Eduard Shevardnadze spoke eloquently of this abiding Soviet interest in Mexico when, during a visit there in October 1986, he referred to the many "erudite connoisseurs of your unique, ancient culture" in the Soviet Union.
6 V. Bushuyev and Yu. Kozlov, untitled article, *Kommunist*, 12 (August 1978); JPRS, 72097, October 23, 1978, p. 134. Throughout the preparation of this study I have used the Joint Publications Research Service's English translations of Russian texts.
7 *Pravda*, April 17, 1973; FBIS-SOV, April 19, 1973, p. G6.
8 *Pravda*, April 12, 1973; FBIS-SOV, April 17, 1973, p. G4.
9 Edmund Jan Osmanczyk, *The Encyclopedia of the United Nations and International Agreements* (Philadelphia and London: Taylor and Francis, 1985).
10 For a recent Soviet criticism of the charter see the comments of V.V. Gorokhov, "Is the 'Force Field' of Dependence Really Omnipotent?" in a roundtable discussion among Soviet scholars entitled "Latin America: Foreign Policy and Economic Dependence," *Latinskaia Amerika*, 10 (October 1987); JPRS 83022, March 7, 1983, p. 39.
11 The shift in policy had caught at least one Soviet scholar on the wrong side of the issue. In a review of a 1979 book on Latin American foreign policy and diplomacy, A.N. Glinkin, a senior analyst at the Latin America Institute in Moscow, criticized the author's treatment of Tlatelolco. The book, by A.I. Kedrov, did not "give attention" to the treaty "or the issue of nonproliferation of nuclear weapons in Latin America, both of which are timely under the present circumstances," according to Glinkin. Kedrov no doubt had completed his book before López Portillo's visit to Moscow when the policy change was announced. See, A.N. Glinkin, review of "Mezhdunarodnaia otnosheniia," Moscow, 1979, in *Latinskaia Amerika*, 6 (June 1980).
12 M. Petrov, "The Soviet Union and the Denuclearized Zone in Latin America," *International Affairs*, (December 1979).
13 *Pravda*, May 26, 1978. FBIS-SOV, May 30, 1978, p. N2.
14 V.V. Gorokhov and P.P. Yakovlev, "Disarmament: Conflicting Tendencies, Different Approaches," *Latinskaia Amerika*, 3 (March 1980), JPRS 75640, May 6, 1980, p.29.
15 FBIS-SOV, June 1, 1981, p. K2.
16 Shirley Christian, *Nicaragua: Revolution in the Family* (New York: Random House, 1985), p.111.
17 *Granma Weekly Review*, May 17, 1981.
18 Havana Radio, May 18, 1979. JPRS 73619, June 5, 1979.
19 *Foreign Broadcast Information Service-Latin America Daily Report* (hereafter FBIS-LAM), August 4, 1980, p. Q6.
20 TASS International Service, August 12, 1982; FBIS-SOV, August 20, 1982, p. K1.
21 *Granma Weekly Review*, November 15, 1981.
22 FBIS-LAM, April 29, 1982, p. M2.
23 *Unomasuno* (Mexico City), October 22, 1986, p. 13.
24 Jerry Hough, "The Evolving Soviet Debate on Latin America," *Latin American Research Review*, 16:1 (1981), p. 136.
25 A major work, *El capitalismo de Estado en México* (Mexico City: Fondo de Cultura Popular, 1969) was translated from the Russian by Armando Martínez Verdugo.

26 V.P. Lukin, "The Concept of 'Centers of Power' and Latin America," *Latinskaia Amerika*, 8 (August 1980). JPRS 76827, November 17, 1980, p. 17.
27 I.K. Sheremetyev, "Foreign and Domestic Factors in Capitalist Development," *Latinskaia Amerika*, 8 (August 1980). JPRS 76827, November 17, 1980.
28 "Latin America: Foreign Policy and Economic Dependence," *Latinskaia Amerika*, 10 (October 1982). JPRS 83022, March 7, 1983, p. 24.
29 M.L. Chumakova, "Mexico: Oil and Foreign Policy," *Latinskaia Amerika*, 2 (February 1982). JPRS 83428, May 9, 1983, p. 123.
30 V.P. Lukin, "The Concept of 'Centers of Power,'" p. 18.
31 Wallace Spaulding, "Shifts in CPSU ID," *Problems of Communism* (July–August 1986), p. 80.
32 FBIS-SOV, June 13, 1977, p. N1 and July 30, 1981, p. K1.
33 K. Brutents, untitled article in *Kommunist*, 3. (1984); JPRS–UKO–84009, May 11, 1984, p. 131.
34 I. Zorina, MEMO, 8 (August 1982). JPRS 82401, December 7, 1982, p. 42.
35 FBIS-SOV, July 29, 1986, p. R11.
36 FBIS-SOV, October 8, 1986, P. K3.
37 FBIS-SOV, October 7, 1986, p. K5.
38 FBIS-SOV, May 7, 1987, P. K6.
39 *Ibid.*, p. K7.
40 *Relaciones Mexicano-Soviéticas, 1968–1980* (Mexico City: Archivo Histórico Diplomático Mexicano, 1981), p. 206–08.
41 FBIS-SOV, October 20, 1983, p. K2. The agreement also provided for Soviet assistance to NOTIMEX "in training technical specialists and the mutual provision of photographic information."
42 FBIS-SOV, June 1, 1981, p. K1. Former Foreign Secretary Castañeda's visit to the USSR in May 1981 was a key step in this regard. *Pravda* emphasized during his trip that "personal contacts and dialogue are an important factor...in the consolidation of mutual trust," (FBIS-SOV, May 28, 1981, p. K1), and the joint communique issued at the end of his tour emphasized "the great significance of personal contacts between the two countries' leading figures."
43 FBIS-SOV, October 3, 1986, p. K1.
44 See, for example, Yu. I. Andreyeva, "Problems of the Country's Development and the Proletariat's Struggle," *Latinskaia Amerika*, 11 (November 1982), pp. 48–59.
45 A. F. Shulgovsky, "The State and Civil Society: New Concepts," *Latinskaia Amerika*, 11 (November 1982). JPRS 82951, February 25, 1983, p.76.
46 Although interviews with four Mexicans were published, the size and placement of those articles clearly indicated that the publishers considered them less significant than bylined articles. The selection of the Mexicans who were interviewed also signaled Soviet displeasure with the Communist party leadership. Two were mid-level officials of the PSUM (presumably more pro-Soviet than the top party leaders); another a radical bishop; and the fourth the leader of the PRJ-affiliated National Movement for Revolutionary Youth.
47 M.L. Chumakova, "Mexico: Oil and Foreign Policy," p. 120.
48 On August 20, 1981 Echeverría was interviewed in Moscow by editors and writers of the Soviet Spanish language journal, *América Latina*, 2 (1982), pp. 83–98.
49 Irina Zorina, "Mexico, 1985...", *MEMO* 11 (November 1985). JPRS-UWE-86003, p. 72.
50 *Ibid.*, p. 73.
51 *Ibid.*, p. 76.
52 Brian Latell, *Mexico at the Crossroads; The Many Crises of the Political System* (Palo Alto: The Hoover Institution, 1986).
53 Jerry Hough, "The Evolving Soviet Debate on Latin America," p. 133.

54 Miguel de la Madrid, "Mexico: The New Challenges," *Foreign Affairs*, 63:1 (Fall 1984).
55 FBIS-SOV, October 7, 1986, p. K8.
56 Karl M. Schmitt, *Communism in Mexico* (Austin: University of Texas Press, 1965), p. 211.
57 Robert Lindsey, *The Falcon and the Snowman* (London: Jonathan Cape, 1980).
58 *Relaciones Mexicano-Sovieticas, 1968–1980*, p. 81.
59 FBIS-SOV, September 30, 1977, p. N1.
60 FBIS-SOV, September 28, 1979, p. K1.

11

Pragmatism and Rapprochement: Soviet Relations with Argentina and Brazil

Aldo C. Vacs

The Soviet Union's approach to Argentina and Brazil has been characterized in recent years by a gradual consolidation of those pragmatic features which aim to generate the highest possible economic and diplomatic returns in exchange for low political and economic investments. The objectives pursued seem to be relatively modest. First, the Soviets seek to establish a stable diplomatic, economic, and cultural presence befitting the Soviet Union's status as a superpower with global interests, but limited by recognition of its inability to assume a dominant role in South America. Second, Moscow wants to develop economic relations that could be economically and politically profitable, helping to alleviate Soviet production problems and reduce its external vulnerability, while consolidating friendly diplomatic ties with its commercial partners. The third objective is to facilitate and promote tendencies toward nonalignment that could weaken Argentine and Brazilian links with the Western powers, but carefully avoiding the generation of hostile reactions from the U.S. or incurring any great political or economic expenses.

In turn, the Argentine and Brazilian approaches to the Soviet Union have been cautious. External factors, such as the evolution of the relationship between East and West and the U.S. role in the Western

Hemisphere have broadened or narrowed their options with respect to the USSR. The fear of Soviet-sponsored ideological and political subversion and concern over negative Western reactions have been weighed against the prospects for obtaining economic gains and offsetting U.S. influences. For a long time after the 1917 October Revolution, the negative side of the equation predominated and bilateral relations with Latin American states, when they existed, remained tense or fluctuated between short periods of rapprochement and longer ones of hostility. Only as the climate of confrontation characteristic of the Cold War years subsided, and the undisputed leadership of the U.S. in the region eroded, was the interest in maintaining stable economic and diplomatic relations with the USSR translated into reality. Thus, while maintaining their military and strategic ties to the Western alliance, Argentina and Brazil reappraised their relations with the USSR on the basis of practical economic and political considerations. Although the timing and intensity of their rapprochement to the Soviet Union varied depending on the nature of their economies and existing political regimes and governments, both countries developed new and closer relations in the 1980s. In both cases the attempt to establish stable and productive relations with the Soviet Union has been guided by the desire to fulfill such aspirations as economic development, political stability, and international independence.

The initial sections of this chapter will analyze the process by which Soviet relations with Argentina and Brazil evolved from hostility to cooperation. The domestic political and economic changes in both countries, the changing Soviet attitude, the transformation of the international environment, the Cuban role, and the changing behavior of the local Communist parties will be highlighted as the main factors which affected the development of cooperative bilateral relations. Based on this analysis, the conclusion will assess the characteristics of the current Soviet foreign policy approach to these countries at the economic, diplomatic, political, and party-to-party levels. The success of this low-profile, risk-avoiding Soviet approach to generating stable and relatively friendly relations with Argentina and Brazil will also be related to the objectives these countries pursue in the international and domestic arenas through their links with the Soviet Union. Finally, the prospects for these relations in the near future are briefly reviewed, concluding that unless highly improbable changes in both Soviet behavior and the international situation take place, the bilateral ties will be preserved and continue to develop as traditional diplomatic and economic state-to-state links.

Aldo C. Vacs

ARGENTINA AND THE SOVIET UNION: FROM HOSTILITY TO COOPERATION

Frustrated Openings and Outright Rejections, 1917–1946

Soviet-Argentine relations have shown a pattern that has remained relatively unchanged up to the present. At the level of state-to-state relations, economic considerations often outweighed political and diplomatic problems. Political differences and diplomatic incidents did not hinder the development of trade so long as powerful economic and political interests were not negatively affected. Moreover, since the beginning of commercial relations in the 1920s, the Soviet balance of trade was deficitary as a result of the nonreciprocal trading pattern adopted by Argentina, which continued to import from Western countries, ignoring Soviet offers of manufactured goods.

The Soviet Union consistently exhibited a pragmatic and flexible attitude in their approach to Argentina, trying to prevent political and diplomatic frictions from affecting economic relations. Successive Argentine rejections of Soviet diplomatic probes and anti-Communist rhetoric in international fora were often met with conciliatory Soviet gestures, even after Uriburu came to power in 1930. Fluctuations between rapprochement and rejection in Soviet-Argentine relations have mostly been the result of changes in the Argentine domestic situation and, consequently, in its foreign policy. In this sense, economic developments (for example, the balance of payments crises and the need for new export markets) and political variations (for instance, military coups or growing internal pressures from the right) within Argentina decisively affected the course of relations. In contrast, the Soviet Union's attitude tended to be more consistently inclined toward rapprochement—the periods of open anti-Argentine hostility were either reactive or tactical in nature, or as in the case when the USSR opposed Argentine admission to the United Nations in order eventually to gain Western approval for admission of the pro-Soviet Polish government.

The Argentine Communist Party's (PCA) role in these relations was practically nil. Used by Argentine governments as a convenient reason for anti-Soviet swings owing to its continuous submission to Soviet dictates and employed as a propagandistic tool and a loyal ally in the Latin American intraCommunist disputes, the PCA remained a marginal actor because of its small membership and inadequate analyses of Argentine political-economic reality.

Soviet Openings and Argentine Fluctuations, 1946–1970

Shortly after Juan Perón's inauguration in 1946, came the announcement of the establishment of diplomatic relations with the USSR.[1] The reasons for the sudden shift were multiple. Perón had recognized the new major power status attained by the Soviet Union during the Second World War and was interested in establishing relations in order to balance, even if only symbolically, U.S. pressures against him. The USSR, interested in acquiring a global presence consistent with its new rank in the international arena, presented the recognition as a natural consequence of its desire to maintain friendly relations with all nations. More important still, both sides perceived the economic opportunities associated with the establishment of diplomatic ties, to the extent that this step was preceded by the visit of a Soviet commercial mission to Argentina which discussed commercial possibilities with Perón before his presidential inauguration.

Nevertheless, throughout Perón's first term in office (1946–52), bilateral relations did not become particularly cordial. As the Cold War progressed, the reluctant but gradual alignment of Argentina with the U.S.—which included signing of the Rio Treaty, acceptance of a U.S. military mission in Buenos Aires, rhetorical support for the U.S. in the Korean conflict, membership in the OAS, and anti-Communist domestic policies— led to cooler relations with the USSR and the multiplication of verbal attacks.

Only in 1953, when the Peronist government faced a severe domestic recession and a balance of payments crisis, did an economic rapprochement with Moscow occur. In August, Argentina and the USSR signed an agreement on trade and payments (the first of its type between the Soviet Union and a nonsocialist Third World country), and in May 1955, the two countries signed an additional protocol promoting closer economic-commercial cooperation. Shortly thereafter, a Soviet industrial and commercial exposition opened in Buenos Aires.[2]

During the Peronist period, the PCA maintained a constant opposition to the government, denouncing its "Nazi-fascist" origins and anti-Communist positions.[3] Peronist control over the trade unions, and Perón's popular support, weakened the PCA and its opposition to the government. Although highly vocal, the Communists did not represent a real threat to the stability of the government nor to its capacity to consolidate working class support. Significantly, at about the same time that the commercial negotiations between Argentina and the USSR began, the PCA briefly toned down its hostility toward the government.

The overthrow of Perón in 1955, and the liberal economic orientation adopted by the new military government, led to the renunciation of the bilateral agreements with the Soviet Union and an impasse in relations.[4] Thereafter, the volume of trade remained stable but low during the military administrations, while showing some tendency to increase during the democratic periods. The administration of General Juan Ongania (1966–1970) represented one of the lowest points in the history of the bilateral relations since 1945. The new government embraced the doctrine of ideological frontiers, claiming that because international communism had made the concept of territorial frontiers obsolete, continuous struggle in defense of national security and against Communist subversion (domestic and international) was necessary.

The Ongania administration outlawed and persecuted the PCA, but its leadership still rejected the armed option. New radical splits—some of them pro-Chinese, others "Guevarist"—were not important enough to affect the organizational solidarity of the party, although it remained small in size and did not make any important inroads in the working class, which was still overwhelmingly Peronist.[5] The PCA remained an orthodox, pro-Moscow party, supporting all Soviet moves from the denunciation of Peking to the invasion of Czechoslavakia. In contrast, groups such as the Armed Liberation Forces (FAL), the Armed Peronist Forces (FAP), the *Montoneros*, and the Revolutionary People's Army (ERP), each with roots in splinter Marxist organizations, Peronism, and Trotskyism, established closer relations with the Cubans, although they seem to have financed their activities primarily through armed actions—kidnappings, bank robberies, extortions, etc.—carried out in Argentina.

The Quest for a Common Ground, (1970–1980)

In the early 1970s, Argentina's military rulers faced a serious political and economic crisis. The urban explosions of 1969, the actions of the guerrilla groups, and the increasing opposition of the political parties to the military government led to crisis within the military, culminating in the ouster of Ongania and his successor, General Levingston. Finally, the new president appointed by the armed forces, General Arturo Lanusse, found a way out of the impasse by permitting free political activities and calling for elections in early 1973. Economically, the military regime also confronted a severe balance of payments crisis caused by abrupt fluctuations in prices for Argentine agricultural exports, as well as by the restrictions imposed by the European Economic Community on Argentine products. In this context, the search for alternative markets for exports became urgent and the USSR appeared as a potential customer of enormous significance.

Domestic political liberalization was coupled with foreign policy flexibility. The doctrine of "ideological frontiers" was abandoned and replaced by a new policy of "ideological pluralism," which called for the development of normal and mutually profitable relations with all countries, regardless of their political-ideological inclinations. From the Soviet Union's point of view, the global climate of "detente" created favorable environmental conditions for a rapprochement whose principal focus would be the strengthening of economic ties rather than political or military considerations.

The Peronist victory in the 1973 elections reinforced the tendency toward closer economic relations with the USSR. In the framework of the nonaligned "Third Position" designed by Perón, the government implemented an economic opening to the East which led to new agreements and expanded commercial exchanges.[6] Argentine exports of grains increased rapidly, and the Soviets in turn won a bid for the supply of turbines for the Salto Grande hydroelectric plant. However, after Perón's death and as the Argentine political and economic situation deteriorated, relations came to an impasse owing to a lack of clear direction from Isabel Perón's administration.

The military government in power after 1976 again deepened economic relations with the USSR and began to develop closer diplomatic ties. Economically, the rationale was the search for reliable customers for Argentine exports of grains and meat. Politically, however, a new element explained the friendly attitude of a self-proclaimed anti-Communist government toward the Soviets: the human rights issue. As Argentina's relations with the U.S. and other Western powers deteriorated as a consequence of continuous violations of human rights, the Soviet Union came to the defense of the country in international fora.[7] Moreover, the PCA, which in a tactical reversal had supported Perón's presidential candidacy in 1973 and then had become harshly critical of Isabel Perón's government, accepted the military coup with few reservations.[8] For its part, the new Argentine government did not outlaw the PCA, and its activities were only "suspended" as with the other "legal" parties. Subsequently the PCA adopted a line defending the "moderate" sectors of the armed forces, praising their disposition to liberalize the regime and establish closer ties with the socialist countries, while emphasizing that ultra-right groups—the Pinochetistas—were not in control of the government.

The Soviet Union also had new reasons to adopt a friendly attitude toward the military government, besides its interest in mutually profitable economic relations. On the one hand, since 1972, Soviet policy had been to cover grain production deficits with massive imports because there was an interest in securing a diversified set of supplies so as to avoid excessive reliance on the U.S. On the other hand, since the early 1970s (with military coups in Chile and Uruguay, and changes in Peru and Bolivia), the Soviet presence in southern Latin America had been severely weakened, and the prospect of a similar decline in relations with Argentina must have been weighed in the decision to ignore the anti-Communist ideology of its military rulers. Finally, during the Peronist administration, Argentina had reestablished diplomatic relations with Cuba, granting credits to promote the export of Argentine manufactured goods to the island.

The Consolidation of Relations, 1980–1986

The grain embargo decreed by the Carter administration after the Soviet invasion of Afghanistan represented a turning point in Soviet-Argentine relations. After brief vacillation during which it mentioned the possibility of joining the embargo if the U.S. abandoned its criticisms of human rights violations and lifted the arms embargo against Argentina, the military government in Buenos Aires decided to satisfy the Soviet demand for grains.[9] A Soviet commercial mission arrived immediately after this decision had been made and negotiated the purchase of all the available Argentine grains, for the first time guaranteeing the purchase of important quantities for the next five years. Argentine exports to the USSR skyrocketed from $418 million in 1979, to $1.6 billion in 1980, and $3.4 billion in 1981. The USSR became Argentina's most important commercial partner, absorbing 80 percent of its grain exports and 33 percent of its total exports in 1981. By contrast, Soviet exports to Argentina remained extremely low, less than $90 million in 1980–81.

Simultaneously, diplomatic and political contacts multiplied, including consultations on topics such as disarmament and issues before the UN General Assembly. More important still, after 1980 the USSR began to supply the Argentine nuclear program with such materials as heavy water and enriched uranium that Argentina had been unable to obtain from Western sources.[10] Military missions exchanged visits, and the number of military attaches was increased.[11] Meanwhile, the Soviets continued to intervene on behalf of Argentina concerning human rights issues before international fora. Argentina, in turn, declined to participate in the Sinai peacekeeping force after the Soviets voiced their opposition to the initiative.

Only during the brief initial period of Leopoldo Galtieri's government did Soviet-Argentine relations once again become tense. Galtieri and his Minister of Foreign Relations, Nicanor Costa Méndez, sought closer ties with the Reagan administration. To this end, Argentina began to support the Salvadoran government with credits and arms, while sending advisors to train the anti-Sandinista rebels. In February 1982, the Argentine ambassadors to Havana and Managua were recalled, and Costa Méndez expressed Argentina's willingness to support the U.S. in any East-West conflict in the hemisphere. Criticism of the USSR mounted after the imposition of martial law in Poland, and government spokesmen raised the possibility of a South Atlantic pact with the United States and South Africa.

The Soviet Union had not reacted to these developments when the Falklands/Malvinas crisis resulted in a complete reversal of the Galtieri administration's foreign policies. The sudden transition from pro-Western positions to anti-U.S. rhetoric was welcomed by the Soviets who immediately supported the Argentine claim to the islands. By the end of the conflict, with Galtieri threatening to ask for military supplies from "any source" the Soviet Union was noncommittal, expressing merely verbal support for Argentina, while denouncing the U.S. and Great Britain.[12] At the same time, Cuban and Nicaraguan support of the Argentine position led both to a rapid rapprochement with these governments and to a common anti-U.S. stance within the Nonaligned Movement.

After the Argentine defeat and the replacement of Galtieri, relations with the USSR remained friendly. Total value of Argentine exports decreased in 1982 and 1983 to approximately $1.6 billion per year (a result of the lifting of the U.S. embargo and the decline of grain prices in the international market), but the USSR was still the largest single purchaser of Argentine grains. Soviet exports, however, remained low, as the debt crisis affecting Argentina lessened the possibilities of increased purchases. Nevertheless, in a gesture of symbolic importance to Soviet authorities, their request for authorization of Aeroflot flights between Moscow and Buenos Aires was finally granted.

The completion of the democratization process and the victory of Raúl Alfonsín in the election of October 1983 did not change the nature of Soviet-Argentine relations substantially. Most probably the Soviets had shared the PCA's preelection assessment about an eventual Peronist triumph, but found no reasons to commit themselves to any candidate. The PCA, however, after having nominated its own presidential candidate, reversed its position and backed the Peronist presidential and vice-presidential nominees, while presenting its own candidates for other offices. The decision was ill-fated. Not only did the Peronists lose, but due to the electoral polarization between them and the Radicals, as well as the PCA's lack of a broad support base, the Communists did not elect any of their own candidates.

Relations with the Soviet Union during the first years of the Alfonsín administration remained friendly. Argentine exports decreased slightly in value, to around $1.3 billion annually in 1984 and 1985, but the volume remained stable.[13] Soviet exports were still extremely low in 1984 ($31 million), but experienced an increase in 1985 (to around $60 million), although still falling short of Soviet expectations. In January 1986, the terms of agreement for Soviet grain purchases were renewed for another five years[14] and in exchange, Argentina offered to buy $500 million in Soviet products during the same period. An interesting recent development has been the contacts between the Soviet commercial missions and several Argentine provincial governments.[15] As a result, the governments of Mendoza, Chaco, Formosa, and Corrientes have signed direct contracts for the supply of Soviet transportation equipment and machinery for road construction. Similar negotiations were established with other provincial governments, and a group of governors visited the USSR in November 1984 in order to explore the possibilities of new agreements.

At the diplomatic level, contacts also intensified with visits of Soviet missions to Buenos Aires and Argentine diplomats and legislators to Moscow. The diplomatic exchanges culminated in January 1986 with the visit of Argentine Minister of Foreign Relations Dante Caputo to the USSR. In the final joint communique, Argentina expressed support for Soviet initiatives on nuclear disarmament, while the Soviets praised the efforts of the Group of Six—Argentina, Greece, Mexico, India, Sweden, and Tanzania—to curtail nuclear armaments, halt nuclear tests, and prevent an arms race in space.[16] Both countries agreed to oppose all foreign pressure and interference in Central America, denounced apartheid, expressed concern on British military bases in the Malvinas, and asked for global negotiations to solve the external debt problems of developing countries. Alfonsín himself went to the USSR in October 1986, a move that was hailed as a landmark in the development of bilateral relations.

The cordiality in Argentine-Soviet contacts did not result, however, in friendly relations between the PCA and the Alfonsín administration. After its 1983 electoral defeat, the PCA turned inward and its leaders criticized earlier political positions for their lack of revolutionary content. Emerging from this period of self-criticism, the PCA turned toward more radical positions, and in mid-1985 established an electoral coalition (FREPU, United People's Front) with the Trotskyist Movement Toward Socialism (MAS) and fractions of the Peronist left embodied in the *Peronismo de Base*, or grassroots Peronism. In the mid-term Congressional elections of November 1985, the FREPU did not elect any congressmen (it only obtained two percent of the votes), but the PCA persisted afterwards in intensifying its opposition to the government whose policies it labeled the "modernization of dependency."[17]

This new, more militant attitude of the PCA should be placed in the context of the issue selected by the party as the main focus of its political campaign: the foreign debt. The Communists presented the debt policies of the Radical government as a clear surrender to foreign pressures, especially after an initial phase of defiance that lasted until the replacement of Alfonsín's first Minister of Economics, Bernardo Grinspun. They denounced the stabilization and adjustment measures embodied in the Austral Plan and the willingness of the government to repay the debt as anti-popular and anti-national. Of consequence here, too, was Cuba's efforts to organize a broad front of progressive and leftist groups supportive of repudiation or moratorium of debt payments.[18] This offered the PCA the possibility of joint action with other political forces, while consolidating its new image as a more radical and dynamic actor in the Argentine political scene. In contrast, the Soviet Union, although denouncing the debt crisis as the result of a U.S. "policy of exploitation," has been less active at the partisan level, preferring simply to call for coordinated action by the Latin American governments in the framework of the Cartagena consensus and the Latin American Economic System (SELA).[19]

Aldo C. Vacs

BRAZIL AND THE SOVIET UNION: FROM MUTUAL REJECTION TO CAUTIOUS RAPPROCHEMENT

Mutual Hostility and Insurrectional Attempts, 1917–1941

As in the case of Argentina, early relations between the Soviet Union and Brazil were plagued by hostility. The Soviet Union made several bids for Brazilian recognition in the first years after the October Revolution, but in this case the results, even at the commercial level, were scarcely successful. The creation of the Communist Party of Brazil (PCB) in 1922 reinforced the distrust of the Brazilian elites concerning the USSR. Relations—or the lack of them—centered from the beginning on political considerations, many of which focused around the role played by the PCB in the domestic Brazilian arena.[20] The single most important event was the PCB's support of an ill-prepared uprising in November 1935. Led by Luis Carlos Prestes, this uprising was rapidly suppressed by the forces loyal to President Getúlio Vargas, and the party, practically destroyed, remained underground for the next ten years.[21]

These events had devastating consequences on relations between Brazil and the USSR for a long time to come. The 1935 uprising would attain a mythical status among the Brazilian armed forces as an event characterized by the treasonous assassination of military officers at night by a band of Communists directed from Moscow. Fostered by Vargas and carefully preserved by the armed forces, high command, the commemoration of the suppression of the uprising represented a powerful obstacle for any rapprochement with the Soviet Union, which was seen as the main instigator of the revolt. Thus, in the following years, as Vargas consolidated his grip on power and established the authoritarian *Estado Novo*, relations with the USSR were nonexistent at all levels, and Brazil wavered between aligning itself with Germany or the United States in the international arena.

Brief Rapprochements and Long Rejections, 1942–1970

When the U.S. entered the war, Vargas finally decided to side with the Allies expecting, in exchange, to receive American supplies of arms and economic aid. The move secured these benefits, satisfying the military demands and accelerating Brazilian economic growth and industrialization. But, for the domestic political scene, joining the Allied side had destabilizing effects on the *Estado Novo* itself. Growing demands for democratization led to Vargas' attempts to liberalize the regime while remaining in control.

Seeking to develop this new progressive image for electoral purposes, Vargas repealed measures taken against the PCB and established diplomatic relations with the USSR.[22] When Prestes and other PCB leaders were freed in late 1944 and allowed to resume their political activities, it became rapidly clear that some agreement had been reached between Vargas and Prestes when the PCB offered its backing to Vargas in the presidential elections scheduled for December 1945. With respect to the USSR, in April of the same year the Brazilian ambassador to Washington offered to establish diplomatic relations, a proposal which was immediately accepted by Soviet representatives.

Actively involved in the *queremista* ('We want Getulio') campaign organized by Vargas' supporters in 1945, the PCB now had an opportunity to become an important actor in the new populist coalition. At the same time, the possibilities for a rapprochement between Brazil and the Soviet Union grew, fostered by the increasingly nationalistic rhetoric of Vargas and growing tensions with the U.S. government, which by this time was showing its distaste for Vargas' permanence in power.

The overthrow of Vargas in October 1945 eliminated the chances for further Communist collaboration with the government, as well as Brazilian rapprochement with the USSR. The PCB participated in the 1945 elections, gathering 10 percent of the votes and electing 1 senator and 14 deputies, but the party was extremely vulnerable in the context of a government headed by a military man, and backed by armed forces which distrusted PCB intentions. Finally, in May 1947, the government banned the PCB, and in October the Congress voted to expel all Communists from elective offices. The party would remain underground for nearly 40 years, although there were periods of relative relaxation during which it participated more openly in Brazilian politics.[23]

The measures against the PCB paralleled Brazil's growing hostility toward the Soviet Union. An open attack published in October 1947 in the Soviet press against President Dutra and the Brazilian armed forces, after which the Soviet Union refused to apologize, led Brazil to sever diplomatic relations. [24] They would not be resumed until 1961.

Mutual indifference and the lack of relations at practically all levels characterized the 1950s. The situation began to change during the Juscelino Kubitschek administration. Following the pragmatic pattern observed in the case of Argentina, these new Soviet-Brazilian contacts focused initially on economic aspects, an approach which generated less resistance from anti-Soviet sectors in Brazil and offered the USSR an opportunity to gain a foothold which could eventually lead to diplomatic, cultural, and political ties.[25]

During the brief presidential term of Janio Quadros, bilateral relations warmed and talks aimed at reestablishing diplomatic ties began. At this time, however, a new element—the Cuban factor—interfered with the completion of the Brazilian rapprochement with the USSR. The Cuban turn to the Soviets, and its growing tensions with the U.S. generated a more acute perception of the "Communist threat" among the Brazilian military and conservative sectors. Quadros' decoration of Ernesto (Ché) Guevara in August 1961 created greater alarm, delayed the reestablishment of diplomatic relations further, and created the conditions for Quadros' resignation.

His successor, João Goulart, finally reestablished diplomatic relations in November 1961.[26] During his administration, bilateral economic links deepened and diversified. Although low in absolute terms (in 1963, Brazilian exports amounted to $43 million while Soviet exports were $29 million), bilateral trade increased rapidly in relative terms.[27] Meanwhile, in the political-diplomatic sphere, the Soviet Union praised the Goulart government's progressive nature. Domestically, the PCB, still illegal, nevertheless enjoyed a relative degree of freedom which it used to consolidate its influence in the labor movement while offering qualified support to the government.

The 1964 military coup which overthrew Goulart had been preceded by a harsh anti-Communist campaign which underscored the leftist inclinations of the government, denouncing its friendly ties to the PCB. The new military government of Castello Branco harshly repressed the Communists and embraced the "doctrine of national security," which called for the elimination of Communist groups controlled by the Soviet Union.[28] This perspective, in turn, led to the establishment of closer political and military ties with the United States, a consistent anti-Cuban position, and a leading role for Brazil in the Dominican Crisis of 1965.

As might be expected, relations with the USSR suffered after Goulart's fall in March 1964. Neither country, however, opted for a complete break of diplomatic and economic links, preferring to keep relations at a very low level of interaction on the economic plane, if openly hostile on the political. Thus, although the Soviet Union granted Brazil a line of credit for the purchase of equipment and machinery in 1966, and renewed it in 1969, less than $6 million were used. Trade volume also declined, being 43 percent lower in 1968 than in 1963.[29] The decline in economic transactions paralleled the intensification of Soviet political criticisms aimed at the military regime. Articles in the Soviet press defined the Brazilian government as "reactionary" and "pro-imperialist," basing itself on an alliance between the command of the armed forces, the bourgeoisie, and multinational corporations.[30]

Notwithstanding the vehemence of Soviet criticisms, with Soviet support the PCB stressed its commitment to peaceful tactics, centering its actions on the creation of a broad democratic front in opposition to the military dictatorship. The party maintained this commitment after it began to lose some of its most active members (among them, Carlos Marighela) who joined urban and rural guerrilla groups. At the same time, the PCB refused to participate in the 1967 Organization of Latin American Solidarity (OLAS) conference in Havana. Afterwards, in what may be seen as one of the clearest manifestations of Cuban-Soviet tactical disagreement during the latter 1960s and early 1970s, numerous Brazilian armed groups—MR-8, ALN, Var-Palmares, etc.—found shelter, training, and support in Cuba, while the old PCB leadership established headquarters in Moscow. The PCB would gradually approach the single tolerated opposition party, the Brazilian Democratic Movement (MDB), eventually coming to exert strong influence (through its participation in the so-called "auténticos" faction), even electing some party members to Congress.

Toward a Rapprochement, 1971-1986

In the 1970s, the Brazilian regime stabilized, promoting a national "economic miracle" while emerging as a middle power. Correspondingly, bilateral relations with the USSR improved. The initial reasons for this slow improvement seem to have been economic: as the Brazilian economy expanded, the need for new markets for its exports led to reappraisals of the convenience of deepening ties to the USSR and other socialist countries. The Soviet Union reacted favorably to this new interest and rapidly engaged in a number of commercial transactions and economic agreements whose aim was to consolidate the economic basis of the relationship.

The first manifestations of the new economic relationship developed in the areas of trade and hydroelectric works:[31] Brazilian exports to the USSR grew from $23 million in 1970 to $158 million in 1973. These exports included a number of nontraditional products such as textiles, medicines, shoes, and clothes, together with agricultural products such as coffee, soybeans, cocoa, and sugar. Soviet exports also increased, but the trade balance remained extremely unfavorable to the Soviet Union. Exports grew from $2.7 million in 1970 to only $12.7 million in 1973.[32]

Up to 1973, Brazil's interest in expanding economic relations with the Soviet Union lay in trade surpluses and hard currency payments made by the Soviets. After the oil shock of 1973, a new factor reinforced its interest in preserving relations as the Soviet Union became a reliable supplier of oil and oil products. Thus, Soviet exports to Brazil increased ten-fold between 1973 and 1975, passing from $12.7 million to $129.3 million—of this total, $123 million was for oil and oil products.[33]

By 1974, the Brazilian desire to develop stable economic links with the Soviets found its complement in a gradual shift of foreign policy toward a relatively more nonaligned position. With the inauguration of General Ernesto Geisel as president came the process of political decompression (*distensão*) and a more flexible foreign policy strategy. The foreign policy of "responsible pragmatism," an approach formulated by the Minister of Foreign Relations, Azevedo da Silveira, implied the abandonment of automatic alignment with the U.S. and instead advocated the search for closer relations with other Western developed powers, Third World nations and, especially, Latin American countries.[34] The diversification of Brazil's external relations was considered essential to consolidating the country's new status as an emergent power. This led to clashes with the United States. Among the most important developments in this regard were the signing in 1975 of an agreement with West Germany for the transfer of nuclear technology and equipment, and the establishment of close diplomatic and economic relations with the former Portuguese colonies in Africa—Angola, Mozambique, and Guinea–Bissau.

The Soviet Union cautiously welcomed the new Brazilian attitude, explaining it as the result of economic imperatives which drove the country to diversify its external links in order to reduce the local dominant classes' dependency on the United States. The increase in Brazilian–U.S. tensions as a result of the pressures applied by the Carter administration on human rights and nuclear policies led to Brazil's abrogation in 1977 of a 1952 bilateral agreement with the United States, strengthening Soviet hopes that the Brazilian trend toward nonalignment was irreversible. Meanwhile, Soviet-Brazilian economic ties deepened as the volume of trade remained high, and Brazil became the USSR's third largest commercial partner in Latin America, after Cuba and Argentina.[35]

During João Figuereido's administration (1979–1985), bilateral relations with the USSR continued to improve as both sides found new reasons for economic and diplomatic collaboration. The process of democratization—*abertura*— and the adoption of measures such as the political amnesty of 1979, provided the opportunity for Prestes and other members of the PCB leadership to return to Brazil.[36] Although not legalized, the Communists were able to develop their activities without being the object of strong repressive measures. After reconstituting its leadership in Brazil, the PCB reaffirmed its commitment to peaceful political tactics and continued to support the MDB as the nucleus of a broad opposition front engaged in the struggle for democratization. Soviet analysts, in turn, deplored the illegality of the PCB, but praised the positive steps taken by the "liberal" sectors headed by Figueiredo against the opposition of the military hardliners.[37]

Soviet pragmatic behavior and its cautious cultivation of friendly relations with the Brazilian regime produced some concrete results in the early 1980s. The Brazilian government refused to join the grain embargo declared by the Carter administration, and instead undertook to increase its exports of soybeans and sugar to the USSR. Going a step further than the Argentines, the Brazilians also refused to adhere to the U.S.-organized boycott of the Moscow Olympics.[38] This new phase of expanding economic relations culminated with the visit of the Brazilian Minister of Planning, Delfim Neto, to Moscow in July 1981, accompanied by a large number of businessmen and government officials. The agreements signed during the visit called for increased Brazilian exports of soybeans, corn, textiles, and manufactures, and for Soviet participation in petrochemical projects, oil exploration, and hydroelectric plants in Brazil.[39] An additional agreement for joint Brazilian-Soviet participation in hydroelectric plants in Brazil and hydroelectric and road projects in Angola, Ethiopia, and Peru was also signed.

By this time, the trade balance leaned heavily to the Brazilian side, with exports in 1981 reaching $621 million, while imports from the USSR amounted to only $20 million.[40] Subsequently, Soviet trade officials concentrated on reducing this imbalance, and by 1984 they had been relatively successful as Brazilian exports of $402 million were balanced by imports of $153 million. Soviet pressures to further diminish their deficit continued, leading to new agreements which bartered Brazilian products for Soviet oil.

On the political-diplomatic plane, the Brazilian positions on various issues of concern to the Soviet Union did not change substantially, even after the Reagan administration's attempts to reestablish closer bilateral co-operation. The Brazilian government maintained its ties with Angola and the other former Portuguese colonies, did not reverse its position on the Palestinian issue, continued to sell arms to Iraq, Iran, and Libya, rejected participation in a South Atlantic security pact, adopted a noninterventionist stand concerning Grenada and Nicaragua, and sided with Argentina in the Falklands/Malvinas conflict. Moreover, economic disagreements on trade, debt, and high-technology issues plagued Brazilian-U.S. relations. The Reagan administration's failure to recreate the "special relationship" strengthened the determination of the Soviet Union to maintain its pragmatic approach and to accept the economic and political costs of this strategy in the hope of deepening the Brazilian nonaligned position.

Indicative of Soviet interest in avoiding any attitude which could have been interpreted by the Brazilian government as an interference in domestic affairs was the Communist Party of the Soviet Union's neutrality with respect to the struggle within the PCB. Soon after the return of the Communist leadership to Brazil, the party split into two factions: a larger "Eurocommunist" tendency headed by Giacondo Días, and a more orthodox pro-Soviet group led by the aging Prestes. The first group was majoritarian, and after a bitter fight replaced Prestes with Dias as Secretary General. The CPSU maintained low-key contacts with both factions, while stressing the progress made by the Communists in the context of the democratization process. In 1984, the PCB, together with most leftist parties and groups, campaigned actively for direct elections and, after these had been rejected by Congress, supported the opposition Democratic Alliance ticket headed by Tancredo Neves and José Sarney.[41]

The Democratic Alliance's victory and the beginning of the Sarney administration—after Tancredo Neves' death—did not result in any substantial change in Soviet-Brazilian relations. Both sides had economic as well as political reasons for maintaining the mutually beneficial links established in the previous years. In December 1985, the Brazilian Minister of Foreign Relations, Olavo Setúbal, visited the USSR. During his stay both countries reaffirmed their intention of strengthening commercial links and promoting diplomatic cooperation.[42] Meanwhile, the PCB was finally legalized in July 1985 after having fulfilled all the requirements for registration before the electoral tribunal. The party participated in the November mayoral elections, presenting candidates on the Brazilian Democratic Movement Party (PMDB) ticket, and electing approximately 100 council-members and 7 mayors. At the same time, it retained ten federal deputies and supported the Sarney administration's implementation of the Cruzado Plan—a heterodox program for stabilization of the economy—in February 1985. In this sense, the PCB had become a reformist party that did not represent a threat to the government, acting instead as a factor for stability by rejecting the more extremist positions of the populist and the radical left.

Unresolved in Brazil's foreign policy was the attitude to be adopted with respect to Cuba. Although the armed groups which had had Cuban support were defeated by the mid-1970s, and all those that were reorganized after the amnesty opted for peaceful methods of struggle (MR-8, PCB, etc), the Cuban issue was still problematic for the democratic government. Cuba's efforts to develop traditional state-to-state ties with Brazil met with distrust in the military, and the new government preferred not to press an issue which could generate domestic tensions without offering any certain economic or political gain. For their part, the Soviets did not make any specific reference to this situation in their public statements about the Brazilian foreign policy, probably out of the conviction that such a move would be interpreted as pressure, reinforcing the military and conservative sectors' opposition to the establishment of relations with Cuba.

THE DYNAMICS OF THE SOVIET RELATIONS WITH ARGENTINA AND BRAZIL

The essential characteristic of Soviet foreign policy toward Argentina and Brazil has been its pragmatism. This cautious Soviet approach has been aimed to establish and consolidate a stable presence in both countries, while trying to reduce the risks and uncertainties associated with more ambitious foreign policy schemes. Pessimism about the revolutionary prospects in either country has reinforced the tendency to develop ties without regard to the orientation of their governments. In brief,

Soviet policy in these cases has been guided by the desire to consolidate traditional economic and political-diplomatic relations, avoiding any type of potentially costly initiatives exploiting whatever opportunities to gradually advance its interests and improve its position in the area.

In this context, Soviet foreign policy behavior shows a pattern that begins with the establishment and, later, consolidation of economic ties.[43] The first bids for closer relations are focused around the possibility of mutually beneficial commercial exchanges. Normally, this implies relatively important Soviet purchases of agricultural products and raw materials that are paid for with hard currency. In the Argentine case, Soviet interest in the purchase of grains is rooted in the deficiencies of its agricultural sector and the need to diversify its foreign suppliers in order to offset possible embargoes. In the Brazilian case, Soviet interest is similarly focused on soybeans and grains, but there is also a clearer political motivation in the diversification of Soviet imports to include tropical and manufactured products. The economic links to both countries not only provide the USSR with the opportunity to offset domestic productive deficiencies using diversified suppliers, but offer the initial chance to attain a stable foothold. For the Soviet Union, creating a concrete economic interest with these countries appears to be the best way to guarantee the stability of the relationship, making it more difficult to break the ties for ideological reasons or external pressures. As different economic groups in Argentina and Brazil develop a material interest in the continuity of the relations, their anti-Communism and anti-Soviet sentiment is countered by the economic profits resulting from bilateral trade.

As exports to the Soviet market become more important for these countries, total foreign trade, Soviet negotiators have exerted more pressure to balance the exchanges. Obviously Soviet leverage is greater with Argentina than with Brazil owing to the markedly different proportion of their respective exports absorbed by the Soviet market. However, in both cases, the pressure for reciprocity, although consistent, has not been extreme. The Soviets have seen the balancing of bilateral trade as a gradual process leading to a relative reduction of deficits. In any case, the main potential customers are not private firms, but rather state enterprises and agencies with whom close relations have been established, especially in the 1970s.

Underscoring the pragmatic character of the Soviet approach to Argentina and Brazil is the circumstance that economic ties, although presented as the foundations of a stable relationship, have not been used to exert open political pressures on either commercial partner. The fears expressed by conservative sectors in both countries concerning the Soviet ability to use its economic leverage to obtain political and diplomatic advantages (or to advance the cause of local Communist parties) have so far been unwarranted.

In the case of Argentina, the initiative in expanding cooperation to other spheres besides the economic came from the Soviet side and found expression mainly in the support provided to the military regime in international fora regarding human rights issues. In the case of Brazil, as economic ties expanded and the country adopted a more nonaligned position, the Soviet Union emphasized agreements on specific topics, while ignoring the areas of dispute. In both cases, however, the basic Soviet objective was similar: to promote tendencies toward more autonomous foreign policies and weaken the links with the U.S. and other Western powers, always in a way so as not to generate domestic backlashes or provoke strong Western reactions.[44] This cautious diversification of links was encouraged by detente and by the multipolarization of the international system. For economic and political reasons, the links thus forged would outlast the demise of detente and the revival of East-West tensions in the 1980s.

Soviet pragmatism was also clear in regard to the bilateral military contacts. The two sides exchanged military missions and offers of armaments, but rejection of closer military ties by both Argentina and Brazil did not affect the cordial climate of the relationships. The Soviet Union welcomed the opportunity to supply weapons to these countries as a way of reducing its trade deficits while consolidating relations at an important level. However, while leaving the possibility of deeper military ties open, the actual initiative was left in the hands of the Argentine and Brazilian governments, with the understanding that any pressure in this direction would generate strong negative reactions by local conservative and military sectors and the United States.

The supply of nuclear materials to Argentina in the early 1980s presented another example of caution. The request for heavy water and enriched uranium came from the Argentine side. The Soviets, appearing somewhat reluctant to comply with the request, strictly limited the shipments. In any case, the main consideration seemed to be that any refusal would have damaged relations without effectively hindering the Argentine nuclear program's completion.

Besides their intrinsic value from the bilateral economic and diplomatic perspectives, Soviet relations with Argentina and Brazil offer the additional dimension of contributing to the erosion of U.S. hemispheric hegemony. The support given to Argentine and Brazilian diplomatic initiatives has reinforced the tendency toward nonalignment evident in both countries' foreign policies since the early 1970s. However, while favoring this trend, the Soviet Union has been careful to avoid outright involvement in situations in which their intervention could have been perceived as provocative by the United States or implied high economic and military costs. Thus, during the Malvinas crisis, Soviet support for Argentina was merely declaratory—it did not even translate into a veto of the UN Security Council's condemnation of the Argentine action.

With respect to Communist party relations, the Soviet attitude toward the PCA and PCB fits into its moderate and pragmatic approach.[45] The CPSU demonstrated its preference for peaceful tactics in both countries by providing support to the orthodox parties that rejected involvement in armed struggles during the 1960s and 1970s, agreeing with the majority of the PCA and PCB leadership in condemning urban and rural guerrilla groups by denouncing them as "adventurous petit-bourgeois ultraleftists." The failure in 1973 of the Chilean experiment in peaceful transition to socialism did not lead to a reappraisal of the peaceful option in the Argentine and Brazilian cases, nor was the *Sandinista* revolution offered as a viable model for these countries later in the decade.

The reasons for supporting the electoral approach as the most appropriate for the Argentine and Brazilian conditions were related to the character of the Soviet state-to-state relations with the countries in question, as well as to the nature of local situations. Open support for armed tactics would have resulted in a complete break of economic and diplomatic relations, and the patient efforts at rapprochement would have been wasted without any possibility of insuring a revolutionary victory.

In contrast, opting for the peaceful path led the military and conservative groups to gradually accept the Communist parties' activities, especially when facing the more dangerous armed groups. At the same time, the Soviet Union's image as the promoter of subversion, if not totally abandoned was considerably softened. As a result, one of the main ideological political obstacles for closer state-to-state bilateral relations was removed.

In this context the Argentine and Brazilian parties were important to the Soviet Union not because of the likelihood they would eventually dominate the domestic political arena, but in their capacity as pro-Soviet propagandizers, as providers of information on local conditions, and as proponents of arguments in favor of the development of state-to-state relations with the USSR. Both parties have defended such controversial Soviet initiatives as the invasion of Afghanistan and Moscow's proposals on nuclear disarmament. They have loyally praised the Soviet system, rejecting attacks from left and right. The PCA and PCB have also been useful in providing the Soviet Union with information on and interpretations of developments in both countries, thus helping to overcome the Soviets' relative lack of acquaintance with the local situations. Finally, through their moderate declarations and analyses, the official Communist parties have justified the Soviet Union's friendly relations with military dictatorships which others on the left, and even Western governments, have repudiated.

In the context of Soviet relations with Argentina and Brazil, the Cuban issue has gradually become less disruptive.[46] Initially, the Cuban Revolution presented the Soviet Union with the first opportunity to establish close ties with a Latin American country and obtain an ally in the hemisphere. But in Argentina and Brazil, the Cuban affair led to a wave of anti-Communism and anti-Sovietism. Cuban support for guerrilla activities in both countries strengthened the tendency to establish closer relations with the U.S. and facilitated the elaboration of national security doctrines (as well as the thesis of ideological frontiers which precluded the establishment of friendly links with the USSR).

As the Cubans diminished their support for the armed groups (although links with them were never totally severed) and tried to reestablish diplomatic and economic relations with most Latin American countries, the response of the Argentine and Brazilian governments differed. The Peronist government established diplomatic and economic ties (these were, in turn, maintained at a low level for almost all of the military period), while the Brazilian regime refused to open relations. In both cases, the Cuban issue was treated independently of the Soviet Union.

Argentina and Brazil looked for Cuban support when it served their interest—for instance, Argentina during the Malvinas crisis—but on other occasions, attacks on Castro and his policies were used with different degrees of success to promote a rapprochement with the U.S. The latter occurred during the first period of Galtieri's administration and when Brazil tried to reduce tensions with the Reagan administration in the early 1980s. The perception of Cuba as extremely dependent on the Soviet Union also explains why the Argentine and Brazilian governments have refused to consider favorably or seriously the Cuban proposal for a moratorium on foreign debt payments.

The objectives pursued by Argentina and Brazil in their relations with the Soviet Union relate more to global North-South interactions than to East-West relationships. From this perspective, three concerns have guided their foreign policies.

First, the search for economic development has been one of the main concerns guiding Argentine and Brazilian foreign policies throughout this period. The USSR represented a potentially large alternative market for Argentine and Brazilian exports. For its part, the Soviet Union was also interested in selling machinery and equipment, and it granted commercial credits under what were sometimes more favorable conditions than those offered by Western firms. The technical assistance that could be provided by the Soviets was also attractive for these countries, as were the possibilities of scientific-technical cooperation. Second, the search for international independence has been another fundamental factor shaping the character of Argentine and Brazilian relations with the USSR. From this perspective, their interest in establishing diplomatic ties with the USSR was related mainly to their desire for increased political autonomy in the international arena. For the Argentine and Brazilian governments, relations with the USSR were one of the most visible manifestations of the right to develop an independent foreign policy guided by calculations of national interest and not subject to external pressures. Finally, the existence of diplomatic and economic relations with the USSR has been accompanied by a degree of Soviet support in the international fora and moderate behavior by the local Communist parties, factors which have helped to reinforce the stability of these governments.

PROSPECTS

The characteristics of the Soviet relations with Argentina and Brazil are not likely to experience any substantial change in the near future. There are no reasons to believe that the pragmatic and cautious Soviet approach will be replaced by a more adventurous type of foreign policy. Conversely, neither Argentina nor Brazil seem to have any concrete interest either in assuming a more hostile stand or in developing much closer relations with the Soviet Union.

In the sphere of economic relations, the volume of trade will probably remain relatively stable. The rise of Mikhail Gorbachev and his stated objectives of modernizing the Soviet economy may have some impact on bilateral relations, but not in the immediate future. If the attempt to increase the productivity in the agricultural sector is successful, for example, there will be fewer opportunities for Argentine and Brazilian exports to increase in volume. In the meantime, however, the medium-term agreements guarantee a stable Soviet demand for grains and other agricultural products.

For its part, the Soviet Union will continue to insist on the need to reduce its trade deficits, while pursuing more aggressive marketing policies for its products. This situation would pose new constraints on both Argentina and Brazil in that up to now triangular schemes have predominated, i.e., using their Soviet export earnings to import from Western countries and to repay their foreign debts. In this context, the debt crisis affecting these countries reinforces the need to preserve commercial relations with the USSR, especially as the possibilities of substantially increasing exports to other countries are not very promising. The Soviet Union has reduced its purchases since the lifting of the U.S. grain embargo and as its hard currency reserves have been drained, but it still represents—especially for Argentina—a market that cannot be substituted easily. The debt crisis thus creates a delicate situation in which Argentina and Brazil are compelled to try to increase their export earnings to increase imports of Soviet products. Because of this situation, and because of Soviet interest in maintaining alternative supply sources while preventing larger trade deficits, the most probable outcome will be a relative stabilization of the economic exchanges at the current level.

In the political-diplomatic sphere, relations will continue to be cordial and characterized by moderation and pragmatism so long as there are no developments which could be perceived as direct threats to the security of any side. The most recent agreements seem to indicate that mechanisms of diplomatic consultation will also be formally consolidated.

The recent democratization of Argentina and Brazil has reinforced the move toward more independent foreign policies and impelled these countries toward greater interest in issues such as disarmament and new international economic arrangements. This new attitude has been praised by the Soviet Union, and if such a trend continues in the future, Argentina and Brazil would probably become more active in their roles as independent actors trying to promote (with explicit Soviet encouragement) the restoration of detente.

The tendency to treat Cuba as a separate actor in the context of Argentine and Soviet relations seems to be a stable feature. There may be a new wave of anti-Cuban hostility if there are reasons to believe that the Cubans are again favoring armed tactics and guerrilla groups in these countries. But so long as the Soviets do not participate actively in such a development, relations will not be essentially affected. With respect to the Central American crisis, the Soviet Union, Argentina, and Brazil have called for nonintervention by external actors and a peaceful settlement of differences in their joint declarations. No radical change of attitude should be expected unless Cuban behavior becomes openly aggressive against El Salvador or other Central American nations.

In the sphere of military relations, the cautious Soviet attitude and the Argentine and Brazilian reluctance to engage in closer contacts seem to be a stable characteristic of the bilateral links. Among reasons for this are the democratization process itself, the armed forces' rejection of Soviet military aid, the ideological opposition of powerful conservative sectors, the interest both countries have in reducing military expenditures, and the economic constraints imposed by the debt on any imports of weapons.

The Argentine and Brazilian Communist parties should also continue to support peaceful tactics. Democratization in both countries has created the opportunity for legal activities by these parties, and it is unreasonable to expect them to abandon, in these more favorable circumstances the commitment to peaceful tactics that they maintained during the authoritarian periods. The only new development appears to be the PCA and PCB's relatively more independent attitude toward the Soviet line. In Argentina, the PCA has developed a policy of alliances with Trotskyite sectors unprecedented among orthodox pro-Soviet parties, while in Brazil, the PCB's "Eurocommunist" orientation implies a deviation from some basic ideological tenets upheld by the CPSU. But, in both cases, relations with the CPSU are still close and the Soviet Union is praised as a model of successful socialism and leader of world progressive causes.

In conclusion, the current characteristics of the Soviet relations with Argentina and Brazil are not likely to change significantly in the near future unless the tensions between East and West rise considerably, causing the Soviets to discard their pragmatic attitude on foreign policy issues. Neither alternative appears probable and thus the trend toward stable economic and diplomatic relations should continue.

Notes

1 On Soviet-Argentine relations during the first Peronista administration (1946–1955) see Vacs, *Discreet Partners: Argentina and the USSR Since 1917* (Pittsburgh: University of Pittsburgh Press, 1984), pp. 12–17.

2 The agreement is reproduced in USSR Academy of Sciences' *América Latina: Estudios de Científicos Soviéticos* (8), Relacíones Sovietico-Latinoamericanas (recopilación documentos), I (Moscow: Redacción Ciencias Sociales Contemporaneas, 1981), pp. 86–93. On the protocol, see Romuald G. Tomberg, *Relaciones económicas de la Unión Soviética con países de América Latina* (Santiago, Chile: E/CEPAL/Proy. 4/R. 12, 1979), p. 53.

3 On the attitude of the PCA with respect to Peronism, see, for the official party interpretation, Oscar Arévalo, *El partido comunista* (Buenos Aires: Centro Editor de América Latina, 1983); and for a highly critical analysis, Jorge Abelardo Ramos, *Historia del stalinismo en la Argentina* (Buenos Aires: Rancagua, 1974).

4 On the characteristics of bilateral relations between 1955 and 1970, see Vacs, *Discreet Partners*, pp. 17–23.

5 On the development of revolutionary tendencies in Peronism and the influence of the Cuban Revolution, see Donald C. Hodges, *Argentina, 1943–1976: The National Revolution and Resistance* (Albuquerque: University of New Mexico Press, 1976), pp. 32–48. Some Peronist groups, on the other hand, found the Cuban option attractive and began to establish contacts with Castro's revolutionary government. Perón did not totally reject these groups or individuals (such as John W. Cooke—for a time Perón's personal representative) who called for more revolutionary tactics, but he continued to offer support to moderate labor leaders and politicians within the movement.

6 On the "opening to the East" see Vacs, *Discreet Partners*, pp. 28–37; and Enrique Estremadoyro, *Relaciones económicas de Argentina con los paises miembros del CAME* (Santiago, Chile: E/CEPAL/Proy. 4/R.3, 1979), pp.59–62.

7 See *Latin American Political Report* 11:7 (February 1977), p. 51; *Ibid.*, 11:34 (September 1977), pp. 267–68; and *Washington Post*, November 11, 1977. The USSR not only abstained from criticizing the Argentine government in its publications and declarations, but beginning in 1977 prevented condemnation of the military regime in the UN Human Rights Commission.

8 For the PCA reaction to the coup see, for instance, Central Committee of the PCA, "The Communists and the New Situation in Argentina," *World Marxist Review Publishers' Information Bulletin*, 7(311): 144 (1976), pp. 36–40; and Rodolfo Ghioldi et al., "Building a Renovated Democracy," *Ibid.*, 10(338): 15 (1977), pp. 19–23.

9 Vacs, *Discreet Partners*, pp. 49–51.

10 *Ibid.*, pp.89–90.

11 *Ibid.*, pp. 86–89.

12 On the Falklands/Malvinas crisis see O. Cardoso, R. Kirschbaum and E. Van der Kooy, *Malvinas: La trama secreta* (Buenos Aires: Sudamericana/Planeta, 1983). On the Soviet attitude, see Victor Lukin, "La Crisis en el Atlántico Sur y sus consecuencias," *América Latina* 11:59 (November 1982) pp. 4–26; and USSR Academy of Sciences' *America Latina: Estudios de Cientificos Soviéticos* (21), "La crisis de las Malvinas/Falklands: orígines y consecuencias," (Moscow: Redacción Ciencias Sociales Contemporaneas, 1983).

13 *Los Andes* (Mendoza), February 11, 1986.

14 *Clarin* (Buenos Aires), January 30, 1986.

15 On the Soviet commercial contacts and agreements with provincial governments, see *Clarin*, January 2, 1984; July 24, 1984; *Los Andes*, December 18, 1983; July 23, 1984; August 18, 1984; November 3, 1984.

16 *La Prensa* (Buenos Aires), February 2, 1986.

17 On the PCA's self-criticisms and new positions, see Maria Seoane, "Autocritica comunista. El puntapie inicial," *El periodista de Buenos Aires*, 68 (December 27, 1985/ January 2, 1986), p. 4; and Patricio Echegaray, "Queremos cambiar el poder, no voltear el gobierno," *ibid*. 79 (March 14–20, 1986), p. 40.

18 On the participation of Argentine delegates in the August 1985 Havana Meeting on the External Debt of Latin America and the Caribbean, see Julian Lemoine, *La deuda externa* (Buenos Aires: Cuadernos de El Periodista de Buenos Aires, 1985) 1:1. For the Cuban position, Fidel Castro, *Ante la deuda y la crisis y por el nuevo orden internacional: Unidad Latinoamericana*, Speech at the Havana Meeting, August 4, 1985.

19 For the Soviet position see, "El yugo de la deuda externa de América Latina es resultado de la política de expoliación de EE.UU.," Documents of the roundtable organized by the Comité Soviético de Solidaridad con los Pueblos de América Latina and Novosti, June 26, 1985, *Panorama Latino-americano: boletín quincenal de la agencia de prensa novosti*, 93.

20 On the origins and early years of the PCB, see Astrojildo Pereira, *Formacão do PCB, 1922–1928* (Rio de Janeiro: Vitoria, 1962); and for a broader perspective, Ronald H. Chilcote, *The Brazilian Communist Party: Conflict and Integration, 1922–1972* (New York: Oxford University Press, 1974).

21 For background in the famous Prestes Column, see Neil Macoulry, *The Prestes Column: Revolution in Brazil* (New York: New Viewpoints, 1974).

22 On the establishment of diplomatic relations, see *América Latina:Estudios de científicos Soviéticos* (8), pp. 71–72.

23 Chilcote, *The Brazilian Communist Relaciones Party*.

24 On the Soviet-Brazilian problems that led to the break in diplomatic relations, see Stephen Clissold, ed., *Soviet Relations with Latin America, 1918–1968. A Documentary Survey* (London: Oxford University Press, 1970), pp. 33–34, 184–88.

25 In 1959 and 1960, unilateral economic ties were initiated with the signing of trade and payments agreements designed to exchange Soviet oil, wheat, and machinery for Brazilian coffee, cocoa, and hides, and the signing of an interbank agreement. See Tomberg, *Relaciones económicas*, pp. 67, 121–124.

26 See Clissold, *Soviet Relations*, pp. 34–35, 188–93.

27 See *América Latina: Estudios de Científicos Soviéticos (8), pp. 118–133.*

28 On the characteristics of the Brazilian national security doctrines, see María Helena Moreira Alves, *State and Opposition in Military Brazil* (Austin: University of Texas Press, 1985), especially pp. 13–53.

29 On the difficulties faced by the Soviets in establishing stable economic ties between 1964 and 1970, see Tomberg, *Relaciones económicas*, pp. 68–74.

30 See the discussions in this regard between Soviet analysts focused on the characteristics of the Latin American authoritarian regimes included in "En torno al problema de los regimenes autoritarios de derecha contemporaneos," *América Latina*, 3 (1976), pp. 76–155, especially the comments by K. Maidanik, A. Karavaev, and M. Chumakova.

31 See Tomberg, *Relaciones económicas*, pp. 72–74.

32 At the same time, the Soviets were able to obtain a contract for the supply of electric equipment for the Capivara hydroelectric plant. In 1972, an intergovernmental agreement on maritime transportation was signed in order to promote the priority use of the ships of both countries for the transportation of their exports.

33 Tomberg, *Relaciones económicas*, pp. 121, 123.

34 On the changes in Brazilian foreign policy strategy after 1974, see, for instance, Alexandre de S. C. Barros, "The Formulation and Implementation of Brazilian Foreign Policy: Itamaraty and the New Actors," in Heraldo Muñoz and Joseph S. Tulchin, eds., *Latin American Nations in World Politics* (Boulder and London:

Westview Press, 1984), pp. 3–44; and "Democratic Transition and Foreign Policy: The Experience of Brazil," in *ibid.*, pp. 216–29.

35 In 1975 and 1977, the Soviets obtained contracts for the supply of turbines and generators for the hydroelectric plant of Sobradinho, and negotiations were initiated in regard to the other hydroelectric projects. See Tomberg, *Relaciones económicas*, p. 73.

36 On the political amnesty and the return of the exiled Communist leaders, see Moreira Alves, *State and Opposition*, pp. 211–12; and Richard F. Staar, ed., *Yearbook of International Communist Affairs, 1980* (Palo Alto: Hoover Institution Press, Stanford University, 1980).

37 See Anatoli Sosnovski, "Brasil: La evolución del régimen y el ejercito," *América Latina*, 1:49 (1982), pp. 26–33.

38 In 1981, Brazil signed a medium-term agreement for the export to the USSR of 600,000 tons of soybeans annually, while the Soviets in turn increased their exports of oil. See Jim Brooke, "Dateline Brazil: Southern Superpower," *Foreign Policy*, 44 (Fall, 1981), pp. 167–81.

39 Augusto Varas, La Unión Soviética en la política exterior de América Latina: los casos de Chile, Argentina, Brasil y Peru (Santiago, Chile: FLACSO, Documento de Trabajo 158, October 1982), pp. 28–29.

40 IMF, *Direction of Trade Statistics Yearbook 1985* (Washington, D.C.: IMF, 1985), p. 393.

41 The evolution of the internal struggle between Prestes and his opponents in the PCB and the line finally adopted by the party in relation to the electoral process may be followed in the sections on Brazil included in Richard F. Staar, ed., *Yearbook of International Communist Affairs* (Palo Alto: Hoover Institution Press, Stanford University) for the years 1981 to 1986.

42 *O Estado de São Paulo*, December 11, 1985.

43 On the general characteristics and evolution of the Soviet economic strategy in Latin America since 1953, see the chapter by Elizabeth Kridl Valkenier.

44 The political objectives pursued by the Soviets in Latin America are assessed in the chapter by David Albright that provides a broader framework of analysis in which the specific cases of Argentina and Brazil should be considered.

45 For the historical background and current characteristics of the interrelations between the CPSU and the Communist parties of the region, see Edmé Domínguez's chapter.

46 The complex nature of the links between the USSR and Cuba and their impact on the state-to-state and party-to-party relations established between the Latin American governments and Communist parties with the Soviet Union since the early 1960s are discussed in the chapter by Jorge I. Domínguez.

12

The USSR and the Andean Countries: Economic and Political Dimensions

Rubén Berríos

The countries of the Andean subregion initiated diplomatic and economic links with the Soviet Union somewhat later than other larger Third World countries. During the first part of the 1960s, Argentina, Brazil, Cuba, and Mexico were the only Latin American countries with diplomatic and economic ties to the USSR. Chile was the first Andean country to exchange diplomatic representatives with Moscow in 1964, but between 1968 and 1970, five neighboring countries (Peru, Bolivia, Colombia, Ecuador, and Venezuela) established diplomatic relations with the Soviet Union and the members of the Council of Mutual Economic Assistance (CMEA).

The late 1960s and early 1970s was a period of rising nationalism throughout the Andean regions, the high points of which were the rise to power of the Peruvian military radicals in 1968, the signing of the Andean Pact in 1969, and the election of Salvador Allende as Chile's president in 1970. The emergence of nationalism led to a marked shift in these nations' approach to foreign relations, and new objectives and guidelines in foreign policy were announced in one country after another. By diversifying their economic ties, the Andean countries sought greater economic independence and a readjustment of their relations to the world economy. Their policies favored domestic capital accumulation and the regulation of foreign investment. Individually and as a bloc they enacted legislation (e.g., Decision 24 of the Andean Pact) to strengthen their bargaining position.[1] Desirous of altering their traditional passivity in foreign affairs and of diversifying their trade relations, these countries embarked on a self-proclaimed independent and "nonaligned" course which involved expanding contacts with the socialist countries and the undertaking of new initiatives toward other Third World nations.[2]

Policies of economic nationalism, agrarian reform, and the strengthening of the nation-state's role in the economy brought some of these countries into conflict with the United States. The nationalizations of U.S.-owned companies, active involvement in the Nonaligned Movement, requests for the reorganization of the OAS, recognition of Cuba, and defense by three countries with a common border (Ecuador, Peru, and Chile) of their claim to a 200-mile maritime limit all caused tension within the United States. Perceiving these developments as politically favorable, Soviet analysts also began to reassess the nature and role of Third World military elites who had previously been dismissed as reactionary.[3]

Despite its view that an anti-imperialist struggle was under way in the Andean region during the late 1960s and the first half of the 1970s, Moscow opted for diplomacy and rejected the radical left's call for immediate socialist revolution. At first, this position put the Soviet Union at odds with Havana. However, after pro-Cuban guerrillas had been decisively defeated in 1965 in Peru and in 1967 in Bolivia, Castro's policy began to swing closer to that of Moscow. For their part, local Communist parties collaborated with and supported elected representatives of moderate parties, as well as the military regimes in power in Peru and Bolivia.[4]

The aforementioned changes in the region presented the USSR with new opportunities for expanded political contact and trade. Although Soviet economic activity in the area accounted for a small percentage of the Andean countries' global exchange, Soviet projects and technicians established a visible presence.[5] Yet Soviet involvement did not turn into a domineering political influence, nor did the purchase of Soviet weapons mean political alignment with Moscow.

An increased Soviet presence in these countries was made possible by significant shifts in the East-West balance of power facilitated by detente, an upsurge of regional nationalism with strong anti-U.S. overtones, and a search for greater diversification and alternative sources of trade. Moscow's aim in the Andean region was not to establish preponderant influence, but rather to undermine Washington's hegemony. The Soviet Union saw nationalizations and internal structural reforms among Andean countries as weakening "imperialism," and it hoped to cultivate economic relations without provoking the United States. Soviet economic interests rested in the expansion of trade. In the case of Peru, for example, arms transfers and the provision of military hardware on favorable terms became a way of enhancing Soviet diplomacy.

This chapter examines the evolution of economic, political and military relations between the Soviet Union and the Andean countries in the last two decades. The emphasis is on Peru and Chile, but reference is also made to Bolivia and Colombia. The section on economic relations focuses on trade and aid, while the section on political relations explores the role played by the Communist parties as well as the regional security implications of Peru's import of large quantities of Soviet weapons. The conclusion examines how the Peru and Andean countries fit into global Soviet perspectives.

THE DIPLOMATIC AND ECONOMIC DIMENSION OF SOVIET-PERUVIAN RELATIONS

Prior to 1969, the only link between Peru and the USSR was through the Communist Party of Peru (PCP) and the sporadic sale of Peruvian fishmeal via London brokers. This changed after the seizure of power in 1968 by progressive military officers. Within a few months (in February 1969), Peru and the USSR established formal diplomatic relations, and the two countries then signed a trade agreement in March 1969, with the Soviets providing credits of $30 million for the purchase of machinery and equipment payable in 10 years at 3 percent interest.[6]

Initially, Soviet and East European trade with Peru was modest. Table 12.1 outlines how commercial exchanges with CMEA countries rose from $37 million in 1970 to $268 million in 1975. As expected, commercial agreements with the other East European members of CMEA followed the establishment of diplomatic ties with Bulgaria, Czechoslovakia, Hungary, Poland, and Romania in late 1968 and early 1969. Total trade with all of Eastern Europe increased from $59 million in 1970 to $253 million in 1975.[7] Trade with the USSR dropped to low levels during the

Table 12.1
Trade between Peru and the CMEA Countries of Eastern Europe
(millions US$)

Year	USSR Exports	Imports	Total Trade	Eastern Europe Exports	Imports	Total* Trade	Total Trade WIR USSR & EE
1970	0.2	0.1	0.3	57.0	2.0	59.0	59.3
1971	0.2	—	0.2	54.3	5.2	59.5	59.7
1972	2.1	0.2	2.3	41.6	5.3	46.9	49.2
1973	18.7	5.2	23.9	53.1	5.0	58.1	82.0
1974	6.2	6.0	12.2	112.4	20.3	132.7	144.9
1975	125.0	39.2	164.2	99.1	35.2	134.3	298.5
1976	24.0	18.4	42.4	84.5	24.3	145.1	187.5
1977	27.7	35.8	63.5	176.9	26.3	203.2	266.7
1978	23.0	24.6	47.6	84.9	24.2	154.1	201.7
1979	15.1	4.3	19.4	93.5	87.4	240.8	260.2
1980	15.7	4.8	20.5	65.3	41.2	116.7	137.2
1981	30.8	18.0	48.8	21.4	37.8	76.3	125.1
1982	14.7	19.9	34.6	40.6	46.3	99.4	134.0
1983	21.8	6.3	28.1	17.6	19.4	60.4	88.5
1984	52.3	30.6	82.9	16.2	16.8	33.0	115.9
1985	187.1	19.4	206.5	55.5	3.1	58.6	265.1
1986	115.6	11.0	126.7	15.2	8.6	23.8	150.5

* Data for some East European countries not always complete, particularly 1976, 1978–1983.
Source: Vneshniaia Torgovlia SSSR, various years from 1970 to 1987; *Kulkereskedelmi Statisztikai Evkonyv*; *Rocznik Statystyczny Handlu Zagranicznego*; *Statistisches Jahrbuch der DDR*; *Anuarul Statistic*; *Statisticke Prehledy*; Anita Tirapolsky, "La Strategie Commerciale du CAEM en Amerique Latine," *Le Courrier des Pays de l'Est*, 299, October 1985. Conversion of Soviet ruble and other currencies to US$ was calculated from the U.N. Monthly Bulletin of Statistics.

conservative administration of Fernando Belaunde (1980–1985), but sharply increased when President Alan García came to office in 1985.

The comprehensive bilateral economic agreements between Lima and Moscow covered trade, economic assistance, and financial arrangements such as credits, soft loans, and barter deals. With the creation of the Ministry of Commerce in 1969, for the first time Peru could negotiate directly on a government-to-government basis, thereby dispensing with both local and foreign private intermediaries in London or New York in selling its commodities. The trade agreements foresaw different modalities of economic cooperation, and a joint intergovernmental commission was assigned the task of finding new areas of cooperation.[8] An important step in the development of economic relations between Peru and the Soviet Union was the signing of a cooperation agreement for supplying machinery and equipment in August 1970.[9] Under this agreement, Peru received an additional credit for $24 million to purchase oil storage tanks, vehicles, and fishing port construction equipment. This was later expanded somewhat, under a fishing agreement signed in September 1971, which provided for Soviet assistance in constructing a fishing complex at Paita designed to process 180,000 metric tons of fish.[10] The USSR was to supply fishing and refrigeration equipment, ice-making facilities, generators, and repair shops, and it would be repaid in fish. Peru also granted Soviet vessels permission to dock in Peruvian ports. In turn, the USSR provided research assistance to study Peruvian fishing resources and began training Peruvian subprofessional specialists in Soviet institutes and universities.[11] The Paita fishing complex, however, never operated at full capacity, because ecological disturbances along the Peruvian coast caused the fish to disappear.

At this time, Soviet-Peruvian economic relations also focused on the Olmos hydroelectric and irrigation project near Peru's northern coast. The Soviet Union agreed to assist Peru in the construction of the first phase of the project designed to irrigate 112,000 hectares of land and generate 600,000 kilowatts of electric energy.[12] The protocol signed in Lima in June 1972 allowed for further cooperation, particularly in carrying out studies of hydroelectric energy resources of the Huallaga, Maranon, and Ucayali rivers. Soviet technical missions, whose task was to study the financial and technical aspects of the project, began arriving in October 1974. The Soviets also became involved in studying geological resources for nonferrous metals and oil, and conducted feasibility studies to build a steel plant in Nazca. In 1980, the USSR proposed to finance $535 million of the Olmos hydroelectric complex. Negotiations, which were reactivated under the Alan García administration, are said to be in their final stages as this book goes to press.

During the 1970s, the Soviet Union achieved a broader and closer relationship with Peru than with any other Latin American country except Cuba, and during these years Peru also became the third largest regional market for the Soviet Union, after Brazil and Argentina (but excluding Cuba). Soviet exports consisted mainly of machinery and equipment, cargo ships, helicopters, oil tanks, and medicines, while Peruvian exports were mainly fish meal and frozen fish, minerals, and agricultural goods. At first, the supply of Soviet machinery and equipment was sold on credit at low interest while Peruvian products were sold on contract using hard currency.

Soviet aid to Peru has come mainly in the form of lines of credits for the purchase of machinery and equipment. According to Soviet sources, between 1969 and 1973, the CMEA countries provided Peru with $204 million in lines of credit.[13] The terms of payment have been generous and interest rates low. Outright grants, on the other hand, have been few.[14] Most have followed natural disasters as, for example, in 1970, when northern Peru was devastated by an earthquake that left 60,000 people dead and thousands more homeless. The USSR donated 100 prefabricated homes, earth-moving equipment, supplies for three nurseries, food, medicine, a fully equipped 200-bed hospital with a team of Soviet doctors, and two MI-8 helicopters to remove the wounded.[15]

An important form of Soviet aid has been the bilateral agreements on cultural, scientific, and technological cooperation. Peru and the USSR have had an active cultural exchange. Particularly significant agreements have provided for the training and education of Peruvians in the Soviet Union. According to the Peruvian ambassador to the USSR, during the last 16 years, 10,000 Peruvian students have graduated from Soviet universities.[16] The U.S. State Department estimates that of the over 90,000 Third World students enrolled in Soviet and East European universities at the end of 1984, 1,185 were Peruvians.[17] The recent cultural and scientific agreement between Peru and the USSR stipulates that particular attention will be placed on training students in specific fields based on Peruvian development needs.

One of the most controversial Peruvian cooperation agreements with the USSR has dealt with fishing. First established in 1971, it has been renewed periodically, the latest was signed in 1987 and is to last until 1990.[18] Recent controversy has centered on whether taxes should be collected on the volume of fish caught by the Soviet fleet and whether a bigger share of the catch should remain in Peru.[19] While the number of Soviet factory trawlers operating in Peruvian waters has been increased to supply EPSEP (the state's food fishing company) with frozen fish, meat, and oil for the local market, Peru has also insisted on better fishing terms.

Under the agreement signed in 1984, the Soviets were to give EPSEP 7.5 percent of the unrefined fish oil, plus all species other than Pacific and horse mackerel netted with a catch (like hake, pilchard, and other table fish). The Soviets keep 85 percent of the fish meal and raw oil for their services, leaving 7.5 percent of the catch to compensate for operating expenses and permits. The Soviet share is shipped to the Soviet Union, but the oil and fish meat is sold through

Pesquera Pacífica and EPSEP. The agreement also includes provisons for training Peruvian fisherman in trawler operations, but this has not been successful because few local fishermen are willing to remain at sea for the 45 to 60 days the trawlers are out.[20]

Following the announcement of Peru's ineligibility for further IMF loans in August 1986, and with the prospect of dwindling trade credits, the government began to use general counter-trade commitments in an effort to finance imports with exports. Although in the early 1970s Peru had been engaged in some triangular deals involving the Hungarian Central Bank, Peruvian exporters of fish meal and other commodities, and Western equipment suppliers, the beginnings of bartering on a regular basis began in 1983 when Finance Minister Carlos Rodríguez Pastor travelled to Moscow to reschedule payments on Peru's Soviet debt, then amounting to $1.1 billion.[21] A counter-trade arrangement to reschedule Peru's debt was agreed to under Belaunde, and went into effect in July 1984. This postponed the repayment period for almost half of the debt—$519 million—and committed the Soviets to marking purchases from a list of Peruvian products, three-quarters of which had to be nontraditional goods. The agreement pushed the USSR above the EEC as the second largest market for Peruvian manufactured goods after the United States. Contracts have since been renewed and new ones have been signed for frozen chickens, textiles, zinc cells, candy, tiles, wood, leather, and IBM-clone microcomputers.[22] During the first half of 1985, this form of payment helped to reactivate the Peruvian textile and footwear industries which were unable to sell their products on the U.S. market owing to protectionism. Repayment of overdue debts with goods was also arranged with Hungary, Yugoslavia, Czechoslavakia, and Romania.

Since the first counter-trade agreement was signed with the Soviet Union (November 1983 through June 30, 1987), Peru has exported some $363 million worth of goods to the USSR and other East European countries. Two-thirds of the payment-in-kind deals were made with nontraditional exports. In January 1988, Peru and the USSR agreed to a ten-year restructuring of Peru's debt at a three percent annual interest. In the most recent agreement approved by President García in March 1988, the Soviets have committed themselves to purchase between $212 and $246 million for the 1980–1990 period.[23] The debt pact paves the way for an expected $600 million export agreement under which the Peruvian navy will build 80 medium-sized fishing vessels for the USSR over the next 5 years. The USSR will also finance and build a $65 million dry dock in the port of Callao to service the 220 vessels of the

Soviet fishing fleet off Peru's coast. Negotiations are also underway to explore the phosphate deposits at Bayovar.[24]

More striking than Soviet-Peruvian trade and economic relations, however, have been the agreements the two countries have signed regarding military assistance. The purchase of Soviet military equipment in the early 1970s further jeopardized relations with the United States, which had already been under strain owing to nationalizations of American-owned firms. Since World War II, Peru had been one of the continent's major recipients of U.S. military aid, third on the list after Chile and Brazil in the period 1953–1966.[25] This pattern had begun to change after 1967 when Peru purchased a number of Mirage jets from France. Though the Velasco Alvarado government began discussions with Moscow on major arms purchases as early as 1972 (when it acquired an initial contingent of 250 T-55 tanks, delivered in 1973), not until the more conservative Morales Bermúdez took office in 1975 did Soviet-Peruvian military relations deepen. Alarmed in 1975 when the Ford administration agreed to sell advanced fighter aircraft (F5s) to Chile, and when Ecuador bought a dozen Jaguar planes from Great Britain, Peru's armed forces also set out on modernizing their defense capabilities with sophisticated new equipment.

Peru first turned to Washington for aircraft and arms, but after waiting seven months for an answer, it went to other suppliers in the international arms market. France and Israel, "the first choices," proved too expensive, and when the Soviets offered lower prices and extended credit facilities, Peru could not resist. The Peruvian air force requested 36 supersonic SU-22 Sukhoi fighter bombers worth $250 million, while the army received a batch of helicopters and tanks. The Soviet Union also provided training and instruction in the use of the equipment. Figures on the exact amount of Soviet arms sales to Peru vary enormously. From 1975–1979, Peru accounted for between 20 percent and 24 percent of all Latin American arms imports; of those, anywhere from 41 percent to 65 percent came from the Soviet Union.[26] There is also disagreement over the terms of Soviet conditions, though it is widely assumed to involve a repayment period of about 10 years at low interest rates of 2.5 percent.[27] According to U.S. government figures, in 1977 there were also approximately 100 Soviet and Cuban advisors in Peru, and it is estimated that, through 1981, some 790 Peruvian officers went to the Soviet Union and Eastern Europe for military training.[28]

From the Soviet point of view, the arrangement provided an ideal opening to the Latin American arms market. Some scholars also believe that Soviet support for the Peruvian military, like the close commercial partnership with Argentina, did exert some pressure on the Pinochet government in Chile.[29] Certainly the Peruvian buildup made Chile apprehensive, and tensions between the two countries ran high around the hundredth anniversary of the War of the Pacific. Although military visits and exchange between Peru and the USSR have been frequent, Peru has strenuously denied Chilean claims of Soviet influence in its armed forces.[30]

More recent Peruvian governments have also downplayed the importance of the military link with the Soviet Union. Attempting to diversify sources of supply and comply with the air force's request for additional weapons, the administration of Fernando Belaunde Terry approved the purchase of 25 French Mirage 2000s, 16 of which were scheduled for delivery in 1985. In the midst of Peru's worst economic recession in this century, the exorbitant cost of the original deal—some $700 million—shocked Peru's foreign creditors.[31] That year Peru also requested $50 million more in arms from the Soviet Union, a sale that included more helicopters and tanks.[32] In his inaugural address on July 28, 1985, President Alan García announced a reduction in defense spending, and Peru began talks with Chile and Ecuador aimed at ending their regional arms race. García also decided to reduce Belaunde's original order of Mirage 2000s from 25 to 12. Historically, however, disarmament proposals in Latin America are characterized by much rhetoric, but few concrete proposals. In 1985 Peru had received 6 MI-17 Hip-Hs in addition to a squadron of 16 MI-24 attack helicopters that arrived in 1984. In 1987, Peru purchased 15 AN-32 planes from the USSR at a cost of $84 million. All this indicates that Soviet military ties to Peru remain strong.

THE DIPLOMATIC AND ECONOMIC DIMENSION OF CHILEAN-SOVIET RELATIONS

Chile established diplomatic relations with the USSR near the end of World War II, on December 11, 1944. As the Cold War intensified, the government swung to the right, the Chilean Communist Party was outlawed, and in October 1947, Chile broke diplomatic relations with the USSR.[33] Relations between Chile and the Soviet Union were virtually nonexistent for the next decade and a half. Relations were reestablished in November 1964 after Christian Democrat Eduardo Frei was elected president, but no trade, financial, or technical agreements were signed until 1967.[34]

The Soviet Union warmly received the election of Salvador Allende as president in 1970, seeing in his triumph a vindication of the "peaceful road" to socialism. Allende, who was a socialist, was the candidate of *Unidad Popular* (UP), a coalition of leftist parties which included the Communists.

During the first year of UP government, the USSR advised Allende not to break with Chile's traditional economic partners, but instead to reduce its dependence gradually.[35] Unwilling to make too great a commitment to Chile, the Soviet Union deliberately kept its relations low-key. As relations with the United States became more difficult, on the other hand, the Allende government sought to strengthen Chile's association with other nations, particularly the socialist countries. During his campaign, Allende had pledged to reestablish ties with the Castro regime and to support ending the embargo on Cuba imposed by the OAS. True to his word in September 1970, Allende renewed diplomatic ties with Cuba, after which Castro made a month-long visit to Chile in November-December 1971. Diplomatic relations with other socialist countries followed.

When Chile nationalized its copper industry, Washington cut off U.S. credits and increased its support to the opposition. Forced to seek alternative sources of trade and finance, a high-level Chilean delegation visited various Soviet bloc countries (as well as China), gaining commitments from them to invest between $300–$400 million in Chile in the next six years. During its visit to the Soviet Union in May 1971, the delegation signed an agreement increasing Soviet credits to Chile. The USSR and Chile also agreed on opening commercial offices in Moscow and Santiago and paved the way for the creation of a Chilean-Soviet trade commission. As a result, trade did increase somewhat, but it was never all that significant since the credits were mainly linked to the purchase of Soviet machinery and equipment. Moreover, credits from the USSR were significantly less than those provided by China ($95 million) and East European countries ($65 million).[36] Although Soviet-Chilean relations warmed, and credits, as well as trade, increased, Moscow was still hesitant to make too great a commitment. When Salvador Allende went to the Soviet Union in late 1972 in search of more aid and additional lines of credit, he was politely turned down: the Soviets were willing to subsidize the Chilean experiment, but not to the same degree they had helped Cuba.

Between 1970 and 1973, Chile's total credits from the USSR amounted to approximately $350 million. However, this came within the framework of traditional Soviet foreign aid, providing credits for technical cooperation in fishing, housing construction, vehicles, mining, etc. Allende welcomed the moderate amount of aid, but Soviet hard currency assistance, which was of vital importance to purchase spare parts and food from its traditional suppliers, never reached the levels desired by the UP government. Moscow's attitude to Allende was characterized by restraint and political caution, and its diplomatic pragmatism was nearly devoid of ideological commitment.[37] The USSR was reluctant to commit massive resources to Chile, considering its government not to be "socialist" and, closer to the "Peruvian experiment" than to Cuba.[38] Moreover, Chile was geographically remote and had little to offer other than copper. Allende's three years in power also coincided with improved U.S.-Soviet relations rising from detente. Under these circumstances, the potential economic and political benefits of peaceful coexistence with the U.S. were more important than USSR-Chilean relations. When Allende sought greater emergency assistance, the country was already in such turmoil that the Soviets had little reason to believe that their aid would save the UP government.

BOLIVIA AND COLOMBIA'S RELATIONS WITH THE USSR

Diplomatic relations between Bolivia and the USSR were established in April 1945, but the two countries did not immediately exchange envoys. Not until nearly a quarter century later (in November 1969) were relations formalized and restored, with the exchange of ambassadors occurring in 1970. Soviet economic ties with Bolivia expanded after trade and techno-scientific agreements had been signed in June and August 1970. In 1971 both countries signed an agreement whereby the Soviets agreed to purchase tin and tin concentrate and to sell mining machinery and equipment to the Bolivians.[39] During the two short-lived military presidencies of Generals Alfredo Ovando (September 1969–October 1970) and Juan J. Torres (October 1970–August 1971), Bolivia took a surprising turn to the left, adopting a form of "military populism" influenced by the military experiment in Peru. Significantly, the fall of General Torres did not terminate Soviet willingness to honor its agreements. The Soviet Union subsequently provided credits for mining projects, particularly with COMIBOL, and signed agreements providing for joint Soviet-Bolivian exploration for oil and natural gas in the Andes as well as for Soviet assistance in the development of the zinc and tin industries.

Since 1971, relations with the East European countries have also made possible the extension of unilateral credit offers to Bolivia, some followed by general bilateral agreements and contracts for specific projects. Both the Soviets and East Europeans have pledged to extend technical and economic cooperation and are importing small amounts of nonferrous metals (including lead, wolfram, copper and zinc) from Bolivia.[40] Moscow's original high expectations of developing flourishing trade transactions with Bolivia were somewhat undermined by the country's extreme financial and economic crisis during the first half of the 1980s.

Like Bolivia, Colombia had a long hiatus in its relations with the Soviet Union, first established in 1935, but broken in 1948. They were not restored until January 1968. Despite the absence of formal relations, the Soviet Union has purchased Colombian coffee since 1959. Colombian exports diversified after 1967, and from 1968 until the mid-1970s, total trade between Colombia and the socialist countries showed some variation, oscillating between $46 million (1968), $66 million (1970) and $57 million (1973). Not until 1974, however, did trade begin to record a considerable increase.[41]

Since 1975, cooperation agreements with the USSR have been concluded in the area of economic, commercial, industrial, scientific, and technical cooperation. These agreements have provided for the supply of machinery and equipment, installation, exchange of patents, licenses, and technical information, supply of services and know-how, sending of experts or specialists, granting scholarships to Colombians, scientific exchange, participation in trade fairs, etc. The projects and areas of cooperation in which the USSR has been involved include the oil and gas industries, production of machine tools, iron and steel industries, coal, cellulose and paper, forestry industry, light industries, medical industries, pharmaceuticals, railway equipment, telecommunications, electricity, atomic power, fishing, harbor equipment, and agriculture.[42]

The most important undertaking for which the Soviet Union has provided economic and technical assistance is the Urra project involving the construction of two hydropower stations in the Upper Sinu river. This project involves a tripartite cooperation agreement with part of the equipment supplied by Western firms. The total cost of the project has been estimated to be $450 million, and the Soviets have agreed to provide one-third of the financing. The project will not only supply electricity to the area, but will irrigate 350,000 hectares of land.

PROMOTING SOVIET INTERESTS THROUGH THE COMMUNIST PARTIES AND THE LEFT

In the Andean region, as in much of Latin America, the Communist parties have been orthodox and pro-Moscow. They have constituted the oldest, most numerous, and strongest element in the Left. By the late 1940s, they had developed extensive influence in the labor movement, and later became the dominant political force therein, but the Communists have rarely been real contenders for national power. Factionalism has been one reason. As a result of the Sino-Soviet split and quarrels between the Soviet leadership and Fidel Castro over guerrilla activity, the Communist parties splintered in the early 1960s. Today dozens of "Communist" groups exist in Peru, Bolivia, and Colombia. Competing with the orthodox parties during the 1960s were numerous Maoist and Castroist organizations. Trotskyism, too, has been present in most Andean countries, but nowhere except in Chile (briefly in the 1930s, Bolivia in the early 1950s, and Peru in the 1970s), have they become a factor of significance in national politics.

The left has had periods of growth and decline in the Andean countries. Because its leaders have been quarrelsome and unwilling to compromise, particularly concerning international issues, the Left has not fared very well. Indeed, except for Chile in the late 1930s and again between 1970 and 1973, and perhaps in Peru at various times since 1980, the Left has been ineffectual. Revolutionary violence has been on the increase, not only in Chile, but also in other Andean nations under civilian leadership. Frustration in the left has led to the emergence of groups like *Sendero Luminoso* in Peru and M-19 in Colombia, but as the Peruvian and Colombian experiences show, terrorism does not necessarily spell an end to civilian government. Increased pressure due to debt payment obligations, economic recession, and increased political polarization have also provided the left with greater opportunities for exploitation.

Soviet Pragmatism and Caution as the Chilean Left Takes Power

The Chilean Communist Party (PCCh) has been a factor of importance in Chilean politics almost since its genesis in 1921, by which time it had already elected two deputies to the lower house of the Chilean congress. For over five decades the Communists have been an important element in the labor movement, and at times a key political force that participated in three government coalitions. The PCCh is one of the oldest and largest Communist parties in Latin America, claiming in 1973 to have 200,000 members.[43] The PCCh was and still is one of the most orthodox Communist parties of its type.[44] The Chilean Left has also included another party of importance, one which emerged in the 1930s as the result of the unification of several small socialist organizations: the Socialist Party of Chile (PSCh). Despite differences with its mercurial rival and often-times reluctant socialist ally, the PCCh joined the PSCh and the Radical Party (among others) in forming the Popular Unity (UP) coalition in the late 1960s.

The election in Chile of a Marxist president was the first such event to occur in any country in the Western Hemisphere. Never before had such attempt been made, and it was only three years after Ché Guevara had failed in his efforts to organize a guerrilla movement in Bolivia. Although the Allende government was not a socialist regime, it attempted to lay down the foundations for building socialism without a violent revolution and through parliamentary rules. As noted earlier, Moscow responded favorably to developments in Chile because these confirmed that the "peaceful road" policy could be successfully implemented.[45]

Within the first coalition cabinet appointed by Allende, Communist representatives were given the ministries of Labor, Finance, and Public Works. Two years later, as the economic crisis worsened, the PCCh also received the Economics portfolio. After his first year in power, Allende encountered growing opposition from both the Left and the Right, and the policy of the PCCh was to seek compromise with the centrist Christian Democrats. Allende had been elected in a three-man field with less than 40 percent of the vote, and the UP coalition did not control a majority in the Congress. Furthermore, he faced strong U.S. pressure. The Nixon administration had begun to use political and economic coercion when the Allende government recognized Cuba, nationalized American-owned mining companies, carried out sweeping agrarian reform, and granted political asylum to left-wing exiles from all over Latin America.[46]

By mid-1973, the UP was severely divided. The Socialists and the pro-Cuban Revolutionary Leftist Movement (MIR) proclaimed there was not alternative but revolutionary armed struggle. Although the MIR was no part of the UP coalition, it played a significant role and offered its critical support to the Allende administration. Formed in 1965 mainly by dissident members of the Socialist Party, the MIR had been particularly active in the universities between 1970 and 1973, becoming as critical of the PCCh as it was of its declared enemies on the right. After 1971, the MIR had become increasingly critical of the UP coalition, forming a "People's Assembly" in Concepción to supersede the "reactionary" National Congress. Allende and the PCCh rejected their arguments, blaming the ultra-left for much of the political chaos and accusing it of "adventurism."

After the right-wing military coup which overthrew the Allende regime, Chile's relations with the USSR and most of the socialist countries were cut off. Ironically, although Chile under the Pinochet regime was one of Latin America's staunchest anti-Communist governments, it maintained normal diplomatic and commercial relations with Romania and the People's Republic of China. Romania, which has insisted on its independence from Moscow, maintained ties to Chile to protect investments made during the Allende administration.[47] China, too, refused to follow the Soviet lead in breaking relations even after the Pinochet government replaced Allende's ambassador to the People's Republic with a lower ranking official.

In September 1973, all parties which had formed the UP were banned and in March 1977, the military decreed all political parties to be "in recess." Marxist cadres went underground or into exile. The PSCh was hard hit by repression and weakened by its own internal divisions. The PCCh was also driven underground, but its well-structured and disciplined organization gave it the ability to survive. After seven years in clandestinity, the PCCh undertook a major strategic shift in September 1980, endorsing "all forms of struggle," both violent and nonviolent.

Frustrated by Pinochet's refusal to negotiate a return to democracy, civilian leaders from a broad spectrum of political backgrounds have agreed to support a campaign aimed at destabilizing the regime through civil disobedience. In 1983 they formed the Democratic Alliance, a broad coalition which included the Right, moderates, and even some socialists. For its party, the PCCh joined a Socialist Party faction headed by Clodomiro Almeyda and the MIR to form the Popular Democratic Movement (MDP). In 1984, a group calling itself the Manuel Rodríguez

Patriotic Front (FPMR) appeared. Although the front has no official links to the CP, it is said to receive support from the PCCh and has claimed responsibility for a number of violent acts, including an attempted assassination of Pinochet. With the MIR, the FPMR is one of the most secretive Chilean organizations.[48]

The PCP and Turbulence in the Peruvian Left

The *Partido Socialista del Peru* (PSP) was founded in 1928 by José Carlos Mariátegui, but on Comintern orders changed its name to the Communist Party in 1930. Mariategui, one of Latin America's most original Marxist thinkers, advanced several theses about the "Indian question" at the Buenos Aires Conference of Communist Parties in 1929, but his views were criticized as "petty-bourgeois romanticist," and labeled "Trotskyist." After his death in April 1930, the PCP succumbed to the organizational and ideological control of the Soviet Union. The party has always been a minority element in Peruvian politics, exerting some influence within the labor movement through the *Confederación General de los Trabajadores del Peru* (CGTP) which it helped found in 1929.[49] Its principal and much more successful rival has been the *Alianza Popular Revolucionaria Américana* (APRA) which espoused a radical, nationalist, populist line. The PCP suffered a sharp blow in 1964 when the party split into pro-Soviet and pro-Chinese factions. Subsequently, there have emerged several pro-Chinese splinter groups, some of them using the PCP name.[50]

In 1968, the military regime of Juan Velasco Alvarado took power. The new government legalized the CGTP again (the organization brought together 19 federations and 66 trade unions, and its leadership was predominantly from the pro-Moscow PCP, now known as the PC Unidad, and it soon became the most important force in organized labor.[51] As state-to-state relations were established with the USSR in February 1969, the PCP threw its support to the military. At first it strongly favored the "anti-imperialist actions of the military government" and the "revolutionary process aimed at building socialism."[52] However, after 1975 the party redefined its position. With Morales Bermúdez now in power, the PCP argued that the "second phase" of the military government was moving towards "bourgeois '*desarrollismo*.'"[53]

Despite general Soviet enthusiasm for Peru's "progressive" military during its first phase (1968–1975), some Soviet analysts remained skeptical about the prospects of a military led transformation. Others expressed distress that the Peruvian armed forces were acting in a corporatist and technocratic manner. Velasco's fall from power in 1975 led to a reassessment of the role of the military and a downplaying of its revolutionary potential. According to one scholar, at first Moscow believed that the palace coup reflected merely a change of personnel rather than ideology. By 1977, however, the USSR did realize that Velasco's fall signalled more than change of leadership.[54]

The PCP has had mixed success since the return of democracy to Peru. In 1980 the conservative candidate, Fernando Belaunde Terry, received a resounding electoral endorsement. The Left had failed to present a common front following a squabble over seats in Congress. However, Belaunde's popularity soon vanished because of the inability of his administration to deal with economic depression. Benefiting more directly from the economic decline was APRA and its leader, Alan García, who was elected president in 1985. Despite setbacks, the PCP increased its electoral presence during the early 1980s. It became an important component of the *Izquierda Unida* (IU), the largest electoral alliance of leftist parties and groups yet formed.[55] In the 1983 and 1986 municipal elections, the IU emerged as the second political force in the country behind APRA. The main source of unity for the IU has been Alfonso Barrantes Lingan, who as an "independent," became its president. From 1983 to 1986 Barrantes was mayor of Lima, and he ran as the IU presidential candidate in the 1985 election. The leftist coalition increased its respectability and legitimacy with the electorate by championing the cause of the *sectores populares* in the urban areas and among unionized workers.

More problematic for the PCP and its leftist allies has been the emergence of *Sendero Luminoso* (Shining Path). The *Sendero* phenomenon has come about as a result of the frustrated modernization process and the socioeconomic decomposition of Peruvian society in recent years. According to one observer, "*Sendero*'s decision to begin armed action in 1980 in isolation from the rest of the left corresponded to its belief that conditions for revolution existed and that the road to Communism in Peru lay through a 'prolonged popular war'."[56] During the last seven years, *Sendero*'s guerrilla campaign and the repression it provoked have created a state of fear and confusion that threatens the viability of parliamentary democracy in Peru.

The origins of *Sendero* date to 1970 when the national leadership of the pro-Chinese PCP (*Bandera Roja*) expelled Abimael Guzmán, along with a number of cadres who later formed the PCP (*Sendero Luminoso*).

The group's nucleus was drawn from student organizations based in the Ayacucho area, particularly from within the University. Run according to a tightly organized cell structure, over the course of the 1970s *Sendero* became increasingly militant and dogmatic.[57]

Although the administration of Fernando Belaunde Terry (1980–85) repeatedly described *Sendero* as part of a "foreign conspiracy" with links to Cuba, China, and the USSR, it did not substantiate these assertions. *Sendero* is unique in that it is not aligned politically or economically to any foreign power. In fact, it has bombed the American, Soviet, Chinese, and Cuban embassies in Lima. *Sendero* has also denounced the current Chinese leadership and Peru's Marxist groups, but has proclaimed support for the "Shanghai Gang of Four" in slogans painted on walls. The IU coalition, and particularly the pro-Soviet PCP, have consistently rejected the terrorist methods of *Sendero* and its supporters. This kind of action, they argue, only erodes popular support for the domestic options that are currently available under the García administration. For the mainstream left, the cause of violence is rooted in sociopolitical problems and the solution is primarily political, not military.

Sendero's actions express a Pol Pot-type of communism. Although its goal is to seize power by force, *Sendero* is a very different kind of group from those which have taken up arms in other Latin American countries. Its orientation is a mixture of radical and messianic fanaticism, and it has mechanically concluded from Mariátegui's analysis of the 1920s that Peru is still a "semi-feudal" and "semi-colonial" society.[58] From this characterization, and also from an adherence to Maoism, *Sendero* views the main force of revolutionary change to be the peasantry, and sees itself as a vanguard of this revolutionary situation in Peru. As *Sendero* does not believe in the process of formal democracy, it is the only group which has abstained from the elections since 1978. *Sendero* characterized the military governments of Velasco Alvarado (1968–75) and Morales Bermúdez (1975–80) as "fascist" regimes engaged in the construction of a corporate state the Belaunde administration (1980–85) was a continuation of fascism behind a "mascarade of apparent democracy." Nor was the election of APRA leader Alan García as president in 1985 considered a change by *Sendero*.

Sendero's strategy of 'prolonged popular war' has involved armed propaganda and sabotage operations, the destabilization of the political system, and the launching of guerrilla war. The recurrence of this type of violence, however, is not exclusively the work of *Sendero*; it has been reinforced by other extreme left groups committed to armed struggle.[59]

These groups have been responsible for a number of isolated terrorist attacks; in 1986 alone, over 2,600 terrorist attacks were recorded.[60]

TRENDS AND PROSPECTS IN RELATIONS BETWEEN THE USSR AND THE ANDEAN COUNTRIES

Since the 1960s, the Soviet Union has enjoyed expanded contact with Peru and other Andean countries, with the concomitant opportunity to increase its presence in the region. This was possible because the Andean countries began displaying a new self-confidence and assertiveness in the late 1960s and early 1970s. Despite disdain for the Soviet system, the Andean nations sought expanded ties with the Soviet Union because the new relationship provided them with a larger and more independent role in world affairs and gave them room to maneuver and potential bargaining leverage vis-à-vis the United States. Along with the expansion of diplomatic ties, there was an expansion of trade. Commercial ties with the USSR have enabled the Andean countries to expand and diversify imports and exports, as well as obtain financing and technical assistance. Even though some Andean governments later turned anti-Communist, relations have remained cordial because of common interest. In this sense the Soviet Union has assumed few political and strategic risks in the area.

In their diplomatic pragmatism, the Soviets have a preference for "progressive" and "anti-imperialist" governments such as those of Velasco Alvarado and Salvador Allende. However, in Peru the Soviets were never able to translate arms sales into significant political influence. In Chile, the Soviets proceeded cautiously without getting too involved, but the UP experiment ended in disaster and only confirmed Soviet doubts about the viability of the "peaceful road to socialism."

While Peru and other Andean democracies favor Soviet trade and aid, the bulk of their economic ties remain outside the Soviet bloc. Economic relations with CMEA countries will continue to serve the Andean region's interest. These relations have yielded certain economic advantages for the Andean countries by expanding export markets and providing a comfortable trade surplus. In addition, Andean countries have benefited from technical assistance in the construction and training of industrial projects. Soviet aid has also been beneficial, even though it is by no means extensive and is often tied to the purchase of goods and services. Overall trade volume with the USSR still remains low, and despite lip service paid to the postulates of the New International Economic Order, the Andean countries are primarily commodity producers and the Soviets exporters of machinery. The expansion of cultural diplomacy with its emphasis on international exchange of scholars and artists (and, as is shown in Table 12.2, particularly involving students) have also strengthened Soviet ties with these countries.

Relations between the Andean countries and the Soviet Union have undergone modifications, with internal developments in each country. During the 1960s and early 1970s, the transformation of traditional political institutions, coupled with a resurgence of nationalism in the region, led to the emergence of left-leaning regimes. The coups which ousted José Torres in Bolivia (1971), Salvador Allende in Chile (1973), and Juan Velasco Alvarado in Peru (1975) eroded, and in some ways reversed, the nationalist developmentalist projects. The fall of Allende was a bitter disappointment to Moscow. By the mid-1970s, too, the climate for foreign investment had changed as the Andean Pact rules were eased.

A traditional vehicle for Soviet policy has been the orthodox Communist parties, but these have had a limited influence on the national politics of the Andean countries. Only in Chile and Bolivia have they participated in the national government. The attitude of the CPs has varied from country to country. While the Chilean and

TABLE 12.2
Students From the Andean Countries in the USSR and Eastern Europe, 1972–1984

	1972	*1977*	*1982*	*1984*
Bolivia	205	205	105	245
Colombia	395	910	2,390	2,140
Ecuador	320	755	825	935
Chile	NA	NA	NA	NA
Peru	260	525	825	1,185
Venezuela	110	85	20	40
TOTAL	1,290	2,480	4,165	4,545

Source: U.S. General Accounting Office, *U.S. and Soviet Bloc Training of Latin American and Caribbean Students: Considerations in Developing Future U.S. Programs*, GAO/NSIAD-84-109, August 16, 1984, p. 5. Data for 1984 taken from U.S. Department of State, *Warsaw Pact Economic Aid to Non-Communist LDCs, 1984*, May 1986, p. 17.

Colombian Communist parties are engaging in "all forms of struggle, both violent and non-violent," in Bolivia (until recently) they formed part of the Siles Suaso government coalition. In Peru, the CP holds several seats in Parliament and participates in the IU. In the absence of strong Communist parties, it is government-to government-relations which have prevailed in the consolidation of a stable Soviet presence in the region.

Soviet relations with the Andean countries have entered a new phase as the latter countries are increasingly overburdened by their foreign debts to the West and internal economic crises. The debt crisis reinforces the need to preserve economic relations with the USSR because of increasing difficulties in placing exports in western markets. But, to take only one example, as the Peruvian government under García attempts to diversify international alliances, it is unlikely to find export earnings to be sufficient to increase further purchases from the USSR. While García has been praised by the Soviets for his attitude on debt renegotiation, the Soviet Union has welcomed the restructuring of their share of Peru's debt under a barter arrangement. Much of the increase in Peruvian exports during 1985–87 is, in fact, part of this deal. Declining oil prices, foreign exchange constraints, and geographical distance will further restrict trade between the Andean nations and the Soviet bloc. Furthermore, most of the Andean countries are faced with a growing insurgency at home which will probably continue to worsen. Setbacks for a return to democracy in Chile, and the obvious uncertainties about long-term prospects and developments in the Andean region, are factors likely to work in favor of the Soviet Union. Despite the limited contacts between the Andean countries and the USSR, relations have proved useful to both sides.

NOTES

1 For a discussion on foreign investment regulations, see Jessica D. Einhorn, *Expropriation Politics* (New York: Lexington Heath & Co., 1974); Shane Hunt, "Direct Foreign Investment in Peru: New Rules for an Old Game," in Abraham Lowenthal, ed., *The Peruvian Experiment* (Princeton: Princeton University Press, 1975); Paul Sigmund, *Multinationals in Latin America: The Politics of Nationalization* (Madison: University of Wisconsin Press, 1980); Lynn K. Mytelko, *Regional Development in a Global Economy: The Multinational Corporation, Technology and Andean Integration* (New Haven: Yale University Press, 1970).

2 On the Nonaligned Movement see Peter Willetts, *The Non Aligned Movement: The Origins of a Third World Alliance* (London: Frances Pinter, 1978) and William LeoGrande, "The Evolution of the Non-Aligned Movement," *Problems of Communism*, 29 (January–February 1980), pp. 35–52.

3 For the Soviet view, see, N.S. Leonov, "Peru: Novaia Rol' Voennykh," *Latinskaia Amerika* 4 (1971); Yuri Zubritsky, "Por el camino de la lucha y la esperanza," *América*

Latina, 2:22 (1979), pp. 53–61; Anna Matlina, "El imperialismo y la 'revolución de los militares,'" *Ibid.*, pp. 62–73; Jan Prazsky, "Armies Against the People and Armies with the People," *World Marxist Review*, 10 (October 1970), pp. 52–57; B. Ponomarev, "Topical Problems of the Theory of the Revolutionary Process," *Kommunist*, 15 (October 1971), pp. 63–72; V. Bushuyev, "New Horizons in Latin America," *International Affairs*, 5 (1973), pp. 35–41.

4 For an interesting analysis, see Cole Blasier, *The Giant's Rival: The USSR and Latin America* (Pittsburgh, University of Pittsburgh Press, 1983); Leon Gouré and Morris Rothenberg, *Soviet Penetration in Latin America* (Miami: Center for Advanced International Studies, University of Miami, 1975).

5 V. Listov and Y. Korionov writing for *Pravda*, June 24 and December 1970, respectively, hailed the Peruvian military for its "progressive" and "anti-imperialist" positions. The military in Bolivia was praised for similar reasons.

6 USSR Academy of Sciences' *América Latina: Estudios de Cientí/ficos Soviéticos* (8), "Relaciones Sociéticos-Latinoamericanas (recopilación documentos), I (Moscow: Redacción Ciencias Sociales Contempuraneas, 1981), p. 204.

7 Ministerio de Economíca, Finanzas y Comercio, *Estadística de Comercio Exterior del Peru*, 1968 to 1975. The data cited is from the Soviet source, the Peruvian figures show a slightly higher volume of trade.

8 Enrique Estremadoyro, "Relaciones económicas del Perú con los país miembros del Consejo de Ayuda Mutua Económica," CEPAL, E/CEPAL/ proy 4/R.9, November 1979; UNCTAD, "Trends, Policies and Prospects in Trade and Economic Cooperation between Peru and the Socialist Countries of Eastern Europe," a study prepared by the UNCTAD Secretariat, TD/B/856, July 1981.

9 *El Peruano* (Lima), July 7, 1980; *The New York Times*, August 28, 1970.

10 See, "Soviet Prommashexport Enterprise and the Ministry of Fisheries Sign Contract for Construction of Paita Fishing Complex," in T. Stephen Cheston and Bernard Loeffke, *Aspects of Soviet Policy in Latin America* (New York: MSS Information Corporation, 1974).

11 A.I. Sizonenko and A.V. Bobrovnikov, *Soviet Soiuzov i Latinskaia Amerika Segodnia* (Moscow: Akademia Nauka SSSR, 1978), p. 44.

12 Anatoli Olshany, "El Perú y los países miembros del CAME," *América Latina*, 4 (1974), pp.52–59.

13 Olshany, A., *Ibid.*

14 For instance, in July 1984, President Fernando Belaunde received heavy-duty machinery (bulldozers, earth moving tractors, and several loaders) donated by the Soviet Union worth $500,000; *La República* (Lima), July 11, 1984.

15 Carlos Muñiz, "Perú-URSS, 10 años de las buenas relaciones," *América Latina*, 4 (1974), pp. 52–59.

16 "Serán mas amplios los vínculos culturales," Interview with the Peruvian Ambassador to the USSR, René Hooper López, *América Latina*, 1 (1986), pp. 49–50.

17 U.S. State Department, *Warsaw Pact Economic Aid to Non-Communist LDCs, 1984* (Washington D.C.: Government Printing Office, May, 1986).

18 "Fishing agreement with USSR extended by 3 years," Foreign Broadcast Information Service Latin America (FBIS-LAM) 171, September 4, 1986; *El Comercio* (Lima), September 30, 1986.

19 *Expreso* (Lima), November 19, 1985, p. 2; *El Comercio* May 10, 12, 24, June 4, 6, 10, 23, November 14, 26, December 17, 1985; *Gente* (Lima), May 5, 1988.

20 *The Andean Report* (Lima), June 1984; *El Nacional* (Lima), March 26, 1986; *El comercio*, September 8, 1986.

21 *The Andean Report*, May 1985, p. 65.

22 *The Washington Post*, August 26, 1985, *The Andean Report*, June 1984 and May 1985; and Woy-Hasleton, "Peru," in *Yearbook in International Communist Affairs 1985*, (Palo Alto: Hoover Institution Press, 1985).

23 *The Andean Report,* April 1988, p. 89; *1/2 de Cambio* (Lima), February 1, 1988; *El Peruano,* February 7, March 3, 1988.

24 Ibid., *1/2 de Cambio; El comercio,* January 20, 1988.

25 Luigi Einaudi, "Peruvian Military Relations with the United States," in Daniel Sharp, ed., *U.S. Foreign Policy in Peru* (Austin: University of Texas Press, 1970).

26 There are frequent major discrepancies between three main sources: the Peruvian government, the Stockholm International Peace Research Institute (SIPRI), and U.S. Arms Control and Disarmament Agency (ACDA). Thus, SIPRI puts Peru's arms imports between 1975 and 1979 at 20 percent of Latin America's total—up from 14 percent in the preceding year period; ACDA claims 24 percent in 1974–1978. For the same periods, SIPRI claims the Soviet Union supplied 41 percent of all of Peru's arms imports; ACDA puts the figure at 65 percent. ACDA estimates that the total Peruvian arms supplies from the Soviet Union by 1980 had reached $900 million. See ACDA, *World Military Expenditures,* p. 162; *SIPRI Yearbook, 1980,* p. 115.

27 José Encinas del Pando, "The Role of Military Expenditure in the Development Process: Peru, a Case Study 1950–1980," *Ibero Americana: Nordic Journal of Latin American Studies,* 12:1–2 (1983).

28 ACDA, *World Military Expenditures and Arms Transfers 1971–1980* (Washington, D.C.: Government Printing Office, 1980), p. 12.

29 Aldo Cesar Vacs, *Discreet Partners: Argentina and the USSR since 1917* (Pittsburgh: University of Pittsburgh Press, 1984).

30 del Pando, "Military Expenditures"; *The New York Times,* April 16, 1975.

31 *Latin American Weekly Report* (London), January 25, 1985; *Latin American Regional Report – The Andean Group* (London), October 5, 1984.

32 *The Washington Post,* July 27, 1984.

33 Memoria Ministerio de Relaciones Exteriores, República de Chile, Correspondencia del año 1944, pp. 121–25; 1947, pp. 60–69; 1964, pp. 43–45 as cited by Jorge Vera Castillo, "Relaciones soviéticas-chilenas," separata *América Latina-Union Soviética,* 2:2 (December 1984–January 1985).

34 Carlos Muñiz O., *La URSS y América Latina* (Lima: Francisco Mancloa Editores, 1968).

35 J.S. Nogee and J.W. Sloan, "Allende's Chile and the Soviet Union: A Policy Lesson for Latin American Nations Seeking Autonomy," *Journal of Interamerican Studies and World Affairs,* 21:3 (August 1979).

36 Isabel Turrent, *La Union Soviética en América Latina: el caso de la Unidad Popular chilena, 1970–1973* (Mexico, D.F.: El Colegio de México, 1985).

37 Nogee and Sloan, "Allende's Chile."

38 For more on the Soviet discussions of these issues, see the chapter by Edmé Domínguez. See also Joan Barth Urban, "Contemporary Soviet Perspectives on Revolutions in the West," *Orbis,* 19:4 (Winter, 1976); Augusto Varas, "La Unión Soviética en la política exterior de América Latina: los casos de Chile, Argentina, Brazil y Peru," Documento de Trabajo 158 (Santiago de Chile: FLACSO), 1982.

39 "Trade Agreements between the USSR and the Republic of Bolivia," *Foreign Trade* (Moscow), 1 (1971).

40 *Boletín Informativo Semanal,* Ministerio de Relaciones Exteriores y Culto, La Paz, 152, October 4, 1983.

41 UNCTAD, "Trends, Policies and Prospects in Trade and Economic Cooperation between Colombia and the Socialist Countries of Eastern Europe," a study prepared by the UNCTAD Secretariat, TD/B/814, August 12, 1980.

42 Marta Luisa Gómez, "Las relaciones económicas de Colombia con los países miembros del Consejo de Asistencia Mutua Económica (CAME)," E/Cepal/proy. 4/5.2, November 1979, and Anatoli Olshani, "Colaboración económica y comercial de los paises miembros del CAME y Colombia," *América Latina* 3 (1982).

43 Carmelo Furci, *The Chilean Communist Party and the Road to Socialism* (London: Zed Books, 1984).

44 During the Sino-Soviet split, quarrels between Castro and the USSR on revolutionary strategy, the Soviet invasion of Czechoslovakia, and the crushing of Solidarity in Poland, the Communist Party of Chile has sided with Moscow.
45 Robert J. Alexander, *The Tragedy of Chile* (Westport: Greenwood Press, 1978).
46 Paul Sigmund, "The USSR, Cuba and the Revolution in Chile," in Robert H. Donaldson, ed., *The Soviet Union in the Third World: Successes and Failure* (Boulder: Westview Press, 1981).
47 Victor C. Dahl, "The Soviet Bloc Response to the Downfall of Salvador Allende," *Inter-American Economic Affairs*, 30:2 (Autumn, 1976).
48 "Chile," *Yearbook of International Communist Affairs 1986* (Palo Alto: Hoover Institution Press, 1986).
49 Denis Sulmont, *El movimiento obrero peruano (1890–1980)* (Lima: Tarea, 1982); José Arico, ed., *Mariátegui y los orígenes del marxismo latinoamericano* (Mexico: Cuadernos de Pasado y Presente 60, 1978).
50 Ricardo Letts, *La Izquierda peruana, organizaciones y tendencias* (Lima: Mozca Azul Editores, 1981).
51 D. Sulmont, *El movimiento obrero.*
52 Jorge del Prado, "Is There a Revolution in Peru?," *World Marxist Review*, 14:1 (January 1971), pp. 17–27; and "The Revolution Continues," *World Marxist Review* 16:1 (January 1973), pp. 64–71.
53 Jorge del Prado, "A Difficult Stage in the Process of Change," *World Marxist Review*, 20:12 (December 1977) pp. 88–95.
54 Ilya Paizel, "The Evolution of Soviet Perceptions of Latin America during the Brezhnev Years," Ph.D. dissertation, School of Advanced International Studies, the Johns Hopkins University, 1987, p. 277.
55 Rafael Roncagliolo, *?Quien Ganó?: Elecciones 1931–80* (Lima: DESCO, 1980).
56 Michael Reid, *Peru: Paths to Poverty* (London: Latin American Bureau, 1985), p. 108.
57 On the origins of Sendero see, Carlos Ivan Degregori, "Sendero Luminoso": I. Los hondos y mortales desencuentros, II. La lucha armada y utopía autoritaria," Documentos de Trabajo No. 4 y No. 6, Instituto de Estudios Peruanos, 1986; David Scott Palmer, "The Sendero Luminoso Rebellion in Rural Peru," in Georges Fauriol ed., *Latin American Insurgencies* (Washington D.C.: Georgetown University Center for Strategic and International Studies and the National Defense University, 1985); Eugenio Chang-Rodríguez, *Opciones políticas peruanas* (Trujillo: Editorial Normas Legales, 1987)
58 See the special section on *Sendero Luminoso* in *NACLA: Report on the Americas*, June 1986; see also Manuel Jesús Granados, "El PCP Sendero Luminoso: aproximaciones y su ideología," *Socialismo y Participación 37*, Marzo, 1987; Cynthia McClintock, "Why Peasants Rebel: The Case of Peru's Sendero Luminoso," *World Politics*, 37 (1984); Raúl Gonzalez, "Para entender a Sendero," *Que Hacer*, 42 (August–September 1986).
59 In the highlands there is PCP-Puka Llacta ('Red Land' in Quechua) and in Lima there are two armed groups that unified in December 1986: the Tupac Amaru Revolutionary Movement (MRTA) and the MIR (Cuarta Etapa).
60 *Caretas* (Lima), December 29, 1986.

Conclusion

Eusebio Mujal-León

The last thirty years have witnessed a slow but steady expansion in the Soviet Union's interest, presence, and influence in Latin America. Since the late 1970s, developments in Central America and the Caribbean Basin have provided most of the fuel for controversy and debate about this process but, as the preceding chapters clearly indicate, the range and scope of Soviet initiatives have grown significantly throughout the continent.

Cautious and opportunistic, the Soviet Union has employed a broad array of policy instruments in its relations with Latin America. At the state-to-state level, these have included political/diplomatic initiatives as well as trade and aid mechanisms. Within individual countries, the Soviet Union has also sought to extend its influence in the region through its relationship with Communist parties as well as with the trade union and university front organizations controlled or influenced by them. Beginning the late 1970s, there were also increased contacts with and support for (mediated and funneled through Cuba) more radical movements, especially in Central America and the Caribbean as well as, more recently, in Chile.

The Soviet Union has clearly distinguished between different Latin American areas and subregions in its elaboration of strategy, in its emphasis on different instruments, and in its choice of tactics. At one end stands Cuba, a plenary member of the Soviet bloc. Its integration allowed Fidel Castro to claim a special relationship with the Soviet Union, to receive massive subsidies and aid, and—particularly in the late 1970s—to bask in the limelight of its prominent "internationalist" assignments. On the other hand, this process also reduced Cuba's room to maneuver and paved the way for active Soviet involvement in Cuban domestic and foreign policy choices. From this perspective, Cuba is in a much different category than any other Latin American country. The dynamics of intra-bloc alliance politics and international patron–client relations stand at the core of its relationship with the Soviet Union. And, if we are to judge from Soviet reticence toward Nicaraguan efforts to join the Council for Mutual Economic Assistance (CMEA), it will not soon be displaced from its unique position.

Cuba and the Castro regime have a special place in Soviet strategy and policy. The island stands astride a strategically vital area. Its leader has his own foreign policy agenda, but as Castro's freedom to operate has shrunk and domestic economic exigencies have compelled him toward normalizing relations with many Latin American countries whose governments he had earlier vituperated and tried to overthrow, Castro has grudgingly accepted his place in the "international" division of labor. That he has tried to carve a special niche for himself in the Non-Aligned Movement (NAM) or has pursued his own (domestic and foreign policy) interests while displaying "internationalist solidarity" in Angola—to take two of the most prominent examples—should not obscure Castro's growing dependence on the Soviet Union. This is most keenly felt in the economic sphere, where Cuba, whose economy could not survive but for large infusions of Soviet aid, has been assigned and cannot in the foreseeable future escape the role of sugar and nickel producer. In the realm of foreign policy, the possibility of autonomous action has increased as the 1980s have worn on, but even here economic and diplomatic exigencies (not to mention the assertive presence of the Reagan Administration) have dictated greater caution in Cuba's policies toward other Latin American countries. The result has been a convergence between Soviet and Cuban foreign policies and increased coordination in their approaches to the region.

Soviet policies toward other Latin American countries must be analyzed from a rather different perspective. At the core of Soviet policy has been a modified and updated version of "geographic fatalism." Viewed through this prism, Latin America is an area where the United States, given its geographical proximity and extensive political and economic ties, has a "natural" and easily exercised, albeit no longer unquestioned, hegemonic advantage. Change in foreign alignment and domestic orientation has been possible (this, Fidel Castro demonstrated and so may the Nicaraguan Revolution), but such processes have been neither easy nor especially likely. Moreover, although Soviet capabilities have increased enormously over the past three decades, they still do not match those of the United States in the region.

From the Soviet point of view, however, a silver lining has existed in this cloud and is found in the conflictual nature of the U.S. relationship with Latin America. Anti-Americanism—whether expressed by revolutionary and/or nationalist elites—is the permanent price that the United States must pay for its hegemony in the region. Such conflicts erode American influence and prestige, but they do not always or even often allow for a necessary and rapid expansion of Soviet influence. There is an ebb and flow to Soviet optimism about developments in Latin America (in the Caribbean and Central America, the euphoria which followed the Nicaraguan Revolution gave way, for example, to pessimism after the October 1983 invasion of Grenada), but the foundation of Soviet policy has been to take prudent advantage of situations that develop and to encourage those trends that whittle American influence. While caution has been a hallmark of Soviet policy in Latin America, it should certainly not be interpreted as a sign of disinterest or passivity. Granted other regions of the world (Eastern and Western Europe, East Asia, and the Middle East) have had more direct significance to immediate Soviet security interests, but over the last three decades Latin America has assumed an increasingly important place in Soviet calculations, not least because of its unique relationship with and relevance to the Soviet Union's foremost global competitor.

Uniform in seeking to diminish American influence, Soviet policy toward Latin America has also been affected by the diverse circumstances and opportunities found in the region. Among those factors that have conditioned Soviet policies toward a given country are the fragility of political institutions, the degree of fragmentation on the Left and the strength of the Communist party, the importance that the USSR attaches to commercial exchanges, its potential for an "independent" foreign policy, its political/strategic significance for the United States, and the range of realistic options that American policymakers have in responding to developments there.

As the chapters in this volume indicate, one aspect of Soviet policy has been to expand state-to-state diplomatic and economic relations. Although this effort has been ecumenical, throughout the 1980s Moscow has paid special attention to the larger, more developed (and capitalist) countries of the hemisphere such as Argentina, Brazil,

Mexico, and Peru. These are countries whose political structures have proved relatively stable and where the prospects for a fragmented and organizationally weak Left have not been great. They are also key regional players whose resources and ambitions have created the potential for disputes with the United States and whose policy choices and alignments can also have an important impact on adjoining countries (Bolivia, Ecuador, and Uruguay). An expanded economic relationship has also been on the agenda. So far, however, trade exchanges have not matched Soviet expectations or hopes, and the USSR has had to accept large commercial deficits in order to sustain the relationship. In a more positive vein, the bulk of Soviet trade with Latin America—which grew from 60 million rubles to 2.5 billion rubles between 1960 and 1987—has been with these countries.

Central America and the Caribbean Basin have provided the other major reference points for Soviet policy. The area is strategically vital to the United States, which has been more willing to intervene militarily than to adopt measures to encourage economic and social development there. Most states in the region are characterized by their vulnerability to external political and economic pressures as well as by the fragility of their domestic institutions. There are also two governments sympathetic to Soviet objectives in the area. Cuba is a "regional influential" with its own foreign policy agenda but also willing (and eager) to serve as a conduit and intermediary for Moscow. Nicaragua, which now appears to have weathered the challenge from the Reagan administration, has provided logistical and other support for insurgent movements in various Central American countries. Strengthening the hand of the radical Left in the region have been the successful efforts—often under Cuban aegis or with its encouragement—to forge political/military fronts in El Salvador, Guatemala, and Honduras. The result has been a cauldron of instability where the Soviet Union, with little direct involvement, has seen its influence grow.

Soviet interest and activities in Latin America are likely to grow over the next decade. Encouraging this trend will be the deepening shift from bipolar to multipolar competition in the international system. The resulting fluidity in alliance patterns will encourage Latin American countries and elites to press forward with their efforts to diversify their political and economic dependence on the United States. Since the late 1970s, in a development that has attested to the pluralization of the international system as well as to the realities of its interdependence, numerous extracontinental actors (Japan and Western European countries, parties, and the political internationals) have become active in the region. The Falklands/Malvinas War and the debt crisis have strained the foundations of the interamerican system. The first decisively weakened the idea that the United States was a natural member of the pan-American community and has given impetus to various efforts at achieving greater intraregional political coordination. A prominent example in this regard has been the efforts to refashion the Organization of American States (OAS) into a purely Latin American organization. For its part, the debt crisis affirmed Latin America's economic vulnerability and dependence on an international financial system which, properly or not, is still widely perceived as dominated by the United States. Although in the short-term the debt crisis has not advanced regional integration and economic cooperation, it has encouraged Latin American elites to think seriously about those processes. The formation of the Cartagena Group and the more recent economic integration agreements between Argentina and Brazil represent important first steps in this regard.

The redirection of Soviet foreign and domestic policies currently being engineered by Mikhail Gorbachev should also encourage Moscow to deepen its engagement with Latin America. The ultimate scope of these changes (whether they are a sign of profound weakness or represent only an effort to *réculer pour mieux sauter*) is very much a matter of debate and conjecture.

Notwithstanding these uncertainties, there can be little doubt that a new era has opened in Soviet politics since Gorbachev assumed the post of CPSU Secretary General in March 1985, and one of its consequences has been a much more dynamic and, in a certain way, unpredictable, foreign policy. Its touchstone has been the primacy accorded domestic modernization and economic development. Several of Gorbachev's predecessors (and, most notably, Yuri Andropov) had openly referred to the importance of domestic priorities and to the Soviet Union's limited ability and obligation to provide aid to its allies and clients. But only under Gorbachev has the economic balance-sheet been so starkly drawn ("The years of stagnation [the Brezhnev era] brought the country to the brink of economic crisis," the theses presented to the 19th Party Conference in June 1988 declared),[1] and the urgency of domestic economic reforms so clearly linked to the need for a foreign policy approach based on "a substantially different kind of international relations."[2]

At the root of *novoe myshlenie* (new thinking) in foreign policy lies the abandonment of Soviet economic autarky and the advocacy of a program for controlled integration into the international economic system. The idea is to modernize the Soviet economy through an infusion of Western capital and technology as well as by means of an internal reorganization that deemphasizes the role of heavy industry and renders manufacturing as well as agricultural production more efficient. The result would be a heightened Soviet (and CMEA) participation in international trade.[3] Exports of raw materials and energy products would be at the core of Soviet trade with advanced Western countries, while sales of machinery and agricultural equipment would lead its exchanges with developing countries.

Linked to this economic imperative has been an effort to reshape Soviet strategy toward the United States and other advanced industrial countries as well as the Third World. The "new style" of Soviet international activity would be to seek "frank and productive dialogue" with the West through which could come "a minimum of trust. . . between representatives of opposing social systems" and a "renunciation of the ideologization of interstate relations."[4] Part and parcel of this effort, as announced in the 1986 CPSU Program, is to seek "normal, stable relations" with the United States as well as "fruitful, mutually advantageous. . .cooperation in various fields."[5] If the accommodation suggested here is one side of the coin, there is also another, more competitive dimension to relations with the United States and other Western countries. As the principal representatives of opposing "social-class values,"[6] the USSR and the United States cannot help but remain locked in an adversarial relationship, each jockeying for international advantage. In the current era of strategic parity and with the emergence of other capitalist "power centers," however, the struggle may be carried on through more "political means."[7]

Here emerges another aspect of Soviet new thinking: its emphasis on the increasingly competitive yet interdependent character of the international system. The USSR has always recognized and tried to take advantage of "intercapitalist" rivalries—witness Soviet policy toward Europe since the 1920s. But the fresh wrinkle under new thinking involves a conscious shift away from the Leninist "strategy of assault" (aimed directly at the United States and played out first in Western Europe and then in the Third World) to a longer-term Gramscian "war of position." The target is still the United States, but given contemporary conditions, the approach is no longer to press forward in search of a rapid, qualitative shift in the global balance of power. Rather the focus is on how to manage and take advantage of the competition between the "main centers of present-day imperialism"[8] (the United States, Western Europe, and Japan) as well as "new economic and political centers of rivalry [which have emerged] especially in the Pacific Basin and in Latin America."[9]

New thinking has also implied a reevaluation of Soviet views and strategy toward the Third World. Concern with the drain on Soviet resources represented by its allies and clients in the developing world (especially in light of a deteriorating economy) became manifest during Yuri Andropov's brief tenure as CPSU Secretary General. He was almost sarcastic in his expressions of "sympathy" with those Third World countries and movements who wanted Soviet aid: "[It is] one thing to proclaim socialism as one's aim and quite another to build it."[10] A similar cost–benefit rationale has been evident under Gorbachev, whose view seems to be that, although the USSR has benefited from its Third World initiatives, its pursuit of a strategy aimed at the weakest links in the imperialist chain has led, in effect, to a drain on the Soviet Union. The 1986 CPSU Program cautioned "socialist-oriented" countries (in the Third World) that they must build a new society "mainly through [their] own efforts," with the Soviet Union helping only "to the extent of its abilities."[11]

Skepticism about the prospects for revolutionary change, concern over the decline in Soviet trade with less developed countries, a realistic assessment of the political and economic costs that such ventures would entail, lessened reliance on military instruments, and greater sophistication in its efforts to become an "equal power" at regional levels[12] are at the core of Gorbachev's revised policy toward the Third World. One arena for initiative has been provided by the larger, economically and geopolitically important capitalist countries (Argentina, Brazil, India, Iran, Mexico, and Saudi Arabia) with whom the Soviet Union hopes to expand trade as well as political relations.[13] "Socialist-oriented" countries and "revolutionary-democratic" parties have provided the other point of reference for Soviet Third World policy under Gorbachev. Given the indigestion prompted by imperial expansion in the 1970s, Gorbachev has been cautious with respect to new targets of opportunity. Established clients have not been jettisoned, but the Soviet Union has been willing to enter into discussions with the United States about various regional conflicts and, in what is the most remarkable turnabout, appears ready to risk at least a short-term defeat in Afghanistan.

What implications does new thinking hold for Soviet policy in Latin America? The short answer is innovation within a broad pattern of continuity. The longer answer begins with a truism: a foreign policy emerges when the more difficult choices are made. The Gorbachev revolution in foreign policy is still long on declarations of intention; its only significant new initiatives have come in the sphere of disarmament and in the decision to withdraw from Afghanistan. On the Latin American front, there have been few major or surprising developments. Notwithstanding apparent differences over *perestroika* and *glasnost*, support for Cuba has been reaffirmed, and a 50 percent increase in assistance announced for the 1986–1990 period. Economic and military aid have continued to flow to the *Sandinistas* and so have oil shipments. But care has been taken to avoid giving the United States a pretext for escalating its conflict with Nicaragua. Proxies (Cuba and Eastern European states) continue to provide training for the security and armed forces; arms shipments have consisted primarily of weapons useful in counterinsurgency warfare. The most visible initiatives have come with respect to the larger, capitalist countries of the hemisphere with whom high-level and very publicized visits (including Gorbachev's much-postponed one to several Latin American nations) have been exchanged.

And what, then, are the most important challenges that the Soviet Union is likely to confront in its dealings with Latin America over the next decade?

The first challenge focuses on Cuba and the dilemma posed by changes in Soviet strategy toward the Third World. The shift from activism to accommodation ("our willingness to make compromises as equals" was the way Gorbachev put it in February 1988)[14] could have important implications for Cuba. Fidel Castro, who has made of "internationalism" both a cause and a *raison d'être* for his regime, may find both his role in the Soviet foreign policy scheme and his capacity to perform on the world stage diminished. The debt crisis may not provide a very adequate outlet for his internationalism. The priority that Gorbachev has assigned to domestic modernization could also have an important impact on Cuba. Certainly, neither he nor any one else in the Kremlin is interested in destabilizing the Cuban regime, but there must be limits to Soviet economic largesse, especially when Castro's policy choices (abolition of the peasant free markets, reliance on moral incentives, and the scrapping of the System of Economic Management and Planning [SDPE]—to mention only the most prominent) run directly counter to Soviet initiatives under *perestroika*.[15] In short, what is to be done about a country whose role as exemplar has certainly dimmed and whose economy is in a tailspin?

The second challenge relates to the Soviet drive for expanded relations with the larger Latin American countries. Such initiatives have made good sense (from an economic and political point of view), and there is every evidence that they will multiply under the "new" thinking. From their side, many Latin American elites and governments have come to view such links in a positive vein, as increasing their room for domestic and international maneuver. If recent developments are any sign, the political side of Soviet efforts will focus on rallying support from such countries as Argentina, Brazil, and Mexico on questions ranging from global armaments reduction to the denuclearization of the Caribbean and South Atlantic.[16] The Anglo–Argentine conflict over the Falklands/Malvinas and the often strained or competitive U.S.-Argentine relationship have encouraged Soviet leaders to draw geopolitical parallels with the case of India. Economic opportunities—the prospect of markets for Soviet manufactured goods and of access to foodstuffs and grains, ample mineral resources, and Western technology—also beckon. But the test will be how to realize this potential. The reorganization of the Soviet foreign trade bureaucracy and the permission now given some state enterprises to export directly are steps in this direction, but there is still much that remains to be done. In seeking a niche for its exports, the Soviet Union must overcome not only the poor reputation (deserved or not) of many of its goods and the hard-currency crunch caused by the debt crisis, but also the competition of more advanced industrial powers like Japan and the Federal Republic of Germany, whose attention is also focused on Latin America. High transportation costs and the current Soviet inability to bid on World Bank-financed projects act as additional constraints. The imaginative use of countertrade arrangements, mixed enterprises (where Soviet equipment is paid off by the sales that the enterprise generates), and trilateral ventures (as in the agreements with Brazil to participate in hydroelectric projects in Angola, Ethiopia, and Peru) may be helpful in solving some of these problems, but the obstacles to an expansion in trade relations cannot be underestimated.

The third challenge focuses on Nicaragua and the model it offers for Third World countries who would embark on a transition to socialism. Soviet analysts no longer exude their previous sense of euphoria about the prospects for revolutionary change throughout Central America.[17] Notwithstanding caution and some ambiguity with respect to the process,[18] however, the FSLN has been extolled for having created a "popular revolutionary democratic power."[19] Since the 1970s, in its dealings with radical parties in the Third World, the Soviet Union has stressed that a *sine qua non* for the development of organic ties is the creation of a "vanguard" party; and in line with this, exchanges and contacts between the FSLN and CPSU have expanded. The Soviet Union has advised the FSLN to maintain a mixed domestic economy as well as Nicaragua's links to the capitalist-dominated world economy. The correlative has been to stress the need for a "vanguard" party able to sustain itself in power during a lengthy transition period during which no extraordinary demands for economic solidarity will be placed on the USSR.[20] Clearly, such advice fits well with the imperatives of new thinking. But, the strategy may unravel, and the choices could become much more difficult, if either developments in other Central American countries get out of hand, or the FSLN leadership proves incapable of resolving the deepening economic and social crisis in Nicaragua.

The final challenge emerges from the *frente unido* alliance strategies that Communist parties have adopted in recent years. Joint initiatives between Communists and radical Left movements (which would congeal into either political-military fronts or electoral coalitions) developed first in Central America during the late 1970s. From there, the example spread to Chile (where the PCCh, MIR, and the Clodomiro Almeyda wing of the Socialists collaborated first in the armed actions spearheaded by *Frente Patriótico Manuel Rodríguez* and, more recently, in the more strictly political *Izquierda Unida*), and then to Argentina, Peru, Uruguay, and Mexico, among others. Compared to the meager showing of a divided Left, the electoral results of the various *frente unido* experiments have seemed impressive. A more careful look, however, reveals often complex situations where there is little political/organizational integration among the various forces. This has led one Soviet observer to warn against "the fetishization of unitary processes."[21] Other, more explosive consequences could develop from situations where political-military fronts try to take power, as may occur in El Salvador or possibly Chile. Such developments could compel Gorbachev to answer the question posed by Anatoly Dobrynin: "How can retaliatory—and completely justified measures, including armed action, by revolutionary forces be kept within national boundaries; what can be done to prevent it from turning into a new seat of international tensions?"[22] The answer to this question could provide a real test of new thinking both in Latin America and for the U.S.-Soviet relationship.

NOTES

1 *Pravda*, May 27, 1988 as translated in FBIS–SOV, May 27, 1988, p. 40.
2 See Gorbachev's speech to the February 1988 Central Committee published in *Pravda*, February 19, 1988 and translated in the *Current Digest of the Soviet Press*, 40: 7 (1988), p. 10.
3 O. Bogomolov, "The World of Socialism on the Path of *Perestroika*," *Kommunist* (Moscow), 16 (November 1987), pp. 92–102.
4 *Pravda*, February 19, 1988, as translated in *op. cit.* (*CDSP*).
5 As translated in *CDSP*, Special Supplement, 38: 2 (1986), p. 22.
6 *Op. cit.* (Footnote 2), p. 10.
7 *Op. cit.* (Footnote 1), p. 48.
8 Mikhail Gorbachev's Report to the 27th CPSU Congress as translated from *Pravda*, February 26, 1988, in FBIS–SOV, p. O6. Elaboration of these arguments may be found in the writings of Aleksandr Yakovlev, Evgeni Primakov, and Karen Brutents cited earlier in this volume, particularly by David Albright and Elizabeth Valkenier. Among many Soviet articles in this vein, see A. Yakovlev, "Inter-imperialist Contradictions—The Modern Context," *Kommunist*, 17 (November 1986), pp. 3–18; E. Primakov, "The Leninist Analysis of Imperialism, *Ibid.*, 9 (June 1986), pp. 102–114; and, V. Razmerov and Yu. Fedorov, "Two Tendencies in Inter-imperialist Relations," *Mirovaia ekonomika i mezhdunarodnye otnoshenia* (*MEMO*), 1 (January 1988), pp. 3–20.
9 Op. cit. (Footnote 5), p. 5.
10 Quoted in Francis Fukuyama, "Soviet Strategy in the Third World" in Andrzej Korbonski and Francis Fukuyama, *The Soviet Union and the Third World—The Last Decades* (Ithaca: Cornell University Press, 1987), p. 41.
11 *Op. cit.* (Footnote 2), p. 21.
12 On this, see Evgeni Primakov's interview with *Al-Hawadith* (Kuwait) [September 25, 1987] as translated in FBIS–SOV, October 1, 1987, p. 29.
13 For a recent argument which links the development of economic relations with these countries to the fate of *perestroika*, see L. Zevin, "Some Questions of Economic Cooperation between the USSR and Developing Countries," *MEMO*, 3 (1988), pp. 41–52.
14 *Op. cit.* (Footnote 2), p. 21.
15 For a remarkable exchange, see the article by V. Chirkov entitled "An Uphill Task," in *New Times*, 33, August 1, 1987, and the reply by the Deputy Chairman of the Cuban Council of Ministers, Carlos Rafael Rodríguez in *ibid.*, 41, October, 19, 1987, pp. 16–17.
16 For recent arguments, see I. Zorina and V. Sheinis, "Brazil and Argentina in the Modern World," *MEMO*, 8 (1987), pp. 68–77; O. A. Zhirnov and N. M. Isakova, "The South Atlantic Should Become a Zone of Peace," *América Latina*, 8 (August 1987), pp. 27–34; and N. Zhdanov-Lutsenko, "Latin America—Part of the Pacific," *ibid.*, 2 (February 1988), pp. 19–26.
17 For example, the articles published by S. Mikoyan, B. Koval, and K. Maidanik in *América Latina* in early 1980.
18 In discussing the paths of development which are open to Latin American countries, for example, V. Sheinis has written" "There does, of course, exist the path upon which Cuba has embarked and upon which, apparently, Nicaragua is entering." *MEMO*, 5 (1985), p. 121. Commenting on Central American revolutionary movements generally, V. Grishin has remarked as to how "the process is not rectilinear and is far from being irreversible due to internal and external factors." *América Latina*, 9 (September 1987), p. 62.
19 Y. Koroliov, "Nicaragua: the Experience of the Transition Period," *América Latina*, 9 (September 1984), p. 52. B. Merin and Y. Vizgunova, "Present Phase of the

Anti-imperialist Democratic Struggle," *ibid.*, 6 (June 1986), p. 32, have described the FSLN as a "revolutionary and democratic movement."

20 Yu. Onufriev, "Nicaragua: The Road to National Reconstruction," *América Latina*, 10 (October 1985), pp. 4–16, and A. P. Strogov and A. P. Klishin, "Democracy—Principal Law of the Sandinista Revolution, *Latinskaia Amerika*, 11 (November 1987), pp. 57–62.

21 The comment was by A. Kuzmishchev from the Institute of the International Working Class in *América Latina*, 9 (October 1987), p. 65. It culminated a set of polemical exchanges which began with the publication of an article by N. Vasetski in *ibid.*, 1 (January 1987).

22 *Pravda*, April 13, 1988 as translated by *CDSP*, 11: 15, p. 16.

List of Contributors

David E. Albright is currently Professor of National Security Affairs at the Air War College in Montgomery, AL. Prior to joining the faculty of the College, he worked at the Council on Foreign Relations (New York) as research associate for the Council's project on the United States and China in World Affairs, and he served as associate editor, and later senior text editor, of the journal *Problems of Communism*. Dr. Albright has written extensively on the USSR and the Third World. His recent works on this topic include *The USSR and Sub-Saharan Africa in the 1980s*, *Soviet Policy Towards Africa Revisited*, and *Vanguard Parties and Revolutionary Change in the Third World: The Soviet Perspective*.

Rubén Berríos is an associate researcher of GRADE (Grupo de Analisis para el Desarrollo—Development Analysis Group) in Lima, Peru. He has published a number of articles on technology and other economic issues, and on Soviet-Latin American relations. He is currently writing a book on the political economy of East-South relations.

Peter Clement is an analyst in the Office of European Analysis at the Central Intelligence Agency. He holds a Ph.D. in Russian History, has published articles on Soviet foreign policy, and is completing work on a study of Soviet domestic politics in the 1930s.

Edmé Domínguez Reyes has been a senior researcher at the Department of International Politics, Center for Research and Teaching in Economics, in Mexico City. She is the author of numerous articles on Latin America. Professor Domínguez is currently teaching at the University of Göteborg, Sweden.

Jorge L. Domínguez is Professor of Government at Harvard University. He has published extensively on Latin America, and was the former president of the Latin American Studies Association. Professor Domínguez received his Ph.D. from Harvard University. One of his most recent works is *Central America: Current Crises and Future Prospects*.

W. Raymond Duncan is Distinguished Teaching Professor in Political Science, State University of New York (SUNY), College at Brockport. He has published numerous articles on Soviet relations with Latin America, and his latest book is *The Soviet Union and Cuba: Interests and Influence.*

Robert K. Evanson is an Associate Professor of Political Science at the University of Missouri–Kansas City. His major research interests at this time are Soviet foreign trade policy and Soviet relations with Latin America and the Third World. He has published on these issues and on Czechoslovak politics in *Soviet Studies, The Journal of Interamerican Studies and World Affairs, Orbis, World Affairs*, and other journals.

Brian Latell is a senior Latin American specialist with the National Intelligence Council in Washington D.C., and an Adjunct Professor at the School of Foreign Service, Georgetown University. He is the author of articles and book chapters on Mexico and Cuba.

Richard L. Millett is a Senior Advisor for Political Risk Analysis to Frost and Sullivan Inc. of New York, and Research Associate of the Center for International Studies, University of Missouri–St. Louis. From 1982–1984, he was Visiting Professor of International Relations at the Air War College. He is the author of over 50 books and articles on Latin America including *Guardians of the Dynasty*, "Central American Paralysis," *Foreign Policy* (Summer 1980), and "The United States and Latin America," *Current History* (February 1984). He has his Ph.D. from the University of New Mexico, and did post-doctoral work at the Mershon Center, Ohio State University.

Carmelo Mesa-Lago is a Distinguished Service Professor of Economics and Latin American Studies at the University of Pittsburgh. He was the Director of the Center for Latin American Studies at Pittsburgh from 1974 to 1986, and has been a Visiting Professor at Oxford University, A Research Associate at the Instituto Torucato di Tella (Buenos Aires) and the University of Miami, he has taught at universities in Havana and Madrid. In 1980 he served as the President of the Latin American Studies Association (LASA). Dr. Mesa-Lago is the author of 25 books and about 100 articles/chapters in books on the Cuban economy, Latin

America's social security and health care, and comparative economic systems.

Eusebio M. Mujal-León is Associate Professor of Government at Georgetown University and the author of *Communism and Political Change in Spain* (Indiana University Press, 1983), *The Cuban University under the Revolution* (University of Miami, 1988), and *European Socialism and the Conflict in Central America* (Praeger, 1989). He is also co-editor of *Spain at the Polls* (Duke University Press, 1985) and editor of *Latin American Politics and Society: A Cultural Research Agenda?* (a special 1988 issue of the journal, *World Affairs*). Currently, he is at work on *Looking Beyond the Pyrenees: Spanish Foreign Policy since Franco.*

Michael Radu is a Research Associate at the Foreign Policy Research Institute in Philadelphia and contributing editor of *Orbis*. He is the editor of *Eastern Europe and the Third World*, coeditor of *Africa in the Post-decolonization Era*, and the author of *Ideology, Violence and the Central American Left: The Case of Guatemala*, as well as of numerous articles on revolutionary movements and Eastern Europe's role in the Third World.

Aldo C. Vacs is Assistant Professor of Political Science at Skidmore College. He has published on Soviet-Latin American relations, including a book on Soviet-Argentine relations, *Discreet Partners: Argentina and the USSR since 1917*. He has also published on the redemocratization process in Argentina, and recently completed a study of the political economy of the external debt of Argentina and Brazil. Vacs completed his Ph.D. in political science at the University of Pittsburgh. He also holds degrees in sociology, planning and economic policies, and political science from the Universidad Nacional de Cuyo (Argentina), Escola de Sociologia e Política de São Paulo (Brazil), and the Economic Commission for Latin America (Chile).

Elizabeth Kridl Valkenier received her Ph.D. from Columbia. Currently, she is Resident Scholar at the Harriman Institute for Advanced Study of the Soviet Union and Adjunct Professor of Political Science at Columbia. She has been a Senior Scholar on a number of official U.S.-Soviet and U.S.-Polish academic exchanges in Moscow, Leningrad, and Warsaw. She has participated in several joint Soviet-American scholarly conferences held under the terms of official cultural exchange agreements. Professor Valkenier is also the author of *Russian*

Realist Art, the State and Society (1977), and *The Soviet Union and the Third World: An Economic Bind* (1983). Her other publications include articles on various aspects of Soviet policies in the Third World which have appeared in *World Politics, Problems of Communism, Survey, Orbis, Europa Archiv, The Christian Science Monitor,* and *The New York Times*. She has contributed chapters to various symposia, most recently to *East-West Tensions in the Third World* edited by Marshall Shulman.

List of Acronyms

ANL	National Liberation Alliance
APRA	American Revolutionary Popular Alliance Alianza Popular Revolucionaria Americana—Peru
CCP	Communist Party of China
CGPT	General Confederation of Peruvian Workers Confederación General de los Trabajadores de Peru
CIA	Central Intelligence Agency—U.S.
CIDE	Center for Research and Economic Education
CMEA	Council of Mutual Economic Assistance
CNS	National Syndical Coordination Coordinación Nacional Sindical—Chile
CNT	National Confederation of Workers Confederación Nacional de Trabajadores
COB	Workers Conference of Bolivia Confederación Obrera Boliviana
CPSU	Communist Party of the Soviet Union
CPUSTAL	Permanent Congress of Syndical Unity of Latin American Workers Congreso Permanente de Unidad Sindical de los Trabajadores de América Latina
CTM	Confederation of Mexican Workers Confederación de Trabajadores Mexicanos
CUT	Workers Central Unity Central Unitaria de Trabajadores—Chile

ECLA	Economic Commission for Latin America and the Caribbean
EGP	Guerrilla Army of the Poor Ejercito Guerrillero de los Pobres—Guatemala
ELN	National Liberation Army Ejercito de Liberación Nacional—Peru
EPS	Sandinista Popular Army Ejercito Popular Sandinista
ERP	Revolutionary People's Army Ejercito Revolucionario del Pueblo—Argentina
FAL	Armed Liberation Forces Fuerzas Armadas de Liberación—Argentina
FAP	Armed Peronist Forces Fuerzas Armadas Peronistas—Argentina
FAR	Rebel Armed Forces Fuerzas Armadas Rebeldes—Guatemala
FARC	Colombian Revolutionary Armed Forces Fuerzas Armadas Revolucionarias Colombianas
FDR	Democratic Revolutionary Front Frente Democrático Revolucionario—El Salvador
FDR	Democratic Front Against Repression Frente Democrático Contra la Represión—Guatemala
FMLN	Morazanista National Liberation Front Frente Morazanista de Liberación Nacional—Honduras
FPL–FMLN	Popular Liberation Front-Farabundo Marti Fuerzas Populares de Liberación-Farabundo Marti—El Salvador
FPMP	Manuel Rodrıguez Patriotic Front Frente Patriotica - Manuel Rodríguez—Chile
FREPU	United People's Front Frente del Pueblo Unido—Argentina
FRTS	Revolutionary Federation of Salvadoran Workers Federación Revolucionaria de Trabajadores Salvadoreños

FSLN	Sandinista National Liberation Front Frente Sandinista de Liberación Nacional
FUSS	United Federation of San Salvador Federación Unitaria de San Salvador
GDP	Gross Domestic Product
GDR	German Democratic Republic
GOSPLAN	Soviet State Planning Commission
GSP	Global Social Product
IC	Intergovernmental Commission for Economic and Scientific-Technical Cooperation
ICBM	Intercontinental Ballistic Missile
IDL	International Division of Labor
ILA	Institute of Latin America
IMEMO	Institute of World Economy and International Relations
IMF	International Monetary Fund
IU	United Left Izquierda Unida—Peru
JUCEPLAN	Central Planning Board (Cuba)
LDC	Less-Developed Country
MAP-ML	Popular Action Movement–Marxist-Leninist Movimiento de Acción Popular–Marxista-Leninista– –Nicaragua
MAS	Movement toward Socialism Movimiento al Socialismo—Argentina
MDB	Brazilian Democratic Movement Movimento Democrático Brasileiro
MHR	Honduran Revolutionary Movement Movimiento Hondureño Revolucionario
MIR	Revolutionary Left Movement Movimiento de Izquierda Revolucionaria—Chile

MPLA	Popular Movement for the Liberation of Angola Movimento Popular de Libertacão de Angola
NJM	New Jewel Movement
NIC	Newly Industrialized Country
NIEO	New International Economic Order
OAS	Organization of American States
OLAS	Organization of Latin American Solidarity Organización Latinoamericana de Solidaridad
ORPA	Revolutionary Organization of the People in Arms Organización Revolucionaria del Pueblo en Armas– –Guatemala
PAN	National Action Party Partido de Acción Nacional—Mexico
PCA	Communist Party of Argentina Partido Comunista de Argentina
PCB	Communist Party of Brazil Partido Comunista do Brasil
PCB	Communist Party of Bolivia Partido Comunista de Bolivia
PCCh	Communist Party of Chile Partido Comunista de Chile
PCE	Communist Party of Ecuador Partido Comunista de Ecuador
PCES	Communist Party of El Salvador Partido Comunista de El Salvador
PCH	Communist Party of Honduras Partido Comunista de Honduras
PCM	Communist Party of Mexico Partido Comunista de México
PCP	Communist Party of Peru Partido Comunista de Peru
PCU	Communist Party of Uruguay Partido Comunista de Uruguay

PDC	Christian Democratic Party Partido Demócrata Cristiano—Chile
PGT	Guatemalan Labor Party Partido Guatemalteco del Trabajo
PIT	Workers' Plenary Inter-Syndicate
PMDB	Brazilian Democratic Movement Party Partido do Movimento Democrático Brasileiro—Brazil
PPM	Mexican People's Party Partido del Pueblo Mexicano
PPSC	Popular Christian Social Party Partido Popular Social Cristiano—Nicaragua
PPP	Panamanian Popular Party Partido del Pueblo de Panamá
PRI	Institutional Revolutionary Party Partido Revolucionario Institucional—Mexico
PRT	Workers' Revolutionary Party Partido Revolucionario de los Trabajadores—Argentina
PSCh	Chilean Socialist Party Partido Socialista Chileno
PSM	Mexican Socialist Party Partido Socialista Mexicano
PSN	Nicaraguan Socialist Party Partido Socialista Nicaragüense
PSP	Popular Socialist Party—Cuba Partido Socialista Popular
PSP	Socialist Party of Peru Partido Socialista de Peru
PST	Socialist Workers' Party—Panama
PSUM	Unified Mexican Socialist Party Partido Socialisto Unificada de México (former PCM)
PT	Workers' Party Partido dos Trabalhadores—Brazil

PVP	Popular Vanguard Party—Costa Rica
SDPE	System of Economic Management and Planning (Cuba)
SELA	Latin American Economic System Sistema Económico Latinoamericano
SIR	International Red Cross Socorro Rojo Internacional
UDL	Democratic Union for Liberation Unión Democrática de Liberación
UNRG	Guatemalan National Revolutionary Alliance Unión Nacional Revolucionaria Guatemalteca
UP	Popular Unity Unidad Popular—Chile
UP	Patriotic Union Unión Patriótica—Colombia
WRM	*World Marxist Review*
WTO	Warsaw Treaty Organization

Index

Index

Index

Index

Index